THE WAVE PRINCIPLE OF HUMAN SOCIAL BEHAVIOR AND THE NEW SCIENCE OF SOCIONOMICS

by

Robert R. Prechter, Jr.

The Wave Principle of
Human Social Behavior
and
The New Science of Socionomics

Printed in the United States of America

For information, address the publishers:
New Classics Library
Post Office Box 1618
Gainesville, Georgia 30503 USA
Phone: 800-336-1618, 770-536-0309
Fax: 770-536-2514
E-mail address for products: customerservice@elliottwave.com
E-mail address for comments: bb@elliottwave.com
Web site: www.elliottwave.com

New Classics Library is the book publishing division of
Elliott Wave International, Inc.

ISBN: 0-932750-49-4
Library of Congress Catalog Card Number: 98-68275

This book is dedicated to
Ralph Nelson Elliott,
who deserves to be recognized as
the father of modern social science.

Acknowledgments

My greatest debts go to four groups of people: the scientists who have so rigorously uncovered so many of nature's secrets as detailed herein, the observant subscribers who have so generously alerted me to new developments and sent copies of articles and studies, Paul Montgomery and Didier Sornette, who critiqued the manuscript, and my colleagues at EWI who aided in production, particularly Sally Webb, who handled the bulk of the project, Pam Kimmons, who produced the jacket art, Gay Doles and Pete Kendall, who researched myriad details, Angie Barringer and Dave Allman, who produced charts and illustrations, and Jane Estes, Betsy Forrester, Beth Parks and Rachel Webb, who helped along the way.

TABLE OF CONTENTS

STATEMENT OF VALUE

I hope that readers will forgive a rather advocative opening statement. However, I fear that without it, too few economists and sociologists will seriously consider this material. Therefore, I will state the following un-equivocally: The social sciences today are where the physical sciences were three hundred years ago. The Wave Principle is to sociology and related sciences what Newton's laws were to physics. It provides a basis and frame-work within which to study and quantify social behavior and thus serves as an anchor for the undertaking of true social science. The resulting break-through is so profound that it requires a new name for the science it makes possible. I think socionomics is a good term.

Ralph Nelson Elliott's great insight is the idea that financial markets have a specific organizational law of patterned self-similarity that is gov-erned by the Fibonacci sequence, which therefore ties it to the laws of nature. If I have an insight to provide, it is the vast implications of that fact.

I believe that the Wave Principle and socionomics are the most impor-tant concepts ever introduced to the field of social science. They *should* change forever the professions of market analysis, economics and sociol-ogy. In fear that it might go unread, I make these bold statements in hopes that they will inspire (or annoy) practitioners of social professions enough to prompt some of them to investigate these ideas and reconsider the old assumptions permeating their fields.

APOLOGIA

I think that the Wave Principle and socionomics are stone cold facts. However, I have worked with and developed them for twenty-five years. Only a fraction of what I know about the field is in this book. It does not come close to conveying the full breadth and depth of either the Wave Principle or socionomics. The nuances of patterns, the remarkable preci-sion of expression, and wider social applications are to be found detailed, to the extent currently possible, in other publications, both extant and forth-coming.

The purpose of this book is to make a case for the validity of the Wave Principle and socionomics as they relate to recent scientific discoveries and the current state of related professions. Despite this narrow goal and my best attempt as a layman who spends most of his time on business, this book may not be up to scientific standards. I am aware that no single chapter in this book proves anything. Worse, some parts of this book present information from fields in which I am an utter novice. However, I believe that when I put all this information together and point out the connections, it makes a substantial circumstantial case. I hope that knowledgeable readers will inform me of any errors I have made so that I may make corrections in the next edition of this book.

WHY NOW?

In Manfred Schroeder's new book, *Fractals, Chaos, Power Laws*, the "Scaling in Psychology" section takes up just one page out of 400. With the knowledge of the Wave Principle and the introduction of socionomics, that representative knowledge ratio should change.

> "Ever since his *Principia*, mathematics has been regarded as the most secure form of knowledge. Newton's successful mathematical descriptions of motion transformed human perception of the structure of the universe beyond recognition. Galileo, on whose shoulders Newton stood, once remarked that the 'great book of nature' is written in the language of mathematics."
> —Peter Coveney and Roger Highfield in
> *Frontiers of Complexity*, 1995

> "Phenomena of mass action [are] under impulsions and controls which no science has explored."
> —Bernard Baruch in the foreword to *Extraordinary Popular Delusions & the Madness of Crowds*, 1932

> "There are no 'Darwin's equations' describing biological evolution in quantitative, mathematical terms."
> —Coveney and Highfield in *Frontiers of Complexity*, 1995

> "There exists no branch of science that deals specifically with an explanation of the subjective self and its relation to the internal and external environment....The successive mentational processes have neither been identified nor shown to obey laws that allow predictable conclusions....Because of the untold number of individuals involved, it would be particularly important to understand the...neural mechanisms...that so galvanize the collective human mind that overnight there

is a round-the-globe spread of fashions in dress (e.g., hair styles, Levis), games (e.g., Hula-Hoops) and reading (e.g., Haley's *Roots*) [or of being] it seems suddenly receptive to some particular 'movement' and inclined to mass demonstrations."
—Paul D. MacLean in *The Triune Brain in Evolution*, 1990

"With these decisions, we have what looks very much like the individual actions of people, with very individual reasons. But statistically, we have some routine [.618] number keep appearing. This is evidence that there is at work some machinery, which corresponds to [a Fibonacci] model. I believe that in a couple of decades, there will be a completely new psychology.... The human being is related to some hidden and unknown laws of the universe."
—Vladimir Lefebvre of the University of California, in
The Los Angeles Times, 1993[1]

"I predict — and I am by no means alone — that one of the most exciting growth areas of twenty-first century science will be biomathematics. The next century will witness an explosion of new mathematical concepts, of new *kinds* of mathematics, brought into being by the need to understand the patterns of the living world. Those new ideas will interact with the biological and physical sciences in totally new ways. They will — if they are successful — provide a deep understanding of that strange phenomenon that we call "life": one in which its astonishing abilities are seen to flow *inevitably* from the underlying richness, and the mathematical elegance, of our universe.... A full understanding of life depends upon mathematics. At every level of scale, from molecules to ecosystems, we find mathematical patterns in innumerable aspects of life. *It is time we put the mathematics and the biology together.*"
—Dr. Ian Stewart in *Life's Other Secret*, 1998

"Never — I do not think that is too strong a word — have social scientists been able to embed their narratives in the physical realities of human biology and psychology, even though it is surely there.... We know that virtually all of human behavior is transmitted by culture. We also know that biology has an important effect on the origin of culture and its transmission. The question remaining is how biology and culture interact, and in particular how they interact across all societies to create the commonalities of human nature. What, in final analysis, joins the deep,

mostly genetic history of the species as a whole to the more recent cultural histories of its far-flung societies?...It can be stated as a problem to be solved, the central problem of the social sciences and the humanities, and simultaneously one of the great remaining problems of the natural sciences. At the present time no one has a solution."
—Edward O. Wilson in *Consilience*, 1998

For a number of reasons, the time is right for this book. With science on its current path, serious minds are becoming open to concepts such as those presented herein. With the social mood trend about to become volatile (as I believe it is), people generally will find themselves more willing to pay attention to hypotheses of endogenous causes of social change.

Finally, as a subscriber of mine recently wrote in a personal note attached to a story about chaos and finance, "Like Alexander King's story of the man in an isolated village in Switzerland who unknowingly reinvented the typewriter, it looks like these people are about to rediscover the Elliott Wave."[2] Presumably that typewriter maker was forced to admit that his feat had already been accomplished. If someone today rediscovers the Wave Principle, he might not feel so constrained. I want to make sure that R.N. Elliott gets his due.

I would like to discuss so much more that pertains, from the structure of music to the success and failure of industries to the history of philosophy. However, presenting a full case will have to wait until my team and I have the time to gather more data than we have amassed so far. Few people would read a 1000-page presentation on the applicability of socionomics without having first become convinced of its validity, or at least of its possible validity. I hope there is enough herein to make socionomics acceptable as a hypothesis that will intrigue research scientists who will then desire to undertake to prove or disprove the thesis. Fortunately or not, it has fallen upon me to make the presentation. To transmute the old joke, "It's a fun job, but someone's got to do it."

Foreword

Several times in my life, I have come across a grand concept that was so beautiful, logical and compelling from the standpoint of its pattern that I decided almost immediately that it was valid. That is not cautious science. However, I did not stop there, but investigated further, often much further because of my conviction and fascination, to make sure that I had not been misled.

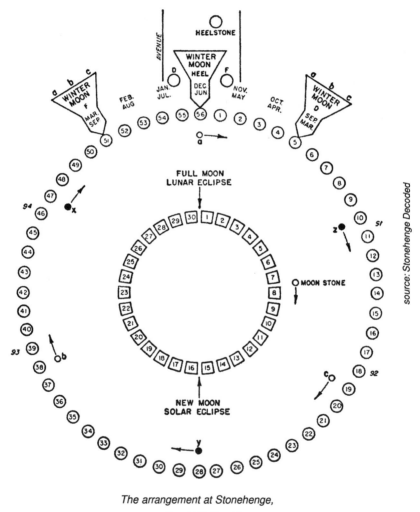

The arrangement at Stonehenge,

per Gerald S. Hawkins

The first such experience I can recall was upon reading the brilliant *Stonehenge Decoded* by professor Gerald S. Hawkins.[3] I was only 17 at the time, but I could see that the pattern of the stones and holes so perfectly matched solar and lunar cycles that thereafter no reasoning person could insist that it was built simply as a chanting ground for druids. When I visited the site the following year, I excitedly mentioned the theory to the official in charge, who had obviously heard about it. "Rubbish!" was his instant reply; "It was a druid temple!" The exquisite coincidence of pattern meant nothing to him.

My next such experience came upon an introduction to the concept of continental drift in a geology course at Yale. The fit among the continents' coastlines is so remarkable and the contour of the ocean floors so compatible with drift that it seemed a compelling deduction at first exposure. It was only a few years ago that I read the story of Alfred Wegener, who postulated the theory in *The Origin of Continents and Oceans* in 1922, and how for decades the profession had not simply challenged but mercilessly derided both him and his idea. The coincidence of pattern meant nothing to them. Then, some forty years later, the concept was quietly slipped into the textbooks by the next generation of experts who, as supporting data accumulated, could see its validity as easily as their predecessors could see its ludicrousness.

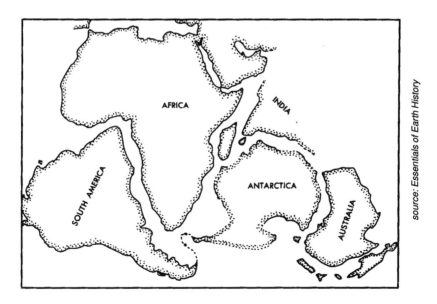

source: Essentials of Earth History

source: The Mysterious William Shakespeare

Edward de Vere, 17th Earl of Oxford

Another time I had this experience was about five years ago upon attending a one-hour speech by Charles Vere, Earl of Burford, about the authorship of the poems and plays written under the pseudonym "Shake-speare." The evidence in favor of the Stratford-Upon-Avon fellow whose name was William Shaksper (as far as anyone can tell, as he was unable to scrawl his own name the same way twice) is essentially nonexistent, and that in favor of Edward de Vere, 17th Earl of Oxford, is so overwhelming as to be definitive. Yet once again, the majority of established scholars, not to mention the tourist trappers in that small town of Stratford, value intricate pattern coincidence between the life and character of an author and the life and character of his plays as naught. In fact, orthodoxy is so bitterly opposed to admitting a lifelong error that its members denigrate, with vicious *ad hominem* attacks, the intrepid detectives of the author's true identity. They almost never argue the facts because frankly, there are no adequate responses. To experience fully the shallowness and prejudice of the Stratfordians' responses, as well as the richness and genius of the Oxfordians' case, you should read the scholarly *The Mysterious William Shakespeare — The Myth and the Reality* by Harvard alumnus Charlton Ogburn and the work of his predecessors. I am convinced that when the tawdry factoids[4] fostered by the current establishment are finally overwhelmed and replaced by the real story, our children will be reading about de Vere's unique accomplishments and genius, immeasurably enriching the experience of his revolutionary literary output.

Previously, in the early 1970s, I had another such experience with respect to technical methods of stock market analysis. Their basis in recurring patterns (of human behavior, this time) seemed so obviously more valid than the conventional approach that I wasted little time with the latter after comprehending the difference. Needless to say, economists are virtually unanimous in their denigration of technical analysis. The derisive arrogance of some random walk enthusiasts has been so egregious in this regard that it has been satisfying to watch their sacred cow get gored by the new academics who have discovered that the market is not random but apparently governed by nonlinear[5] mathematics, which can produce patterns and thereby provide a basis for technical analysis.[6] Has this breakthrough changed random walkers' minds? Of course not. Max Planck said, "A new scientific truth does not triumph by convincing its opponents and making them see the light, but rather because its opponents eventually die, and a new generation grows up that is familiar with it."[7] As with the Stonehenge curator, the anti-continental drifters and the Stratfordian Shakespeare orthodoxy, random walkers are just going to have to die off to allow the truth to flourish.

My acceptance of the Wave Principle actually came a bit less suddenly. I began trying to apply a rudimentary understanding of it as part of my investigation of technical methods of stock market analysis. By the mid-1970s, I was keeping an hourly chart of the Dow and becoming more fascinated watching the waves unfold as R.N. Elliott described and seeing many of my forecasts on that basis come to pass. In 1976, I read Elliott's original works and was on fire. Here was something not only true but *important*. It just needed some more thought and research.

I will not dwell on the resistance to the idea of the Wave Principle that I have encountered. The good news is that the light of understanding is beginning to shine through the mist. The October 1993 issue of *The Economist* contained a special section called "Frontiers of Finance," which told readers that market prices may not be random; they might reflect nonlinear mathematics. The page 1 sidebar reads, "The idea that a financial market can be predicted is no longer confined to cranks." To me, that is like a 17th century chronicler observing, "The idea that sun lies at the center of the solar system is no longer confined to cranks." In this context, one wishes to be a crank because it means you are a guy who, against a herd of mythologers, came up with the right answer.

Furthermore, many brilliant people have become intrigued with the idea. Dr. John Shea of Memphis's Shea Clinic (who at the age of 30 developed the stapedectomy operation for deafness), arranged for me to join a group of distinguished scientists in addressing "Symmetry in its Various Aspects" at the 21st International Congress on the Unity of the Sciences (ICUS) in Washington, D.C. in 1997. A few months later, I was intrigued to see that two studies of large financial crashes by scientists from the Institute of Geophysics and Planetary Physics at the University of California and the Niels Bohr Institute in Copenhagen use *Elliott Wave Principle* as a reference, a welcome event. (See citations later in this book.) Though work on this book precluded my attendance, I was honored that Daniel Shechtman, the discoverer of quasi-crystals, invited me to address the International Society for the Interdisciplinary Study of Symmetry (ISIS) conference this year in Haifa, Israel. These are marvelous signs of progress in attention paid to the Wave Principle by the scientific community.

I am prepared for backlash from the entrenched old guard of the professional establishment, but I don't care about that. I had my share of both adulation and derision in my "guru" years on Wall Street, times when I could do no wrong in my forecasting and times when I could do little right (that anyone would acknowledge, anyway). Rarely does derision have much real substance, and smart people can see that. I hope I am still young enough to be able to wait, if necessary, for the old guard to die off and to see the new guard start from a fresh perspective. I hope more fervently that upon reading this book and observing the pattern connections, you will experience that same reaction that I have upon occasion and say to yourself, "Yes, of course this is true. How could anyone doubt it?"

SUMMARY

The purpose of this book is to establish the idea that in humans, an unconscious herding impulse impels social mood trends and changes that are specifically patterned according to a natural growth principle and which in turn is the engine of cultural expression and social action. Following is a summary of the main points in this book:

In the 1930s, Ralph Nelson Elliott (1871-1948) discovered that price changes in stock market indexes produce a limited number of definable patterns, or waves, that are robustly self-affine[8] at different degrees, or sizes, of trend. He described how waves at each degree become the components of waves of the next higher degree. Elliott called this phenomenon "The Wave Principle." The essential form is five waves generating net movement in the direction of the one larger trend followed by three waves generating net movement against it, producing a three-steps-forward, two-steps-back form of net progress. Because the basis of the essential form is a repeated 5-3, the numbers of waves at different degrees reflect the Fibonacci sequence. This model has produced a substantial documented success in both accounting for and forecasting stock market trends. Stock market indexes are important because they record man's valuation of his own productive enterprise. The fact that this valuation follows an intricate Fibonacci-based pattern indicates that there is a single essential cause of that valuation, the social mood that underlies it, and the enterprise that results from it.

There is some evidence that the cause of the pattern may be the unconscious herding impulse generated by the brain's limbic system. This impulse determines men's social mood and is independent of outside influence. Fractal, spiral and Fibonacci phenomena in biology and human perception and mentation suggest a biological basis for the phenomenon.

Social mood trends represent changes in human attitudes. Changes in social mood trends precede compatible changes in history and culture, indicating that the former causes the latter. Thus, there is powerful evidence that the pattern of mood change produced by the social interaction of men is the underlying engine of the trends of social progress and regress. This orientation has allowed successful forecasting of financial, economic, political and cultural events. The relationship of the pattern to Fibonacci mathematics suggests that the Wave Principle is another manifestation of a type of growth pattern found throughout nature in processes of growth and decay, expansion and contraction.

DEFINITIONS

The Wave Principle or *The Elliott Wave Principle*

The Wave Principle is the pattern of progress and regress characteristic of social (and apparently other) phenomena in which progress occurs in specific patterns of five waves and reaction occurs in specific patterns of three waves or combinations thereof.

Elliott wave

An Elliott wave (or *wave*, in context) is any one of the patterns that occurs as a fundamental component of the Wave Principle.

wave

The term "wave" is used as part of the designation of a particular manifestation of an Elliott wave. It is followed by a term describing its position within at least the wave of one larger degree, for example, "wave 1," "wave A," "wave ⓒ of 4," etc.[9] Each wave must allow the movements preceding, following and encompassing it also to be so designated.

From a socionomic perspective, each wave is a unit of social expression and experience.

Elliotter or *Elliottician*

Using what is becoming conventional terminology, an Elliotter or Elliottician is one who analyzes data series in terms of the Wave Principle.

socionomics

Socionomics is the study of social trends based upon the following understanding: There are biologically based psychological impulses within individuals that relate to human interpersonal dynamics. These dynamics contribute to patterns of fluctuation in collective mood that are *formological* in that they have consistent Fibonacci-based mathematical properties and produce the Wave Principle.[10] This patterning of social mood creates a *sociological imperative* that mightily guides and influences the character of individual and social behavior. The resulting human actions in turn cause the trends and events of history. The overall process that may be termed *historical impulsion*. As opposed to the traditional mechanistic models of aggregate behavior that are based upon presumptions of multiple exogenous causes and ultimate effects, socionomics recognizes that patterns of aggregate human behavior are endogenous, self-causing, self-regulating, self-reinforcing and, to a far greater degree than has heretofore been imagined, predictable.

socionomist

A practical *socionomist* develops and analyzes indicators of social mood in order to forecast the character of social events, occasionally actual social events, and, when possible, the path of social mood itself in light of its following the Wave Principle.

sociometer

A sociometer is a direct reflector of the states and trends of social mood, such as a stock market average. (Other types are proposed in Chapter 15.)

formological system

A *formological system* is neither linear nor nonlinear in terms of event causality because the cause of its processes is not events. A formological system is formologically causal, meaning that the form of the system determines the shape of its process. (For more, see Chapter 20.)

robust fractal

As opposed to self-identical fractals, whose parts are precisely the same as the whole, and indefinite fractals, which are self-similar only in that they are similarly irregular at all scales, a *robust fractal* is one of intermediate specificity. Though variable, its component forms, within a certain defined latitude, are replicas of the larger forms. Both waves and arbora (see below) are robust fractals. (For more, see Chapter 3.)

arborum, etc.

I use the term *arborum* (plural *arbora*) to denote a robust branching fractal common to nature (as opposed to a self-identical or indefinite branching fractal). An *arbum* (plural *arba*) will denote one of the branches of an arborum. The verb, *to aborate* will denote "to proceed in a robust branching fractal." The process of robustly branching will be termed *arboration*. The adjective *arboral* will mean "having the properties of an arborum." (For more, see Chapter 3.)

Social Mood

I would like to have a single word to stand for "social mood," but have been unable to find one. Words such as "zeitgeist" and "archetype" tend to be stereotyped quickly, and I want to avoid trendiness. The best word I could come up with is *maiesthai*. Maiesthai is the Greek word for "to strive" and is one of the roots of the word "mood," according to Webster's. The combination of mood and striving is a perfect synthesis to express what the Wave Principle governs, so we could make it an English noun. Unfortunately, it is not an easy word to cozy up to. Suggestions are welcome.

Notes on the Definition of Wave

Instead of *Elliott wave*, we could choose always to use the term *wave*, as R.N. Elliott did. However, there are so many types of waves — sine, ocean, light, radio, micro, etc. — that the particular form described as the Wave Principle requires a specific designation. The use of the term wave in the context of a discussion of Elliott waves is no problem. Indeed, the definitions of that and related words in the unabridged *Webster's New International Dictionary* (1976) are remarkable in combining so many of the features of Elliott waves. Here are pertinent excerpts:

As a noun:
- A surge of sensation or emotion.
- An undulating or jagged line constituting a graphic representation.
- One of the vicissitudes of life or fortune.
- A tide of opinion or sentiment carrying many with it: a movement sweeping large numbers in a common direction.
- A disturbance or variation that transfers itself and energy progressively from point to point in a medium or in space in such a way that each particle or element influences the adjacent ones....

As an intransitive verb:[11]
- (Of a crowd): to move in a restless, irregular or fluctuating way likened to that of sea waves.

Waver (the archaic form of which is *wave*):
- To...alternate between...objects [or] conditions (a mood that wavered between uncertain cheer and blackest gloom).
- To vacillate irresolutely between options or attractions.
- To fluctuate in opinion.

NOTES

1 Washburn, J. (1993, March 31). "The human equation." *The Los Angeles Times*.

2 (1993) Personal letter to R. Prechter from J. Barnes, Wetumpka, Alabama.

3 Hawkins, G.S., and White, J. (1965). *Stonehenge decoded*.

4 This useful word originally and properly meant an oft-repeated apparent fact that is false. Journalists have transformed the word to mean "small fact," an egregious error that makes their new definition itself a factoid.

5 Actually, I challenge this terminology in Chapter 20.

6 See Brock, W., *et al.* (1992, December). "Simple trading rules and the stochastic properties of stock returns." *Journal of Finance*.

7 Planck, M. (1949). *Scientific autobiography and other papers*.

8 Fractal objects whose properties are not restricted display self-*similarity*, while those that develop in a direction such as price graphs display self-*affinity*. The term "self-similar" is often employed more generally to convey both ideas. In this book, I sometimes use this term in its general sense.

9 See Chapter 1 for a brief discussion of wave notation.

10 See Chapter 3 for a brief discussion of Fibonacci mathematics.

11 It also means "to gesture in greeting." Elliott waves may be nature's way of doing just that. An archaic synonym for wave is *bob*, which I like.

NOTE TO THE READER

I have often added italics in cited quotations to highlight pertinent words and passages. I do not note "emphasis added" after each one.

PART I:

AN INTRODUCTION TO
THE IDEA OF
THE WAVE PRINCIPLE

In the first three parts of this book, I will explain the theory of the Wave Principle, connect it to fractals and spirals, show that it can be modeled and quantified, relate it to indicators of market behavior, demonstrate its utility in forecasting, and then explore its biology, psychology and sociology.

Part I is the "bear with me" section. It travels far afield in directions whose relevance may not be immediately apparent but which will be bolstered and clarified as the book progresses.

Chapter 1:

Basic Tenets of the Wave Principle

This chapter provides a succinct overview of the Wave Principle so that those new to the concept can get the idea as quickly as possible. That way, we can move on to address the validity of the concept of the Wave Principle and then discuss its implications and application. Full details are available in *Elliott Wave Principle* (1978/1998). This chapter is necessarily dry as a bone, but I promise that the steam will rise as we move along.

R.N. Elliott's Discovery

In the 1930s, Ralph Nelson Elliott discovered that aggregate stock market prices trend and reverse in recognizable patterns. The patterns he discerned are repetitive in *form*, but not necessarily in time or amplitude. Elliott isolated and defined thirteen patterns, or "waves," that recur in market price data. He named and illustrated the patterns. He then described how they link together to form larger versions of themselves, how they in turn link to form the same patterns at the next larger size, and so on, producing a structured progression. He called this phenomenon The Wave Principle.[1]

Many areas of mass human activity display the Wave Principle, but it is most popularly applied to stock market averages. There is voluminous, meticulously tabulated data on financial markets because people deem them important. Actually, the stock market is far more significant to the human condition than it appears to casual observers and even to those who make their living by it. The level of aggregate stock prices is a direct and immediate measure of the popular valuation of man's total productive capability. That this valuation has a *form* is a fact of profound implications that should ultimately revolutionize the social sciences.

While Elliott progressed to the recognition of patterns and their link-age by a painstaking process of cataloging the minute details of price movement, we will forego such exercises and proceed directly to a de-scription of the overall pattern.

The Five-Wave Pattern

In markets, progress ul-timately takes the form of five waves of a specific structure. Waves (1), (3) and (5) in Fig-ure 1-1 actually effect the di-rectional movement. Waves (2) and (4) are countertrend interruptions. The two inter-ruptions are apparently a req-uisite for overall directional movement to occur.

Elliott noted three con-sistent aspects of the five-wave form. They are: Wave two never moves beyond the start of wave one, wave three is never the shortest wave,

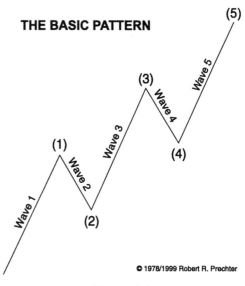

THE BASIC PATTERN

Figure 1-1

© 1978/1999 Robert R. Prechter

and wave four never enters the price territory of wave one. The stock mar-ket is always somewhere in the basic five-wave pattern at the largest de-gree of trend. Because the five-wave pattern is the overriding form of market progress, all other patterns are subsumed by it.

Component Structures

Figure 1-2 shows the first two waves of Figure 1-1 *in greater detail*. Notice the difference in their subdivisions, which reflect the two modes of wave development: *motive* and *corrective*. The two modes are fundamen-tally different in both their roles and construction.

A motive wave (also called a "five") has a *five*-wave structure. Its subwaves are denoted by numbers (in this case, 1, 2, 3, 4, 5). Both the five-wave pattern of Figure 1-1 and its *same-directional components*, i.e., waves (1), (3) and (5), employ motive mode. Their structures are called "motive" because they powerfully impel the market.

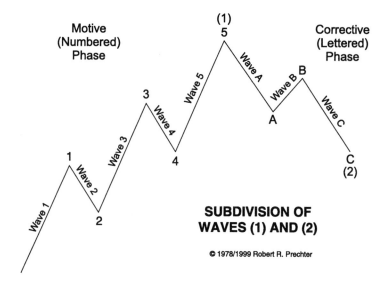

Figure 1-2

A corrective wave (also called a "three") has a *three*-wave structure or a variation thereof. Its subwaves are denoted by letters (in this case, A, B, C). All countertrend interruptions, which include waves (2) and (4) in Figure 1-1, employ corrective mode. Their structures are called "corrective" because each one appears as a response to the preceding motive wave yet accomplishes only a partial retracement of the progress it had achieved, "correcting" its extremity.

Self-Similarity and Degree

When the motive wave in Figure 1-1 ends, a corrective wave of corresponding size follows, so that overall, the result looks like Figure 1-2. Figure 1-3 shows the detail of this development. Observe that the overall form of Figure 1-3 is the same as that of its own subwaves (1) and (2), depicted in Figure 1-2. The only difference is that Figure 1-3 represents a pattern of *one degree* (i.e., relative size) *larger* than the waves of which it is composed.

The word "degree" has a specific meaning and does not mean "scale." Component waves vary in size, but it always takes a certain number of them to create a wave of the next higher degree. Thus, each degree is identifiable in terms its relationship to higher and lower degrees. This is unlike the infinite scaling relating to say, seacoasts (see Chapter 2).

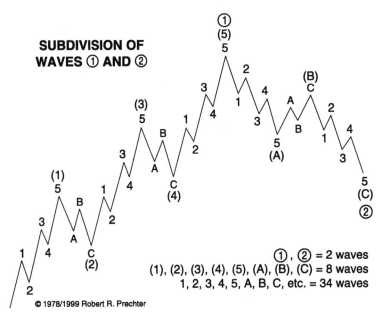

Figure 1-3

As Figure 1-3 illustrates, then, *each same-direction component of a motive wave* (i.e., wave one, three or five) *and each full-cycle component* (i.e., waves one + two, or waves three + four) *of a complete cycle is a smaller version of itself.*

At this juncture, the significant point to understand is that Figure 1-3 not only illustrates a *larger* version of Figure 1-2, it also illustrates *Figure 1-2 itself,* in greater detail. In Figure 1-2, each subwave 1, 3 and 5 is a motive wave that must subdivide into a "five," and each subwave 2 and 4 is a corrective wave that must subdivide into a "three." Waves 1 and 2 in Figure 1-3, if examined under a "microscope," would take the same form as waves (1) and (2), and in further detail, waves ① and ②. *Regardless of degree, the form is constant.* We can use Figure 1-3 to illustrate two waves, eight waves or thirty-four waves, depending upon the degree to which we are referring.

The Essential Design

Now observe that within the corrective pattern illustrated as wave ② in Figure 1-3, waves (A) and (C), which point downward, are each composed of five waves: 1, 2, 3, 4 and 5. Similarly, wave (B), which points

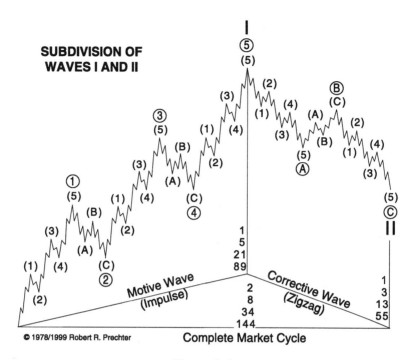

Figure 1-4

upward, is composed of three waves: A, B and C. This construction discloses a crucial point: Motive waves do not always point upward, and corrective waves do not always point downward. The mode of a wave is determined not by its absolute direction but primarily by its *relative* direction. Aside from four specific exceptions, which are discussed in the literature, a wave divides in *motive* mode (five waves) when trending in the *same* direction as the wave of one larger degree of which it is a part, and in *corrective* mode (three waves or a variation) when trending in the *opposite* direction. Waves (A) and (C) are motive, trending in the same direction as wave ②. Wave (B) is corrective because it corrects wave (A) and is countertrend to wave ②. In summary, the essential underlying tendency of the Wave Principle is that *action in the same direction as the one larger trend develops in five waves, while reaction against the one larger trend develops in three waves,* at all degrees of trend.

These phenomena of *form, degree* and *relative direction* are carried one step further in Figure 1-4. This illustration reflects the general principle that in a market cycle, waves will subdivide as shown in the table below.

Number of Waves at Each Degree

	Impulse	+ Correction	= Cycle	
Largest waves	1	1	2	
Largest subdivisions	5	3	8	
Next subdivisions	21	13	34	
Next subdivisions	89	55	144	, etc.

As with Figures 1-2 and 1-3, neither does Figure 1-4 imply finality. Following the form, this larger cycle automatically becomes two subdivisions of the wave of *next* higher degree. As long as progress continues, the process of building to greater degrees continues. The reverse process of subdividing into lesser degrees apparently continues indefinitely as well. As far as we can determine, then, all waves both *have* and *are* (or at the largest degree, *will be*) component waves.

Why 5-3?

Elliott himself never speculated on why the market's essential form was five waves to progress and three waves to regress. He simply noted that it was happening. Does the essential form have to be five waves and three waves? I think so.

First, were there no fluctuation, there would be no progress. A steadily increasing trend of 3% per year, for instance, would be stasis; nothing would ever change. Fluctuation in a net sideways trend, i.e., one with no net change, would also be stasis. Progress must include setbacks *and* net change over time. From the point of view of a participant, *punctuated* progress is the only kind of progress that is possible to perceive.

Second, the 5-3 pattern is *the* minimum requirement for, and therefore the most efficient method of, achieving both *fluctuation* and *progress* in linear movement when the only constraint is that the lengths of odd-numbered waves of each degree be longer than those of the even-numbered ones. One wave does not allow fluctuation. The fewest subdivisions to create fluctuation is three waves. Three waves in both directions do not allow progress. To progress in one direction despite fluctuation, movements in the main trend must be at least five waves, simply to cover more ground than the three waves. While there could be more waves than that, the most efficient form of punctuated progress is 5-3, and nature typically follows the most efficient path.

Notation and Nomenclature

Waves are categorized by degree. The degree of a wave is determined by its size and position *relative to component, adjacent and encompassing waves*. Elliott named nine degrees of waves, from the smallest discernible on an hourly graph of stock prices to the largest he could assume existed from the data then available. He chose the following terms for these degrees, from largest to smallest: Grand Supercycle, Supercycle, Cycle, Primary, Intermediate, Minor, Minute, Minuette, Subminuette. Cycle waves subdivide into Primary waves that subdivide into Intermediate waves that in turn subdivide into Minor waves, and so on. This specific terminology is not critical to the identification of degrees, although out of habit, longtime practitioners have become comfortable with Elliott's nomenclature.

When labeling waves on a graph, some scheme is necessary to differentiate the degrees of waves in the stock market's progression. The most desirable form for a scientist might be 1_1, 1_2, 1_3, 1_4, 1_5, etc., with subscripts denoting degree. We use this form in our computer program (see Chapter 4), although it is difficult to read a large number of such notations on a graph. Elliott Wave International has standardized a sequence of labels involving numbers and letters. The following notations, for instance, denote first waves from Grand Supercycle degree down to Subminuette: Ⓘ, (I), I, ①, (1), 1, ⓘ, (i), i. This standard provides for rapid visual orientation.

It is important to understand that these names and labels refer to specifically identifiable degrees of waves. By using a nomenclature, an analyst can identify precisely the position of a wave in the overall progression of the market, much as longitude and latitude are used to identify a geographical location. To say, "The Dow Jones Industrial Average is in Minute wave ⓥ of Minor wave 1 of Intermediate wave (3) of Primary wave ⑤ of Cycle wave I of Supercycle wave (V) of the current Grand Supercycle" is to identify a specific point along the progression of stock market history.

Variations on the Basic Theme

The basic model is simple, but reality is a bit more complex, as there are specific variations on the underlying theme that Elliott catalogued in detail. He also noted the important fact that each pattern has identifiable *rigidities* as well as *tendencies*. From these observations, he was able to formulate descriptions of typical wave behavior and therefore *rules* and

A REALISTIC ELLIOTT WAVE

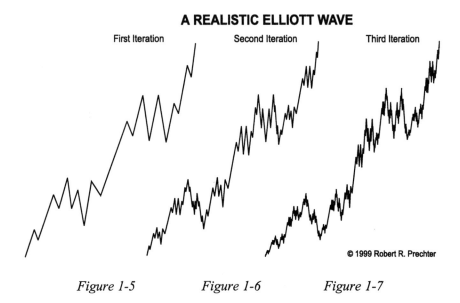

First Iteration   Second Iteration   Third Iteration

© 1999 Robert R. Prechter

Figure 1-5   *Figure 1-6*   *Figure 1-7*

guidelines for proper wave identification. For example, in the five-wave pattern (termed an "impulse"), the middle wave is usually the longest, and the two corrective waves usually alternate in form, the first "sharp," the second "sideways," as shown in Figure 1-5. Figures 1-6 and 1-7 then take this form to two and three iterations respectively.

A thorough understanding of such details is necessary to know what the market can do, and at least as important, what it does not do. However, as the purpose of this chapter is limited to introducing the general hypothesis, a discussion of such nuances is omitted. Chapter 3 will present a highly detailed representative list of wave-formation rules for impulses to give you a flavor of their intricacy. Some readers may wish to peruse a short list of fine points in order to understand more precisely the reasons behind some aspects of the labeling in the historical graphs shown throughout this book. If so, see endnote 2.[2]

Modern Science Comments on the Wave Principle Hypothesis

1996 was an important year for the Wave Principle. In that year, the *Journal of Physics* published a scientific study entitled "Stock Market Crashes, Precursors and Replicas" by Didier Sornette and Anders Johansen, then of the Laboratoire de Physique de la Matière Condensée at the University of Nice, France, and collaborator Jean-Phillippe Bouchaud. The authors make this statement:

It is intriguing that the log-periodic structures documented here bear some similarity with the "Elliott waves" of technical analysis [citation *Elliott Wave Principle*]. Technical analysis in finance can be broadly defined as the study of financial markets, mainly using graphs of stock prices as a function of time, in the goal of predicting future trends. A lot of effort has been developed in finance both by academic and trading institutions and more recently by physicists (using some of their statistical tools developed to deal with complex times series) to analyze past data to get information on the future. The "Elliott wave" technique is probably the most famous in this field. We speculate that the "Elliott waves"...could be a signature of an underlying critical structure of the stock market.[3]

In this book, I further speculate that the Wave Principle could be a signature of the underlying structures of a whole lot of things. Let us begin our journey.

NOTES

1 Elliott, R.N. (1938). *The wave principle.*

2 **Summary of Additional Technical Aspects**: Additional technical aspects of waves, which are discussed in detail in *Elliott Wave Principle – Key to Market Behavior* by A.J. Frost and Robert R. Prechter, are herewith stated as briefly as possible: Impulses, i.e., five-wave patterns like those shown in Figures 1-1 through 1-7, are typically bound by parallel lines. One wave in an impulse, i.e., 1, 3 *or* 5, is typically extended, i.e., much longer than the other two. In impulses, waves 2 and 4 nearly always alternate in form, where one correction is typically of the zigzag family and the other is not. There are two rare motive variations called diagonal triangles, which are wedge-shaped patterns that appear in one case only at the start (wave 1 or A) and in the other case only at the end (wave 5 or C) of a larger wave. Corrective waves have numerous variations. The main ones are named zigzag (which is the one shown in Figures 1-2, 1-3 and 1-4), flat, and triangle (whose labels include D and E). These three simple corrective patterns can string together to form more complex corrections (the components of which are labeled W, X, Y and Z). Corrections usually terminate within the span of wave 4 of the preceding impulse. Each wave exhibits characteristic volume behavior and a "personality" in terms of attendant momentum and investor sentiment.

3 Sornette, D., Johansen, A., and Bouchaud, J.P. (1996). "Stock market crashes, precursors and replicas." *Journal de Physique I France* 6, No.1, pp. 167-175.

Chapter 2:

Universal Forms: Fractals, Power Laws and Spirals in Self-Organizing Systems, and Their Connection to the Wave Principle

Fractals and Their Relationship to the Wave Principle

A fractal is an irregularly shaped object that is nonrandom in the sense that its discontinuities (i.e., fluctuations) at all scales are similarly irregular. For example, if someone were to show you a line representing the indentations of land along a coastline, you would not be able to say, without other evidence, whether the coastal section was 1 mile long, 10 miles long, 100 miles long or 1000 miles long. A fractal displays the property of self-similarity (or self-affinity, depending on its form) at different scales. The jaggedness of a coastline is self-similarly irregular at different scales. So it is with price graphs of financial markets. As R.N. Elliott pointed out in 1938, the patterns of the Wave Principle take a similarly jagged shape whether viewed on an hourly, daily, weekly, monthly or yearly graph.

In 1689, Jakob and Johan Bernoulli were able to "discern the minute in infinity" in a mathematical progression that foreshadowed the discovery of the fractal geometry of nature.[1] Perhaps the first person specifically to advance the idea of self-similarity at different scales in natural forms was the German poet and naturalist, Johann Wolfgang von Goethe, who in 1790 described the self-similarity of parts to the whole of plants.[2] A century later, from 1874 to 1897, mathematician Georg Cantor studied self-similar sets as mathematical phenomena.[3,4]

In 1919, Felix Hausdorff invented the idea of fractional dimensions to describe the plane- or space-filling property of complex fractals.[5] A fractional dimension (called a Hausdorff dimension prior to the 1980s) describes objects that share properties of two sets of dimensions. For example, if a sheet of paper is considered as a two-dimensional plane, is a partially compressed ball of paper two-dimensional or three-dimensional? It is still a plane, but it has been folded so as to appear to fill space, giving it three-dimensional properties. Its dimension can be measured as a fraction between 2 and 3. In the same way, plots of financial market prices can be considered as a one-dimensional line or as taking up space on a two-dimensional plane.

It is quite certain, since he was careful to name sources that inspired his later ideas, that Elliott never studied Bernoulli, Goethe, Cantor or Hausdorff, so it is acceptable to say that in the 1930s, R.N. Elliott independently rediscovered the idea of self-similarity at different scales. More important, he was unquestionably the first to describe self-affinity as a fundamental property of social phenomena and to recognize its implication for social causality. Here is some of Elliott's commentary that introduced these revolutionary ideas:

> Extensive research in connection with what may be termed human activities indicates that practically all developments which result from our social-economic processes follow a law that causes them to repeat themselves in similar and constantly recurring serials of waves or impulses of definite number and pattern. It is likewise indicated that in their intensity, these waves or impulses bear a consistent relation to one another and to the passage of time.
>
> The expression "human activities" includes such items as stock prices, bond prices, patent (application)s, [the] price of gold, population [growth], movements of citizens from cities to farms and vice versa, commodities prices, government expenditures, production, life insurance [purchases], electric power produced, gasoline consumption, fire losses, price of seats on the stock exchange, epidemics, and real estate [prices].[6] It is particularly evident in those free markets where public participation in price movements is extensive.
>
> Those who have attempted to deal with the market's movements have failed to recognize the extent to which the market is a psychological phenomenon. They have not grasped the fact that there is regularity underlying the fluctuations of the market, or, stated otherwise, that price movements in stocks are subject to rhythms, or an ordered sequence. The wild, senseless and apparently uncontrollable changes in prices from year to year, from month to month, or from day to day, link themselves into a law-abiding rhythmic pattern of waves. The same rules apply to the price of stocks, bonds, grains, cotton, coffee and all the other activities previously mentioned.

The student should recognize that there are cycles within cycles. Major waves subdivide into intermediate waves [, which] subdivide into minor waves. One cycle becomes but the starting point of another, or larger, movement that itself is a part of, and subject to the same law as, the lesser movement. This fundamental law cannot be subverted or set aside by statutes or restrictions. Current news and political developments are of only incidental importance, soon forgotten; their presumed influence on market trends is not as weighty as is commonly believed. Underlying this progression, in whatever field, is a fixed and controlling principle, or the master rule under which nature works.[7]

It has been decades since similar words, more precisely stated, have emerged as a result of studies in fractal geometry. I believe that, especially along with his pioneering diagrams, they are more than sufficient to credit Elliott with having introduced the idea that self-affinity governs social processes and is fundamental to nature. As these words imply, though, and as we shall see more clearly in Chapter 3, Elliott explained that there is much more to the Wave Principle than mere self-affinity.

Examples of the Basic Pattern from the Lowest Extreme of Available Data Duration to the Highest

Elliott pointed out that the impulse-correction pattern, which subdivides into five waves then three waves, is manifest at all degrees of trend. Figures 2-1 through 2-7 illustrate this observation with real-life examples.

The shortest duration of available data is that which shows every single price change in a financial index. Such changes sometimes register in less than a second and are called "ticks." Figure 2-1 shows a "tick" graph from October 6, 1997. Figure 2-2 shows an hourly graph from September 1997. Figure 2-3 is a daily graph from 1962. Figure 2-4 is a weekly graph from 1974-1975.

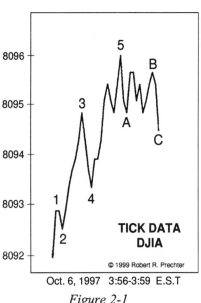

© 1999 Robert R. Prechter

Oct. 6, 1997   3:56-3:59 E.S.T

Figure 2-1

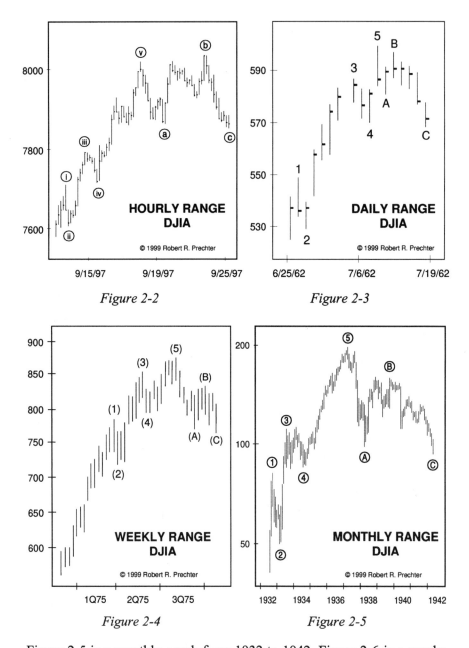

Figure 2-2

Figure 2-3

Figure 2-4

Figure 2-5

Figure 2-5 is a monthly graph from 1932 to 1942. Figure 2-6 is a yearly graph from 1929 to the present. Figure 2-7 is a decade-by-decade graph from 1700 to the present. There are no data prior to 1690. All these plots show similar patterns of movement despite a difference in time span of over 30 million to 1. The longer-term formulations depicted in Figures 2-6 and 2-7 are still unfolding, but to date the pattern is following the same form as the smaller-degree plots.

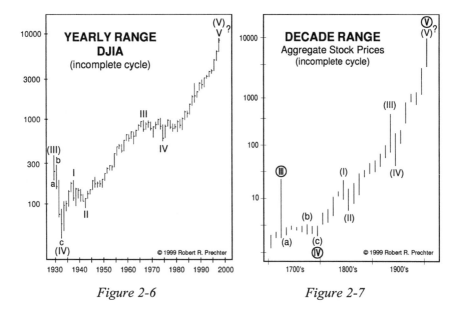

Figure 2-6   *Figure 2-7*

The Ubiquity of Fractals in Nature

The modern science of fractal geometry reveals that nature is replete with self-similar patterns. The pioneer in the recent furthering of this concept is Benoit Mandelbrot, an IBM researcher and former professor at Harvard, Yale and the Einstein College of Medicine. What Mandelbrot has demonstrated is the *ubiquity* of fractals and self-similarity in nature. This discovery has dispelled the idea of randomness in natural forms. Before Mandelbrot, most scientists had presumed that no single geometry governed clouds, seacoasts, mountain ranges, cotton prices and trees. Mandelbrot said that in fact they display a relational form, an orderliness that comes from the fact that they possess self-similarity at different scales.[8]

Countless natural forms are self-similar. Waves on the ocean range from huge swells hundreds of meters in length that are generated by gravitational fluctuations to so-called capillary waves of about one centimeter in length that are controlled by surface tension.[9] In trees, branches off the trunk look like small versions of the tree, as do the twigs off the branches and the veins in the leaves. River systems look like trees, as they branch from rivers to streams to creeks to runoff ditches. Lightning takes a similar form. Manganese oxide creates a fractal branching pattern when it undergoes a reaction-diffusion process on the surface of limestone. Bacteria create similar patterns when growing in a petri dish.

It is tempting to begin viewing almost *everything* as a fractal. A house is a box composed of smaller boxes called floors, which have smaller boxes called rooms. All the houses together in a small geographical area make a neighborhood, and all the neighborhoods in a larger geographical area make a city. Reflecting the same idea, a library has rooms that subdivide into racks that subdivide into bookcases that subdivide into bookshelves that subdivide into books that subdivide into chapters that subdivide into paragraphs that subdivide into sentences. Reverse that list, and you can see how the body of human knowledge grows and how it is stored, all the way up to today's largest encapsulation, the Internet. Psychiatrist Montague Ullman suggests that dreams are fractals, wherein the central concern of the dreamer is expressed both in the overall "story" of the dream and separately in its component parts.[10] Figures 2-8 through 2-15 depict three types of fractals. Chapter 3 will explore their differences.

Fractals in Finance

This excerpt from a 1985 article in *The New York Times* summarizing Mandelbrot's exposition brings us closer to the subject of social fractals:

> When you zoom in, looking closer and closer, the irregularities don't smooth out. Rather, they tend to look exactly as irregular as before. Some of Mandelbrot's fractal patterns looked indistinguishable from records of stock market prices. Economists needed to understand the heretical idea that prices don't change in a smooth, continuous flow. They can change abruptly in instantaneous jumps.[11]

Similarly, Elliott contended that major bull markets are no different in shape from short-term rallies, and big bear markets are no different in shape from short-term reactions. They are just of a larger degree and thus occur less often. A headline-making market "crash," for instance, is simply a large version of what happens all the time on smaller scales. The article continues:

> Daily fluctuations are treated [by economists] one way, while the great changes that bring prosperity or depression are thought to belong to a different order of things. In each case, Mandelbrot said, my attitude is: Let's see what's different from the point of view of geometry. What comes out all seems to fall on a continuum; the mechanisms don't seem to be different.

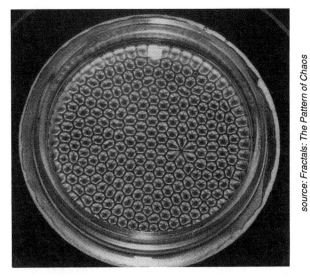

source: Fractals: The Pattern of Chaos

*A self-identical fractal: silicone oil heated to a critical state —
a collection of identical hexagons of increasing size*

Figure 2-8

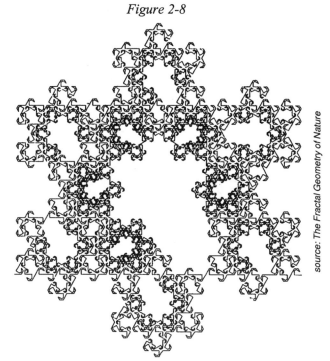

source: The Fractal Geometry of Nature

*A self-identical fractal: computer-generated snowflake —
a collection of identical hexagonal forms of increasing size*

Figure 2-9

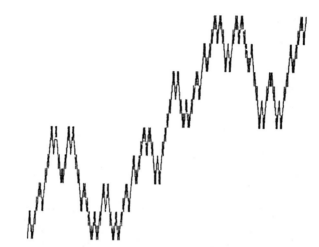

A self-identical fractal: line Iteration – repeating patterns of increasing size

Figure 2-10

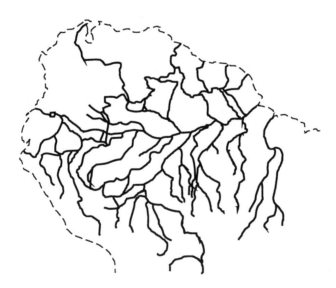

A branching fractal: South American river system

Figure 2-11

A branching fractal: lightning

Figure 2-12

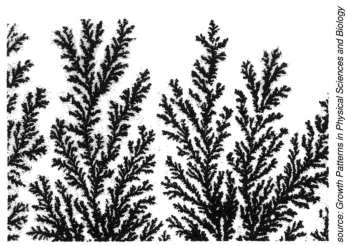

A branching fractal: manganese oxide diffusion

Figure 2-13

source: Growth Patterns in Physical Sciences and Biology

source: http://gordonr.simplenet.com

An indefinite fractal: clouds
Figure 2-14

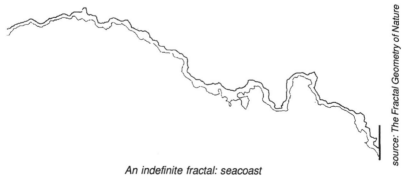

source: The Fractal Geometry of Nature

An indefinite fractal: seacoast
Figure 2-15

This is precisely what R.N. Elliott said about the stock market, and he said it sixty years ago. The following quote, from *Insight* magazine, throws some light on the enormity of Elliott's feat. He discovered all this (and much more; see Chapter 3) in the 1930s using hand-drawn charts of hourly to yearly market data:

> Because of the complexity of the images [scientists] are studying, they use virtually millions of numbers in their calculations. These numbers, says, Quentin Dolecek of Johns Hopkins's Applied Physics Laboratory, would be impossible without computers.[12]

The Ubiquity of Power Laws in Nature

A power law is a formula that when graphed produces a curve whose height is inversely proportional to its distance raised to a power. For instance, the frequency (f) of earthquakes is inversely related to their energy (e) raised to a power (x), as in the formula $f = 1/e^x$. In other words, if a logarithm of the number of events is plotted against the logarithm of their energy, the result is a straight line. Power laws have no intrinsic scale, meaning that graphs of such phenomena appear the same regardless of the size of measurements one might take to assess them.

Much has been made of the fact that power laws govern fractals, although the very idea of a fractal seems naturally to imply a power law. Self-similarity *at all scales* implies that the *frequency* of events, fluctuations or patterns in a fractal will vary inversely with their *size*.

The Gutenberg-Richter law, identified a half-century ago, states that the severity of earthquakes as measured by the Richter scale is related to their frequency according to a power law.[13] Also in 1949, G.K. Zipf found that the distribution of wealth throughout a society follows a power law.[14] In the 1990s, scientists are discovering that power laws govern an immense number of fractal formations and events, both animate and inanimate, including avalanches, earthquakes, mountain sizes, zigs and zags in the flights of bees, economic fluctuations and financial market fluctuations. Richard Voss of IBM's T.J. Watson Research Center found a power law in the structure of DNA.[15] H. Eugene Stanley of Boston University, says *New Scientist,* has found a power law "in the dynamics of the human heart and lungs."[16] Stephen Wolfram of Wolfram Research in Champaign, Illinois, has developed a computer program, "Mathematica," that applies power-law aspects of complexity theory (see Chapter 20) to fields as diverse as "designing the bicycle track at the 1996 Olympic games, predicting the flow rates of molecules in commercial shampoos, determining how tidal waves evolve...and 'how biological systems can be constructed.'"[17] Wolfram's research began with a search in the 1980s to investigate "patterns on mollusk shells, the behavior of molecules swirling in a turbulent fluid, and fluctuating prices on the stock market." Norman Packard, an associate who with Wolfram set up the Center for Complex Systems at the University of Illinois, applies the fundamentals of complexity theory "to help Swiss banks play the stock market."[18] Scientists today are studying complex systems to find out how matter can organize itself into more complex forms (Per Bak of the Neils Bohr Institute in Copenhagen), how life originated (Stuart Kauffman at the Santa Fe Institute), and how complex systems, from a collection of bacteria to a group of competing companies, behave (Christopher Langton at the Santa Fe Institute). Power laws are everywhere in such systems, including financial markets.

A Power Law in the Stock Market

R.N. Elliott's depiction of the progress of the stock market unequivocally implied that while larger stock market reactions occur less often than small ones, they do not occur less often *relative to the size of advances that precede them*, but in fact just about as often. In other words, Elliott implied that the stock market follows a power law. In 1995, Boston University physicists Gene Stanley and Rosario Mantegna found that the fluctuations in the Standard & Poor's Composite index of the 500 highest capitalized stocks do follow a power law. This particular power law is a Levy stable law (named after a French mathematician of the early 20th century), which produces a bell curve with "extended wings," indicating that far-from-normal fluctuations in terms of size occur a bit more often than they would if they followed a one-to-one relationship to the duration of the data sample. Figure 2-16, from Mantegna and Stanley's article in *Nature,* demonstrates that the S&P's fluctuations are quite uniform throughout the time scale, from 1 minute to 1000 minutes.[19] This finding is consistent with the Wave Principle, which creates the same forms at all sizes of trend, with the added wrinkle that large fluctuations, at least in this data sample, occurred a bit more often than smaller ones relative to the time intervals between them.

Levy laws also govern birds' flying and landing patterns, drips from leaky faucets, the wanderings of ants, and fluctuations in cotton prices and heartbeats. Stanley is applying the behavioral similarities of complex systems to understanding landscape formation, traffic patterns, Alzheimer's disease and the behavior of neutron stars. Like fractals, power laws suffuse nature.

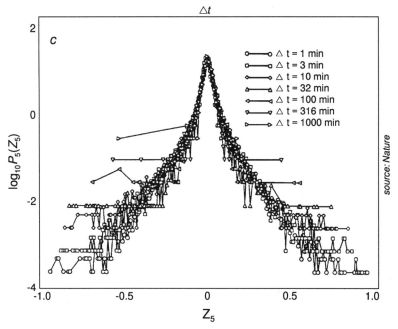

Consistent fractal fluctuation at varying time intervals in the S&P 500

Figure 2-16

Quantity and Quality in Fractals and Power Laws

Fractals involve sizes, but specific sizes do not matter in describing or defining a fractal object. In the same way, power laws relate to sizes and frequencies, but the specific sizes and frequencies do not matter to the formulae. Quantitatively, what matters in each case is *relative* sizes and frequencies, i.e., *relationships*, not absolutes.

Qualitatively, what matters in fractals and power laws is *form*, not size. Trees are governed by form, not absolute branch size. Heartbeat is governed by pattern, not absolute frequency. The spirals of Nautilus sea-shells and the galaxies are governed by a single form, not their size. As we said in *Elliott Wave Principle*, "The patterns that Elliott discerned [in financial markets] are repetitive in *form* but not necessarily in time or amplitude." A fractal is not the only ubiquitous natural phenomenon whose essence is its form. The other is the spiral.

The Ubiquity of Spirals in Nature

Like fractals and power laws, spirals appear throughout nature. While Euclidean geometric forms (except perhaps for the ellipse) typically imply stasis, a spiral implies motion: growth and decay, expansion and contraction, progress and regress.[20] The logarithmic spiral, which depicts constant geometric expansion, is the quintessential expression of growth in the universe and is reflected in structures as diverse as pine cones, sunflowers, sea shells, whirlpools and hurricanes. It covers scales as small as the motion of atomic particles and as large as galaxies. The spiral is also one of biology's most ancient body forms. The exoskeletons of early sea animals developed Fibonacci-based spiral shapes that have persisted through to today, as you can see in Figures 2-25 and 2-27. A fossilized Lake Ivo fern is virtually identical to its present-day counterpart, as you can see in these two photographs from *The Smithsonian* (Figure 2-17). If you would like to see a counterpart to this form in fauna, hold up your arm so that your hand is at eye level, then make a fist (holding your thumb inside), and bend your wrist inward. Looking at the side view, do you see the fern? Figures 2-18 through 2-28 illustrate more of these forms.

Does the Wave Principle, which already incorporates two aspects shared by common patterns in nature, i.e., fractals and a power law, reflect spiral growth as well? The idealized depiction of the stock market's progression, as presented in Figure 1-4, is an excellent base from which to

source: Smithsonian, Nov. 84

Lake Ivo fern, modern and fossilized

Figure 2-17

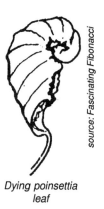

Dying poinsettia leaf

Figure 2-18

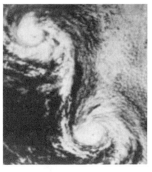

source: Fascinating Fibonacci

Whirlpool

Figure 2-19

source: Omni Magazine

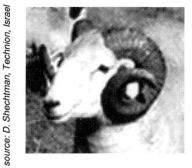

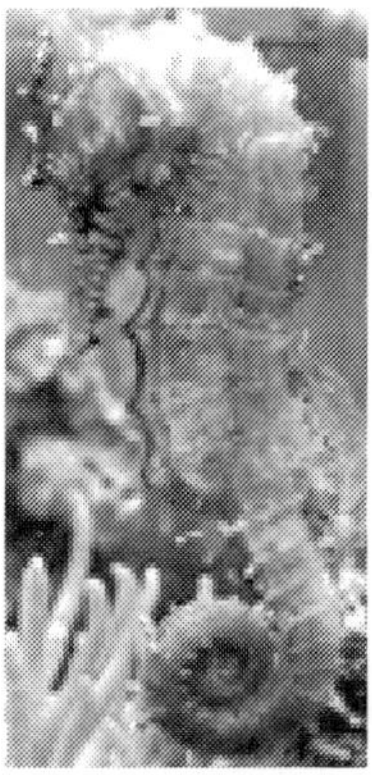

Sea horse

Figure 2-20

source: Jay Frase, http://home1.gte.net/frasej/

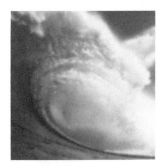

Ocean waves

Figure 2-21

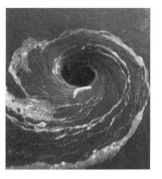

Hurricane

Figure 2-22

source: Omni Magazine

Quasi-crystal under an electron microscope

Figure 2-23

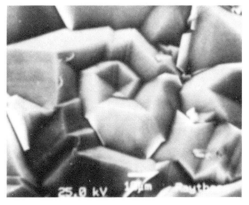

source: D. Shechtman, Technion, Israel

Horn

Figure 2-24

source: www.ansi.okstate.edu

source: Omni Magazine

Spirals in shells
Figure 2-25

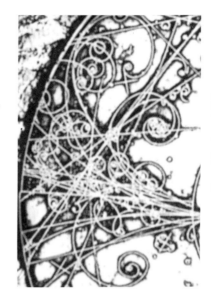

source: Nova-Adventures in Science

Atomic particles in bubble chamber
Figure 2-26

Nautilus
Figure 2-27

source: Hale Observatories

Spiraling galaxy
Figure 2-28

construct a logarithmic spiral, as Figure 2-29 illustrates. In this construction, the top of each successive wave of higher degree is the touch point of the exponential expansion. The further time extends, the larger the degrees of trend get, implying a geometric expansion in the size of the advances and retrenchments that form mankind's progress.

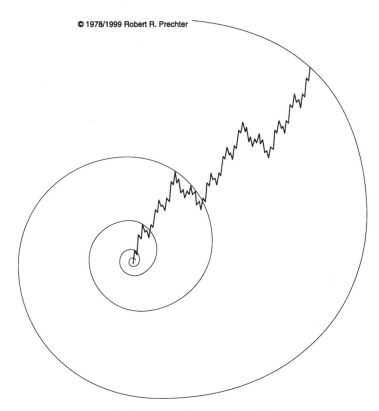

Elliott waves reflect spiral growth

Figure 2-29

The propagation of the *lowest* form of animal, bacteria, can be plotted as a logarithmic spiral. Figure 2-29 implies that the growth of the *highest* form of animal can also be plotted as a logarithmic spiral. While it may seem a wild concept that the progress of life, including human life, can be mapped as a logarithmic spiral, some recent scientific endeavors support this depiction, which was originally published in *Elliott Wave Principle* in

1978. For example, *Physics Reports* has just published a ground-breaking paper by Didier Sornette of the Department of Earth and Space Science and the Institute of Geophysics and Planetary Physics at the University of California at Los Angeles. "Discrete Scale Invariance and Complex Dimensions"[21] demonstrates log periodicity and complex dimensions in the stock market, which are exactly what Figure 2-29 implies. Two years ago, Sornette collaborated on a published study that specifically identifies the shape that results when such distributions, which are common in certain self-similar systems, are graphed. The report concludes, the "trajectory describing a discrete self-similar system [such as the stock market] in the complex coupling constant plane [such as a price graph] is a *spiral*."[22]

Scientists are finding the spiral shape in the natural processes of even broader aggregations such as ecologies. Here is an example, as described by *Newsweek*:

> Population biologists, for instance, were among the first to notice chaos. Lions and zebras, ferrets and prairie dogs — their numbers can careen off into wild and seemingly random oscillations. Was this chaos? To find out, researchers sought strange attractors for these predator-prey systems — the fingerprint of chaos that shows the behavior of each population through time. Unfortunately, data on natural populations is lousy. Finding chaos requires several generations worth of clean data, and scientists don't have it. So chaoticians turned to lab and computer experiments. Researchers led by Oxford's [Robert] May recently built a computer model of parasites that lay eggs in insects. They input rules for how many parasites and hosts move to adjacent patches of grass each generation. Then they hit "go." When they mapped the relative abundances of hosts and parasites, they got diagrams resembling such emblems of chaos as intricate *spiral waves* and crystal lattices. "Simple interactions among species may lead...[to] chaotic patterns in space," says zoologist Anthony Ives of the University of Wisconsin, "where population booms and busts occur in a *seemingly random* pattern" — yet one that is actually a highly ordered lattice or spiral.[23] [see Figure 2-30.]

In other words, spiraling appears to be a fundamental aspect of growing systems that involve bipolarity, stress and fluctuation. This correlation is not only compatible with the Wave Principle's depiction of the human social experience but also with the fact that species fluctuations also apparently follow the Wave Principle, as Chapter 13 will demonstrate.

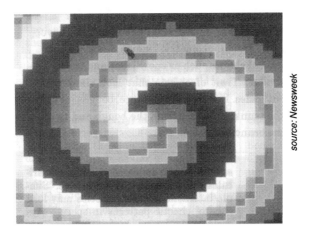

A mathematical simulation of a predator-prey balance in nature shows a spiral design

Figure 2-30

R.N. Elliott said sixty years ago that the phenomenon he described as the behavior of financial markets was a universal principle of nature. Scientific discoveries in the 1980s and 1990s are leading to the same conclusion. To put it summarily, it is no longer acceptable to label this aspect of the Wave Principle as grandiose or mystical; its general nature reflects discoveries of modern mainstream science. Now let us progress to some more pertinent specifics.

NOTES

1 Dunham, W. (1990). *Journey through genius.*

2 Goethe, J.W. (1790). "On the metamorphosis of plants."

3 Dauben, J.W. (1990). *Georg Cantor: his mathematics and philosophy of the infinite.*

4 For more on the pioneers in fractals, see *Classics on Fractals.* G.A. Edgar, ed. (1993), Addison-Wesley, Reading MA.

5 Hausdorff, F. (1919). "Dimension und äusseres mass." *Mathematische Annalen,* 79, pp. 157-179.

6 Elliott showed graphs of these activities in *The Wave Principle* (1938).

7 These sentences are collected from pp. 92, 147, 157, 183, 192, 217, 218, 228, 229 of *R.N. Elliott's Masterworks — The Definitive Collection* (1994), which includes *The wave principle* (1938), The *Financial World* articles (1939), "The basis of the wave principle" (1940) and *Nature's law* (1946). I have omitted ellipses and one-letter brackets for reading clarity.

8 Mandelbrot, B. (1988). *The fractal geometry of nature.*

9 Glazman, R. (1988, April). "Fractal features of sea surface...." *OE Reports.*

10 Briggs, J. and Peat, F.D. (1989). *Turbulent mirror,* p.110.

11 Gleick, J. (1985, December 29). "Unexpected order in chaos." *This World.*

12 Hanson, G. (1990, October 8). "A world that is graphically real." *Insight.*

13 Gutenberg, B. and Richter, C.F. (1949). *Seismicity of the earth.*

14 Zipf, G.K. (1949). *Human behavior and the principle of least action.*

15 Voss, R. (1992). "Evolution of long range fractal correlations and 1/f noise in DNA base sequences." *Phys. Lett.* 68:3805-3808.

16 Buchanan, M. (1997, November 8). "One law to rule them all." *New Scientist.*

17 Hotz, R. (1997, October). "A study in complexity." *Technology Review.*

18 *Ibid.*

19 Mantegna, R. and Stanley, H.E. (1995, July 6). "Scaling behaviour in the dynamics of an economic index." *Nature.*

20 As with nonlife and life (see near the end of Chapter 13), stasis and growth may not be that unrelated. There is an intimate connection between the governing ratio of the circle (*pi,* represented by π, which is 3.1416...) and the governing ratio of the golden spiral (*phi,* represented by ϕ, which is

1.618034...). One formula illustrating the relationship between *pi* and *phi* is:

$$F_n \approx 100 \times \pi^2 \times \phi^{(15-n)},$$

where n represents the numerical position of the term in the sequence and F_n represents each term in the Fibonacci sequence. The number "1" is represented only once, so $F_1 \approx 1$, $F_2 \approx 2$, $F_3 \approx 3$, $F_4 \approx 5$, etc. (For more on *phi* and the Fibonacci sequence, see Chapter 3.)

21 Sornette, D. (1998). "Discrete scale invariance and complex dimensions." *Physics Report,* No. 297, pp. 239-270.

22 Saleur, H. and Sornette, D. (1996). "Complex exponents and log-periodic corrections in frustrated systems." *Journal de Physique I France* 6, No. 3, pp.327-355.

23 Begley, S., *et al.* (1992, May 25). "Finding order in chaos." *Newsweek.*

Chapter 3:

Robust Fractals and Fibonacci Mathematics

R.N. Elliott went *far* beyond the comparatively simple idea that financial prices form an indefinite fractal with an implied power law. His big achievements were in discovering *specific component patterns* within the overall form[1] as well as its connection to *Fibonacci mathematics*.[2] First we will explore pattern.

Types of Fractals

Until very recently, it has been generally presumed that there are two types of self-similar forms in nature: (1) *self-identical* fractals, whose parts are precisely the same as the whole, and (2) *indefinite fractals*, which are self-similar only in that they are similarly irregular at all scales.

Nature does produce fractals of the first type. When magnets, oils, crystals and water are at a critical state bordering on phase transition (i.e., between magnetic and nonmagnetic, a different cellular arrangement, a different molecular arrangement, and gas-liquid, respectively), the components are, except for size, "precisely, exactly, mathematically identical" to the whole.[3] In each case, the whole is not simply as irregular as its parts; it is *exactly the same form* as its parts, from the largest size component to the next and the next. Figures 2-8 through 2-10 illustrate this idea: The oil forms hexagons that make up larger hexagons; the snowflake is a precisely repeating hexagonal form; the rigidly repeating line pattern mimics the shape of a financial market.

Figures 2-14 and 2-15 are depictions of a seacoast and clouds, which are presumed to be fractals of the second type. The literature on natural fractals concludes that nature most commonly produces indefinite fractal forms that are orderly only in the extent of their discontinuity at different scales and otherwise disorderly. Scientific descriptions of natural fractals detail no specific patterns composing such forms. Seacoasts are just "jagged lines," trees are composed simply of "branches," rivers but meander, and heartbeats and earthquakes are merely "events" that differ in frequency. Likewise, financial markets are considered to be self-similarly discontinuous in the relative sizes and frequencies of trend reversals yet otherwise randomly patterned. These conclusions may be due to a shortfall in empirical study rather than a scientific fact.

Robust Fractals: Elliott's Discovery of a Third Type of Self-Similarity

R.N. Elliott described for financial markets a third type of self-similarity. By meticulously studying the natural world of social man in the form of graphs of stock market prices, Elliott found that there are *specific patterns* to the stock market fractal that are nevertheless *highly variable* within a certain definable latitude. In other words, some aspects of their form are *constant* and others are *variant*. If this is true, then financial markets, and by extension, social systems in general, are not vague, indefinite fractals. Component patterns do not simply display *discontinuity* similar to that of larger patterns, but *they form, with a certain defined latitude, replicas of them*.

Elliott defined waves in terms of what makes them identical, thereby allowing for their variability in some aspects of detail within the scope of those definitions. He was even able to define some of the patterns' variable characteristics in probabilistic terms. Elliott's discovery of *degrees* in pattern formation, i.e., that a certain number of waves of one degree are required to make up a wave of the next higher degree, is vitally important because it links the building-block property of self-*identical* fractals to the Wave Principle, revealing an aspect of self-identity among waves that indefinite fractals do not possess.

The fact that both waves and (as we shall soon see) natural branching systems are fractals of *intermediate specificity* implies that nature uses this fractal style to pattern systems that require highly adaptive variability in order to flourish. Therefore, I think the best term for this variety of fractal is *robust* fractal.

Elliott's discovery of specific hierarchical patterning in the stock market is fundamental. Even fractals and power laws, which go to the essence of form, are only a vague comment about that form. They do little to define the object. *If you can describe the pattern, you have the essence of the object.* The more meticulously you can describe the pattern, the closer you get to knowing what it is.

Although Elliott came to his conclusions fifty years before the new science of fractals blossomed, the very idea that financial markets comprise specific forms and identical (within the scope of their definitions) component forms remains a revolutionary observation because to this day, it has eluded other financial market researchers and chaos scientists. Elliott's work shows that the general relationship between sizes and frequencies of financial movements, currently considered a breakthrough discovery, is not the essence, but a by-product, of the fundamentals of financial market patterns.

The end of Chapter 2 commented that due to the new science of fractal geometry, the Wave Principle can no longer be considered fantastic on the grounds of the unlikelihood of self-similarity at different scales. There is good news pertaining to our current discussion as well. A group of scientists (see Arneodo, *et al.* in "The Robust Fractal Reappears" section later in this chapter) has very recently recognized that there is a type of fractal in nature whose self-similarity is intermediate between identical and indefinite. As far as I know, theirs is the only published study on the subject. Nevertheless, science is once again edging toward confirmation of another important aspect of the Wave Principle that heretofore, to skeptics, appeared to reflect either undue imprecision or undue complexity. In fact, it reflects reality. I believe that *robustness will prove to be the essence of fractals that matter most in nature.*

Describing in What Ways Waves Are Identical and in What Ways They Are Variable

The concept of a robust fractal is difficult to depict visually because a single illustration cannot convey both those aspects of an Elliott wave that are invariant and those that are variable, i.e., what its manifestations have in common and what they need not. We can draw the essence of an Elliott wave but not state the precise path that any manifestation of it will actually take. Elliott waves in reality always conform to a few simple rules of patterning, but vary considerably within that format. The advancing and declining patterns throughout Figure 1-4 are depicted as self-identical, like the forms in Figures 2-8 through 2-10, simply because there is no better way to convey the essential idea. Presenting the full description of what actually happens requires verbal discussion and/or many illustrations.

Elliott described five elementary patterns in the stock market, which he called impulse, diagonal triangle, zigzag, flat and triangle. The first two occur in motive mode (i.e., when prices are moving in the direction of the trend of one larger degree, effecting the larger wave's progress), while the latter three occur in corrective mode (i.e., when prices are moving opposite the direction of the trend of one larger degree, punctuating its progress). Figure 3-1 summarizes these five patterns. In corrections, sometimes two of the patterns will occur side by side, interrupted by an intervening zigzag, as noted under the heading, "Double Three."

One Example of a Detailed Description of an Elliott Wave

This section should give you a flavor of Elliott's powers of observation as well as an idea of how robust fractals may be defined. He noted, for instance, the following characteristics of an impulse, the most common form of motive wave, as depicted in Figure 1-1 and in the top left of Figure 3-1. Do not bother to memorize these traits; the point is that the description is quite detailed.

> The impulse subdivides into five waves, which may be labeled 1, 2, 3, 4 and 5.
> Wave 2 never moves beyond the start of wave 1.
> Wave 3 is never the shortest wave.
> Wave 4 never moves beyond the end of wave 1.
> Waves 1, 3 and 5 each subdivide into five waves.
> Waves 2 and 4 each subdivide into a corrective pattern.
> Wave 3 always takes the form of an impulse.
> Wave 1 always takes the form of an impulse.[4]
> Wave 5 may be an impulse or a diagonal triangle (an Elliott wave that is defined elsewhere; see illustration in Figure 3-1).
> Typically, wave 1 or 3 or 5 is an extension, which means that it is substantially longer than each of the others and contains larger subdivisions than each of the others does.
> Wave 3 is most commonly the extended wave.
> Wave 1 is least commonly the extended wave.
> When wave 3 is extended, waves 1 and 5 tend toward equality of amplitude.

SUMMARY OF MOTIVE PATTERNS

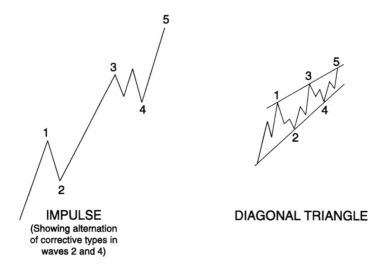

IMPULSE
(Showing alternation
of corrective types in
waves 2 and 4)

DIAGONAL TRIANGLE

SUMMARY OF CORRECTIVE PATTERNS

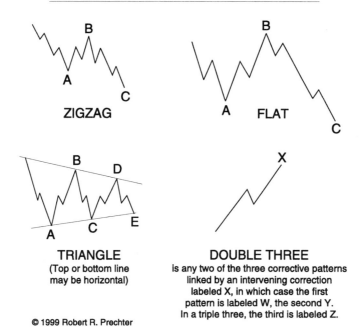

ZIGZAG

FLAT

TRIANGLE
(Top or bottom line
may be horizontal)

DOUBLE THREE
is any two of the three corrective patterns
linked by an intervening correction
labeled X, in which case the first
pattern is labeled W, the second Y.
In a triple three, the third is labeled Z.

© 1999 Robert R. Prechter

Figure 3-1

The center of wave 3 has the steepest slope of any equal period within the larger impulse.

Among the three basic types of corrective waves (see Figure 3-1), wave 4 will almost always be a different type than wave 2.

Wave 4 typically ends when it is between the starting and ending levels of subwave four of 3.

Wave 4 often divides the entire impulse into .618/.382 proportion.

Sometimes wave 5 does not exceed the level of the end of wave 3.

Wave 5 often ends when meeting or slightly exceeding a line drawn from the end of wave 3 that is parallel to the line connecting the ends of waves 2 and 4, on either arithmetic or semilog scale.

When wave 5 is extended, it is often 1.618 times as long as the net travel of waves 1 through 3.

When wave 1 is extended, it is often 1.618 times as long as the net travel of waves 3 through 5.

This list covers only the main rules and guidelines of form for this one Elliott wave. Go back to Chapter 2 and examine Figures 2-1 through 2-7. You will see that all of those illustrations incorporate these rules and guidelines.

Each of the five elementary patterns shown in Figure 3-1 has its own description as well as a short catalog of variations that are similarly delineated by differences in form. For instance, sometimes both boundary lines of a triangle slope toward each other, and sometimes either the top or bottom line is horizontal. As another example, sometimes wave B of a flat ends at the level of the start of wave A, and sometimes it ends beyond it. Elliott attached a name to each of these differences in form so that with his terms, we know immediately what form and variation we are talking about.

If Elliott was anything, he was meticulous. His description of waves, their positions within larger waves, and their relative frequency of occurrence have stood the test of sixty years' intensive application by some very dedicated practitioners,[5] with only minor modifications.[6] Additionally, I have quantified on sliding scales all of the patterns' variable features in the process of building our Elliott wave computer program, which I discuss in Chapter 4, and have formulated additional guidelines for discriminating among waves, some of which are referenced in Chapters 5 and 6.[7]

The essence of the Wave Principle is "5-3," but there is quite a bit more to know about it. There are reasons to believe that there is more to know about the form of natural branching systems, and perhaps other natural fractals, as well. Before we make that connection, we have to investigate another aspect of waves.

The Fibonacci Sequence and Ratio

The Fibonacci sequence[8] is 1, 1, 2, 3, 5, 8, 13, 21, 34, 55, and so on. It begins with the number 1, and each new term from there is the sum of the previous two. The limit ratio between the terms is .618034..., an irrational number variously called the "golden mean" and "divine proportion," but in this century more succinctly *phi* (ϕ) after the architect Phidias, who designed the Parthenon. Both the Fibonacci sequence and the Fibonacci ratio appear ubiquitously in natural forms ranging from the geometry of the DNA molecule to the physiology of plants and animals, as we will see in this chapter and in Chapter 11. This book will not present a treatise on Fibonacci; you can find a pretty good one in Chapter 3 of *Elliott Wave Principle* and other sources.

In the past few years, science has taken a quantum leap in knowledge concerning the universal appearance and fundamental importance of Fibonacci mathematics. Chapters 10, 11, 12 and 21 will explore the wider scope of this new knowledge and its implications. For the time being, it might interest readers to know that some of the greatest intellects in Western thought, from Pythagoras to Isaac Newton, held a special reverence for the role of *phi* in nature.[9] (For more on this subject, see Chapter 3 of *Elliott Wave Principle*.) Some of history's greatest minds might have agreed with R.N. Elliott's rather incautious contention that *phi* is the secret of the universe,[10] but for now, let us simply explore how it relates to waves.

The Fibonacci Sequence in the Wave Principle

Elliott's publisher, renowned investment advisor Charles Collins, first realized that the Wave Principle is connected to the Fibonacci sequence, and communicated that fact to Elliott. After researching the subject to the small extent possible at the time, Elliott presented the final unifying conclusion of his theory in 1940,[11] explaining that the progress of waves has the same mathematical base as so many phenomena of life.[12]

The Fibonacci sequence governs the numbers of waves that form the movement of aggregate stock prices in an expansion upon the underlying 5-3 relationship. Figure 3-2 shows the progression. The simplest expression of a corrective wave is a straight-line decline. The simplest expression of a motive wave is a straight-line advance. A complete cycle is two lines. At the next degree of complexity, the corresponding numbers are 3, 5 and 8. This sequence continues to infinity.[13] We will now explore why this fact is important.

THE SUBDIVISION OF WAVES
REPRODUCES THE FIBONACCI SEQUENCE

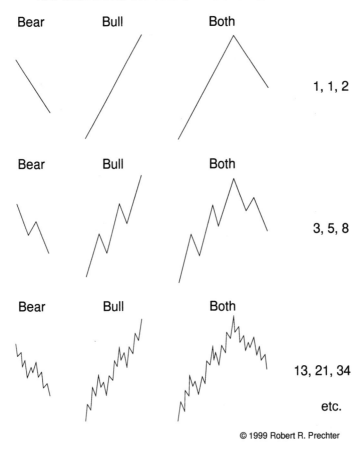

© 1999 Robert R. Prechter

The subdivision of waves reproduces the Fibonacci sequence

Figure 3-2

The Fibonacci Sequence and Ratio in Plant Life

A grand connection between Fibonacci and life has been proposed from time to time. In the seventeenth century, mathematician Jakob Bernoulli, the father of probability analysis, was the first modern European to observe the importance of the Fibonacci ratio in nature. Early in the twentieth century, several publications reported on Fibonacci expressions in plant and animal physiology, including *The Curves of Life* by Theodore Cook (1914), *On Growth and Form* by Scottish zoologist D'Arcy Thompson (1917), *The Elements of Dynamic Symmetry* by Jay Hambidge (from articles published by the Yale University Press in 1919), and papers by Oxford professor A.H. Church on "Phyllotaxis in Relation to Mechanical Law."

There are many expressions of Fibonacci mathematics in plants, from leaf arrangements to branching tendencies to the numbers of petals in flowers. For instance, lilies have 3 petals, buttercups 5, delphiniums 8, marigolds 13, asters 21, and most daisies 34, 55 or 89. While flowers occasionally reveal non-Fibonacci numbers, says Professor Ian Stewart, "you don't find any other numbers anything like as often," and when you do, they often reflect the family of numbers called the Lucas sequence:[14] 1, 3, 4, 7, 11, 18, 29, etc., which is the Fibonacci phenomenon of additive growth starting with two different numbers, 1 and 3, instead of 1 and 2. Figure 3-3 is an idealization of a plant showing the number of its branches on various planes proceeding along the Fibonacci sequence as it climbs upward. Figure 3-4 is a photograph of the candy lily plant at the entrance to my driveway. From stem to tip, it subdivides 1, 2, 3, 5.[15] Its berries tend to have 21 kernels. Not all Fibonacci expression in plants is numerical. Figure 3-5 is a depiction of the baby's breath that came with the roses I bought for my wife recently. At every furcation, it branches into three stems that take the rough shape of an upwardly expanding cone. Can you spot how Fibonacci governs this form? If not, read endnote 16.[16] Stephane Douaday and Yves Couder of the Laboratoire de Physique Statistique and the Laboratoire de Physique in France explain that phyllotaxis, the Fibonacci-based structure of plants, is a self-organized growth process.[17] As we shall see, many (if not all) self-organized growth processes involve Fibonacci mathematics.

Fibonacci numbers appear in the tiniest first cells of a growing plant, called primordia, which grow outward from an apex along a spiral called a "generative spiral" that ultimately produces the plant. Two researchers, the Bravais brothers, found the mathematical rule that governs the spacing of the primordia along the generative spiral.[18] It turns out that the angles be-

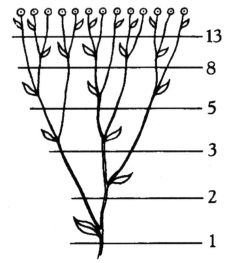

source: Fascinating Fibonaccis

Sneezewort (*Achillea ptarmica*), with number of
stems at each horizontal level of development.
(Adapted with permission from E.H. Huntley,
The Divine Proportion.)

Figure 3-3

A candy lily branches 1, 2, 3, 5

Figure 3-4

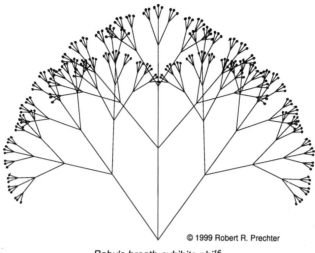

Baby's breath exhibits phi[16]

Figure 3-5

tween the center of the apex and successive primordia is always the same, approximately 137.5 degrees. This angle is .382 (1 - ϕ and ϕ^2) of the full circle of 360 degrees and is called the golden angle. G. Van Iterson[19] in 1907 showed that this angle produces two families of interlocking Fibonacci spirals, one clockwise and the other counterclockwise (see Figures 3-9 through 3-11). In 1979, H. Vogel explained why: The golden angle is the only divergence angle at which seeds may pack without gaps, making it the most efficient method of packing and the only way to achieve full density in the seed head.[20,21]

Efficiency is not the only advantage that Fibonacci has for life forms. It is also the best sequence for robustness, which is to say, for providing the greatest latitude for variability and growth in an integer-based system. The reason is that the Fibonacci ratio has a unique property that sets it apart from all other irrational numbers. When using increasingly large whole numbers in fractions to approach limits, the differences between the result and the limit shrink more slowly for *phi* than for any other irrational number.[22] I infer from this fact that *phi* allows for more and longer growth in real-world entities, which must be counted in whole numbers, than any other limit.

To summarize the above paragraphs, nature uses Fibonacci for *efficiency* and *robustness* in plants, which are *self-organizing growth forms*. As this book progresses, we shall investigate the possibility that social man is participating in a self-organizing growth form whose progress is governed by Fibonacci mathematics because it allows the greatest efficiency and robustness.

Meticulous observers have related the Fibonacci sequence specifically to the growth and form of plants for some time. Now there is evidence that Fibonacci mathematics regulate *all* fractal branching systems.

Fibonacci in Diffusion-Limited Aggregations (Branching Systems)

In the early 1990s, five scientists from the Centre de Recherche Paul Pascal and the Ecole Normale Supeieure in France investigated the diffusion-limited aggregation model, which is a set that diffuses via smaller and smaller branches. Arneodo *et al.* state at the outset that it is "an open question whether or not some structural order is hidden in the apparently disordered DLA morphology."[23] To investigate the question, they use a wavelet transform microscope to examine "the intricate fractal geometry of large-mass off-lattice DLA clusters." (See Figure 3-6.) In the first linking (as far as I can discover) of the two concepts of fractals and Fibonacci since Elliott, they demonstrate that their research "reveals the exist-

source: *Growth Patterns in Physical Sciences and Biology*

DLA cluster
Figure 3-6

ence of Fibonacci sequences in the internal 'extinct' region of these clusters." These mathematics pertain to "apparently randomly branched fractals that bear a striking resemblance to the tenuous tree-like structures observed in viscous fingering, electrodeposition, bacterial growth and neuronal growth," which are "strikingly similar to trees, root systems, algae, blood vessels and the bronchial architecture," i.e., *the typical products of nature*. The study shows that these apparently random fractals are in fact *more orderly than previously realized*. Specifically, the authors find that the branching characteristics of off-lattice DLA clusters "proceed according to the *Fibonacci recursion law*," i.e., they branch in intervals to produce a 1-2-3-5-8-13-etc. progression in the number of branches. The authors of this study, then, have found the Fibonacci sequence in DLA clusters *in the same place that R.N. Elliott found the Fibonacci sequence in the Wave Principle*: in the increasing numbers of subdivisions as the phenomenon progresses.

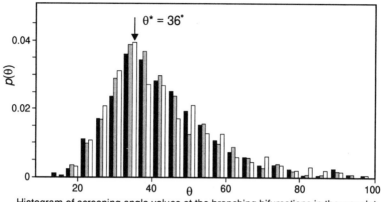

Histogram of screening angle values at the branching bifurcations in the wavelet transform representation of 4 off-lattice DLA clusters; three magnifications a^{-1} (black), $(2.2)\ a^{-1}$ (grey) and $(2.2)^2\ a^{-1}$ (clear) are shown, corresponding respectively to three successive generations of branching. A single maximum is observed for $\theta^* \sim 36°$.

source: Growth Patterns in Physical Sciences and Biology

Figure 3-7

The authors find even more evidence of Fibonacci. They have discovered that the most commonly occurring "screening angle" between bifurcating branches of these DLA clusters is 36 degrees, which holds *regardless of scale*. (See Figure 3-7.) This is the ruling angle of geometric phenomena that display Fibonacci properties, from the five-pointed star (see Figure 3-8) to Penrose tiles (see Figure 21-4). The authors elaborate:

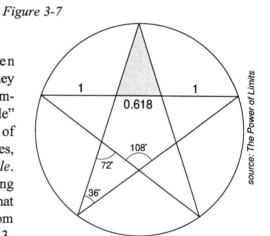

source: The Power of Limits

Fibonacci in the five-pointed star

Figure 3-8

The intimate relationship between regular pentagons and Fibonacci numbers and the golden mean $\phi = 2\cos(\pi/5) = 1.618...$ has been well known for a long time. The proportions of a pentagon approximate the proportions between adjacent Fibonacci numbers; the higher the numbers are, the more exact the approximation to the golden mean becomes. The angle defined by the sides of the star and the regular pentagons is $\theta = 36°$, while the ratio of their length is a Fibonacci ratio (F_{n+1}/F_n).

The authors conclude, "The existence of this symmetry *at all scales* is likely to be a clue to a structural hierarchical fractal ordering." Indeed, it is. In not a dissimilar way, Elliott found that the price lengths of certain waves are often related by .618, *at all scales*, revealing another, though perhaps less fundamental, Fibonacci aspect of waves.

There is another link between these two phenomena, though it is a bit amorphous conceptually. 36 degrees is 1/**5** of a semicircle, is the ruling angle of the **5**-pointed star, and is half the angle of the **pent**agon, whose 72-degree angles are 1/**5** of a circle. The average bifurcation angle, then, links the property of "fiveness" to DLA clusters just as Figure 1-1 displays the importance of "fiveness" to the Wave Principle. The formula for *phi* itself, which is ($\sqrt{5}$ - 1)/2 or ($\sqrt{5}$ + 1)/2 depending upon the inversion, is grounded upon the square root of **5**. Apparently, among all Fibonacci numbers, the number 5 has the most fundamental importance to *phi*. The reason may be its necessity in creating progress in the form of waves as explained in Chapter 1 under the heading,"Why 5-3?"

The authors announce that their "wavelet analysis provides the first numerical evidence for the existence of a 'Fibonaccian' quasi-fractal structural ordering in DLA clusters." This is terrific news because DLA structures occur in countless of nature's living forms and processes, one of which the Wave Principle purports to depict.

The Robust Fractal Reappears

In a brilliant concluding proposal, Arneodo, *et al.* determine from just this data that they are working with a type of fractal that scientists had not yet found, an intermediate form between perfect self-identity and vague, indefinite self-similarity:

> The intimate relationship between regular pentagons and Fibonacci numbers and the golden mean...has been well known for a long time.... The recent discovery of "quasi-crystals" [see Figure 2-23 and Chapter 21 —ed.] in solid state physics is a spectacular manifestation of this relationship. This new organization of atoms in solids, *intermediate between perfect order and disorder*, generalizes to the crystalline "forbidden" symmetries, the properties of incommensurate structures. *Similarly, there is room for "quasi-fractals" between the well-ordered fractal hierarchy of snowflakes and the disordered structure of chaotic or random aggregates.*"[24]

This is the same type of intermediately ordered fractal that R.N. Elliott described for the stock market. Of course, Elliott managed to detail many more aspects of that fractal, showing to a far greater degree how substantially its form is self-identical within a certain definable latitude of expression. As implied earlier, I prefer the term *robust* fractal to quasi-fractal since it has been established (to my satisfaction at least) that nature's processes of growth and expansion produce this type of fractal. Its connection to natural phenomena indicates that there is nothing quasi about it. I expect that it will eventually be found to be so common that other types of fractals should be called quasi.

To summarize, what we have here is a study that observes the Wave Principle's characteristics of fractality, fiveness and Fibonacci in a phenomenon (DLA clusters) that shares with the Wave Principle the fundamental aspect of robust self-similarity.

I will add that this is yet another study among many in the past twenty years that shows more order in apparently random processes than previously believed, which is what this book proposes about human social behavior. I would guess that more and greater such surprises are forthcoming in the sciences, both natural and social.

Arboration

The science of robust branching fractals is brand new. The literature has yet to settle on a noun for a branching fractal, a verb for its progress or an adjective for the property of being tree-like. ("Diffusion-limited aggregation" is rather a mouthful.) Taking a hint from Eugene Stanley of Boston University, who used the word "arborization" in one of his studies, I would like to suggest a nomenclature. Specifically to refer to the robust branching fractals common to nature (as opposed to self-identical or indefinite branching fractals), perhaps we can use the term *arbora*, a single one being an *arborum*. The branches themselves will be termed *arba*, one being an *arbum*. The verb *to arborate* will mean "to proceed in a robust branching fractal." The process will be called *arboration*. The adjective *arboral* will mean "having the properties of an arborum." As we shall soon see, waves and arbora have so much in common that they may be differing manifestations of the same underlying theme.

Degrees in Arboration and the Possibility of Other Specifics in Their Form

Recall that while indefinite fractals have infinite variability in their successive subdivisions, *waves* display an order in their relative sizes, as each manifestation has specific degrees of subdivision. Similarly, while trees, bronchial tubes and other arbora (see Figures 10-2 through 10-10) have branches of all sizes, each specific manifestation appears to have *degrees* of arboration. With respect to trees, there is the trunk, arms off the trunk, branches off the arms, twigs off the branches and leaf veins off the twigs. There is an order to the relative sizes in each manifestation of the branching process. One never sees branches that are, for instance, the same width as, or larger than, the trunk, just as one never sees an Elliott wave that is smaller than its components. In fact, there often appears to be a rough characteristic ratio between the size of each branch and its offshoots. This property appears to hold for the DLA model (see Figure 3-6) and all of nature's arbora. In this regard, arbora are very much like waves.

Whorls of seashells (see Figures 2-25, 2-27 and 3-12), which spiral according to Fibonacci mathematics, also display the phenomenon of degree, as each chamber and each whorl increases according to a ratio of the previous one. (Unlike waves and arbora, however, the relationships between them are mathematically rigid, producing an identical fractal.)

Once again, the very latest science may be uncovering this phenomenon. In just the past year, Sornette[25] has proposed that in most complex systems, the infinite number of scales that are present do not play an equivalent role. Rather, there are discrete levels in a global hierarchy. His work on log periodicity (see Chapter 2) has led him to propose a mechanism for the natural emergence of discrete scale invariance (DSI) that applies to a host of examples. There is evidence of DSI in systems ranging from dust devils to cyclones in weather, from joints to plate boundaries in tectonics, from primary to quaternary structures in proteins, from molecules to systems in physiology, from neurons to hemispheres in the brain and from individual traders to national trading blocs in the global economy. DSI is a property of the examples of dwelling spaces (from rooms to cities) and knowledge blocks (from sentences to the internet) that I gave in Chapter 2. The Wave Principle is the only hypothesis that *from the start* proposed hierarchical degrees in the stock market's price structure.[26]

There may be more details to discover in DLA clusters and natural arbora. Taking a clue from waves, we might investigate whether arbora are composed of a limited number of specific component forms of arba. We might ask whether they have common ratios of length, common ratios of width, a limited number of shapes, or rules for the specific number of arba that sprout. For now, I am content to observe that this shared property of DLA clusters and the Wave Principle suggests that one important characteristic of *all* robust fractals may be their development via specific degrees, just like their self-identical cousins.

To summarize all these findings, it appears that fractality, *phi*, the number 5 and the phenomenon of degree all appear to be factors in the morphology of robust fractals.

Fibonacci Spirals

The spiral is not only nature's premier growth/expansion form, but also one of biology's most fundamental. The DNA molecule, the code for life, is made up of two intertwining spirals. The .618 ratio between its width and cycle length (see Figure 11-1) makes it a Fibonacci-related spiral. Its form apparently carries forward into the final forms whose growth it governs. Daisies, pine cones and sun-

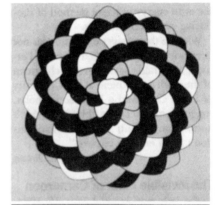

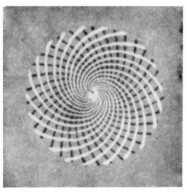

source: Mathematics

A SPIRALED FLOWER
The diagram above reveals the double spiraling of the daisy head at right. Two opposite sets of rotating spirals are formed by the arrangement of the individual florets in the head. They are also near-perfect equiangular spirals. There are 21 in the clockwise direction and 34 counterclockwise. This 21:34 ratio is composed of two adjacent terms in the mysterious Fibonacci sequence.

Fibonacci spirals in the daisy

Figure 3-9

source: Science 86 Magazine, May 1986

Pine cone

Figure 3-10

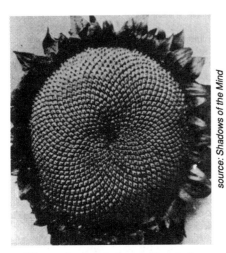

Fibonacci spirals in the seedhead of a sunflower

Figure 3-11

flowers provide famous examples, as spirals in one direction are composed of a Fibonacci number of seeds (or kernels), while spirals in the other direction are composed of the next Fibonacci number of seeds, and both sets of spirals exist simultaneously in one set of seeds, as shown in Figures 3-9 through 3-11. Many seashells grow in successive spirals, each of which is larger than its predecessor by the Fibonacci ratio (see Figures 2-27 and 3-12).

While a substantial portion of the form of these plants and animals is a Fibonacci spiral, for other species, the influence is less obvious. Architect György Doczi demonstrates a subtle golden-spiral correspondence between the style of growth of plants and animals. The sacrum in animals from frogs to humans, he says, is the center that corresponds to the apex of the generative spiral in plants. Out of each grow spiral-compatible forms that correspond to the divisions of the seashell (see Figure 3-12).

> Figure [3-12] shows a man's hand, traced from an X-ray photo. ...The hand is a microcosm of the body. It grows out of the wrist as the spine grows out of the sacrum, and as wings grow out of a butterfly, *or as leaves and flowers grow out of their stems. ...The unity we share with plants* and animals is...[also] visible from the fact that our growth, like theirs, seems to unfold from a single center."[27]

Without belaboring the evidence, we can surmise that it is not just seashells that manifest Fibonacci-based spirals as a whole form, or heart muscles and ear canals (see Chapter 11) that manifest Fibonacci-related spirals in body parts. As Chapter 11 further demonstrates, all forms of life may have Fibonacci spiral aspects both in their parts and in their whole expression. The fact that the Wave Principle is Fibonacci-based and produces a logarithmic spiral (see Figure 2-29) connects it to the Fibonacci-spiral growth phenomena of life.[28] Next, I hope to show a unity among all these concepts.

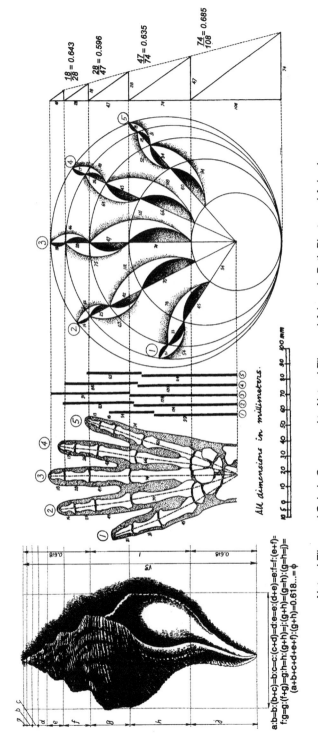

$$\frac{18}{28} = 0.643$$

$$\frac{28}{47} = 0.596$$

$$\frac{47}{74} = 0.635$$

$$\frac{74}{108} = 0.685$$

All dimensions in millimeters.

a:b=b:(b+c)=b:c=c:(c+d)=d:e=e:(d+e)=e:f=f:(e+f)=
f:g=g:(f+g)=g:h=h:(g+h)=i:(g+h)=(g=h)=(g−h)=
(a+b+c+d+e+f):(g+h)=0.618...= φ

Natural Fibonacci Spirals Correspond to Natural Fibonacci Arbora in Both Plants and Animals

Figure 3-12

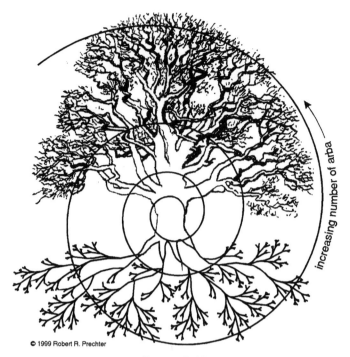

Figure 3-13

Figure 3-14

Nature's Developing Waves, Branching Arbora and Expanding Spirals — All the Same Thing?

Waves and arbora become *more complex*, and spirals *more expanded*, *as time proceeds*. These growth-related robust fractals reflect Fibonacci mathematics, robustness, fiveness and degree. In contrast, static fractals such as magnets, crystals and water in a critical state, and snowflakes (see Figures 2-8 and 2-9) *do not become more complex over time* and do not reflect Fibonacci mathematics. The difference appears to be that static fractals are phenomena of *space*, while robust fractals are growth patterns through *time*.

It could be that nature's developing waves, branching arbora and expanding spirals (and perhaps other robust fractals as well) share properties of robustness, degree, fiveness and Fibonacci because they are fundamentally all the same phenomenon. The only difference between them may be nature's manifestation or depiction, i.e., how the underlying process is "plotted" on reality's three-dimensional grid.

Waves reflect an expanding spiral, as shown in Figure 2-29. Arboration reflects an *expanding* spiral in terms of the *number* of arba and a *contracting* spiral in terms of the *size* of arba, as depicted in Figures 3-13 and 3-14.

Figures 3-15, 3-16 and 3-2 express the Fibonacci sequence in three different ways: as a *tree*,[29] a *spiral* and a *wave*.

The Fibonacci sequence as a tree

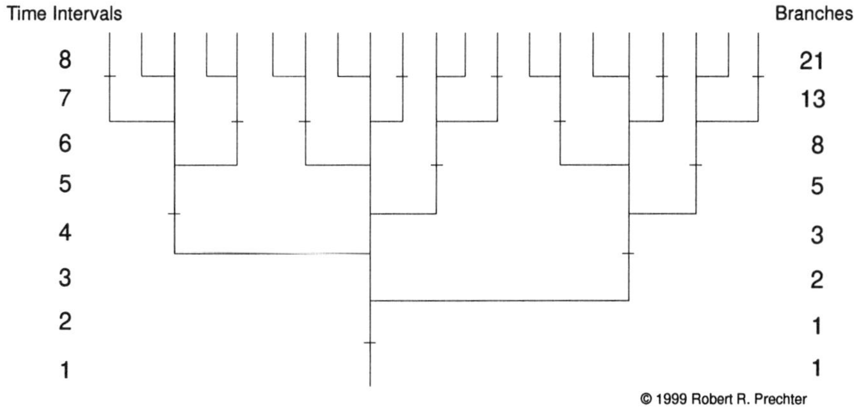

Figure 3-15

The Fibonacci sequence as a spiral

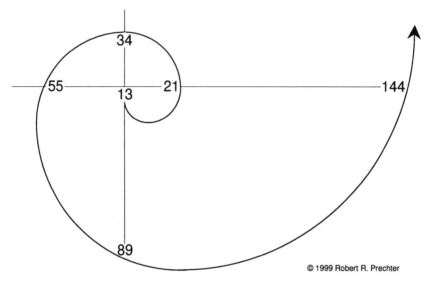

© 1999 Robert R. Prechter

Figure 3-16

Nature's Fibonacci-based growing forms have the same cross-repre-sentational property. Figure 3-12 shows how Fibonacci spirals and arbora are translated in plants and animals. We can see that in some sense, the *same thing* is going on, although the components of the spirals grow *larger* and the components of the arbora grow *smaller* while in each case making the entire form larger.

Natural *processes* express this cross-representational property as well. For example, evolution is a process that makes *waves, spirals and arbora*. Successful species branch out into subspecies, and so on, making arbora, as depicted in Figures 3-17 through 3-19, while the total number of species ebbs and flows in waves, as depicted in Figures 13-1 through 13-3. We can also depict the increasing number of species on earth as a spiral, as we did the Wave Principle in Figure 2-29 and the arbora in Figures 3-13 and 3-14, or we can extrapolate from population simulations such as depicted in Figure 2-30.

Phylogeny of Reptiles
from 300 Million Years Ago to the Present

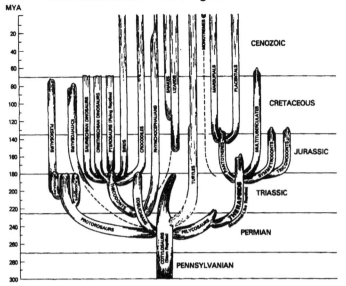

Figure 3-17

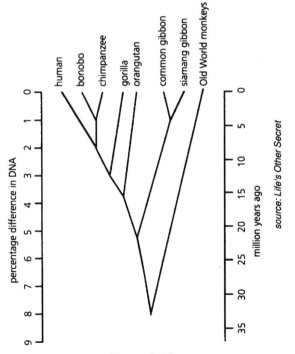

Figure 3-18

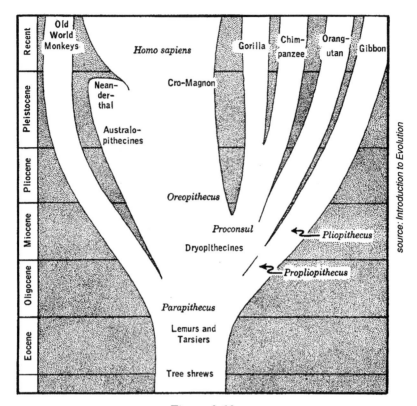

Figure 3-19

The propagation of language apparently makes both arbora and waves as well. Linguistic theory, whether by design, luck or sloppiness, closely relates two terms, *stammbaumtheorie* and *wellentheorie*, which translate into English as *family-tree theory* and *wave theory*, to describe the furcation of a parent language into branches and sub-branches via "waves of linguistic change."[30]

This transformation property may cover other types of fractals as well. For example, when is a topographic fractal (mountains, hills, hillocks, etc.) also an arborum? Answer: when water, snow or flowers fill the cracks. See Figure 3-20.

Figure 2-29 shows that a spiral can be superimposed upon a graph of the idealized wave form. It is also true that price trends can be graphed in such a way as to reveal not a line, but a spiral. Figure 3-21 shows the stock market's advance from 1942 to 1966, plotted by annual averages on a typical graph. We can plot the same data on a graph on which the X axis moves

source: Great Performance, Beaverton OR

Figure 3-20

incrementally clockwise, as shown in Figure 3-22. The resulting plot is a roughly-shaped outwardly-moving spiral. Figure 3-23 shows the stock market's decline from April 1930 to July 1932, plotted by monthly close on a typical graph. Figure 3-24 shows the same data graphed on a rotating axis, which produces a roughly-shaped inwardly-moving spiral. In other words, waves in the stock market may be conceived of as countless overlapping spirals of different sizes when time is graphed as a circle rather than a line. When economists say offhandedly that the economy "spirals" into depression, they are quite right. However, there is no reason to avoid saying (as to a man, they do) that it also spirals into advances.

There are two points of rest in our spiral depictions: the outer circle and the inner point. These points relate to Elliott waves, as they correspond conceptually to the peak moment at the end of wave 5 and the trough moment at the start of wave 1, respectively.

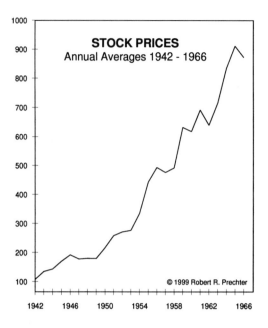

Figure 3-21

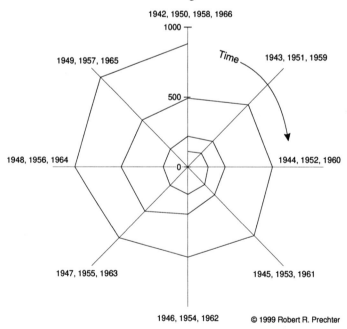

Figure 3-22

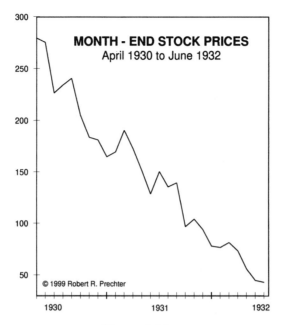

Figure 3-23

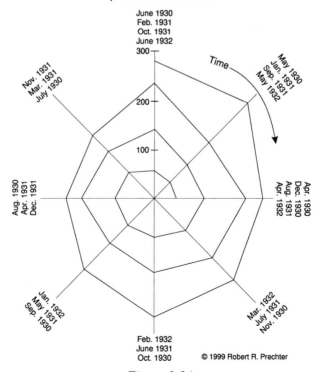

Figure 3-24

All these pictures resemble many natural expressions of growth and expansion, from life forms to galaxies. In terms of their essence, then, there may be little difference among nature's progressing forms. The only difference may be the template upon which nature projects them. That, in turn, may depend upon whether time is accounted as a line (as in waves), an advancing disk (as in branches) or a circle (as in spirals). In the context of this interconnectedness, the idea of Elliott waves is not radical, but perhaps to be expected.

The Opposing Duality of Spirals, Waves and Arbora

I would like to make one last observation because it might be important, though I do not know why. A logarithmic spiral divides a plane in two, with the area inside the line and that outside each conforming to the spiral shape where they meet. All the space on the plane is involved in adapting to the spiral pattern. Waves are manifest as a jagged line dividing a plane, with the entirety of the two resulting areas joined as opposing shapes. Similarly, arbora are not just lines. They are actually a division of a plane in such a way as to fill an entire space with compatible branches *from two directions*. The dual nature of arboral systems is clearer when the arba are "fat," as in the photo of the embryo shown as Figure 3-25. Here,

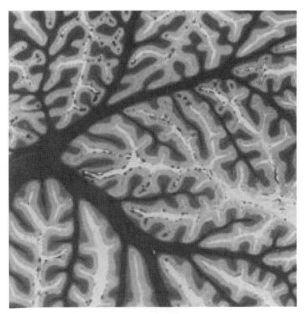

Arboral embryo

Figure 3-25

you can see the darker arboral system emanating from the left *and* the lighter arboral system emanating from the right, filling all the space. You can see the same effect when you hold up your hand and spread your fingers slightly apart. Space fills in the gaps with arba that are very much like the fingers themselves.

In other words, every phenomenon that arborates also makes the space around it arborate in response. Spirals, arbora and waves are simply a *division of plane-space that produces a like but opposing form* on both sides. I am not sure what this means, but it would surely delight the yin/yang philosophers in the Orient who taught centuries ago that reality derives from opposing duality.

A Connection to the Human Social Experience

The Wave Principle reveals that the human social experience follows a form that derives from the tension between the opposing dualities of progress and regress. Its ruling ratio is *phi*, the same number that governs nature's arbora and spirals, making it fundamental to nature's arrangements. In its broadest sense, then, the Wave Principle communicates the seemingly outrageous idea that the same law that shapes living creatures and galaxies is inherent in the mentation and activities of men *en masse*. We will explore the biological, perceptual and mentational origins of this phenomenon in Chapters 10 through 12.

As Chapter 16 later argues, the mass psychological fluctuations revealed by the stock market are not only *correlated* with mankind's actual progress and regress through history, but in fact *produce* them. What the Wave Principle ultimately says, then, is that mankind's progress, which results from his social nature, does not occur in a straight line, does not occur randomly, and does not occur cyclically. Rather, progress takes place in a Fibonacci-related arborating, spiraling or wave-fractal style that nature uses for all its robust forms. As the activity of social man has form, it is apparently no exception to the general law of order in the universe.

Professor Ian Stewart of Warwick University makes a case in his book, *Life's Other Secret*, that the cardinal code of life is mathematical, not biomechanical. He begs his readers, "We must turn at least some of our attention to life's other secret — the universal mathematical principles of growth and form that DNA exploits."[31] As the research throughout this book attests, it is exactly a "universal mathematical principle of growth and form" that the Wave Principle of human social behavior reflects. This is a tall claim, which it is the purpose of the rest of this book to verify.

NOTES

1 Elliott, R.N. (1938). *The wave principle.*

2 Elliott, R.N. (1940, October 1). "The basis of the wave principle."

3 Buchanan, M. (1997, November 8). "One law to rule them all." *New Scientist.*

4 There is one rare exception, which I pointed out in *Elliott Wave Principle.*

5 To read the original works of R.N. Elliott, Charles Collins, A. Hamilton Bolton, A.J. Frost and Robert Prechter, please see the list of sources at the end of this book.

6 For details on the few additions and corrections made by Frost and Prechter, see *Elliott Wave Principle.*

7 See also "Wave Personality" in Chapter 2 and "Ratio Analysis" in Chapter 4 of *Elliott Wave Principle.*

8 The sequence is named for the 13th century Pisan mathematician, Leonardo, son of Bonacci, or Fibonacci for short.

9 It has become fashionable in recent years to disparage the "simplistic, Newtonian" view of the universe as being "mechanical." Newton, however, may not have been entirely the Newtonian that his detractors would have us believe. When perhaps the greatest scientist of all time has the golden spiral carved on the headboard of his bed, you can bet, if the character of a man's life means anything, that he admired it for good reason.

10 It is also fashionable to dismiss as a mystical fixation the fascination that earlier scientists had for *phi.* Such dismissal would make sense if we were talking about Madame Blavatsky and Piazzi Smyth, but we are talking about people who rank among the few dozen greatest intellects of the ages. Dare we say they were fools in this regard, all of them?

11 Elliott, R.N. (1940, October 1). "The basis of the wave principle."

12 It is perhaps possible that R.N. Elliott was not the first person to observe a connection between Fibonacci numbers and financial markets. Harvard Emeritus Professor Barry Fell, whose book *Saga America* (1980) details the activities of North Americans around 300 B.C., made this observation:

> Mathematical notation in North America was revolutionized in the fifth century A.D., when the Nevada voyagers brought the newly invented Sanskrit system of decimal notation back from India. In this replica of a mathematical petroglyph from Massacre Lake, northwest Nevada, the annual crop report on maize is given in ancient Libyan script ... By far the

most sophisticated of the checkerboard patterns found at Nevada petroglyph sites are the grouping at the Whiskey Flat site..., [which] yield a sequence of numbers called by mathematicians the Fibonacci series.

Perhaps forecasting corn prices using Fibonacci ratios is not something new!

13 So far in this book, I have mentioned **1** overall form, **2** elementary patterns in motive mode, **3** elementary patterns in corrective mode, and **5** elementary patterns in all. This progression is a hint that the organization of the Wave Principle itself reflects the Fibonacci sequence. Figure 3-14 in *Elliott Wave Principle* depicts one such conceptual organization.

14 The Lucas sequence is named for 19th century French mathematician Edouard Lucas, who also coined the term "Fibonacci numbers."

15 It flowers at the number "5," which is where collective human behavior flowers under the Wave Principle. See Figure 18-6.

16 Each successive set of stems is approximately 2/3 of the length of the preceding set.

17 Douaday, S. and Couder, Y. (1993). "Phyllotaxis as a self-organized growth process." *Growth patterns in physical sciences and biology.*

18 Prusinkiewicz, P. and Lindenmayer, A. (1990). *The algorithmic beauty of plants.*

19 Thompson, D. (1917). *On growth and form.* p.857.

20 Vogel, H. (1979). "A better way to construct the sunflower head." *Mathematical Biosciences*, No. 44, pp. 145-174.

21 The main exception to this manifestation in plants is an angle that corresponds to the near-Fibonacci Lucas sequence, 1, 3, 4, 7, 11, 18, etc.

22 Khinchin, A. Ya. (1964). *Continued fractions*, p. 36.

23 Arneodo, A., *et al.* (1993). "Fibonacci sequences in diffusion-limited aggregation." *Growth patterns in physical sciences and biology.* All quotes in this section are from this source.

24 *Ibid.*

25 Sornette, D. (1997, October 15). "Generic mechanisms for hierarchies." *InterJournal Complex Systems*, No. 127. And (1998, June 30-July 3). "Discrete scale invariance in turbulence?" Proceedings of the 7th European Turbulence Conference. And "Discrete scale invariance and complex dimensions." *Physics Reports* No. 297, pp. 239-270. And (1999). "Critical crashes." *Risk*, Vol. 12, No. 1.

26 Sornette proposes that there is a discrete set of laws and tools for each level in a DSI hierarchy. The Wave Principle does not imply such differences in the underlying psychology that produces waves of social mood. However, there are some differences in the rules and tools one employs to analyze the

stock market at different degrees. For example, below Minor degree, the relative size of each wave does not necessarily correspond to the relative size of its degree. The best overall labeling sometimes requires allowing Subminuette movements to be larger than Minuette ones. This never happens at larger degrees. Similarly, there are rare times that wave four will slightly overlap the price territory of wave one at Subminuette degree. Again, this never happens at larger degrees. This difference might simply be a function of the inaccuracy of stock averages in reflecting waves of social mood. Arboration, which appears generally to proceed according to the same law regardless of which degree is developing, has exceptions as well. For instance, the leaf on a tree, at the end of the arboration process, is different in construction from the branches.

27 Doczi, G. (1981). *The power of limits*.

28 **The Dearth of Data on *Phi* and Spirals**. Many scientists have an aversion to *phi*, perhaps because mystics have sometimes waxed eloquent over its properties. In many studies quoted later in Chapters 11 and 12 in which *phi* has obviously appeared, researchers do not even mention it. This is akin to finding that the ratio pertaining to a particular set of natural processes is 3.14 and not mentioning that it approximates *pi*. This aversion has led to a sad dearth of data about *phi* in nature, which forces me in this chapter to work with limited information, quoting architects instead of biologists. It is time for science to get over the fear of *phi*ing. When that fear is overcome, I believe we will see an explosion of *phi*-related research and discovery.

The same problem exists for natural spirals. I have seen no work dedicated to their assessment. Once again, this dearth of study forces me simply to make the observation that they are everywhere in nature. If the resulting vagueness bothers you, it does me, too. Unfortunately, until scientists tackle natural spirals as a field of study, we are stuck with little more than commenting on their repeated appearance.

29 Given this connection between waves and trees, perhaps when people say, "Wall Street is a jungle," they are more correct than they know.

30 (1976). *Webster's Third New International Dictionary*.

31 Stewart, I. (1998). *Life's other secret*.

PART II

VALIDATING THE
WAVE PRINCIPLE BY ITS
OWN OPERATION

Theoretical support for the Wave Principle continues later, in Part III. I could have arranged that section to follow Part I, but some readers at this point might require something concrete to justify their continuing investigation. Part II is dedicated to demonstrating the validity of the Wave Principle. Thereafter, we will venture further, and more solidly, into scientific support for it.

Chapter 4:

Modeling and Quantification Support the Validity of the Wave Principle

A Simple Model Reflects Reality

In 1995, Michael Buettner of Elliott Wave International constructed a simple computer model of the Wave Principle without considering any actual market behavior. The model incorporates the three main rules as well as four guidelines of behavior for the impulse pattern, as follows:

(1) Wave two does not carry past the beginning of the preceding wave one.

(2) Wave three is not the shortest wave.

(3) Wave four does not enter the price range of wave one.

(4) Wave four usually has a form different from that of wave two. (This model uses a "zigzag" for wave two and a "flat" for wave four, which are their most common positions.)

(5) One motive wave is usually extended, and it is usually wave three. (Wave three is always extended in the model, which arbitrarily makes it equal to .618 times the summed lengths of waves one and five.)

(6) Waves five and one tend toward equality when wave three is extended. (The model makes them equal.)

(7) Waves are often related by Fibonacci ratios. (This model incorporates two common tendencies in having wave two retrace .618 of wave one and wave four retrace .236 of wave three.)

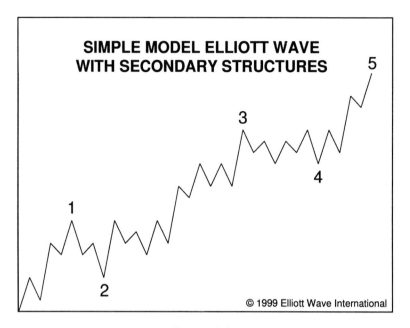

Figure 4-1

Figure 4-1 shows the picture created by the computer from this model. Figure 4-2 shows the same picture to five degrees of iteration. Below it is the actual plot of the Dow Jones Industrial Average from 1932. Understand that our model excludes numerous important subtleties among the Wave Principle's rules and guidelines and forces several rigidities not shared by the actual stock market. Nevertheless, as Buettner concludes, "The market model formulated in the 1930s, even when converted into a highly simplified mathematical idealization, reproduces to a remarkable degree the overall structure of the real market during the subsequent six decades."[1]

While it would be interesting to determine the fractal dimension of this model, it is an extreme simplification of the Wave Principle. A simulation incorporating all of the pattern variability that the Wave Principle is capable of modeling would provide a better match to the real-world behavior, which is what Elliott's definitions are designed to do. Perhaps our "expert system" computer program, discussed in the next section, will provide this opportunity.

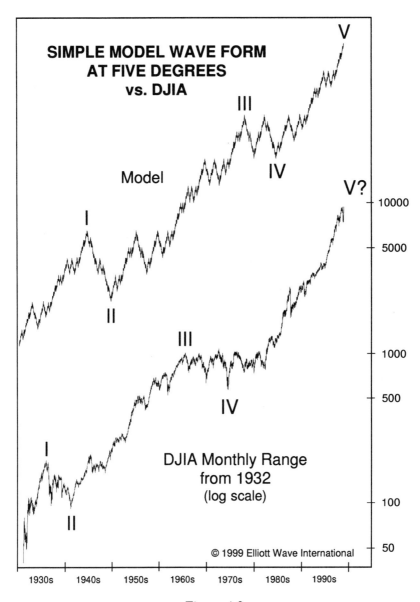

Figure 4-2

Computerization Reflects Objectivity, Consistency and Forecasting Value

Brock, Lakonishok and LeBaron have recently shown that two simple trend-following techniques can make money in markets. The authors conclude as follows:

> When work on nonlinearities in financial time series began, it was seen by many technical traders as justification for their work. They saw a clear connection between technical trading rules and nonlinearities. *For some rules, this connection is indisputable.* Rules that look for general patterns such as "head and shoulders" or more complicated figures are clearly attempting to find some kind of nonlinearity in these series.... We would like to emphasize that our analysis focuses on the simplest trading rules. Other *more elaborate rules may generate even larger differences between conditional returns.*[2]

So far, attempts to develop computer trading models based on fractals, chaos, power laws and so on have failed. As *The Economist* magazine put it in 1996, "Fund managers had hoped that chaos theory would lead them to finance's holy grail. It has delivered remarkably little."[3] The reason that attempts to date have failed is that they have no basis upon which to generate the elusive "more elaborate rules" to which the above study refers. They presume that the market is an indefinite fractal, as described at the start of Chapter 3, and proceed from there to nowhere. In contrast, the Wave Principle model provides a detailed set of rules of pattern formation that are derived from empirics and justified with a hypothesis.

To demonstrate the validity of that hypothesis, my firm, Elliott Wave International, is developing an "expert system" computer program called the Elliott Wave Analysis and Validation Expert System (EWAVES™). The program incorporates all the rules and guidelines currently believed to be valid for interpreting price action under the Wave Principle. To achieve this goal, I had to define each wave pattern *quantitatively.*

Since the market's precise position in the wave structure is always in question, and since one's interpretation of a pattern is only a probability until it is certifiably complete, the computer must be able to judge whether to label, for instance, an ongoing correction as a developing triangle or more likely something else, or whether to label an ongoing impulse as probably ending or not. It is one thing to draw an acceptable pattern called a "contracting triangle" and quite another to state exactly what is allowed within its definition and what is not, and then to differentiate quantitatively between good triangles and unlikely triangles among those allowed.

Taken in its entirety, the labeling of all the waves that conforms best to ideal forms is the working model for the market's current position. Conformity is reevaluated with each new data point and changed whenever the ideal balance tips in favor of another labeling. This approach keeps the analysis and outlook adaptive to the developing pattern and bypasses the human flaw of stubbornness in the face of opposing information.

The task of quantification was not too difficult, but it was based upon my years of experience in viewing wave relationships, not statistical data on them. However, we had to start somewhere, as there was no way to generate statistics until we had defined the patterns we wanted to investigate. Now that the program is written, we can use it to *get* those statistics (for instance, a curve of common retracement percentages for each wave within a contracting triangle) and adjust our quantification parameters as they dictate.

The project began in the Artificial Intelligence Project Office at Lockheed Engineering Science Company in Houston, Texas. It was the only non-government project being handled by the company at the time. From there, the project was transferred, along with the head of the project, to our headquarters.

We utilized no "data fitting" in constructing the program. In other words, we did not fit the pattern, rules, guidelines or labels to any market's action. We simply quantified Elliott's rules and guidelines for pattern development, about 80% of which had been established by 1938. We tested the program in real markets for debugging purposes. It will run on any set of financial or other type of data. Our tests satisfy us that the program usually gives answers that are substantially the way we would analyze the data ourselves.

The first important fact about EWAVES is that it shows that the Wave Principle itself is an *objective* observation. Some critics have misrepresented the concept of the Wave Principle as a fantasy construct forced onto the market. Others have accused it of requiring subjective judgment. Both of these views are false. Objectivity in dealing with probabilities is not the same as subjectivity, and this computer program has now proved that the Wave Principle involves the former.

The next important fact about EWAVES is that it demonstrates the *consistency* of interpretation under the Wave Principle. In many cases, the

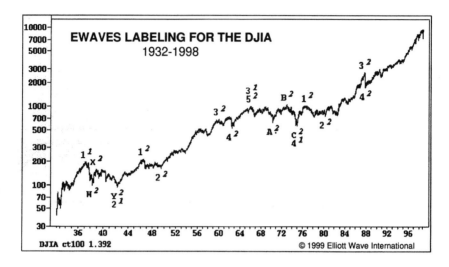

Figure 4-3

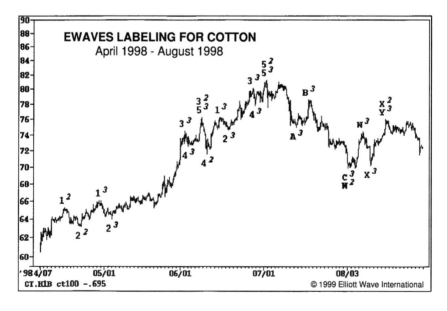

Figure 4-4

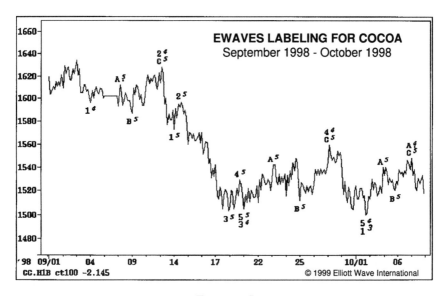

Figure 4-5

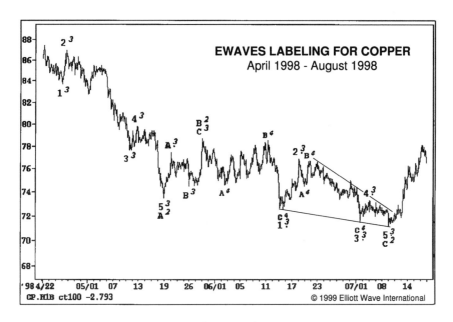

Figure 4-6

wave labeling that the program chooses in each instance as the most reflective of the rules and guidelines of the Wave Principle is the same as that chosen by a human expert. For example, its interpretation of the waves in the DJIA over the past 70 years, shown in Figure 4-3, is the same as that described in Chapter 5 via the analyses of Elliott, Bolton, Collins, Frost and Prechter that was summarized in Figure 4-2. In almost all cases, *one* labeling produced by the computer is the same as that chosen as best by a human expert. Figures 4-4 through 4-6 show additional examples. In no cases does EWAVES produce a labeling that a human would reject as impossible.

Another important aspect of EWAVES is that its operation is compatible with the larger theory of the Wave Principle. The program finds all the patterns so far described under the Wave Principle and is able to link them into a complex self-similar structure.

Finally, EWAVES is demonstrating a fairly reliable forecasting ability. For instance, it consistently and accurately called for rising DJIA prices from 1990 through today, and it accurately called for mostly lower prices in gold from 1996 to the present.

We have yet to quantify these forecasts to prove our point, but we are approaching that goal. Our plan is to develop a "signal" module that in essence would simplify EWAVES' conclusions into buy, sell and stop orders pertaining only to one or two degrees of trend. The program's output through this module would not be the Wave Principle and would provide far less information than a comprehensive wave interpretation, so any results would be a minimum expression of the forecasting value of the analytical engine of the program. Given our knowledge of real-world markets and the avoidance of false assumptions that have disappointed other programmers, we have reason to be optimistic.

The above paragraphs speak to the validity of the Wave Principle but hardly cover the value of the program. Practitioners of the Wave Principle, myself included, are often subjectively influenced, as all humans have their emotions and biases. This is not to support the false accusation that the Wave Principle *is* subjective or *requires* subjectivity. Nor does human subjectivity with respect to applying the Wave Principle make it different from any other approach. However, the fact that the Wave Principle can be computerized gives it an advantage over many other approaches. With an unemotional computer, interpreting price movements in markets is an entirely consistent exercise.

Equally important is EWAVES's volume advantage. The human mind can manipulate only a certain number of concepts at a time. EWAVES, on the other hand, simultaneously takes into account all patterns through several degrees when making its assessment of the best consistency score for labeling purposes. EWAVES lists (and can graph) *all* allowable wave counts and then rank them by accordance with ideal forms, producing an objective roster of outcomes ranked by probability.

Best of all for academic purposes, EWAVES is a wave analysis laboratory that can be used to test any question relating to the Wave Principle, including pattern frequency, characteristics, price targeting, etc., to help refine the Wave Principle through a more detailed empirical study. That is how we hope to use it to help launch this new science.

EWAVES identifies data series that do not reflect the Wave Principle and reports them as "uncountable." Undoubtedly, the program might at times produce a wave labeling for a series of random numbers, as the definition of random means numbers that can reflect anything, in this case including a wave sequence. (For more on this topic, see Chapter 19.) Nevertheless, if we have accurately computerized a valid concept, EWAVES's consistency score for random data would have to average significantly less than that for financial data. While we have yet to test such questions, at least we are developing the means to do so.

The computer history of the Wave Principle, as you can see by this discussion, is so new that it has barely begun. On the other hand, there is a fairly long history of application by people. The next two chapters examine some of that history as another indicator of the Wave Principle's validity.

NOTES

1 Buettner, M. (1995). "An evolutionary model of market growth: The *Elliott wave principle*." Unpublished paper.

2 Brock, W., *et al.* (1992, December). "Simple technical trading rules and the stochastic properties of stock returns." *Journal of Finance.*

3 "Chaos under a cloud." (1996, January 13). *The Economist.*

Chapter 5:

Forecasting Pattern on the Basis of Pattern

As L.F. Richardson pointed out, the length of a seacoast is dependent upon your method of measuring and your scale.[1] A ruler placed on a globe will give one answer; the same ruler applied to every indentation as one traverses the coast itself will give a vastly different one. Similarly, when people ask me where the stock market is going or even what its trend has been, I have to ask, "What degree are you talking about?" There can be multiple answers, as in, "The Minor trend is *down* within a *sideways* Intermediate trend within a *rising* Primary trend."

My colleagues and I spend our time assessing waves lasting minutes to those lasting centuries. For this chapter, I have chosen to chronicle forecasts that pertained to fairly long trends. There are several reasons for this decision. First, if I were to show only a few near-term predictions, readers would rightly assume that the results were due to luck. After all, with so much time within which to choose one's examples, a few would have to turn out right. Second, I want to relate the model shown in Chapter 4 to what practitioners expected along the way, from the first days of the Wave Principle's application. Third, fractals and complex systems are presumed to be unpredictable over any significant time, and I want to demonstrate the contrary before explaining in Chapter 20 why I disagree with that presumption. Finally, successful long-term forecasting is just plain impressive; no one but Elliott wave practitioners can do it.

One important test of a scientific hypothesis is its ability to predict outcomes. Although the Wave Principle hypothesis is difficult to quantify on the basis of predictability because it forecasts only *probabilistically* (see Chapter 20), there is nevertheless substantial evidence of its unique value. While reviewing the following excerpts, it is important that you honestly consider the *utter uncertainty* that exists in real-time forecasting. Psychological experiments show that most people who review events in retrospect consider them to have been obviously implied at the time.[2] As Lee Simonson once said, "Any event, once it has occurred, can be made to appear inevitable by a competent historian."[3] That goes for all of us. "Fine," I always reply to protestations that previous trends were easy to predict, "then how do you forecast the *next* ten years?" Usually I do not get much of an answer. I think that after you read these statements and consider them in the proper light, you will agree that the authors' accuracy in describing the future is due to their knowing something useful.

Forecasting the DJIA over Half a Century

In *The Elliott Wave Principle — A Critical Appraisal*, Hamilton Bolton made this opening statement:

> As we have advanced through some of the most unpredictable economic climate imaginable, covering depression, major war, and postwar reconstruction and boom, I have noted how well Elliott's Wave Principle has fitted into the facts of life as they have developed.

The twists and turns of the plot of stock prices from 1932 to the present are history now, but before each one happened, the path that the DJIA was to take was considered utterly unpredictable or violently debatable. More accurately stated, the consensus at each major trend change was (and always is) *wrong*, for reasons to be discussed in Chapters 8 and 18. However, five people in succession applied a crude young science to forecasting the market's movement during that time with results that are unprecedented.[4]

As you read the excerpts that follow, notice that each analyst operated under the assumption of the Wave Principle. Each therefore consistently maintained the same essential conclusions regarding the wave position of the Dow Jones Industrial Average, namely: (1) 1932 marked the low of a *fourth* wave in a five-wave structure that began in the late 1700s. (2) The Dow required a *fifth* wave in that structure. (3) That fifth wave would itself subdivide into five waves of the next lower degree.

Locate the years 1942, 1953, 1960, 1966, 1970 and 1982 as marked in Figure 5-1. In each of those years, the foremost proponent of the Wave Principle at the time published the commentary that follows. To get a better feeling for the uncertainty of the outlook at the time, please take a piece of paper and cover the remainder of the graph forward from each date. Of course, even this exercise is inadequate to convey the full extent of the

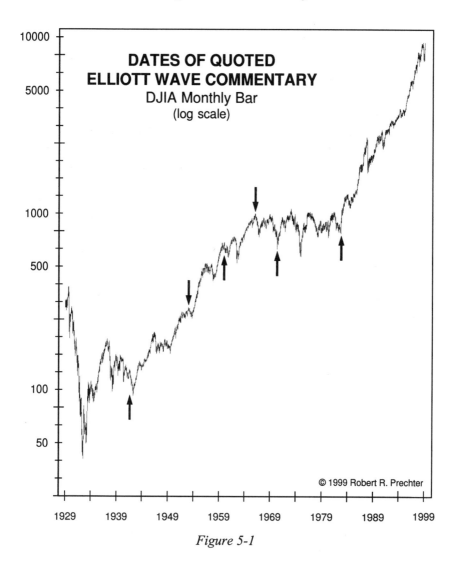

Figure 5-1

real-time uncertainty, as its very shape communicates something about the future that people did not know at the time.

Note: Wave notations were not standardized until very recently, so I have amended some of these presentations to maintain degree-label consistency. Also, some ellipses and minor edits are unmarked for ease of reading. For those interested, everything that each practitioner said about the long term outlook for stocks is reprinted in four volumes, as listed at the end of this book.

August 11 and 25, 1941

Ralph Nelson Elliott, recognizing the end of the wave (IV) corrective process (later labeled wave II of (V),) and forecasting the entire wave (V) advance:

The earliest available stock record is the Axe-Houghton Index, dating from 1854. The essential "change" characteristics of the long movement from 1854 to September 1929 are shown in the accompanying graph [Figure 5-2]. The wave from 1857 to 1929 may be either Supercycle wave (I), (III) or (V), depending upon the nature and extent of development of the country before 1854.[5] There is reason to believe, however, that the period from 1857 to 1929 can be regarded as Supercycle wave (III). The market since 1929 has outlined the pattern of a gigantic thirteen-year triangle of such tremendous scope that these defeatist years may well be grouped as Supercycle wave (IV) of an order dating back to as early as 1776. My observation has been that orthodox triangles appear only as the fourth wave of a [five-wave trend].[6]

Nature's inexorable law of proportion accounts for the recurrent 0.618 ratio of swing-by-swing comparison, [as you can see from] the following tabulation of important movements since April 1930:

The Cyclical Relativity of Market Trends

Wave No.	Dates From	To	Points From	To	Change			Ratio
R	April 1930	July 1932	296.0	40.5	255.5			
S	July 1932	March 1937	40.5	196.0	155.5	155.5/	255.5=	60.9%
T	March 1937	March 1938	196.0	97.0	99.0	99.0/	155.5=	63.6%
U	March 1938	Sept. 1939	97.0	158.0	61.0	61.0/	91.0=	61.6%
								Avg. 62.0%

These ratios and series have been controlling and limiting the extent and duration of price trends irrespective of wars, politics, production indices, the supply of money, general purchasing power, and other generally accepted methods of determining stock values. This feature proves that current events and politics have no influence on market movements.

Since the causes of this phenomenal market behavior originate in the relativity of the component cycles compressed within the triangular area, it is distinctly encouraging to be able to point out that the rapidly approaching apex of the triangle should mark the beginning of a relatively long period of increasing activity [i.e., price increase] in the stock

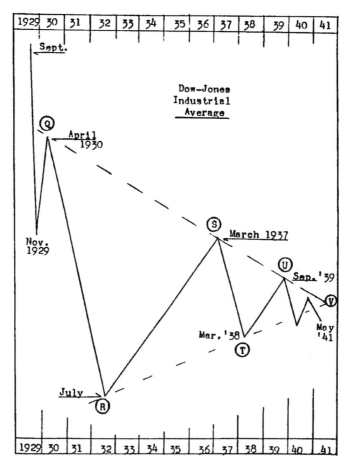

R.N. Elliott's wave interpretation from 1941

Figure 5-2

market. Triangle wave E [shown as Ⓥ on the chart] is well advanced,
and **its termination**, within or without the area of the triangle, **should
mark the final correction of the 13-year pattern of** *defeatism*. This
termination will also mark the beginning of **a new Supercycle wave (V)**
(composed of a series of cycles of lesser degree), **comparable in many
respects with the long [advance] from 1857 to 1929.** Supercycle (V) is
not expected to culminate until about 2012.[7] (See dashed line in the graph
[Figure 5-3].) [8,9]

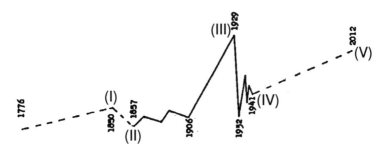

R.N. Elliott's interpretation of the long-term wave position
(not to scale or perspective)

Figure 5-3

[Note: The DJIA touched its low eight months later, in April 1942, during the darkest days of World War II. It has not looked back since.]

First Quarter, 1953

Arthur Hamilton Bolton, recognizing the position, and forecasting the extent, of wave III:

The late R.N. Elliott in 1941 projected a pattern of future stock market behavior which has not varied in fundamentals from his original outline years ago. This last prediction, or hypothesis, is vitally important, because if Elliott is right, we will not see again probably in this century stock prices as low "in dollar price" as they were in 1942. Of course, inflation will take care of a great deal of that hypothesis anyway, but it does mean that **no major depression of the 1929-32 variety is in the cards in our lifetime** (although there may well be 1921s, 1896s, 1873s again within this span). Further, it is as well to keep the background in perspective; Elliott's projection was made at a time when deflation and not inflation was the current fear.

The significance of Elliott's projection should now become more apparent.

(1) Elliott's hypothesis calls for a series of bull markets from 1942 similar in degree to those between 1857 and 1929, in the pattern of 5 waves (3 up and 2 down in between), followed by 3 down (2 down and 1 up), all moving on to successively higher levels.

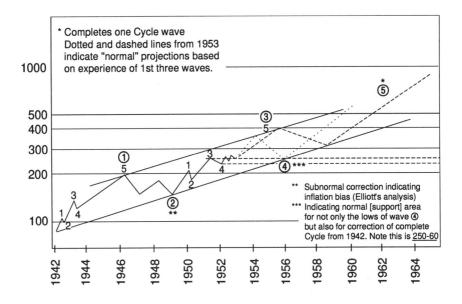

Figure 5-4

(2) Wave ① of the first Cycle bull market was completed in 1946 (Elliott's analysis [before his] death in 194[8]), and its correction (wave ②) was completed in June 1949.

(3) Because of both the time element (a third wave according to Elliott is never shorter in time than the first wave) and amplitude indicated, we must now still be in wave ③ of the 1942-? bull market (one Cycle wave).

(4) Following completion of wave ③ (not likely before 1954 because of time and amplitude elements), there should be a correction (wave ④) on the order of 1946-49, which, however, should not break the base line of the 1942-1949 lows, according to one of Elliott's tenets. (This is a normal expectation only and might in an extreme case be violated slightly.)

(5) Following wave ④, wave ⑤ should close out the first upward Cycle from 1942. Because of the time element again, **it looks like the 1960s before we face a correction to the whole rise from 1942 and anything approaching a major depression in stock prices.**[10]

[Note: Bolton's dashed line in Figure 5-4 called for a top near Dow 1000 by 1965.]

First Quarter, 1960

Hamilton Bolton, continued:

The ratio of 61.8 to 100 and 100 to 161.8 became a central part of Elliott's theories in regard to both *time* and *amplitude*. Thus, Elliott pointed out a number of other coincidences. For instance, the number of points from 1921 to 1926 (i.e., the first three waves) was 61.8% of the number of points of the last wave from 1926 to 1928 (the orthodox top). Likewise in the five waves up from 1932 to 1937. Again, the wave from the top in 1930 (297 DJIA) to the bottom in 1932 (40 DJIA) is 1.618 times the wave from 40 to 195 (1932 to 1937). Also, the decline from 1937 to 1938 was 61.8% of the advance from 1932-37 in DJIA points. Should the 1949 market to date adhere to this formula, then the advance from 1949 to 1956 (361 points in the DJIA) should be complete when 583 points (161.8% of the 361 points) have been added to the 1957 low of 416, or a total of **999 DJIA**. [See Figure 5-5.][11]

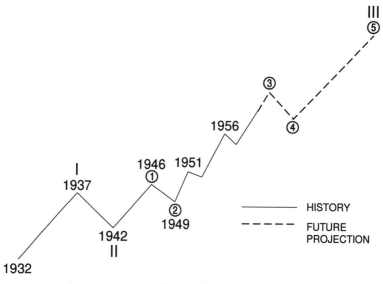

Figure 5-5

[Note: This was a perfect call not only for continuation of the bull market but for the level of its ultimate top. The daily closing high for the Dow in February 1966, thirteen years after the first quotation and six years after the second, was **995.14**. From that point, the stock market experienced its largest bear market since 1937-1942, exactly as forecast.]

First Quarter, 1966; published in April

Charles Joseph Collins, identifying the end of wave III and forecasting the extent of wave IV:

> In the count of Supercycle wave (V) from 1932, I find that two Cycle waves have been completed and a third may have completed in January 1966 or, if not (see subsequent discussion), then it is in the process of completion. These Cycle waves are illustrated in [Figure 5-6].
>
> Cycle wave III, beginning 1942, which is the wave of current interest, I break down as shown in [Figure 5-7]. Incidentally, the upward slant of Primary wave ④ between 1956 and 1962 carries inflationary implications.
>
> Primary wave ⑤ (1962-1966?) of Cycle wave III is shown in [Figure 5-8] by giving the monthly swings of the Dow Industrials. Since Intermediate wave (3) of this Primary wave extended, it would appear that **Intermediate wave (5), and thus Primary wave ⑤ as well as Cycle wave III, ended in January 1966**, as the market has subsequently developed a downthrust. (Those who might argue that such a downswing constitutes wave 2 of an extension of wave (5) are faced with Elliott's dictum that an extension can occur in any one of waves 1, 3 or 5, but

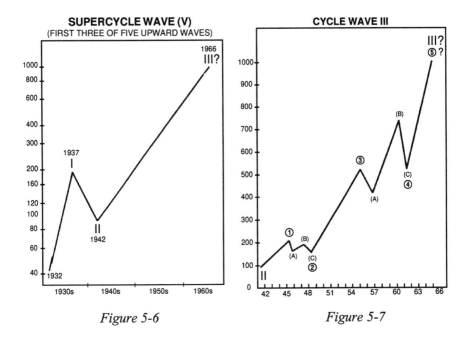

Figure 5-6   Figure 5-7

never in more than one. The extension in Intermediate wave (3), under Elliott's rule, would thus preclude an extension in Intermediate wave (5).)

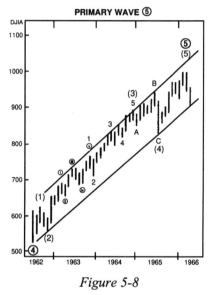

Figure 5-8

The third wave of Primary wave ⑤ extended, and Elliott states that an extension will be retraced twice. Such being the case, this would call for the "C" wave of Cycle wave IV to carry back at least to 770-710 on the Dow, in other words, to the approximate area within which the extension of Intermediate wave (3) began (see points 1 and 2 of [Figure 5-8]). The decline could carry further, however, under Elliott's rule that the correction of a wave should normally carry back to around the terminal point of the fourth wave of the five lesser waves that characterized the swing. The terminal point of the fourth Primary wave of Cycle wave III (see [wave ④ in Figure 5-7]) was established in 1962 at 524 on the Dow. **Purely as a speculation, might not the "A" wave of Cycle wave IV carry to the 770-710 area, the "C" wave to around the lower 524 point, with a sizable intervening "B" wave?**[12]

[Note: This was a perfect call of the Cycle degree top that had just occurred after 24 years of rise. It was also a perfect call of the extent of the first decline into the 1966 daily closing low, which was **744.31**, and a nearly perfect forecast of the ultimate low eight years later in 1974 at **577.60** basis daily closing figures.]

May 1970

Alfred John Frost, forecasting the low of wave IV:

A. Hamilton Bolton in May 1960 said, "Should the 1949 market to date adhere to the Fibonacci formula, then the advance from 1949 to 1956 (361 points in the DJIA) should be complete when 583 points (161.8% of the 361 points) have been added to the 1957 low of 416, or to

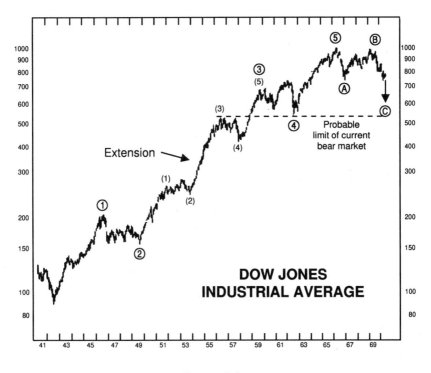

Figure 5-9

a total of 999 DJIA." This forecast was made almost six years before the great bull market peaked at approximately 1000 DJIA. Applying the same formula to determine the extent of the current bear market, we get a number of possibilities, each indicating that a severe market lies directly ahead. A drop of 61.8% from the recorded high of 1000 DJIA would bring the Dow back to 381, its 1929 high. This doesn't seem probable, [as] the current Cycle wave from 1966 should not overlap the 1929 high. Should the current C-wave from December 2, 1968 (DJIA 986) drop 414 points (161.8% of the 1966 A-wave decline of 256 points), **the market would bottom out at 572.** [See Figure 5-9.][13]

[Note: The low of the bear market occurred on December 9, 1974 with a daily close of 577.60 and a low hourly figure of **572.20.**]

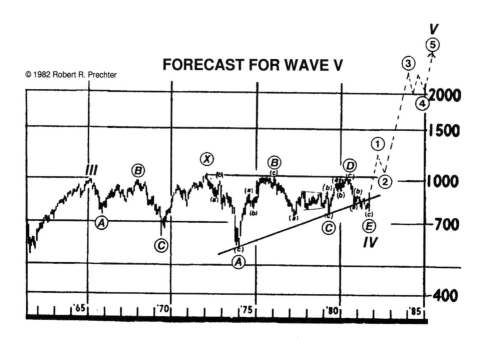

Figure 5-10

September 13, 1982

Robert Rougelot Prechter, Jr., identifying the onset of wave V and projecting its substantial extent:

This is a thrilling juncture for a wave analyst. For the first time since 1974, some incredibly large wave patterns may have been completed, patterns that have important implications for the next five to eight years. The technical name for wave IV by this count is a "double three," with the second "three" an ascending triangle. [See Figure 5-10.] **This wave count argues that the Cycle wave IV correction from 1966 ended last month (August 1982).** The lower boundary of the trend channel from 1942 was broken briefly at the termination of this pattern. A brief break of the long term trendline, I should note, was recognized as an occasional trait of fourth waves, as shown in *R.N. Elliott's Masterworks.*[14]

The task of wave analysis often requires stepping back and taking a look at the big picture and using the evidence of the historical patterns to judge the onset of a major change in trend. Cycle and Supercycle waves move in wide price bands and truly are the most important structures to take into account. [They indicate that] **a period of economic stability**

and soaring stock prices has just begun. One must conclude that a bull market beginning in August 1982 would ultimately carry out its full potential of five times its starting point, thus targeting 3885.[15]

[Note: In the midst of the most extreme stock market pessimism since 1942, Prechter identified the end of a 16-year period of net loss for the Dow a month after its end at 777 and projected a climb to what was perceived as an absurd level of nearly 4000.]

November 8, 1982

Robert Prechter, continued:

Surveying all the market's action over the past 200 years, it is comforting to know exactly where you are in the wave count. [See Figure 5-11.]

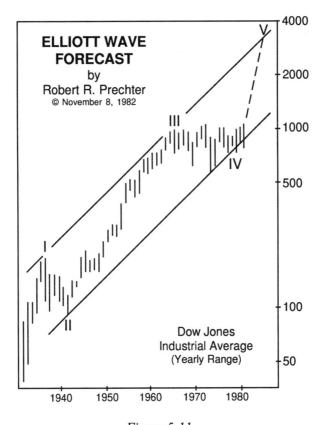

Figure 5-11

April 6, 1983

Robert Prechter, continued:

A normal fifth wave will carry, based on Elliott's channeling methods, to the upper channel line, which in this case cuts through the price action in the 3500-4000 range in the latter half of the 1980s. Elliott noted that when a fourth wave breaks the trend channel [as this one did in 1982], **the fifth will often have a throw-over, or a brief penetration through the same trend channel on the other [i.e., top] side.**

What might we conclude about the psychological aspects of wave V? As the last hurrah, it should be characterized, at its end, by an almost unbelievable institutional mania for stocks and a public mania for stock index futures, stock options, and options on futures. In my opinion, the long term sentiment gauges will give off major trend sell signals two or three years before the final top, and the market will just keep on going. In order for the Dow to reach the heights expected by the year 1987 or 1990, *and* in order to set up the U.S. stock market to experience the greatest crash in its history, which, according to the Wave Principle, is due to follow wave V, **investor mass psychology should reach manic proportions, with elements of 1929, 1968 and 1973 all operating together and, at the end, to an even greater extreme.**[16,17]

[Note: A financial mania is a rare event, occurring on average about once a century. This is the only prediction of a financial mania ever attempted. It has come to pass, as public and institutional desire to own corporate shares has been unprecedented. In fact, it is the greatest stock mania ever, as average U.S. stock valuation here in the second half of 1998 with respect to dividend yield and corporate book value is the highest in history by a substantial margin. Also as anticipated, the Dow has produced a "throw-over" of the upper channel line of the Supercycle advance and has met its upper channel line at Cycle degree (see Figures 5-12 and 18-5). The entire process has taken a decade longer and carried far further than originally imagined.]

Summary

No one has ever conducted market forecasting as a scientific experiment. Neither have Elliotters, so there is no data to quantify the value of these forecasts. Moreover, each of the practitioners cited above made errors along the way, an experience that is shared by everyone who attempts to forecast market prices. Nevertheless, to anyone but a random walker

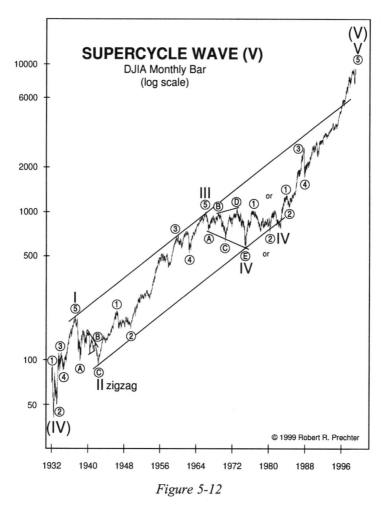

Figure 5-12

who blithely likens such commentary to coin-tossing (an invalid analogy), this is one powerful legacy, particularly when compared to the product of conventional methods, which we will explore in Chapter 19.

The three points that matter with respect to the above quotations are as follows: (1) No other approach to market forecasting has allowed any-one even to adopt a *perspective* such as these forecasts reflect. (2) No approach to market forecasting has produced a degree of *success* remotely approaching that cited above. (3) The outlook through these practitioners has maintained *consistency* throughout this sixty-year period, as each ana-lyst held the same view of the ultimate path for prices and followed through accordingly. Only a valid theory of market behavior could do such things.

NOTES

1   Richardson, L.F. (1961). "The problem of contiguity." *General Systems Yearbook*, Vol. 6, pp. 139-187.

2   One experiment involved subjects forecasting the outcome of a supposed battle between the British and Africans in the 1800s. Those off-handedly informed of the "actual" outcome skewed their answers mightily toward what then became "obvious" from the details supplied, while those not so informed split their decisions 50/50. I regret to say that I do not have a reference for that study, so please enlighten me if you can and I will include it in the next edition.

3   Prochnow, H. (ed.) *The public speaker's treasure chest.*

4   To this list we might add the remarkable Edson Gould, who knew and used the Wave Principle but never said so. For details, see "A Biography of R.N. Elliott" in *R.N. Elliott's Masterworks*.

5   Data prior to 1854 was unavailable at that time.

6   Elliott accomplished this forecast with very limited data, encompassing only 1857 to 1942. He could not see the entire Grand Supercycle wave structure up to that time, which began in 1784. However, he could see the triangular nature of the corrective process from 1929, which shows up in inflation-adjusted data (see Figure 16-3 inset and Figure 16-6). Triangles, he had already observed, appear only in the fourth wave position. From his intimate knowledge of how smaller patterns had linked together, then, he knew where the market was in its larger pattern despite having only a partial recording of it. Frost and I later attained the pertinent back data and validated his conclusion in *Elliott Wave Principle*.

7   Elliott's "2012" forecast was an offhand remark that meant, "it will be the same degree, and therefore about as long, as Supercycle wave (III)." 2012 is the year when their lengths would be exactly the same. He did not actually expect that precise a match. What he meant to convey was that he was predicting a *Supercycle* rise closer to *seven* decades rather than a Cycle degree rise closer to *one* decade or a Grand Supercycle closer to *twenty*. So far, the rise has lasted more than 5½ decades from 1942 and more than 6½ decades from 1932, putting it comfortably in the duration of a Supercycle degree advance.

8   Elliott, R.N. (1941, August 11). "Market apathy – cause and termination." (Educational bulletin*)*.

9   Elliott, R.N. (1941, August 25). "Two cycles of American history." *Interpretive Letter* No. 17.

10   Bolton, A.H. (1953). "Elliott's wave principle." Supplement to *The Bolton-Tremblay Bank Credit Analyst.*

11   Bolton, A.H. (1960). "The *Elliott wave principle* — a critical appraisal." Supplement to *The Bolton-Tremblay Bank Credit Analyst.*

12   Collins, C.J. (1966). "The *Elliott wave principle* of stock market behavior." Supplement to *The Bolton-Tremblay Bank Credit Analyst.*

13   Frost, A.J. (1970). "The *Elliott wave principle* of stock market behavior." Supplement to *The Bolton-Tremblay Bank Credit Analyst.*

14   Elliott, R.N. (1938). *The wave principle.*

15   Prechter, R. (1982, September 13). "The long term wave pattern — nearing a resolution." *The Elliott Wave Theorist.*

16   Prechter, R. (1983, April 6). "A rising tide — the case for wave V in the Dow Jones Industrial Average." *The Elliott Wave Theorist.*

17   All of Prechter's comments from this time are reprinted in the Appendix to *Elliott Wave Principle.* The next logical question was and is, "If all goes according to expectations, what happens after wave V tops out?" This question was addressed well in advance, in 1978 in *Elliott Wave Principle*, in more detail in the April 6, 1983 report quoted here, and in even greater detail in the 1995 book, *At the Crest of the Tidal Wave.* I mention this because it is not just the great 20th century bull market that was in focus throughout the progression of comments cited throughout this section, *but its position in the even larger wave structure.*

Chapter 6:

Forecasting Price Extremes on the Basis of Typical Wave Relationships

As suggested by some of the commentary in Chapter 5, the Fibonacci ratio recurs in certain price relationships among waves. This fact provides a basis for creating guidelines applicable to very specific price forecasting. R.N. Elliott discovered several such relationships, and I have found a number of others. There is no point in cataloguing them in this book; for a list, see Chapter 4 of *Elliott Wave Principle*.

Bolton, Collins and Frost used this type of analysis to produce forecasts of pinpoint accuracy months or years in advance. The quoted excerpts from *The Elliott Wave Theorist* below present two detailed examples of applying wave ratio relationships to the forecasting puzzle. They relate actual situations in the two most important markets covered by the publication: the DJIA and U.S. Treasury bonds. These are striking examples because they went utterly contrary to majority opinion and preceded dramatic market action. You need not take the time to understand every nuance of these discussions. The point is to see that precise forecasting on this basis is possible.

Forecasting the DJIA Using Fibonacci Relationships

November 7, 1983

A break of Dow 1206 will virtually confirm that Primary ① has peaked and assure a continuation of the decline. If 1158 is broken, the next point of support is **1090**, which marks a .382 retracement of Primary ①. [See Figure 6-1.]

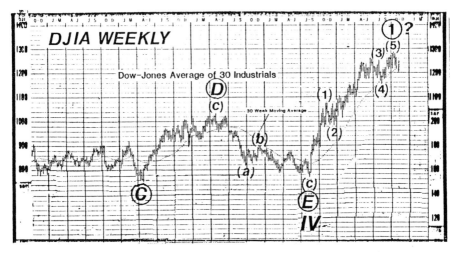

Figure 6-1

March 5, 1984

As the correction progresses, we should be able to get closer and closer to estimating where the final bottom will actually occur. Here are the calculations:

(1) Primary wave ② will retrace .382 of Primary wave ① at **1094.20**.
(2) Within the A-B-C decline, wave C will be .618 times as long as wave A at **1089.19**.

April 3, 1984

Already I am receiving in the mail Elliott-based arguments for an immediate collapse to Dow 200-500, a phenomenon that repeats every time the Dow falls 100 points or more. However, Primary wave ②, which is now in force, should bottom this year.

April 30, 1984

Primary wave ② has *not bottomed yet*. The stock market appears to be on the verge of a 100-point collapse, with a final intermediate term low expected in the May 30-June 4 time period. [See Figure 6-2, from the April 3 issue.]

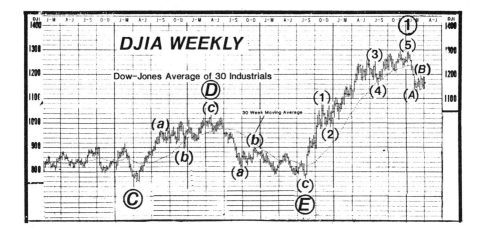

Figure 6-2

June 4, 1984

In terms of *price*, the downside target of 1090 was first computed *seven months ago*, in the November 7, 1983 issue. That basic target was reiterated in the March and April issues, with a "buy" strategy outlined (with minor variations) for the **1087-1099** area. The hourly low on May 30 was **1087.93**. The list of Fibonacci wave relationships now in place is so perfect as to be a compelling argument all by itself that a low is in the making [see Figure 6-3]:

(1) Wave (C) at 90.99 points, is .22 of a Dow point from being exactly .618 times as long as wave (A) at 146.88 points, a typical relationship in zigzags.

(2) Wave (B) at 35.27 points, is ½ point from being exactly .382 times as long as wave (C).

(3) Not only is wave (A) 1.618 times as long as wave (C), which is 2.618 times as long as wave (B), but the actual lengths are remarkably close to Fibonacci numbers: 146.88 points (Fibonacci 144), 90.99 points (Fibonacci 89), and 35.27 points (Fibonacci 34).

(4) Wave (A) lasted 5 weeks, wave (B) lasted 13 weeks, and wave (C) lasted 3 weeks, just as forecast in the May issue. The two impulse waves totaled 8 weeks. The entire correction lasted 21 weeks. Thus, the time lengths create the Fibonacci sequence, 3, 5, 8, 13, 21, re-

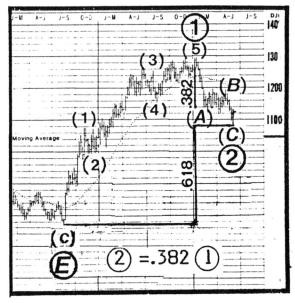

Figure 6-3

vealing that each time period, *as precisely defined by their Elliott Wave structures*, is related to each of the others by a Fibonacci ratio.

(5) Even the Minor moves are related precisely by Fibonacci ratios (see March and April issues).

July 11, 1984

The wave count from the June 15 low is not particularly bullish since it has not traced out a *clear* five waves up. The [price] parameters have not changed, however. The next cyclic lows of importance are due July 24-26.

July 24, 1984

Today's slight new closing low in the Dow at 1086.57 generated "sell signals" all over Wall Street. However, it appears to me that, just like the May 30 low and the June 15 low, this minor decline is actually providing another excellent opportunity to buy. The wave count is completing a *triple* zigzag from the January high and indicates a potential turn to the upside *within a few trading hours*. Taking in all the price action to the present, **Dow 1083 (+ or - 5)** is a very strong support level.

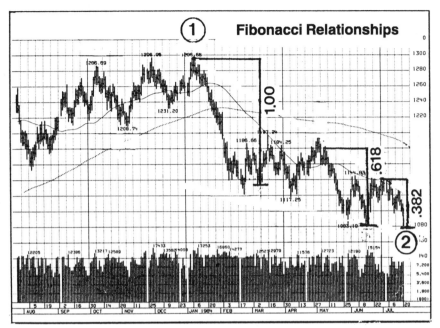

Figure 6-4

Based on typical Fibonacci relationships [see Figure 6-4, from the August 6 issue], I doubt that our stop at Dow 1070 hourly reading will be taken out.

August 6, 1984

The leap out of that bottom [at **1083.59** hourly reading on July 25, 1984], as if you hadn't heard, has been one for the record books and is powerful enough virtually to confirm that Primary wave ③ has begun. [See Figures 6-5 and 6-6.]

To contrast this approach with conventional wisdom, Chapter 11 of *At the Crest of the Tidal Wave* chronicles how historically unpopular a long-term bullish stock market opinion was at that time. The bond forecast recounted below concludes with a description of the consensus opinion of economists. It ties in with the discussions in Chapters 8 and 19.

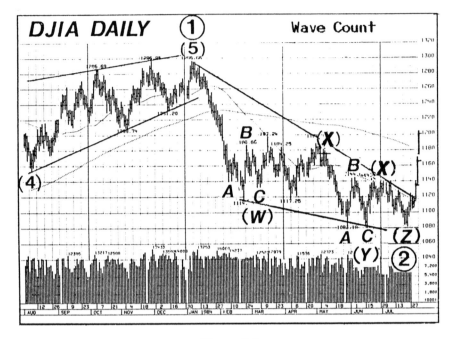

Figure 6-5

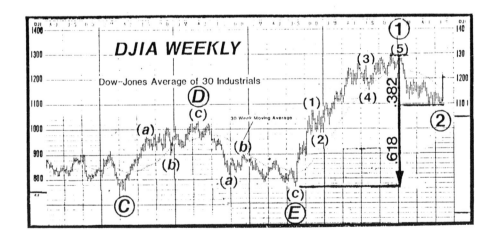

Figure 6-6

Forecasting Bond Prices Using Fibonacci Relationships

November 1983

Now it's time to attempt a more precise forecast for bond futures prices. Wave (a) in December futures dropped 11¾ points, so a wave (c) equivalent subtracted from the wave (b) peak at 73½ last month projects a downside target of 61¾. It is also the case that alternate waves within symmetrical triangles are usually related by .618. As it happens, wave B fell 32 points. 32 x .618 = 19¾ points, which should be a good estimate for the length of wave D. 19¾ points from the peak of wave C at 80 projects a downside target of 60¼. Therefore, *the 60¼ - 61¾ area is the best point to be watching for the bottom of the current decline.* [See Figure 6-7.]

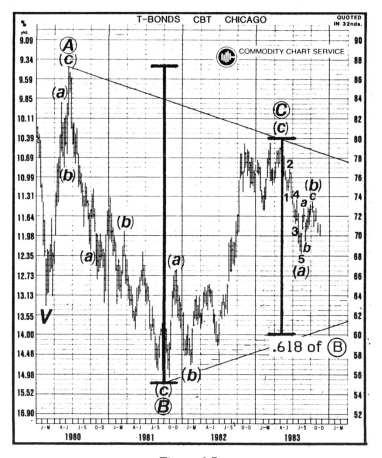

Figure 6-7

April 3, 1984 [after (b) ended in a triangle]

The ultimate downside target will probably occur near the point at which wave D is .618 times as long as wave B, which took place from June 1980 to September 1981 and traveled 32 points basis the weekly continuation chart. Thus, if wave D travels 19¾ points, the nearby contract should bottom at 60¼. In support of this target is the five-wave (a), which indicates that a zigzag decline is in force from the May 1983 highs. Within zigzags, waves "A" and "C" are typically of equal length. Basis the June contract, wave (a) fell 11 points. 11 points from the [slightly lower wave (b)] triangle peak at 70¾ projects 59¾, making the **60 zone (+ or - ¼)** a point of strong support and a potential target. As a final calculation, thrusts following triangles usually fall approximately the distance of the widest part of the triangle.[1] Based on [Figure 6-8], that distance is 10½ points, which subtracted from the triangle peak gives 60¼ as a target.

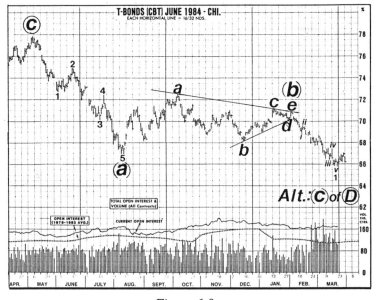

Figure 6-8

June 4, 1984

The most exciting event of 1984 is the apparent resolution of the one-year decline in bond prices. Investors were cautioned to hold off buying until bonds reached the **59¾-60¼** level. On May 30, the day that level was achieved, rumors about Continental Illinois Bank were flying, the 1100 level on the Dow was smashed in the morning on -650 ticks, and the June bond futures contract, amid panic selling, ticked briefly to as low as **59½**, just touching the triangle support line drawn on the chart last month. It stopped cold right there and closed at **59 31/32**, just 1/32 of a point from the exact center of our target zone. In the two and a half days following that low, bonds have rebounded two full points in a dramatic reversal. [See Figures 6-9 and 6-10.]

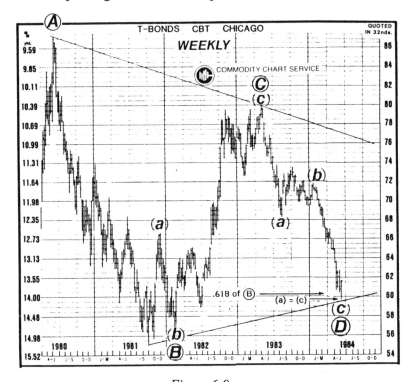

Figure 6-9

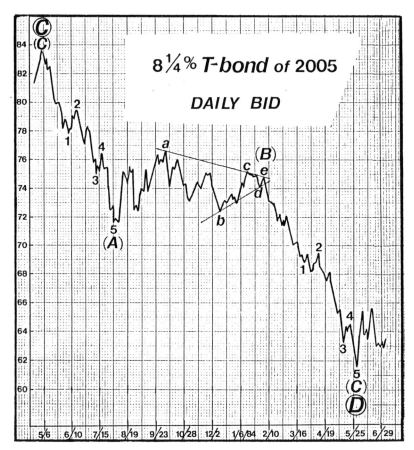

Figure 6-10

Are bonds truly making an important low? The technical evidence argues emphatically that they are. In reaching the Fibonacci support level, bonds traced out an impeccable wave pattern, with a five-wave (a), an a-b-c-d-e triangle (b), and a five-wave (c) from the May 1983 high.

The hourly chart shown [as Figure 6-11] illustrates how the Wave Principle operates even on the smallest level. Notice that all impulse waves are fives and all corrective waves are threes, as required. What's more, each of the Minor waves 1, 3 and 5 hit the lower channel line *precisely*, even though the powerful panic in wave iii of 3 broke the trendline briefly before snapping back into the channel. The channel itself has somewhat of a wedge shape, which is common in *ending* moves.

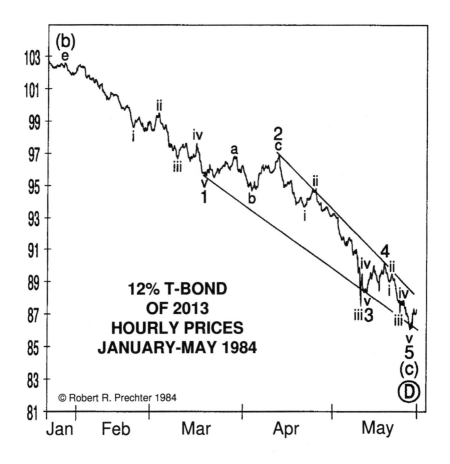

Figure 6-11

July 11, 1984

    The background of investor psychology is very suggestive of an important bond market low. In fact, if this were the only measure I followed, it would appear that bonds are the buy of a lifetime. The news media, which all but ignored the rise in interest rates until May 1984, have been flooding the pages of the press with "higher interest rate" [meaning lower bond price] stories. Most of these came out, in typical fashion, *after* the May low, which was tested in June. During second waves, investors typically relive the fears that existed at the actual bottom while the *market* demonstrates an understanding, by holding above the previous low, that the worst has passed. The last five weeks have demonstrated this phenomenon vividly. On June 11, the WSJ headline read, "Fed Move to Tighten Credit is Expected During the Summer by Many Economists." On June 18, two full articles, including a front page feature, focused on the prospects for higher interest rates: "Cooler Economy Seen Failing to Stem Further Rise in Interest Rates This Year" and "Interest Rates Begin to Damp Economy; Many Analysts See Further Increases." On June 22, the WSJ featured an incredible *five-page* indepth report entitled "World Debt in Crisis," complete with a picture of falling dominoes and quotes like these: from a congressman, "I don't think we're going to make it to the 1990s"; from a V.P. at Citicorp, "Let's be clear — nobody's debts are going to be repaid"; and from a former assistant Secretary of State for economic affairs, "We are living on borrowed time and borrowed money." On July 2, the WSJ reported, without saying so, that economists have panicked. Their forecasts for higher rates now extend halfway into next year! The headline read, "Higher Interest Rates Are Predicted for Rest of Year and Further Rises Are Seen for 1985's First Six Months." Says the article, *"Some say it would take a miracle for rates to fall."* The WSJ is not alone in taking the pulse of economists. *Financial World* magazine's June 27 poll listed the forecasts of 24 economists against their beginning-of-year predictions. *Every single one of them* has raised his forecast in a linear-logic reaction to the rise in rates that has already occurred. They are using the same type of thinking that led them to a "lower interest rates ahead" conclusion a year ago, at the bottom [in rates, top in prices]. This overwhelming consensus based on fundamental analysis is no guarantee that rates have peaked, but history shows that this type of analysis will rarely result in market profits. I prefer to bet on an overlooked theory that recognizes that market patterns repeat themselves over and over again because people are people.

As further developments proved, that low marked the last buying opportunity prior to the start of a historic advance in bond prices that has gone from 59½ to over 134 today, more than a 100% gain. Figure 6-12 shows the updated graph.

As the above excerpts show, wave ratio analysis, applied with knowledge of where such relationships are to be expected, forecasted the exact level of the 1984 lows in both stocks and bonds and then affirmed them as they occurred. In contrast, economists extended their gloomy bond market

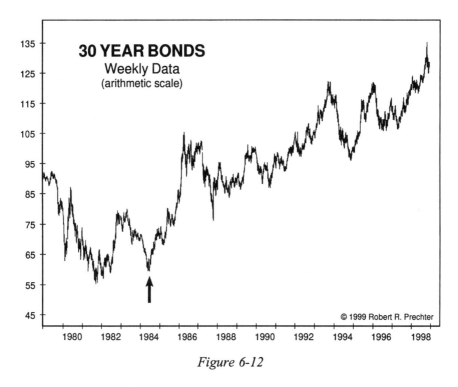

Figure 6-12

outlook to the stock market because of the belief that their forecasted higher interest rates would hurt the economy, which would hurt stocks. This conventional analysis provided exactly the wrong answer, while Elliott wave analysis accurately anticipated *and* recognized, via an *independent* analysis of each market, concurrent lows in both bond and stock prices.

Much More

Chapters 7 and 17 detail a few more long-term financial, economic, monetary and social forecasts that the Wave Principle has made possible. Chapters 4, 5 and 8 and the Appendix in *Elliott Wave Principle* present additional examples of stock market forecasting. The opening parts of Chapters 17, 18 and 19 in *At the Crest of the Tidal Wave* offer a condensed history of my forecasts for gold, the commodity index and collectibles. That book also presents current long-term forecasts for the monetary trend, gold, precious metals mining issues, the commodity index, copper, high-yield ("junk") bonds, high-grade bonds, real estate investment trusts, stock market breadth, mergers & acquisitions and the relative performance of secondary stocks that so far have followed the expected scenarios, despite their dramatic divergence from the consensus outlook. Even if those scenarios go awry from here, their accuracy to date, which is beyond anything that conventional economics can offer, is an adequate demonstration of the Wave Principle's exceptional value. Expectations for the North American and European stock markets, real estate and the world economy, I remain convinced, are on the way to general fulfillment as well, notwithstanding any and all inaccuracies and errors that may occur with respect to postulated specifics.

I stated at the outset of this volume that my stance in this book is advocative. That word is not in the dictionary, but it should be. I intend it to mean that I have chosen to focus on validating the Wave Principle and on the unique accomplishments it makes possible. I am omitting a chronicle of my forecasting errors, while alerting you to the fact that there have been plenty of them, including looking for tops too early and too often in both stocks and bonds.

I plan to publish all of my commentary of past years along with a discussion of what I have learned from errors about both the principle and the limits of forecasting with it. The full record will serve those who wish to judge my errors or to hone their practice of the new science of socionomics by avoiding pitfalls that I did not. In the meantime, if you harbor any doubt as to the value of the Wave Principle *relative to any other extant approach*, Chapter 19 should disabuse you of that concern.

NOTES

1   The width of a contracting triangle is the distance between its boundary lines, measured vertically on the date of the triangle's inception.

Chapter 7:

Relating Aspects of Market Behavior
to Wave Degrees

Besides adding to and quantifying Elliott's rules and guidelines of wave pattern formation, I have spent a good deal of time relating indicators of market behavior to wave degrees. The fact that extremities in these indicators vary in accordance with degree is powerful evidence that wave degrees reflect something *real* in terms of human emotion and behavior. Chapter 14 will carry this theme much further. Herewith are four examples, involving (1) rate of price change, (2) investor psychology, (3) relative trading volume, and (4) the advance-decline disparity, or breadth.

Relating the Rate of Price Change to Wave Degree

One might expect that waves would exhibit power in relation to their degrees, and that is in fact the case. The amount of price change in aggregate stock prices over a specified duration reflects the power of a wave.

Figure 7-1 shows the DJIA plotted against a simple percentage difference between each month-end valuation and the one twelve months prior.[1] Observe that the *52-week rate of change in prices* for the S&P 500 index during the lift-off of each noted wave *is commensurate with the largest degree of the wave that has begun*. When an advance of Supercycle degree began in 1932, the rate of change (ROC) quickly reached +108%. When smaller advances of Cycle degree began in 1942 and 1982, the ROC reached +48% and +53% respectively. When still smaller advances of Primary degree began, the ROC reached lesser peaks.

Declining waves show the same relativity in their extremes of speed. In the Supercycle degree decline that began in 1929, the ROC reached

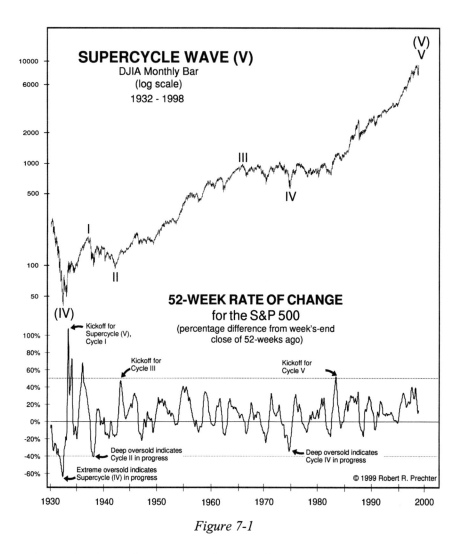

Figure 7-1

-64%. In the Cycle degree corrections that began in 1937 and 1966, the ROC reached -41% and -35% respectively. When still smaller declines of Primary degree began, the ROC reached lesser troughs. Although it is not shown on this graph, the Grand Supercycle corrective wave that began in the year 1720 had the greatest declining rate of change on record, as stock values in London fell 98% in two years.

To conclude, *waves appear to have quantifiable rate-of-change properties that reflect degree.* The higher the degree of the wave that has begun, the more extreme will be the initial speed of price movement.

I use a series of ROCs spanning 14 hours to 20 years to provide a profile of wave speed covering all degrees. These speed indicators are extremely helpful in assessing the progress of waves.

Relating Investor Psychology to Wave Degree

Aggregate dividend payout is a measure of the mental state of investors along the optimism-pessimism continuum. The greater their pessimism, the higher is the payout they demand to make up for perceived risk of capital loss. The greater their optimism, the lower is the payout they require to find stocks attractive, since they expect substantial capital gain.[2]

In Figure 7-2, observe that the *valuation of dividends* paid by the stocks in the Dow Jones Industrial Average at the end of each noted wave is *commensurate with the largest degree of the wave that has ended*. When an advance of Supercycle degree ended in September 1929, the annual dividend payout was 2.89% of the value of the index. When a smaller advance of Cycle degree ended in March 1937, the dividend payout was 3.63%.[3] The 1966 high was a *Cycle* degree top in nominal terms and *Grand Supercycle* degree top in inflation-adjusted terms. In a perfect compromise, its payout of 2.88% matched that of 1929's *Supercycle* high. When

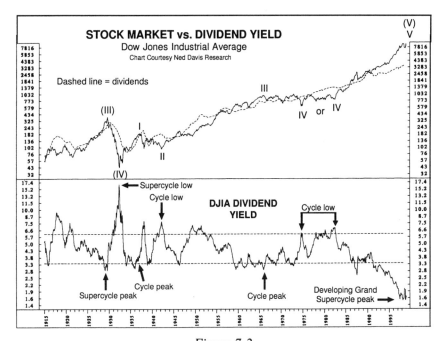

Figure 7-2

still smaller advances of Primary degree ended, the dividend payout reached lesser peaks. The latest low reading of 1.51%[4] in May 1998 fits the interpretation, supported by the sixty years of forecasting presented in Chapter 5, that the market is approaching the end of a wave of Grand Supercycle degree.[5]

Declining waves show the same relativity in ending valuation. When a decline of Supercycle degree ended in July 1932, the payout was 17.35%. When corrections of Cycle degree ended in April 1942, December 1974, and August 1982, the dividend payout reached 7.93%, 6.56% and 7.12% respectively. When still smaller declines of Primary degree ended, valuation reached lesser troughs.[6]

Countless other indicators of investor sentiment reach extremes that relate to the degree of the wave that is ending. These include the ratio of trading volume in puts vs. calls, the ratio of open interest in puts vs. calls, futures premiums and discounts, and the ratio of the number of published books, advisory services, articles and magazine covers that reflect a bullish vs. bearish market opinion.

To conclude, *waves have quantifiable mass-sentiment properties that reflect degree.* The higher the degree of the wave that is ending, the more extreme will be the expression of social mood that produced both the sentiment reading and the wave itself.

Relating Trading Volume to Wave Degree

Now look at Figure 7-3, which is a graph of the dollar-valued trading volume in the stock market divided by the prevailing gross domestic product. This volume/GDP ratio is a measure of trading activity in the stock market compared to the value of the production of goods and services in the economy. It reflects the degree of national interest and activity in the stock market.

Observe that the *volume/GDP ratio* also reaches end-of-wave extremes *commensurate with the largest degree of the wave that is ending.* The larger the degree of an advancing wave, the higher the ratio. The Cycle degree tops of 1937 and 1966-1968 had ratios of 22% and 20% respectively. The Supercycle degree top of 1929 had a ratio of 135%. The currently developing top, which will be of Grand Supercycle degree, has already reached a ratio of 179%, the highest yet.

Declining waves show the inverse tendency. The larger the degree of the wave, the lesser is the volume/GDP ratio at some point late in its development.[7]

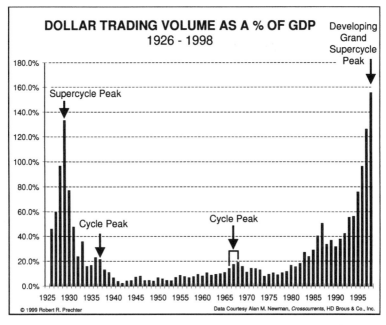

Figure 7-3

To conclude, *waves have quantifiable properties of relative volume that reflect degree.* The higher the degree of the wave that is ending, the more extreme will be the value of trading activity relative to the value of production.

Relating Breadth to Wave Number

The term "breadth" refers to the percentage of component segments of a market that are participating in its trend. In the overall stock market, for instance, such components include sectors, groups and individual stocks. *Every* advancing *fifth* wave, regardless of degree, has narrower breadth, i.e., a lower ratio of segment participation, than its corresponding *third* wave. This is just as true of Supercycle waves as Minor waves.

One measure of breadth is the cumulative sum of the ratios of the number of stocks up each day divided by the number down, normalized for total issues traded. This indicator is called the advance/decline line. If you study Figure 7-4, you will see that the a/d line's performance is better in any wave labeled with the number three than in the subsequent wave of the same degree labeled with the number five. The flat advance-decline line of the 1920s signaled the end of the entire advance from 1857. Similarly, the

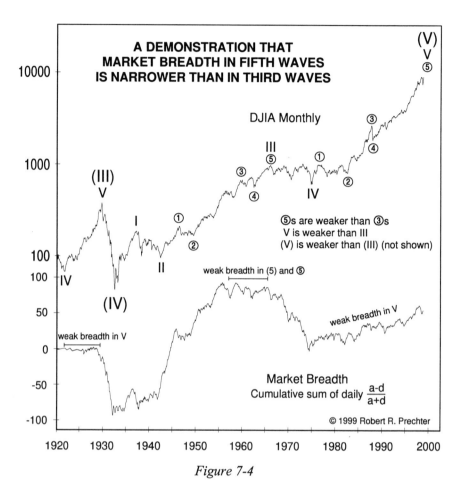

Figure 7-4

flat line in the mid-1960s signaled the end of the 1942-1966 bull market. The inability of this line in the past 24 years to surpass its 1966 high both reflects and supports the labeling that it has been a fifth wave, wave V.

Value in Forecasting

With quantifiable indicators of speed, mood, volume and breadth, we can validate or amend conclusions regarding the present position of the wave structure. For example, since the speed of liftoff has implications as to the degree of the wave that has begun, it implies a continuation of the trend until a movement of sufficient size has occurred. Also, since dividend valuation and volume extremes have implications as to the degree of the wave that is ending, the next wave in the opposite direction will have to be of sufficient magnitude to reflect a change of that degree. In addition, expanding breadth precludes the possibility that a top is nigh.

Furthermore, each indicator helps to predict the others. For instance, extremes in valuation and relative volume can allow us to predict the relative extremity of the next major move in the ROC, and vice versa.

It is the case not only that each of these measures is a powerful indicator of the market's position but also that the market's outlook based upon an analysis of its wave structure is a powerful indicator of how each measure will behave. For example, once we label Cycle wave IV as over, we can expect the next peak reading in the ROC to reflect the power of a wave of Cycle degree. Similarly, once we call for a bull market that will register a Grand Supercycle high, we can expect dividend yield to fall below that of 1929's Supercycle high, and so on.

Forecasting with Indicators of Market-Related Behavior

These quantifiable aspects of waves not only allow for more reliable analysis and categorization but also increase our ability to forecast market behavior. This sentence is more than a claim. The following examples of actual forecasts demonstrate the value of this aspect of socionomics. They show both that the indicators are useful in forecasting waves and that a knowledge of waves is useful in forecasting the indicators. The following excerpts are reprinted from issues of *The Elliott Wave Theorist*. As you read through this commentary, consider that these indicators' intimacy with the very idea of the Wave Principle further validates it.

Forecasting with an Extremity of Sentiment

Elliott Wave Principle was published in 1978, with the Dow at 790. In that book, A.J. Frost and I were long-term bullish for many reasons, but one of them was the low valuation of dividends (i.e., the high dividend yield). As we said then,

> One of our objections to the "killer wave" occurring now or in 1979, as most cycle theorists suggest, is that the psychological state of the average investor does not seem poised for a shock of disappointment. Most important stock market collapses have come out of optimistic, high-valuation periods. Such conditions definitely do not prevail at this time, as eight years of a raging bear market have taught today's investor to be cautious, conservative and cynical.[8]

Take a look at Figure 7-2 and locate the high payout ratios of 1978 to 1982. This forecast called not only for rising stock prices but by implication, falling dividend yields. As you can see, both of these outlooks came to pass. The specific labeling of the advance as *wave V* of (V) implied that dividend yields would fall below any reading on the graph. That has happened as well.

My current analysis of the stock market with respect to dividend valuation should be evident from the notes on Figure 7-2. For details, see Chapter 10 of *At the Crest of the Tidal Wave.*

Forecasting Breadth

Taking for granted that the stock market would soar for years, *The Elliott Wave Theorist* a few months after the 1982 low turned its attention to forecasting the *relative quality* of the advance in terms of the average number of advances vs. declines on a daily basis.

November 29, 1982

Breadth measures almost always begin to show weakness during a fifth-wave advance when compared to the first through third waves. For this reason, I would expect a very broad market through wave ③, then increasing selectivity until the peak of wave ⑤, by which time the leaders in the Dow may be almost the only things going. For now, play any stocks you like. Later on, we may have to pick and choose more carefully.

April 6, 1983

Breadth during wave V should be unexceptional, if not outright poor relative to the spectacular breadth performance in the monolithic markets of the 1940s and 1950s, during wave III. Since it is an impulse wave, however, it will certainly be broader than anything we saw within wave IV from 1966 to 1982. ...A relatively poorly performing a-d line from 1982 to (I expect) 1987 will be a "sell signal" for the entire Supercycle from 1932. The lesson for now is, *don't use that underperformance as a reason to sell too early* and miss out on what promises to be one of the most profitable uplegs in the history of the stock market.

Figure 7-4 adds fifteen years of advance/decline data to the picture I had then, updating it to the present (December 1998). As you can see, Cycle wave V has indeed been weak relative to wave III, and Primary wave ⑤ has been weak relative to wave ③. Intermediate wave (5) (not shown) has been weak relative to wave (3). All of these developments were exactly as forecast.

Forecasting with the Rate of Price Change

A year after the 1982 low came confirmation from the 12-month rate-of-change indicator that a rise of Cycle degree, *not* one either larger or smaller, had begun. Here is my real-time analysis of the event.

August 18, 1983

Indicators of stock market momentum almost always "announce" the beginning of a huge bull market. They do so by creating a tremendously overbought condition in the initial stage of advance. While this tendency is noticeable at all degrees of trend, the Annual Rate of Change for the S&P 500 is particularly useful in judging the strength of "kickoff" momentum in large waves of Cycle and Supercycle degree. This indicator is created by plotting the percentage difference between the average daily close for the S&P 500 in the current month and its reading for the same month a year earlier. The peak momentum reading is typically registered about one year after the start of the move, due to the construction of the indicator. What's important is the *level* the indicator reaches. As you can see [in Figure 7-5], *the level of "overbought" at the end of July 1983, approximately one year after the start of the current bull market, is the highest since May 1943, approximately one year after the start of Cycle wave III.* The fact that they each hit the *50%* level is a strong confirmation that they mark the beginning of waves of equivalent degree. In other words, August 1982 marked the start of something more than what has come to be regarded as the norm, a two-year bull market followed by a two-year bear. On the other hand, it has *not* indicated the start of a glorious "new era," either. If a wave of *Supercycle* degree were beginning, we would expect to see the kind of overbought reading generated in 1933, when the indicator hit 124%[9] one year after the start of wave (V) from 1932. There is now no chance that such a level can even be approached. Thus, the highest overbought condition in forty years signals to me that our Elliott Wave forecast for the launching of wave V is right on target.

Remember, this is just the setup phase. As I have argued since the early days of the current advance, the sentiment indicators should reach much more extreme levels than they ever saw in the 1970s. Put/call ratios and ten-day averages are valuable as far as they go, but they are best interpreted within the context of the broad sweep of market events.

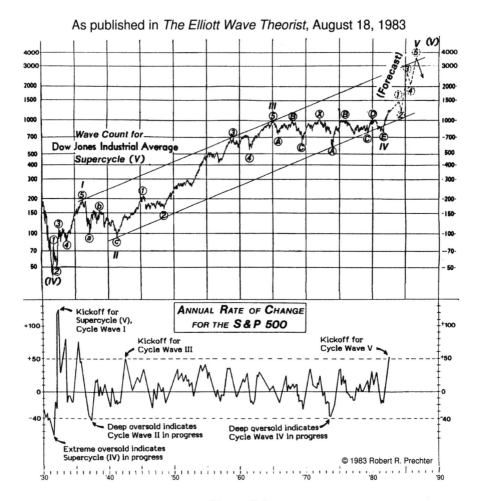

Figure 7-5

Take another look at the long-term Dow chart and ask yourself a few questions about some points that are considered common knowledge.

— Is the market really "more volatile" today than it has ever been in the past? No. A look at 1921-1946 throws that idea right out the window.

— Is the 1000 level a "high" level? For that matter, is 1200 a "high" level? Not any more! The long period spent going sideways since 1966 has put the Dow back at the lower end of its fifty-year uptrend channel in "current dollar" terms (and down to a point of very low valuation in "constant dollar" terms).

— Is the current bull market an "old" bull market that began in 1974 and therefore is "running out of time"? Hardly. Both in "constant dollar" terms and with reference to the 40-year uptrend, the Dow was more undervalued in 1982 than at the crash low in 1974.

— Is my Elliott-based expectation of a 400% gain in 5-8 years a wild one? It appears to be, when compared to recent history. But not when compared to 1921-1929, a 500% gain in 8 years, or 1932-1937, a 400% gain in 5 years.

— Can you always extrapolate current trends into the future? Definitely not. The one rule of the market is change.

— Is any cycle ever "just like the last one"? Not too often! In fact, Elliott formulated a rule about it, called the Rule of Alternation. Broadly interpreted, it instructs the investor to look for a different style of pattern as each new phase begins.

— Is recent market action "too strong," "overextended," "unprecedented," or even a "new era"? No, variations on today's theme have all happened before.

— Is the market a random walk or an erratic wild ride, whipping back and forth without form, trend or pattern? If so, it has "wandered" into long-lasting periods of clear trend, rhythmic cyclical repetition and impeccable Elliott Wave patterns.

At the very least, [Figure 7-5] helps you picture the market's action within the broad sweep of history, thus making next week's money supply report appear as irrelevant as it really is. Furthermore, it helps you visualize why a bull market that is larger than the 30%-80% gains of the upward swings of the last sixteen years is probable, while illustrating the *potential* for a bull market bigger than any in the last *fifty* years. So far, the market is behaving in such a way as to reinforce our original wave V forecast. As long as the market fulfills expectations, we can assume we're still on track.

———————

At this point, I have explained the theory of the Wave Principle, connected it to fractals and spirals, showed that it can be quantified and modeled, related it to indicators of market behavior and demonstrated its utility in forecasting. Now we turn our attention to exploring its basis in biology, psychology and sociology.

NOTES

1 We chose a 12-month span for the ROC indicator to reflect the degrees being examined, but its exact span is arbitrary; an 11.9-month ROC would have a similar profile.

2 As a corollary phenomenon, the greater investors' pessimism, the more dividend payout *matters*, and the greater their optimism, the less relevant or necessary it is deemed. In today's market environment, dividends are actually considered a *detriment* to stock ownership, the theory being that it is better for management to put the money back into the company to make it grow faster. As far as I can determine, this attitude is unprecedented.

3 A year earlier, in March 1936, payout was briefly as low as 2.88% because companies were just recovering from the depression and temporarily had very low payouts that the market knew were about to increase.

4 The S&P 500 yields only 1.34% (July) the Dow Transports only .79% (March) and the NASDAQ over-the-counter index only .29 (December)!

5 For details, see my 1995 book, *At the Crest of the Tidal Wave.*

6 A quick comparison of both the dividend payouts and the ROC percentages suggests the possibility that the average maximum liftoff speed and psychological power exerted at each degree is not far away from a Fibonacci 2.618 multiple of that exerted at the next lower degree.

7 While the end of a declining wave often marks the low in the volume ratio, it sometimes reaches its nadir at the end of wave two *following* the larger correction, as it did in 1942, which was the low of wave II. This expression of apathy fits the description of "wave two" personality as described in Chapter 2 of *Elliott Wave Principle.*

8 Frost, A.J. and Prechter, R. (1978). *Elliott wave principle.*

9 This calculation was based on monthly averages of daily closing figures, which is why it differs from the 108% of the 52-week weekly closing measure.

PART III

THE BASIS OF
THE WAVE PRINCIPLE
IN BIOLOGY, PSYCHOLOGY
AND SOCIOLOGY

The formal construction of the stock market's path implies a mechanism of impulsive cooperation on the part of market participants and therefore of society at large. Because aggregate stock price movement is intricately patterned, there must be primary causes of its behavior, forces that shape it. Part III argues that the primary mover of aggregate stock market prices is mass emotional change, which itself must be, and demonstrably is, independent of outside influence. The specifics of market action are determined by the naturally occurring direction, speed and extent of social mood changes.

If the Wave Principle were the only basis for making this claim, then proof would rest entirely upon demonstrating the validity of the Wave Principle. I believe the literature (including Chapters 5 through 7 of this book) has done a fair job of doing so. For many people, though, that is not enough to dispel skepticism. Is there any other basis to believe that mass emotional change is independent of social events and conditions? Are there biological and psychological sources of these emotional imperatives? Science provides insights that respond to this question in the affirmative.

Chapter 8:

Unconscious Herding Behavior as the Psychological Basis of the Wave Principle

The Triune Brain

Over a lifetime of work, Paul MacLean, former head of the Laboratory for Brain Evolution at the National Institute of Mental Health, has developed a mass of evidence that supports the concept of a "triune" brain, i.e., one that is divided into three basic parts. The primitive brain stem, called the basal ganglia, which we share with animal forms as low as reptiles, controls impulses essential to survival. The limbic system, which we share with mammals, controls emotions. The neocortex, which is significantly developed only in humans, is the seat of reason. Thus, we actually have three connected minds: primal, emotional and rational. Figure 8-1, from MacLean's book, *The Triune Brain in Evolution*, roughly shows their physical locations.

These three areas of the brain apparently followed an evolutionary path of development in that order, as evidenced by several observations. First, reptiles have a brain similar to humans' brain stem, mammals' brains have both that and a limbic system, and certain primates have both these and a significant neocortex. The fossil record reveals the same progression of appearance on earth for each of these groups of animals. Second, in humans, these three sections of the brain are stacked upon each other outward into the head as if the brain were a growing entity. An evolutionary progression explains this "piled-on" form. Third, the skull sizes of later and later hominids are larger and larger, accommodating this expansion. Larger brain size per se would be otherwise unnecessary, as absent evolution, all man would require relative to animals would be a more efficient

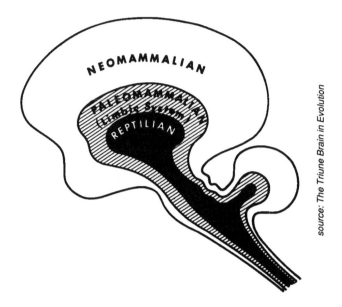

source: The Triune Brain in Evolution

The three sections of the triune brain

Figure 8-1

and powerful mind. Evolution proceeds from forms already available. Fourth, in the human fetus, each portion of the brain develops in the above-described order, as cells of the neocortex organize directly from the cells of the lateral ventricle of the limbic system, which in turn sprouts from the reptilian complex.[1] This chain of events suggests that genetically encoded instructions for forming each more advanced portion of the brain joined an already existing list. Fifth, neural development in children is such that the lower areas of the brain *mature* in earlier years than the upper ones do.[2] This sequence of maturation gets the primitive neural necessities of survival out of the way before developing the higher mental functions. Finally, clinical tests, often in association with serious brain injuries, have produced a large body of evidence indicating that each portion of the triune brain handles functions and behaviors that are common to the animal ancestors that share it and which are absent in those that do not.

The "thinking" done by the brain stem and limbic system is primitive and pre-rational, exactly as in animals that rely upon them. The connection to evolution is important because it explains *why* man has a mind that includes unconscious, impulsive mentation.

The Impulsivity of the Basal Ganglia and Limbic System and Their Independence from the Neocortex

The neocortex is involved in the preservation of the individual by processing ideas using reason. It derives its information from the external world, and its convictions are malleable thereby. In contrast, the styles of mentation outside the cerebral cortex are unreasoning, impulsive and very rigid.

The basal ganglia control brain functions that are often termed instinctive: the desire for security, the reaction to fear, the desire to acquire, the desire for pleasure, fighting, fleeing, territorialism, migration, hoarding, grooming, choosing a mate, breeding, the establishment of social hierarchy and the selection of leaders. More pertinent to our discussion, this bunch of nerves also controls coordinated behavior such as *flocking, schooling* and *herding*. All these brain functions insure lifesaving or life-enhancing action under most circumstances and are fundamental to animal motivation. Due to our evolutionary background, they are integral to human motivation as well. "The limbic system," says MacLean, "underlies the *subjective experience of...emotional feelings* that guide behavior required for self-preservation and the preservation of the species."[3] In other words, it produces powerful emotions as a spur to further the objectives of the basal ganglia.

These two portions of the brain do not learn from new experience. For example, the limbic system houses the brain's pleasure center, which is activated by the neurotransmitter dopamine. In the 1950s, biologist James Olds[4] found that given a lever with which a rat could turn on the electric current that stimulated this portion of its brain, the animal would forgo every other activity — including eating and sleeping — to receive stimulation and would continue to work the lever until it died. Subsequent animal studies have demonstrated that profound pleasure has virtually no satiation point. A cat or monkey will press a bar 10,000 times an hour, for hours on end, to get such stimulation. Olds found that hungry rats were deterred from obtaining *food* if they had to cross a grid giving off 60 microamperes of electricity. To obtain *brain stimulation*, on the other hand, rats have crossed grids charged with 450 microamperes. "We couldn't go higher than that," Olds said, "the shock would knock them out." When they regained consciousness, the rats would resume their path toward the reward. Olds describes a colleague's project in which rats were given only one hour daily in which to eat or to stimulate their brains. After one rat starved to death, the experimenters withdrew rats from the study once they dropped to 70 percent of their original body weight. John Cull, a San Antonio clinical psychologist, referring to human beings, says, "[this portion of] the brain doesn't make value judgments. It just says, 'I'm not getting enough dopamine.' And since there are a whole bunch of ways to make it, *we do whatever we have to do*."[5] This is impulsive, not reasoned, behavior. To differentiate this style of thinking from reason, I will use MacLean's term, *paleomen-tation*, to denote impulsive thought patterns derived from the primitive portions of the brain.

The emotional brain can be triggered by a walnut-sized structure called the amygdala. If the amygdala senses a threat, it reacts instantaneously, signaling crisis and setting off emotional alarms in the limbic system. In 1989, Dr. Joseph LeDoux, a psychologist at the Center for Neural Science at New York University, performed anatomically-related studies at the Laboratory of Neurobiology at Cornell Medical Center and found neural pathways for emotional response that do not go through the cortex and which are faster than the cortex. "The amygdala is just one synapse away from the thalamus, while the hippocampus is several additional synapses away," he explains. This physical difference produces "a difference of as much as 40 milliseconds...in the time it takes a sensory signal to reach the amygdala as compared with the hippocampus." LeDoux's research confirms that *emotion and corresponding reaction can occur both independently of, and prior to, thought*. Because paleomentation is quicker on the draw than the neocortex, emotions are often not reactions to considered *ideas* but immediate reactions to *perceptions* relayed by the senses. As LeDoux points out, "those extra milliseconds may be lifesaving. [However,] it's a very raw form of sensory information...it's quick and dirty process; the cells are fast but not very precise."[6] Harvard psychologist Daniel Goleman, author of *Emotional Intelligence*, says succinctly, "Certain emotional reactions occur before the brain has even had time to fully register what it is that is causing the reaction; the emotion occurs before thought."[7] The result is *immediate responsive action* before the neocortex has time to mull over what is going on or what the consequences of the action will be. Suddenly endangered, we don't think first; we run like hell and then reflect on it later.

Because the goals of the limbic system in motivating behavior associated with self-preservation are so fundamental, it has the capacity to attach extremely compelling emotions to the impulses of the primitive brain. In fulfilling this function, the limbic system holds four trump cards over the neocortex. First, as we have just seen, it is *faster* than the neocortex. Second, it regulates the *amplitude* of emotions as if it held the volume knob on a noise generator. Incredibly powerful emotions thereby *drown out* other signals, such as those from the rational cerebral cortex. Third, the limbic system is disassociated from the concept of time. Whatever it wants, it wants *now*. This disassociation disarms the neocortex, which plans in terms of achieving long-range values. Fourth, the limbic system has proved to be *"essential for a sense of personal identity and reality."*[8] People who have lost portions of that area in the brain lose the crucially important *feelings* attached to both their own identity and that of their environment. This is why the limbic system's feelings are taken so seriously by people and why challenges to them are typically met with fierce resistance, even if that challenge comes from reality itself. In a battle for the soul of a man in an emotionally charged situation, the limbic system usually wins. If you doubt its power and speed, try to envision how you would react if someone suddenly dumped a dozen writhing three-foot blacksnakes in your lap. Understanding that they are harmless, try to decide how long it would take you nevertheless to train yourself not to budge upon being surprised that way in the future.

There is not only a *physical* distinction between the neocortex and the primitive brain but a *functional dissociation* between them as well. The intellect of the neocortex and the emotional mentation of the limbic system are so independent that "the limbic system has the capacity to generate out-of-context, affective feelings of conviction that we attach to our beliefs *regardless of whether they are true or false.*"[9] Epileptics experience storms of emotion that have nothing to do with the reality of the moment; it is just the limbic system firing in a frenzy. Epileptics also experience feelings of immense conviction about an "absolute truth" that is unconnected with any associated idea or thing whatsoever.[10] In normal people, too, feelings of certainty can be so overwhelming that they stand fast in the face of logic and contradiction. They can attach themselves to a political doctrine, a social plan, the verity of a religion, the surety of winning on the next spin of the roulette wheel, the presumed path of a financial market or any other idea.[11] This tendency is so powerful that Robert Thatcher, a neuroscientist at the University of South Florida College of Medicine in Tampa, says, "The limbic system is where we live, and the cortex is basically a slave to that."[12]

A soft version of that depiction, which appears to be a minimum statement of the facts, is that most people do live in the limbic system, particularly with respect to fields of knowledge and activity about which they lack either expertise or wisdom. Informed men may live substantially in the neocortex, but their choice of a field of expertise was probably induced by the limbic system in the first place. Regardless, in every case, the limbic system can still utterly overwhelm the neocortex when it perceives it must.

In effect, then, portions of the brain are "hardwired for certain emotional and physical patterns of reaction"[13] to insure survival of the species. Presumably, *herding* behavior, which derives from the same primitive portion of the brain, is similarly hardwired and impulsive. If so, how do these impulses join together to produce collective agreement in thought and action?

Herding Psychology and Financial Markets

As a primitive tool of survival, emotional impulses from the limbic system impel a desire among individuals to seek signals from others in matters of knowledge and behavior and therefore to align their feelings and convictions with those of the group. The desire to belong to and be accepted by the group is particularly powerful in intensely emotional social settings, when it can overwhelm the higher brain functions.

The less that reality intrudes on the thinking of a group, the stronger is its collective conformity. Dependence most easily substitutes for rigorous reasoning when knowledge is lacking or logic irrelevant. In a realm such as investing, where so few are knowledgeable, or in a realm such as fads and fashion, where logic is inappropriate and the whole point is to impress other people, the tendency toward dependence is pervasive. Trends in such activities are steered not by the rational decisions of individual minds but by the peculiar collective sensibilities of the herd.

In the 1920s, Cambridge economist A.C. Pigou connected cooperative social dynamics to booms and depression.[14] His idea is that individuals routinely correct their own errors of thought when operating alone but abdicate their responsibility to do so in matters that have strong social agreement, regardless of the egregiousness of the ideational error. In the realm of finance, as R.N. Elliott phrased it, Pigou maintained "that an error of optimism tends to create, throughout the community, a certain measure of psychological interdependence until it leads to crisis. Then the error of optimism dies and gives birth to an error of pessimism."[15] In Pigou's words,

> Apart altogether from the financial ties by which different business-men are bound together, there exists among them a certain measure of *psychological interdependence*. A change of tone in one part of the business world diffuses itself, *in a quite unreasoning manner*, over other and wholly disconnected parts.[16]

"Wall Street" certainly shares aspects of a crowd, and there is abundant evidence that herding behavior exists among stock market participants. Myriad measures of market optimism and pessimism[17] show that in the aggregate, such sentiments among both the public and financial professionals wax and wane concurrently with the trend and level of the market. This tendency is not simply fairly common; it is ubiquitous. Most people get virtually all of their ideas about financial markets from other people, through newspapers, television, tipsters and analysts, without checking a thing. They think, "Who am I to check? These other people are supposed to be experts." Many people are emotionally dependent upon the ticker tape, which simply reports the aggregate short-term decision-making of others. This dependence is nearly universal, even among long-term investors. Financial markets induce a form of hypnosis in most people. Outwardly, they appear rational. Inside, their unconscious is in control. They are driven to follow the herd because they do not have firsthand knowledge adequate to form an independent conviction, which makes them seek wisdom in numbers. The unconscious says: You have too little basis upon which to exercise reason; *your only alternative is to assume that the herd knows where it's going.*

In 1987, three researchers from the University of Arizona and Indiana University conducted sixty laboratory market simulations using as few as a dozen volunteers, typically economics students but also, in some experiments, professional businessmen. Despite giving all the participants the same perfect knowledge of coming dividend prospects and then an actual declared dividend at the end of the simulated trading day, which could vary more or less randomly but which would average a certain amount, *the subjects in these experiments repeatedly created a boom-and-bust market profile*. The extremity of that profile was a function of the participants' lack of experience in the speculative arena. Head research economist Vernon L. Smith came to this conclusion: "We find that inexperienced traders never trade consistently near fundamental value, and most commonly generate a boom followed by a crash...." Groups that have experienced one crash "continue to bubble and crash, but at reduced volume. Groups brought back for a third trading session tend to trade near fundamental dividend value." In the real world, "these bubbles and crashes would be a lot less likely if the same traders were in the market all the time," but novices are always entering the market.[18,19]

While these experiments were conducted as if participants could actually possess true knowledge of coming events and so-called fundamental value, no such knowledge is available in the real world. The fact that participants create a boom-bust pattern *anyway* is overwhelming evidence of the power of the herding impulse.

It is not only novices who fall in line. It is a lesser-known fact that the vast majority of professionals herd just like the naïve majority. Figure 8-2 shows the percentage of cash held at institutions as it relates to the level of the S&P 500 Composite Index. As you can see, the two data series move roughly together, showing that professional fund managers herd right along with the market just as the public does.

Apparent expressions of cold reason by professionals follow herding patterns as well. Finance professor Robert Olsen recently conducted a study

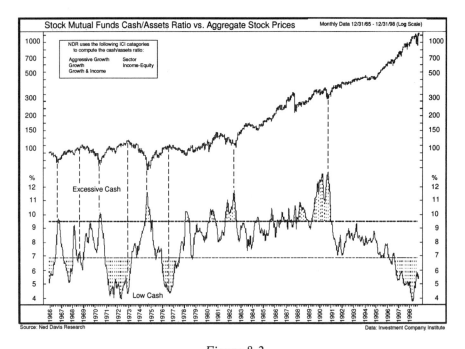

Figure 8-2

of 4000 corporate earnings estimates by company analysts and reached this conclusion:

> Experts' earnings predictions exhibit positive bias and disappointing accuracy. These shortcomings are usually attributed to some combination of incomplete knowledge, incompetence, and/or misrepresentation. This article suggests that the *human desire for consensus* leads to herding behavior among earnings forecasters.[20]

Olsen's study shows that the more analysts are wrong, which is another source of stress, *the more their herding behavior increases*.[21] Equally important, the more their herding behavior increases, *the less accurate their estimates get*. This is a self-reinforcing system with failure the motivator of further failure.

The reason that forecasters' inaccuracy worsens with herding is that the net valuation of the stock market is the *result* of herding. To forecast on the basis of the current sentiments of the herd is to "forecast" the present mood, not future events. Success is simply a matter of whether the present mood maintains, which it usually does not. (For more on this point, see Chapter 18.)

How can seemingly rational professionals be so utterly seduced by the opinion of their peers to the effect that they will not only hold, but *change* opinions collectively? Recall that the neocortex is functionally disassociated from the limbic system. This means not only that feelings of conviction may attach to utterly contradictory ideas in different people, but that they can do so *in the same person at different times*. In other words, the *same brain* can support *opposite views* with equally intense emotion, depending upon the demands of survival perceived by the limbic system. This fact relates directly to the behavior of financial market participants, who can be flushed with confidence one day and in a state of utter panic the next. As Yale economist Robert Schiller puts it, "You would think enlightened people would not have firm opinions" about markets, "but they do, *and it changes all the time*."[22] In each case, they are fully capable of explaining their new conviction, all such utterances being simply (yet sometimes superficially brilliant) rationalizations obediently generated by the neocortex. As market analyst Paul Macrae Montgomery explains, "to the limbic system, the phrase 'net present value of future cash flows' is meaningless because its *only sense of time is now and only value is pleasure or relief from stress*."[23]

Throughout the herding process, whether the markets are real or simulated, and whether the participants are novices or professionals, the conviction of the *rightness* of stock valuation at each price level is powerful, emotional and impervious to argument. Gustave Le Bon, a pioneer in the study of crowd psychology, said a century ago, "It were as wise to oppose cyclones with discussion as the beliefs of crowds.... Time alone can act upon them."[24]

Falling into line with others for self-preservation involves not only the pursuit of positive values but also the avoidance of negative values, in which case the reinforcing emotions are even stronger. Reptiles and birds harass strangers. A flock of poultry will peck to death any individual bird that has wounds or blemishes. Likewise, humans can be a threat to each other if there are perceived differences between them. It is an advantage to survival, then, to *avoid rejection by revealing your sameness*. D.C. Gajdusek researched a long-hidden Stone Age tribe that had never seen Western people and soon noticed that they mimicked his behavior; whenever he scratched his head or put his hand on his hip, the whole tribe did the same thing.[25] Says MacLean, "It has been suggested that *such imitation may have some protective value by signifying, 'I am like you.'*" He adds, "This form of behavior is phylogenetically *deeply ingrained*."[26] Thus, another advantage of herding behavior is the avoidance of seeming difference in order to defuse an excuse to attack.

This tendency toward mimicry is hardly confined to Stone Age tribes. Psychology professor Irving Janis of Yale University, after studying the dynamics of group decision making in the modern political setting, concluded, "In general, the greater the number of those in the decision maker's social network who are aware of the decision, the more powerful the incentive to avoid the social *disapproval* that might result from a reversal." What's more, "The greater the commitment to a prior decision, the greater the anticipated utilitarian losses, social disapproval and self-disapproval from failing to continue the present course of action and hence a greater degree of stress."[27]

That is why, in financial markets, when the best time to buy or sell is at hand, *even the person who thinks he should take action experiences a strong psychological pressure to refrain from doing so*. He thinks, if only half consciously, "When my neighbor or advisor or friend thinks it's a good idea, then I'll do it, too. If I do it now, and I'm wrong, they will all call me a dope, *and I'll be the only dope*." Pressure from, and influence by, peers, then, is at least one reason why most people cannot bring themselves to change from a bullish to bearish orientation or vice versa if to do so would go against the ideas of their associates and contacts. It also explains why a market or other social trend can continue for a long, long time and why financial valuations can become so extreme as to appear outrageous to those who believe that people ought to base their decisions upon some calculable fundamental value.

The discomfort of being alone in one's convictions is so great that it involves physical reactions. "Emotional mentation," says MacLean, "represents the only form of psychological experience that, *by itself*, may induce pronounced autonomic activity" such as sweating, twitching, flushing, muscle tightening and hair standing on end. A person's reaction just *thinking* about taking an action apart from the herd can produce tenseness or even nausea. He knows from experience that anyone who shares a prevailing majority opinion on any subject, particularly one that is intensely attended by the emotions of the limbic system (such as politics, religion, wealth or sex), is treated with the respect due his obvious intelligence and morality. One who utters an opposing opinion is immediately punished by a chorus of deprecating smiles, cackles, mooing, snorting, nipping or outright hostility. It may sound funny, but if you are not used to verbal viciousness or rejection by the group, they are painful experiences, and most people cannot abide either.

Emotionally removed historians sometimes decry the lack of prescience among a population prior to a long-ago financial crisis or the lack of vocal critics in countries that are taken over by fascists, communists, inquisitors or witch-burners. Yet unless one is there, it is nearly impossible to imagine the social pressure to go along with the trend of the day. In many political and religious social settings, for example, "I am not like you" can mean death. The limbic system bluntly assumes that all expressions of "I am not like you" are infused with danger. Thus, herding and mimicking are preservative behavior. They are powerful because they are impelled, regardless of reasoning, by a primitive system of mentation that, however uninformed, is trying to save your life.

The evolutionary advantage of herding, the reason it is incorporated into our paleomentation, is probably that, for animals, it (1) increases the success of life-enhancing activities such as food gathering and preparation, (2) increases the odds of survival in case of attack by a predator, and (3) decreases the odds of being killed because of perceived strangeness.

The resulting actions of herding prior to neocortextural mulling have saved many a life. Unfortunately for humans in modern times, there are important exceptions to that benefit. MacLean worries, "It is one thing to have the anciently derived limbic system to assure us of the authenticity of such things as food or a mate, but where do we stand if we must depend on the mental emanations of this same system for belief in our ideas, concepts, and theories?"[28] As with so many useful paleomentational tools, herding behavior is counterproductive with respect to success in the world of modern financial speculation. If a financial market is soaring or crashing, the limbic system senses an opportunity or a threat and orders you to join the herd so that your chances for success or survival will improve. The limbic system produces emotions that support those impulses, including hope, euphoria, cautiousness and panic. The actions thus impelled lead one inevitably to the *opposite* of survival and success, which is why the vast majority of people lose when they speculate.[29] In a great number of situations, hoping and herding can contribute to your well-being. Not in financial markets. In many cases, panicking and fleeing when others do cuts your risk. Not in financial markets. Paradoxically, then, it is not a confirmation of your correct posture when you look around and can comfortably say, "Everybody out there agrees with me." It is a warning. As John Spooner said, "If you sit in on a poker game and you don't see a sucker at the table, get up, because you're the sucker." The important point with respect to this aspect of financial markets is that *repeated failure does little to deter the behavior*. If repeated loss and agony cannot overcome the limbic system's impulses, then it certainly must have free rein in comparatively benign social settings.

Pointing both to long, persistent financial trends and to sudden giant changes in valuation, neither of which are ever generally anticipated, author J. Orlin Grabbe, straight to the point of this chapter, says, "It would seem that changing images of the future...are endogenous.... They are neither rational or irrational; they are pre-rational.[30] In other words, they are within men, not brought about by outside events. They are not irrational because they have a purpose, no matter how ill-applied in modern life. Yet neither are they rational, as they are within men's unconscious minds, i.e., their basal ganglia and limbic system, which are equipped to operate without and to override the conscious input of reason.

The Super-Organization of Crowds as Distinct from Their Individual Constituents

We have identified unconscious, impulsive mental processes in individual human beings that are involved in regulating behavior with respect to one's fellows in a social setting. Is it logical to expect such impulses to be patterned? When the unconscious mind operates, it could hardly do so randomly, as that would mean no thought at all. *It must operate in patterns peculiar to it.* This is clearly the case in individuals, whose limbic systems produce the same patterns of behavior over and over. Can we link such patterns to the formation of a super-organic pattern such as the Wave Principle? There is evidence to support this hypothesis as well.

Gustave Le Bon said a hundred years ago, "The psychological crowd is a provisional being formed of heterogeneous elements, exactly as the cells which constitute a living body form by their reunion a new being which displays characteristics very different from those possessed by each of the cells singly."[31] Le Bon proposed a "law of the mental unity of crowds," whereby individuals cease to think independently and instead participate unconsciously in "a sort of collective mind."

Is this the outmoded view of a nineteenth-century empiricist who theorized a bit too glibly? Modern researchers are coming close to confirming his view. The November 1997 issue of *Physica A*, published by the European Physical Society, presents a study that specifically connects the stock market with the primitive mentation of animals, including their occasional collective mentation. Didier Sornette, along with Anders Johansen of the Niels Bohr Institute in Copenhagen, propose these relevant conclusions in their paper, "Large Financial Crashes":

> "Stock markets are fascinating structures with analogies [to what is] arguably the most complex dynamical system found in the natural sciences, i.e., the human mind. Instead of the usual interpretation of the efficient market hypothesis in which traders extract and incorporate consciously (by their action) all information contained in market prices, we propose that the market as a whole can exhibit an "emergent" behavior not shared by any of its constituent[s]. In other words, *we have in mind the process of the emergence of intelligent behavior at a macroscopic scale that individuals at the microscopic scale have no idea of.* This process has been discussed in biology *for instance in animal populations* such as ant colonies or in connection with the emergence of consciousness."[32]

This postulation is utterly compatible with the Wave Principle. The behavior that a crowd as a whole exhibits is indeed "intelligent," being a mentation distinct from that experienced by each individual. However, it is not rational; it is impulsive, and that is why only students of crowd psychology, who have observed the difference between crowd behavior and individual behavior, have been comfortable with the very idea. When a herd "thinks," the result is not reason but an emotional interpersonal superorganic dynamic that must be the source of waves. A person's *patterned psychological dynamics as they relate to the social environment* produce an unconscious impulse to herd, which in combination with like minds produces global patterns of interactive dynamics in a social setting. The resulting pattern of collective conduct apparently takes the form of the Wave Principle.

In general, social mood change need not necessarily involve every individual. A person is drawn in to the unconscious, unreasoning, psychologically interdependent social dynamic when he allows himself to be influenced primarily by the emotional state of others rather than by independent research, adequate knowledge and utter rationality. Most people are too busy and unmotivated to fulfill such a tall order. Even those committed to rationality find these requirements difficult to fulfill even in tailor-made situations and impossible to fulfill in all situations.

Even if one wishes to assert the utter rationality of some participants in society, their influence can only matter if most others share that rationality in weighing arguments *and* if the arguments of the rational participants are identical. This utopian situation never exists in real societies, where the sum of people's shared impulses overwhelms the power of logical yet often conflicting entreaties from various individuals. Indeed, those conflicts themselves provide an excuse for people to abandon the hard work of reason and succumb easily to commandeering by the limbic system. Regardless of the divergent thoughts and actions of any individual, then, the crowd will follow its characteristic patterns of behavior.

One way or the other, socially induced mood changes in most individuals are able to progress uninterrupted by intrusion from an independent cerebral cortex. That is why, *in the aggregate*, human interpersonal dynamics are immutable.

NOTES

1 Larsen, W.J. (1997). *Human embryology.*

2 Wright, K. (1997, October). "Babies, bonds, and brains." *Discover,* p. 78.

3 MacLean, P. (1990). *The triune brain in evolution,* p. 247.

4 Nesmith, J. (1996, September 14). "The roots of personality..." *The Atlanta Journal-Constitution.*

5 *Ibid.*

6 Goleman, D. (1989, August 15). "Brain's design emerges as a key to emotions." *The New York Times.*

7 *Ibid.*

8 MacLean, P. (1990). *The triune brain in evolution,* p. 17.

9 *Ibid,* p. 569.

10 *Ibid,* pp. 453, 578.

11 We will explore some of these in Chapters 15 through 19.

12 Wright, K. (1997, October). "Babies, bonds and brains." *Discover,* p. 78.

13 Scuoteguazza, H. (1997, September/October). "Handling emotional intelligence." *The Objective American.*

14 Pigou, A.C. (1927). *Industrial fluctuations.*

15 From Charles J. Collins's foreword to *Elliott Wave Principle.*

16 Pigou, A.C. (1920). *The economics of welfare.*

17 Among others, such measures include put and call volume ratios, cash holdings by institutions, index futures premiums, the activity of margined investors, and reports of market opinion from brokers, traders, newsletter writers and investors.

18 Bishop, J.E. (1987, November 17). "Stock market experiment suggests inevitability of booms and busts." *The Wall Street Journal.*

19 Smith also notes that when he imposes artificial trading curbs that limit downside movement during any one session, it encourages people to generate a stronger-than-normal boom, which in turn makes the ensuing crash worse. Such mandated trading halts, which are in force today, are bound to make crashes worse from another perspective. When people are invested and know that with a few more percent down they will lose their option to exit and be stuck with their shares, they panic even more than they would have otherwise. Potential new buyers will be reluctant to enter because they, too, might get stuck.

20 Olsen, R. (1996, July/August). "Implications of herding behavior..." *Financial Analysts Journal,* pp. 37-41.

21 Just about any source of stress can induce a herding response. MacLean humorously references the tendency of governments and universities to respond to tension by forming *ad hoc* committees.

22 Passell, P. (1989, August 25). "Dow and reason: distant cousins?" *The New York Times.*

23 Montgomery, P. (1991, September 19). Speech, "Stocks and the irrational: possible sub-cortical influences on contemporary equity market pricing." and (1992, September 13) Speech, "Capital markets and the irrational: possible non-cortical influences on the price structure of investments."

24 Le Bon, G. (1895). *The crowd.*

25 Gajdusek, D.C. (1970). "Physiological and psychological characteristics of stone age man." *Symposium on Biological Bases of Human Behavior, Eng. Sci.* 33, pp. 26-33, 56-62.

26 MacLean, P. (1990). *The triune brain in evolution.*

27 Janis, I. (1972). *Victims of groupthink.*

28 MacLean, P. (1990). *The triune brain in evolution,* p. 453.

29 There is a myth, held by nearly all people outside of back-office employees of brokerage firms and the IRS, that many people do well in financial speculation. Actually, almost everyone loses at the game eventually. The head of a futures brokerage firm once confided to me that never in the firm's history had customers in the aggregate had a winning year. Even in the stock market, when the public or even most professionals win, it is a temporary, albeit sometimes prolonged, phenomenon. The next big bear market usually wipes them out if they live long enough, and if they do not, it wipes out their successors. This is true regardless of today's accepted wisdom that the stock market always goes to new highs eventually. Aside from the fact that this very conviction is false (Where was the Roman stock market during the Dark Ages?), what counts is *when people act,* and that is what ruins them.

30 Grabbe, J.O. (1995). *International financial markets.*

31 Le Bon, G. (1895). *The crowd.*

32 Sornette, D. and A. Johansen. (1997, November). "Large financial crashes." *Physica A.*

Chapter 9:

Theories and Observations Relating to Impulsivity and Herding

Encoded Behavioral Rules as a Possible Impetus for Herding

Many families of animals herd, flock, school and swarm, including fish, insects such as ants and bees, birds, many grazing mammals and apparently, humans. "There is something utterly awe-inspiring," says Ian Stewart, "...about [the] apparent unity of purpose [of] large groups of...social animals."[1] It is due, he argues, not to "instinct," but to mentally encoded *rules*. Paul MacLean observes that "reptiles are slaves to *routine, precedent and ritual*,"[2] strongly implying embedded behavioral rules. H. Hediger notes that the habits of a tree porcupine that he observed for seven years "were of almost clock-like regularity."[3] In other words, there may be no genetic code to "join a herd," but there may be a genetic code that imparts individual rules of behavior that *result* in herding.

The behavior of animals is mightily akin to that of units within systems that are programmed to follow certain simple rules. When Mark Tilden, in his Los Alamos laboratory, fed three rules into a robot, it behaved in a seemingly complex way that made it appear to be "thinking" about following sunlight around to maintain its solar power input.[4] Zoologist Fritz Vollrath[5] and Kate Douglas[6] have created "cyberspiders" that, with a short list of rules, construct all the webs made by actual spiders. These experiments show that the mental encoding of rules can account for why animals engage in apparently complex yet rigidly performed behavior. It seems a cogent explanation of why birds migrate and turtles swim to islands that have continental-drifted a thousand miles away. They are obviously not working out their behavior on a slide rule or with a map. If three or four embedded mental rules could produce the course of action, then their mentation need not be that complex.

Inputting goals into a computer program can even cause sets of rules to evolve. Perhaps such rules evolved in the genetic code of plants and animals to further the goals of survival and reproduction. If so, it is likely that a few simple rules embedded in human genes and executed in the basal ganglia and limbic system originally to enhance the survival of all the organisms that preceded man through evolution are the source of human herding behavior.

Indeed, many human beings follow rules so slavishly that the response, "But we've always done it this way!" is often considered of self-evident weight in an argument over procedure. Says MacLean about human beings, "the stress generated by an actual or threatened change in routine is many times compounded when entire organizations are involved." In other words, rules that are shared by a human herd are all the more resistant to suggestions of change.

There are probably two types of rules, the hard-wired and the temporary-derivative. A hard-wired rule might be, "Go along with what most other people think, say or do." A temporary-derivative rule might be, "Most people agree that the stock market always goes up," or "we all know that country X is our enemy." Given the limbic system's role in asserting feelings as truth, initial evidence to the contrary of such learned rules would be (and typically is) perceived literally as unreal. This is why social trend changes always come as a surprise. To conclude, while generally a human does not consciously plan to herd or think he is herding, his unconscious mind may harbor *a few simple rules relating to the behavior of others* that tend to make him an unknowing participant in the herd.

Mental Contagion

One theory of the spread of ideas, which could be a mechanism employed by the herding impulse, is that ideas are units of cultural transmission that have the property of self-replication, like a living thing that "propagates from brain to brain." Says Oxford zoologist Richard Dawkins, "When a craze, say for pogo sticks, paper darts, slinkies or jacks sweeps through a school, it follows a history just like a measles epidemic."[7] This mechanism is not related only to fads. Yale economist Robert Schiller uses the word contagion to describe the psychological mechanism behind financial market trends. Attitudes about every imaginable thing sweep through the population.

Elaine Showalter, Avalon Foundation Professor of the Humanities at Princeton, offers a theory of social hysteria in terms of contagion. Her thesis is particularly important to our discussion because social hysteria is a pure case of *unreasoning emotion*, in this case aimed at inappropriate entities. Her book, *Hystories – Hysterical Epidemics and Modern Media*, chronicles the disease-like transmission of images that people incorporate mentally as if they were real, including alien abductions, satanic ritual abuse, recovered memories and multiple personality syndrome. Like the witch craze of the 1600s, all of these crazes have proved baseless, yet thousands of people insisted for quite awhile that they were real and dedicated immense energy to them. Social hysteria sometimes involves persecution of helpless victims who are demonized in socially transmitted paranoid visions, be they women (in the case of witches), fathers (in the case of recovered memories of child abuse), or people of other religions (such as Jews in Nazi Germany or Muslims in the Balkans). I would add that such demonization can include inanimate objects. In the early 1970s, people were obsessed with the evil of business conglomerates, and many deeply feared that the International Telephone and Telegraph company (ITT) would take over the world. In the 1980s and 1990s, there have been countless hysterical episodes over food, from Alar in apples to pesticide sprays to salmonella in chicken and eggs to cancer-causing meats to the evil of fats and oils, all of which have provided countless hours of discussion on TV talk shows. Today, people are beginning to panic over the coming "Y2K" disaster, which supposedly will bring the modern world to a screeching halt, just as people approaching the last millennium panicked over religious prophecies of the end of the world. Eventually, each incidence of social hysteria subsides, just as epidemics subside.

These observations pertain to our discussion in Chapter 8 of the *independence* of the limbic system and its ability to translate *emotions into images and images into perceived reality*. In the individual, these images are conjured to give the neocortex something to do, as otherwise the welling emotion of anxiety, for example, would have no referent. In the social context, images spread from one person to another, perhaps out of desire to join in group experience, a desire for attention, or perhaps simply by contagion, any of which reasons reflects a *dependence* upon the thoughts and actions of others not unlike the dependence that investors display. Showalter regards hysteria as "a cultural symptom of anxiety and stress..requir[ing] at least three ingredients: physician-enthusiasts and theorists, unhappy, vulnerable patients and supportive cultural environments."[8] These prerequisites certainly fit the world of investing. As I argue in Chapter 14, though, it is unlikely that the sharing of cultural images is restricted to hysteria or the stock market and probable that it pertains to all social experience.

Mental contagion is an ugly idea to some people. Philosopher Daniel Dennett complains, "I'm not initially attracted to the idea of my brain as a sort of dung heap in which the larvae of other people's ideas renew themselves before sending out copies of themselves in an informational Diaspora."[9] Of course, one is not *attracted* to the idea, as independence is the hallmark of a rational man. However, it is folly to dismiss the idea of mental contagion, because ignorance of it is exactly how one becomes most susceptible to its expression in himself. It is a paradox (like so many truths) that one must recognize this aspect of one's mind in order even to attempt to rise above it and watch with a new understanding what is going on in society. That is what the Wave Principle makes possible.

Feedback as Characteristic of Financial Markets and Society

Like societies as a whole, financial markets are a quintessential example of systems whose results feed back into the system as new cause. As the most widely followed market index in the world, the Dow Jones Industrial Average not only *reflects* the pulse of investors, it *affects* the pulse of investors. Not only do investors' decisions make the Dow move in a direction, but the direction of the Dow often causes investors to make those very decisions. Every day, investors watch the same ticker tape, read the same newspapers, listen to the same financial television shows and watch the same market indices go up and down. The same information, opinions and emotional expressions are absorbed and reflected by millions of people involved in the market. It is almost as if the participants are in a town square, and an orator trying to whip up revolution is standing on a balcony, making the crowd's emotions wax and wane with each change in content, tone and volume. In the case of markets, however, the orator and crowd are mostly one and the same. Much of Wall Street's information, such as price level, direction, speed of price change and volume, is self-generated, and just like a mob, the financial community feeds off its own emotions. The reason is that every market decision is both *produced by* information and *produces* information. Each transaction, while at once an *effect*, becomes part of the market and, by communicating transactional data to investors, joins the chain of *causes* of others' behavior. This process produces a mass feedback loop, which is governed by man's unconscious social nature. Since he *has* such a nature, the process repeatedly generates the same forms.

Stock averages even allow the crowd to monitor itself, like fashion-conscious people watching each other at a shopping mall. In their function as monitors, averages such as the Dow Jones Industrial Average must be maintained as a standard. Let us explore this idea as it relates to the integrity of the DJIA. There is an oft-cited and not unreasonable objection to using the Dow in analysis or forecasting, which is that its components are not constant. For instance, Dow Jones & Co. replaces stocks in its averages from time to time, and occasionally one of the stocks splits. Either event changes the relative weightings of the individual issues in the average. Many people call such changes "distortions," implying that this stock average is a rubber yardstick.[10]

A spokesman for Dow Jones & Co. who maintains the Dow averages, admittedly a partisan on this issue, says, "The components may change with the times, but what the Dow represents remains constant."[11] The precision of the DJIA's long-term wave structures and price relationships over the years supports this view unequivocally. The constancy of the Dow is also revealed by its continually constructing long-term parallel trend channels according to Elliott's observation, for instance, in Figures 18-1 through 18-5. The constancy of the Dow is a necessity in accounting for the success of three specific forecasts recounted in Chapter 5. There are others on the record. For instance, even though Dow Jones & Co. substituted MMM for Anaconda in its premier average 1976, the 1977-1978 decline still took the Dow exactly to a .618 retracement of the 1974-1976 advance, reaching a target I published in advance, as detailed in Chapter 4 of *Elliott Wave Principle.* Despite several splits and substitutions, the Dow's rise from 1974 nevertheless topped in 1987 within 0.07% of a level that made the 1974-1987 advance in percentage terms precisely equal to that of 1932-1937, fulfilling a wave relationship that A.J. Frost called for nine years in advance in *Elliott Wave Principle.*

Because of all this experience, it is clear to me that investors have a complex emotional relationship with the Dow *as such*, as an entity in itself, much as fans remain loyal to a sports team despite the continual replacement of individual players. Professional investors' actions reflect this loyalty when they adjust their portfolios after a change in Dow (or S&P) components. They make such adjustments either to mimic what Dow Jones & Co. did or under the assumption that other people will do so. Each of these reasons conforms to the herding impulse.

Social Visioning as an Aspect of Herding

Why does a vast plurality of observers find extremely high or low financial market valuations utterly justifiable during their occurrence yet so obviously crazy in retrospect? That the majority (of money, actually, and therefore usually people) at the time of the extreme valuation believes it to be sensible is true by definition, or the pricing would not exist. Years later, historians look back at the time and cluck about how absurd prices were. Yet "every age," said Charles Mackay in 1852, "has its peculiar folly; some scheme, project or fantasy into which it plunges, spurred on either by love of gain, the necessity of excitement, or the mere force of imitation."[12]

Mackay uses the word "fantasy," as have a number of psychologists since. While *mood* definitely precedes action (see Chapter 16), it is not necessary that fantasy images precede that action. Herding people *feel* a certain way and can express themselves impulsively to reflect those feelings. They need not share any specific fantasy or image, just a mood. Nevertheless, the idea does *fit* the Wave Principle, so it may be that shared fantasy images are an *intermediate step* between mood change and resulting action.

Several social scientists have proposed models that involve people sharing a social vision that serves as a benchmark against which they judge the world. Unlike physical benchmarks, social visions *change*. Trends based upon subjective mental imagery undergo violent reversals when that imagery dissolves. The unconscious use of an inconstant benchmark explains why people may believe fully in a dream of perpetual prosperity one decade and succumb fully to a despairing nightmare of imminent doom the next. Their minds adapt to the group's changes in attitude as if reality itself had changed (and as a result, it usually does; see Chapter 16).

In 1952, Wilfred R. Bion presented a paper to the *International Journal of Psychoanalysis* on small-group dynamics. He characterized them as based upon primitive, shared unconscious fantasies, images or myths that come about as a way of relieving the pressure of, and evading the effort of, maintaining a rational, problem-solving orientation.[13] Psychologist Carl Jung, many of whose ideas are controversial for good reason, nevertheless addressed the idea of human herding in terms that are not incompatible with this view. He proposed that all individuals inherit, both genetically and by cultural transmission, ideational forms, or "archetypes," that are "collective, universal and impersonal" and which together form a "collective unconscious" social mind that rules emotionally-charged social behavior.[14] Jung's "archetype" is essentially an unconsciously shared social dream, fantasy, image or myth.

Psychologist Lloyd deMause presents a case for a "psychogenic theory of history," whereby adults in groups first generate shared fantasies based upon childhood experience, then project them as images, and then act them out.[15] He cites as evidence the fact that social images in news photographs, cartoons, advertisements, political speeches, entertainment media and so on *precede* events that then appear to mimic those images. This theory is not incompatible with the Wave Principle. Socionomics is based upon the idea that social mood is responsible for the character of social action. Since mood is expressed immediately in countless ways other than buying or selling stock (see Chapter 14), expressions of the prevailing mood probably do include public visual images. These images would reflect mood quite immediately, before the public could mobilize itself enough to act in the economic and political arenas (see Chapter 16). However, I expect that the hypothesized connection of these images to childhood experience is derived from Freudian ideas, making that aspect of the theory highly conjectural. In light of the information in Chapter 8, I suggest that such images would necessarily coalesce around the concerns of the limbic system and therefore be *evolutionarily primitive* in their nature. The resulting images might appear to a psychologist as childlike, although children are not typically obsessed with wealth, death, survival or sex (which concerns shape many social images), and the limbic system is.

Regardless of any associated psychoanalytics, the essential idea of social visioning has had staying power, finding its way into such modern social words as "paradigm." Science historian Thomas Kuhn, for instance, defines this term as "the entire constellation of beliefs, values, techniques, and so on shared by the members of a given community."[16]

Swiss economist Eugene Bohler brings us closer to the subject of finance when he says, "The modern economy is as much a dream factory as

Hollywood."[17] Terms such as "fantasy" and "social dream" might appear overdone to many readers. As a close observer of the public's view of the stock market for many years, I find these terms utterly compatible with reality. What words better describe the results of a poll in late 1997 showing that *on average*, U.S. mutual fund investors expect their funds to gain *34% per year for the next ten years?*[18]

If social visioning is an intermediate step between social mood and social action, the dynamics of its manifestation would have to follow the Wave Principle, which governs its cause. It may well do exactly that. In 1965, B.W. Tuckman presented research on the developmental sequence of the psychological dynamics of small groups.[19] Expanding upon his observations in the 1980s, psychiatrist Philip Wells Shambaugh of the Harvard Medical School, an expert on small-group dynamics, observed a certain style of progress in the images that such groups share and made this report:

> The development of small groups, in its simplest form, proceeds in a series of five waves, alternatingly positive and negative. I began to wonder why such an undulation occurs and hypothesized that each stage of group development is patterned by an underlying shared fantasy. The first is the primordial paradise fantasy, the second, [a] negative phase, includes a number of competing fantasies, all marked by anger and hatred, the third [is marked] by the image of a Morean utopia, the fourth, again negative, is not often described but probably involves the decay of the utopian image, and the fifth, positive, is of a democratic group structure. If one accepts [Prechter's] thesis that the Elliott wave form is based on mass psychology, it makes sense. ...The homologizing between the fantasies of small and large groups [becomes] quite essential in this unexpected context.[20]

If social visioning occurs, and if it follows the Wave Principle, then people must share images and their associated feelings *all the time*, just as the Wave Principle is operating all the time. There is no reason to believe that people share images only at extremes in valuation or emotion, which only reflect their intensity. People often do share visions of boundless abundance or certain destruction, but these are the poles of the scale. In between, there are various degrees of optimism or pessimism and of uncertainty about the future, whose associated images would be correspondingly moderate. Pricing extremes in the stock market would reflect the power of social visions, and trend durations their persistence.

Habituation

Why is the mind so plastic with respect to financial valuation? Apparently, people adopt the recent past as normal no matter how unusual historically. Pathologist Frederick A. Hottes has a suggestion as to why:

> Sensory receptors experimentally have been shown to have the property of adaptation. Basically, if a continuous sensory stimulus is applied, the receptors respond at a very high pulse rate at first, then at a progressively lower rate until finally many of them no longer respond at all. Would the same response in the brain explain why the recent past is a stronger stimulus for behavior than older experiences/history books?[21]

Habituation is common in life forms as low as the sea-slug, whose six attendant neurons will eventually cease to cause a withdrawal of its gill when touched, as if it is getting used to the stimulation to the point that it is no longer stimulation. Humans' physical sensory apparati show the same diminution of response. If the brain reacts the same way, it would explain why people get used to new settings, whether physical or cultural, why they get bored with sameness in entertainment, and why they find new social events and trends shocking while accepting old social events and trends as normal.

University of South Florida College of Medicine's Dr. Robert Thatcher, founder and former director of the Applied Neuroscience Research Institute of the University of Maryland School of Medicine, suggests a mechanism for *long-term* habituation: periodic "waves" of nerve growth and brain restructuring.

> The new model of neural development holds that the primitive areas of the brain mature first; in the first three years of life, the regions in the cortex that govern our sensory and motor skills undergo the most dramatic restructuring, and these perceptual centers, along with instinctual ones such as the limbic system, will be strongly affected by early childhood experiences.
>
> But the frontal cortex, which governs planning and decision making, and the cerebellum, a center for motor skills, are also involved in emotional development. And those parts of the brain don't get rewired until a person is five to seven years old. What's more, another major restructuring of the brain occurs between ages nine and eleven, says Thatcher. Suddenly, the brain is looking less like a sculpture in stone and more like a work in progress.

Thatcher's readings of the EEGs of adolescents and adults have revealed that some reorganization of the brain may occur about every two years from birth to death. He proposes that these reorganizations happen in response to waves of nerve growth factor that sweep across the cerebral hemispheres in two-year cycles, revamping up to one-fifth of the brain's synaptic connections at the leading edge of the wave. The idea of the traveling waves is just a theory now — but it's a theory that's making more sense to more scientists.[22]

Such periodic restructuring would offer an adaptational advantage to survival. If a person's environment changes, his brain can adjust to it. This adaptability with reality as a reference may explain why one generation of people is utterly at home with farming, another with machines, another with electronics and another with computers.

Periodic waves of restructuring would explain why people fight *new* long-term social trends as abnormal while embracing *old* ones as normal. It takes time for brains to restructure themselves to fit the new social environment, which they invariably do, *as if it is a new environment in reality to which they must adjust to survive.* That is why each new level of financial prices, whether higher or lower, after some time is accepted as normal regardless of what might be considered historically reasonable value. As a result, few people are induced to sell at a market top or buy at a bottom.

The sliding response curve of habituation and the plasticity of waves of brain restructuring are marvelous adaptive mechanisms most of the time, but not in finance. As with the paleomentation of the limbic system, this otherwise very useful mental ability is counterproductive to successful financial speculation. By the time it becomes crucially important for people to recall the significance of a similar market environment or juncture in the past, they have forgotten it and have adjusted to the new one as if it were normality. Waves of brain restructuring might also account for why people are mostly oblivious to their own cycles of attitude. Incorporating the Wave Principle into one's thinking is an excellent way to be aware of one's own changes in attitude so that they do not mislead and also to anticipate social changes so that they are not a shock.

A Hypothesis of Dynamic Herding as a Function of a Fibonacci Bipolar Impulse to Imitate or Deviate

I would like to offer a hypothesis of the creation, maintenance and reversal of human social trends (whether involving the stock market, hair styles, musical preferences, skirt lengths, tie colors, or whatever). You may be better served reading this section after reading Chapter 12, which presents the work of Lefebvre and Adams-Webber.

These psychologists posit and demonstrate that people's mental decision model is bipolar and that on average, people have a built-in bias, by a ratio of .618 to .382, toward the positive or optimistic end of the pole. One bipolar decision continuum might be, at one end, an impulse to *imitate* others, and at the other end, a capacity to *deviate* from the behavior of others. The research cited in Chapter 12 suggests that any such impulses would be biased toward imitation in a .618/.382 ratio.

Because imitation has the stronger tendency in this hypothesis, any initial random fluctuations in people's preferences in a neutral context would quickly lead to a slightly higher density of preference for one object or idea. That preference in turn would invoke the bias to imitate, which would increase that density and cause a trend toward agreement. Soon, that trend would culminate in a one-sided stance. After a state of preference was established in the majority of the population, individuals would deviate from time to time, but their number would usually be too small to attract enough imitation to change the group's orientation. Eventually, random impulses to deviate would, at some point, result suddenly in a large number of people deviating. If the imitation that then resulted were to involve enough people, a change in trend would occur. At the critical point, the change in overall orientation that establishes the new polarity would be very rapid.

While this model would work as described if imitation and deviation impulses were random, I believe that in the real world, they are not. Too long a time of consensus breeds reaction in people. Eventually, a long-standing condition of social agreement *fosters* deviation in many human beings. Therefore, to adjust the hypothesis slightly, I would contend that at some point, the neglected pole becomes attractively charged out of the desire for newness and the excitement of change, tipping the Fibonacci balance in its favor. Such a model might account for why voters slosh back and forth from conservatism to liberalism, generally reaching 62%/38% extremes before galloping in the other direction. This model might be termed the dynamic herding hypothesis.

In support of this possibility, one of Poulton's experiments cited in Chapter 12 asks subjects to rate the "lightness" of a gray sheet of paper against the poles of black and white.[23] Subjects tend very strongly to rate the paper at 62%, but 62% *of which pole* varied, producing data spikes at 38% and 62% of the white-black spectrum. Lefebvre offers this explanation:

For some subjects, the white sample played the role of the positive pole, and for others, the black one. The former marked 0.62 of the scale from point 0, and the latter from the point 100.[24]

The black/white dichotomy is quite reflective of the battle between liberals and conservatives in the political arena or bulls and bears in a financial market. Like the left-right spectrum in politics, the up-down spectrum in stock market belief is mostly a function of feeling, which is the realm of the limbic system.[25] In the former case, "left" and "right" are the poles of belief that alternate between positive (attractive) and negative (unattractive) in people's minds. In the latter case, "up" and "down" are the poles of belief that alternate between positive (probable) and negative (improbable). The recessive tendency to deviate triumphs when a majority adopts the previous negative pole as the positive one.

The Individual's Place in the Herd

The idea of patterned collective behavior is not easy for many people to accept because it appears *inhuman* in the sense that it does not reflect what *makes* people human — the rational faculty — while social action reflects impulses from an evolutionarily pre-human portion of the brain. Philosopher Friedrich Nietzsche bluntly stated the difference: "Madness is rare in individuals, but in groups, parties, nations and ages, *it is the rule*."[26] Nevertheless, it is the impulsive mind that is essentially identical in almost every person. Our conscious minds make us human and different from each other, but it is our unconscious minds that make us the same.

Research shows that the power of the limbic system to override the neocortex varies a great deal among individuals. Some people find it difficult to control their emotions. Others, such as criminals, find it nearly impossible to resist their impulses.[27] The same fact may apply to herding behavior. For some people, imitation may be anathema. Others seem nearly incapable of independent rational exertion and soak up all their ideas from society. Everyone herds somewhat, and most people herd a lot. As lay philosopher Eric Hoffer said, "When people are free to do as they please, they usually imitate each other."[28]

Regardless of how rational some individuals in a financial market may be, *it is the most impulsive participants that wield absolute control over its trends*. Even if, say, only 30% of investors are prone to panic, that is quite enough to precipitate one. When panic ensues, those less prone to panic know that if they do not act, they may be driven bankrupt by those who do. This knowledge creates a chain reaction as otherwise calm people succumb to the fear that the panic will ruin them. They capitulate because others are capitulating.

Alternatively, if, as I suspect, people run the gamut of panicability, then an initial panic by those most impulsive will draw in those next most disposed, which will increase the selling, which will trigger the next most disposed, and so on. The reverse is true in an uptrend with respect to confidence. As the trend extends and extends, less and less susceptible individuals succumb. Supporting this view is the illustrative fact that the great genius Isaac Newton was finally baited into the famous South Sea Bubble near its peak, losing the equivalent of a million 1998 dollars. His resulting loss caused him to remark, "I can measure the motions of bodies, but I cannot measure human folly." Now, with the Wave Principle, we have a basis for measuring that property and unraveling its mystery.

In the face of such impulses, our struggling neocortex has only two possible functions. The first is to eliminate conflict among the brain's parts by rationalizing, *ex post facto*, the decisions made by the limbic system. Gallons of ink and miles of transmission wires are wasted on this exercise daily. Brains engaged in this unconscious goal can reach a heated pitch. To anyone versed in the Wave Principle, the endless discussion and analysis of the news as it relates to the stock market appears fruitless and even bizarre. (For more on this topic, see Chapter 18.)

For the first time ever, the neocortex now has a second function. With knowledge of the Wave Principle, the neocortex may attack the problem of market analysis and social forecasting using reason. Understanding that financial market behavior is governed by the patterned unconscious, then, is precisely what, for the first time ever, allows analysis of it to be objective.

We can now postulate that paleomentational thought processes are the psychological motor of the trends and patterns of social mood that produce Elliott waves. How do we account for the fractal, Fibonacci-based, spiral-related pattern of Wave Principle dynamics? In Chapters 10 through 12, we will examine the biological origins of those aspects of nervous system behavior.

NOTES

1 Stewart, I. (1998). *Life's other secret.*

2 MacLean, P. (1990). *The triune brain in evolution,* p. 237.

3 Hediger, H. (1950). *Wild animals in captivity.*

4 The rules are: (1) If your solar cells are not generating more than X amount of power, spin at random and move 10 centimeters forward. (2) If they have been generating power above X for less than five seconds, move forward in a straight line at constant speed. (3) If they have been generating power above X for more than five seconds, stop.

5 Vollrath, F. (1992, March). "Spider webs and silks." *Scientific American,* pp. 52-58.

6 Douglas, K. (1996, August 10). "Arachnophilia." *New Scientist,* pp. 24-28.

7 Dawkins, R. (1993, December 15). "Is religion just a disease?" *The Daily Telegraph.*

8 Showalter, E. (1997). *Hystories – hysterical epidemics and modern media.*

9 Dennett, D. (1991). *Consciousness explained,* p. 202.

10 A presentation of this objection can be found in *Stock Market Logic,* by Norman Fosback (1976), The Institute for Econometric Research, Fort Lauderdale, pp. 282-284.

11 Reference unavailable.

12 Mackay, C. (1841). *Extraordinary popular delusions and the madness of crowds.*

13 Bion, W. (1952). "Group dynamics: a review." *International Journal of Psychoanalysis,* No. 33, pp. 235-247.

14 Jung, C. (1959). *The archetypes and the collective unconscious.*

15 deMause, L. (1982). *Foundations of psychohistory,* pp. 172-243.

16 Kuhn, T. (1962). *The structure of scientific revolutions,* (2nd ed. 1970).

17 Grabbe, J.O. (1995). *International financial markets.*

18 From a poll conducted by Montgomery Asset Management (San Francisco), released October 1997.

19 Tuckman, B.W. (1965). "Developmental sequence in small groups." *Psychology Bulletin* No. 63, pp. 384-399.

20 From a personal letter from P. Shambaugh to Robert R. Prechter, Jr., June 15, 1986.

21 From a personal letter from F.A. Hottes to R. Prechter, August 21, 1996.

22 Wright, K. (1997, October). "Babies, bonds, and brains," *Discover,* p. 78.

23 Poulton, E.C., *et al.* (1968). "Response bias in very first judgments of the reflectance of grays." *Perception and Psychophysics*, Vol. 3, pp. 112-114.

24 Lefebvre, V. "Sketch of reflexive game theory," from the proceedings of the Workshop on Multi-Reflexive Models of Agent Behavior conducted by the Army Research Laboratory.

25 See "The Extent of Impulsivity in Political Action" section in Chapter 16.

26 Nietzsche, F. (1886). *Beyond good & evil.*

27 Samenow, S. (1984). *Inside the criminal mind.*

28 Hoffer, E. (1955). *The passionate state of mind.*

Chapter 10:

Biological Connections to the Robust Fractal Aspect of the Wave Principle

Fractals in the Body

Why does the unconscious herding impulse produce a *robust fractal* pattern of social interaction? It might appear surprising if the brain were *not* associated with a robust fractal form of behavior. The human body, like much of nature, is a mass of robust fractals.

In 1992, researchers at Boston University, MIT and Harvard Medical School discovered that the fractal pattern in the nucleotide sequence of

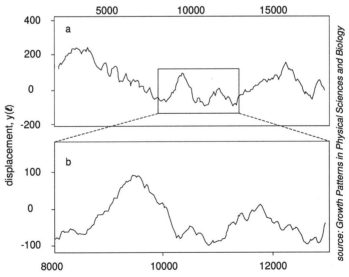

The DNA walk representation for the rat embryonic skeletal myosin heavy chain gene (α = 0.63) (a) The entire sequence. (b) The magnification of the solid box in (a).

Figure 10-1

DNA links its parts over long stretches of the molecule in such a way as to produce "a remarkably long-range power law correlation."[1] Figure 10-1 shows both an *entire* sequence and a magnified *portion* of it. Their similarity is like that of the Elliott wave pattern at various degrees shown in Figures 2-1 through 2-7, suggesting at least the possibility that DNA is not an indefinite fractal but a patterned *robust* fractal.[2]

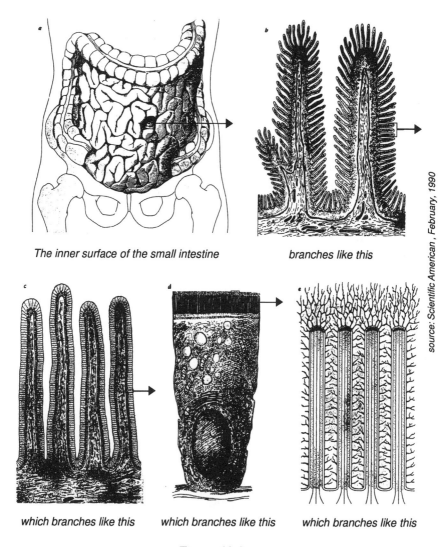

The inner surface of the small intestine

branches like this

which branches like this   which branches like this   which branches like this

source: Scientific American, February, 1990

Figure 10-2

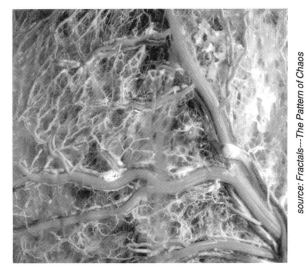

source: Fractals---The Pattern of Chaos

Blood vessels form an arborum

Figure 10-3

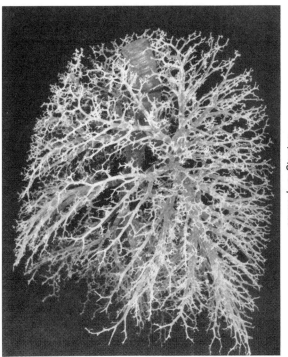

source: Lung Structure

Air passages in the lung form an arborum

Figure 10-4

The fractal aspect of DNA carries through to the forms it governs. For example, the circulatory system, the lungs, certain cardiac muscles, the surfaces of hemoglobin, the bile duct system, the urinary connecting tubes in the kidney, the placenta and the absorption surface of the small intestine are all fractal branching systems, or arbora. Figures 10-2 through 10-4 show examples.

Fractals in Nervous System Physiology

Well, guess what. The brain, and the forms to which it is directly connected, reflect this same design. An arborum suffuses the retina (see Figure 10-5), which is directly connected to the nervous system. Dr. Ary L. Goldberger of Harvard Medical School's Beth Israel Hospital made this observation in the February 1990 issue of *Scientific American*:

> Certain neurons, for instance, have a fractal-like structure. If one examines such neurons through a low-power microscope lens, one can discern asymmetric branches, called dendrites, connected to the cell bodies. At slightly higher magnification, one observes smaller branches on the larger ones. At even higher magnification, one sees another level of

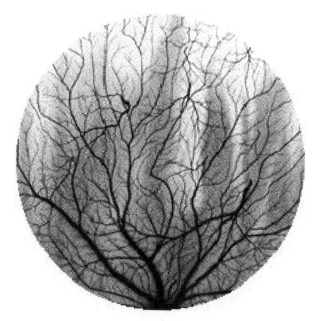

The retina forms an arborum

Figure 10-5

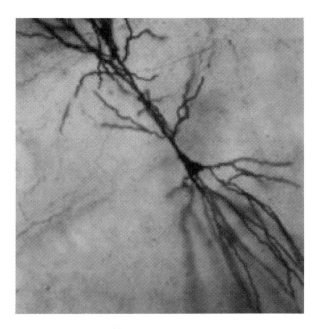

Neurons form arbora

Figure 10-6

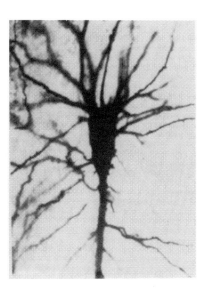

source: Journal of the American Medical Association

The giant pyramidal Betz cell of the motor cortex forms an arborum.

Figure 10-7

detail: branches on branches on branches.... If one saw two photographs of the dendrites at two different magnifications (without any other reference), one would have difficulty in deciding which photograph corresponded to which magnification.[3] [See Figure 10-6.]

Along with Dr. Lewis A. Lipsitz, also of Beth-Israel, Goldberger adds to the list of neurological arbora "the branching pattern of the Betz cells in the frontal cortex, spiny cells in the caudate, and anterior horn cells in the spinal cord."[4] (See Figure 10-7.) The same structures that we see at these micro scales occur at macro scales. The white tissues of the cerebellum, called the arbor vitae, or tree of life (see Figure 10-8), as well as the blood vessels in the brain (see Figure 10-9) arborate in a pattern not unlike that of a solitary oak tree (see Figure 10-10), which is apparently the way it has "grown" through evolution.

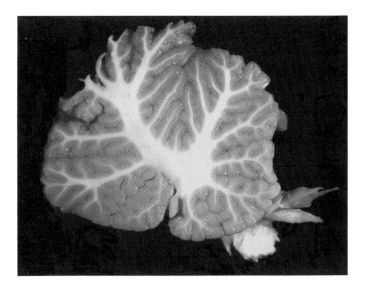

A sheep's cerebellum is an arborum

Figure 10-8

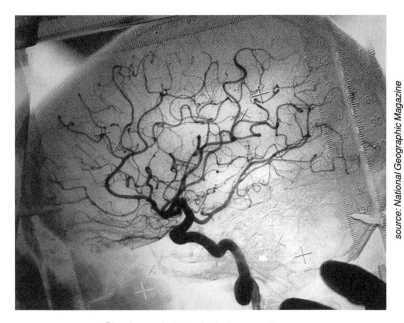

source: National Geographic Magazine

Blood vessels in the brain form an aborum
Figure 10-9

An oak tree is an arborum
Figure 10-10

Fractals in Nervous System Function

Iterated Systems president Michael Barnsley, who, with Dr. Alan Sloan, pioneered the development of fractal imaging systems for data compression software in the late 1980s, recently mused on PBS, "The most important fractal in the human body is the incredibly complex wiring circuit, the brain. We may never understand how our brains *work*, but if we do, I suspect that it will depend upon some application of fractal geometry."[5] Indeed it may, because it is not only the *structures* of the brain and nervous system that reveal fractals. Recent studies show that some of their impulsive *functions* do as well. For instance, the nervous system controls the human heartbeat. Researchers from Boston University and Harvard Medical School report that a healthy human heart beats irregularly. As reported by the *Dallas Morning News*,

> Plotting the time intervals [between beats] on a graph creates an interesting pattern. It's a complex, jagged line looking a little like a mountain range. The nature of the jagged pattern looks the same when it's graphed for a short time period – say minutes – or over a longer time, like 24 hours, corresponding to thousands of heartbeats. This similar structure persisting over different scales is what mathematicians call a fractal.[6]

Head researcher Dr. Ary Goldberger makes this observation:

> A fractal pattern in heartbeats implies some *long range correlations in nervous system activity*, since the involuntary (or "autonomic") nervous system regulates heartbeat. *And since the involuntary nervous system controls lots of things, the fractal pattern may appear elsewhere*, and in fact, the data that we have from other systems suggest that it applies more broadly to respiration, blood pressure control *and so forth.*[7]

Following up on that presumption, Dr. Jeffrey M. Hausdorff of Beth Israel Hospital, in cooperation with Harvard Medical School, has employed a special device to monitor striding patterns of healthy people. He finds that variations in stride display long-range self-similar correlations extending over hundreds of steps; in other words, their patterns are fractals. Echoing the conclusion of Dr. Goldberger's heartbeat study, he states, "each stride interval depends upon stride intervals at remote previous times."[8] This conclusion based upon the fractal nature of the nervous system's regulatory functions is exactly the same as that necessitated by the Wave Principle about financial markets: each movement depends upon movements in the past, both recent and remote. Our brains, then, "work" in accordance with fractal geometry, just as the Wave Principle does.

These studies reveal that fractals are crucial to the short- and long-range behavior and self-organization of man's nervous system. The Wave Principle reveals that fractals are crucial to the short- and long-range behavior and self-organization of man's social system. Is it farfetched to postulate a direct connection between the two?

Fractals as Tools of Efficiency, Efficacy and Robustness

Why does the body employ fractals? Three reasons appear to be efficiency, efficacy and robustness. As Goldberger explains with respect to other bodily systems,

> Fractal branches or folds greatly amplify the surface area available for absorption (as in the intestine), distribution or collection (by the blood vessels, bile ducts and bronchial tubes) and information processing (by the nerves).... Fractal structures, partly by virtue of their redundancy and irregularity, are robust and resistant to injury.[9]

Similarly, IBM physicist Richard Voss proposes that the fractal pattern in DNA might be involved in enhancing copying accuracy from one generation to the next.[10] I would postulate that DNA's fractal nature makes it active in ensuring the robustness of the species as well. Its copying "errors," which are commonly presumed to be random mistakes, are far more likely to be vital discontinuities, regulated fractally, that ensure adequate mutation to provide for the adaptability of the species to changing environments.

How do fractals contribute to the efficiency of human mentation? Fractals in the physical and functional aspects of the nervous system may help the brain *understand* fractals. It can certainly recognize clouds and trees and mountains in a flash. In contrast, it might take some time to teach a computer the difference between a cloud, a bird and an airplane. Then it might be confused by a blimp or a falling star. But the brain can usually tell the difference between the natural and the man-made in an instant. Perhaps it is able to recognize and deal with nature so intimately because of its parallelism with nature in both design and function. As Briggs and Peat summarize Nobel laureate Ilya Prigogine's view, "The brain is the nonlinear product of a nonlinear evolution on a nonlinear planet."[11] In 1990, Dr. Larry R. Vandervert proposed to the national convention of the American Psychological Association a chaotic/fractal dynamical unification model for psychology, in which he argues that the ability of the *mind* to understand fractals in the *world* may be a reflection of the fractal structure of the *brain*.[12]

Societies cluster for reasons of efficiency as well. People travel, congregate and settle in such a way as to produce a fractal cluster in the very organization of crowds, societies and cultures. Zipf discovered in 1949 that the distribution of the populations in towns cluster according to a power law.[13] Supporting that conclusion, Dr. Peter Grassberger of the University of Wuppertal in Germany demonstrates that epidemics spread throughout the population in a fractal pattern. That is to say, the distribution of people infected with a communicable disease within a small segment of the population looks much like the distribution throughout a larger segment.[14] This result is due to the fact that the social interaction of people produces a fractal, which is apparently the most efficient and robust arrangement for their interaction. Diseases, like computer viruses on the internet, occasionally take advantage of this efficient distribution system. The apparent value of fractals and power laws to social aggregations is consistent with the appearance of fractals in all kinds of social data, including financial market pricing data, as mentioned in Chapter 2.

The fractal nature of the *physiology* and *function* of the brain and mind is compatible with the fractal nature of its *product* in concert with like minds: the Wave Principle. Likewise, the primitive brain may impel mentational interdependence among humans in the pattern of the Wave Principle because this cooperative social fractal is valuable in terms of efficiency, efficacy and robustness. As Le Bon said in 1895, "Crowds are always unconscious, but this very unconsciousness is perhaps one of the secrets of their strength. In the natural world, beings exclusively governed by instinct accomplish acts whose marvelous complexity astounds us."[15]

Fractals as Necessary for Viability

The value of fractals in living forms may be even greater than efficiency, efficacy, robustness and other such utilitarian advantages to life; they may be necessary for life itself. Lipsitz and Goldberger have conducted studies demonstrating that *aging* coincides with a *reduction in the arboration of the nervous system* and that a reduction in the fractal irregularity of the heartbeat is a signal of an impending heart attack. In other words, health and vitality require fractal physiology and function. Prigogine says this about the brain:

The brain has to be largely irregular; if not, you have epilepsy. This shows that irregularity, chaos, leads to complex systems. It's not at all disorder. On the contrary, *I would say chaos is what makes life and intelligence possible.* The brain has been selected to become so unstable that the smallest effect can lead to the formation of order.[16]

In other words, perhaps not only the efficiency and adaptability of a complex system, but its very existence, depends upon its fractal patterns of irregularity.

As it happens, the life of a stock market uptrend also depends upon persistent fluctuation. Studies on trend-reaction frequency show that a paucity of reactions after a long uptrend is a reliable sign of an impending reversal.[17] As with an unnaturally smooth stride, heartbeat or brainwave, an unusually smooth rise in stocks is a precursor to the death of a bull market from old age or to a market heart attack or epileptic fit in the form of a crash. Apparently *what is true for individual life forms in this regard is true for super-organic social clusters as well.* They both depend upon fractals for health and perhaps even existence.

Conclusion

Fractals permeate individuals' nervous systems, the congregation of people, and their patterns of interaction. These facts are consistent with the discovery that these same people's minds, in combination with like minds, produce a fractal of collective mentation called the Wave Principle. Physiologist and Nobel laureate Sir Charles Sherrington calls the brain a self-organizing system that appears as "an enchanted loom, where millions of flashing shuttles weave a *dissolving pattern*, always a meaningful pattern [and] a shifting *harmony of sub-patterns*."[18] This description matches that of social behavior under the Wave Principle, where a harmony of sub-patterns weave together to form larger meaningful patterns that dissolve only to lead to the development of the next ephemeral pattern, all as a result of the self-organization of many individuals. To conclude, the brain may be disposed to participating in a fractal of collective sentiment because circumstantially, it, along with the rest of the human body's structures and functions, is of and for fractals in so many ways.

NOTES

1 Stanley, H.E., *et al.* (1993). "Fractal landscapes in physics and biology." *Growth patterns in physical sciences and biology.*

2 Goldberger, A., *et al.* (1990, February). "Chaos and fractals in human physiology." *Scientific American,* pp. 42-49.

3 *Ibid.*

4 Lipsitz, L. and Goldberger, A. (1992, April 1). "Loss of 'complexity' and aging." *Journal of the American Medical Association.*

5 Lesmoir-Gordon, N. (1994). "Fractals: the colors of infinity."

6 Siegfried, T. (1993, March 29). "Healthy hearts have complex rhythm." *The Dallas Morning News.*

7 *Ibid.*

8 Browne, M. (1997, April 15). "Variations in stride." *The New York Times.*

9 West and Goldberger point out in another article that branching in the lungs "approaches the more favorable ratio of surface to volume enjoyed by our evolutionary ancestors, the single-celled microbes." [ref: Goldberger, A., *et al.* (1990, February). "Chaos and fractals in human physiology." *Scientific American,* pp. 42-49.] Perhaps all of the body's fractal patterns are a method of reconstructing the environment of ancient life. For instance, the fractal nature of the absorption surface of the intestine might serve to approximate the surface/volume ratio of ancient unicellular microbes as well. Blood vessels likewise bring nutrients to all parts of the body as the sea did long ago to microbes. (Indeed, the body's regulation of salinity mimics the ancient environment of the sea. Our eyes are washed with a saline solution for the same reason.)

10 Voss, R. (1992, June). "Evolution of long range fractal correlations and $1-F$ noise in DNA-based sequences." *Physical Review Letters.*

11 Briggs, J. and Peat, D. (1989). *Turbulent mirror,* p. 166.

12 Vandervert, L. (1990, August 12). Presentations: "A chaotic/fractal dynamical unification model for psychology" and (1989, May) "Systems thinking and neurological positivism: further elucidations and implications."

13 Zipf, G.K. (1949). *Human behavior and the principle of least action.*

14 "The practical fractal."(1987, December 26). *The Economist.*

15 Le Bon, G. (1895). *The crowd.*

16 Prigogine, I. and Stengers, I. (1984). *Order out of chaos.*

17 Eliades, P. (1998, May 4). "Danger: bear may be crossing." *Barron's.*

18 Sherrington, C.S. (1940). *Man on his nature.*

Chapter 11:

Biological and Perceptual Connections to the Fibonacci Foundation of the Wave Principle

Fibonacci in the Body

Why does man's unconscious herding impulse produce a *Fibonacci*-based pattern of social interaction? Consider that the human body, like most plant and animal life forms, is a mass of Fibonacci expression, from micro to macro scales.

The DNA molecule, which is the data source for the developing human being, spirals in Fibonacci proportion. Given current best measurements, the length of one cycle is 34 angstroms, and its height is 20 angstroms, very nearly producing the Fibonacci ratio 34/21 (see Figure 11-1).[1] Fibonacci may be hidden more deeply in the structure of DNA. Stanley *et al.* note parenthetically in their power-law study, "The DNA walk representation for the rat embryonic skeletal myosin heavy chain gene [has a long range correlation of] *0.63*"[2] (see Figure 10-1), which once again is quite close to *phi*.[3]

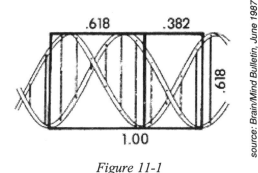

Figure 11-1

Biochemistry professor Guido Pincheira of the University of Chile argues that symmetry in DNA produces symmetry in the intermediate and final forms it governs. That symmetry, he says, includes Fibonacci expression.[4]

Fibonacci certainly does appear in the final form. One of the lowest forms of animal life, the starfish, mimics the Fibonacci-based five-pointed star shown in Figure 3-8. The highest form of life, man, also mimics this form when arms and legs are spread, as depicted in Figure 11-4.[5]

The golden section is found throughout the human body. The navel, which marks the source of life for a developing fetus, divides the average adult body into Fibonacci proportion. The neck divides the distance from navel to head into Fibonacci proportion (see Figure 11-2). Dr. Robert M. Ricketts of the University of Illinois in Chicago has

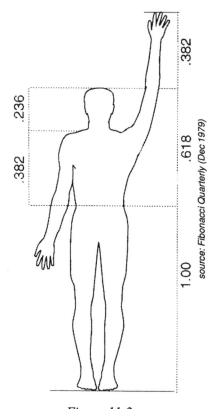

Figure 11-2

produced an exhaustive description of Fibonacci relationships in the human head (see Figure 11-3).[6] Heart specialists confirm that the muscles of the left ventricle of the heart are made up of a series of spirals that repeatedly contract to a point that is approximately *62%* of the long axis from the aortic valve to the apex."[7] In the early 1960s, Drs. E.R. Weibel and D.M. Gomez meticulously measured the architecture of the lung and reported that the mean ratio of short to long tube lengths for the fifth through seventh generations of the bronchial tree is *0.62*, again the Fibonacci ratio.[8] Bruce West and Ary Goldberger have found that the diameters of the first seven generations of the bronchial tubes in the lung decrease in Fibonacci proportion.[9] Figure 11-4 is the famous drawing by Leonardo da Vinci pointing out the human body's Fibonacci proportions. Architect György Doczi summarizes the pervasive appearance of Fibonacci in the human body:

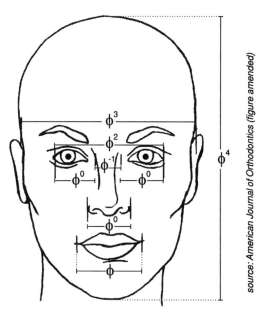

Figure 11-3

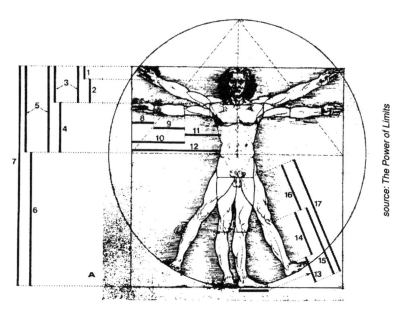

1 : 2 = 2 : 3 = 3 : 4 = 4 : 5 = 6 : 7 = 8 : 9 = 9 : 10 = *0.618±*
10 : 12 = 11: 10 = 13 :14 = 14 : 15 = 16: 15 = 15 : 17 =

Leonardo da Vinci's depiction of Fibonacci relationships in the human body

Figure 11-4

All parts of the human body share the same proportional limitations. The length relationships of hand to arm to trunk...are shared...by the relationships of head to neck, trunk, legs and feet. The entire human bone structure fits neatly into three golden rectangles and a reciprocal, the latter containing the head. We find an astonishing unity between the proportional harmonies of the whole body and its diverse parts.[10]

From our most intimate genetic coding to our full body proportion, we reflect the Fibonacci ratio. Is the brain so disposed as well? The answer appears to be yes, both physiologically and functionally.

Fibonacci in the Physiology of the Brain and Nervous System

Oxford professor of mathematics Roger Penrose, who shared the Wolf Prize for Physics in 1988 with cosmologist Stephen Hawking, presents this discussion in his 1994 book, *Shadows of the Mind*:

> The organization of mammalian microtubules is interesting from a mathematical point of view. The number 13 might seem to have no particular mathematical significance, but this is not entirely so. It is one of the famous Fibonacci numbers: 0, 1, 1, 2, 3, 5, 8, 13, 21, 34, 55, 89, 144, ... where each successive number is obtained as a sum of the previous two. This might be fortuitous, but Fibonacci numbers are well known to occur frequently (at a much larger scale) in biological systems. For example, in fir cones, sunflower heads, and palm tree trunks, one finds spiral or helical arrangements involving the interpenetration of right-handed and left-handed twists, where the number of rows for one handedness and the number for the other handedness are two successive Fibonacci numbers. [See Figures 3-9 through 3-11.] (As one examines the structures from one end to the other, one may find that a "shunt" takes place, and the numbers then shift to an adjacent pair of successive Fibonacci numbers.) Curiously, the skew hexagonal pattern of microtubules exhibits a very similar feature — generally of an even more precise organization — and it is apparently found (at least normally) that this pattern is made up of 5 right-handed and 8 left-handed helical arrangements, as depicted in [Figure 11-5]. In [Figure 11-6], I have tried to indicate how this structure might appear as actually "viewed" from within a microtubule. The number 13 features here in its role as the sum: 5 + 8. It is curious, also, that the double microtubules that frequently occur seem normally to have a total of 21 columns of tubulin dimers forming the outside boundary of the composite tube — the next Fibonacci number!

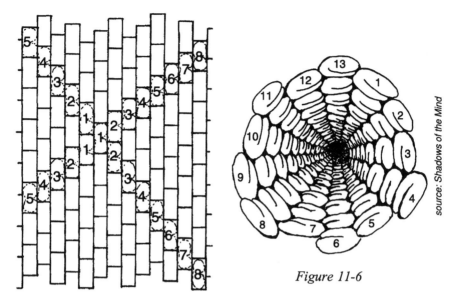

source: Shadows of the Mind

Figure 11-6

Figure 11-5

(However, one should not get carried away with such considerations; for example, the "9" that occurs in the bundles of microtubules in cilia and centrioles is *not* a Fibonacci number.)

Thus, the mammalian brain has an intricate Fibonacci expression in its microbiology.

Led by Stanley of Boston University, fifteen researchers from MIT, Harvard and elsewhere recently studied the physiology of neurons in the central nervous system with the goal of quantifying the arboration of the neurites, which are the arba of neurons. Taking the ganglion cells of a cat's retina as a model system, they find that the fractal dimension of the cells is "*1.68 + or - 0.15* using the box counting method and *1.66 + or - 0.08* using the correlation method."[11] Although the authors do not mention it, this is quite close to *phi*. Stanley *et al.* point out that this is the same as the fractal dimension for the diffusion limited aggregation (DLA) model, the generic model of diffusion through arboration (see Chapter 3). In other words, a fractal dimension of *phi* is apparently shared by all sorts of phenomena that grow according to a diffusion equation, specifically arbora such as the circulatory system, bronchial system, trees, bacteria, chemical reactions, and so forth, not the least of which is our very own brain's neurons.

Fibonacci in the Electrical Impulses of the Nervous System

It is not only the *physiology* of neurons and microtubules that reflects Fibonacci mathematics. Fibonacci appears to be expressed in the ratio of *electrical charges* within the cells of the body's nervous system. Here is a description of the electric charges of neurons from Coveney and Highfield:

> The membrane that cloaks each and every cell in the body is electrically charged because of a difference in numbers of electrically charged atoms — ions — inside and outside [of the cell].... Neurons, unlike other cells, are able to alter their electrical properties. When a signal is received from another neuron, the properties of the cell membrane change, allowing ions to travel across. Sodium ions flood in through large protein-based ion channels and the membrane potential changes rapidly *from -70 thousandths of a volt to +40 thousandths of a volt.* Although the local membrane properties change again to restore the status quo, this triggers similar changes in adjoining membrane so that a spike of electrical activity is sent out. This impulse, called an action potential, ripples along the length of the nerve.[12]

Although it does not seem to have been pointed out before, what this means is that the *peak negative charge* of the cells in each neuron is 70/110ths, or .636, and the *peak positive charge* is 40/110ths, or .364, of the entire range of its charge. These ratios are very close to the Fibonacci ratios, .618 and .382. While neuron potentials are variable from these values, the peak negative charge is always more than the peak positive charge. Given all the Fibonacci-related properties of the body, it might be prudent to investigate whether measurements of nerve cell electrical charges consistently, or on average, reflect the Fibonacci ratio.

Fibonacci as a Tool of Efficiency

Why do the brain and nervous system's innermost forms and functions exhibit Fibonacci proportions? It may be for the same reason that collective human interaction produces punctuated progress in the form of 5-3: Nature prefers the most efficient path. Quoting Penrose,

> Koruga (1974) has suggested that these Fibonacci numbers may provide advantages for the microtubule in its capacity as an "information processor." Indeed, Hameroff and his colleagues have argued, for more than a decade, that microtubules may play roles as cellular automata, where complicated signals could be transmitted and processed along the

tubes as waves of differing electric polarization states of the tubulins....
Koruga argues for a *special efficiency* in the case of a Fibonacci number-
related structure of the kind that is actually observed for microtubules.
There must indeed be some good reason for this kind of organization in
microtubules, since although there is some variation in the numbers that
apply to eukaryotic cells generally, 13 columns seems to be almost universal amongst mammalian microtubules.[13]

The Fibonacci-based style of *collective* human action that results from interactive mentation may also be a "special efficiency" of nature, just as its
inner structure and processes may be. In the case of the Wave Principle,
though, its goal is not the efficiency of an individual's biology but efficiency in the progress of the species.

Fibonacci Spirals in Neurology and Perception

Why does man's unconscious herding impulse produce a *spiral* pattern of social interaction, as revealed in Figure 2-29? The answer is that
spirals appear to be crucial to the functioning of our nervous system and
organs of perception, which at some level must be involved in the production of waves.

Like so many aspects of life,
our faculties of *perception* are replete
with spirals. As we all know from
high school biology, the cochlea of
the inner ear is spiral shaped (see Figure 11-7). The sense of touch is also
associated with spirals. According to
an article on a presentation by neurophysiologist Dr. Robert Thatcher,
"The receptive fields of the neurons
in our arms, legs and fingers wrap
around these surfaces in spiral bands,
similar to the sandal laces of a Roman soldier."[14]

*source: "Physiology in Fractal
Dimensions," American Scientist, Vol. 75*

Spiral cochlea of the ear

Figure 11-7

All physiologic sensors, including hearing, touch, taste, vision and
pain receptors, have not only spiral physiology, but also *response curves*
that are logarithmic. Hottes points out a possible larger connection:

Cellular action membrane potentials, which are important for muscles and the nervous system, have a voltage equal to the log of the ratio of the ion concentration outside the cell to that inside the cell. The brain and nervous system are made from the same type of cellular building units and look similar microscopically, *[so the response curve of] the central nervous system is probably also logarithmic.*[15]

The logarithmic-spiral nature of both the physiology and response curves of our faculties of perception apparently extends to our perception itself. Studies by E.L. Schwartz[16] show that when the brain receives spiral signals from curved surfaces on the retina, ear canal and so forth, it stores them as straight lines in a process called logarithmic conformal mapping.[17] This model of human perception, whereby the cerebral cortex translates the shapes of objects against a picture of the logarithmic spiral, offers a single answer to how the brain maintains size invariance, maintains rotational invariance, compresses information, perceives depth, perceives forms, perceives visual illusions and compares intersensory information.

What mathematical relationship do the curves on the retina have to the straight lines they represent both in reality and in the brain? A hint may come from Schwartz's estimate of the value of the parameter that characterizes the *difference* between the shape mapped on the retina and that in the brain, both in terms of magnification and deformation. Extrapolating the data from cats and monkeys, he has determined that the value of the parameter is *1.6 to 1.7.* Though he does not mention it, this is once again an expression of the Fibonacci ratio. From such data, Dr. Thatcher argues that the mind's processing and storage functions utilize as a standard against which objects are compared not just any spiral, but the *golden* spiral, whose radius increases by *phi* with each 90 degrees of rotation.

Thatcher further proposes that "Aesthetic feeling is the product of the complexity of an object and the degree of match of that object with the logarithmic spiral form in the brain." If this conclusion is true, it might explain why so many studies show that people consistently demonstrate a preference for Fibonacci proportions in objects and why so many artists throughout history, from ancient Egyptian and Greek architects to Leonardo da Vinci, have held a special fascination for Fibonacci relationships, consciously including them in their creations.

The link between all the forms and processes discussed in this Chapter is their Fibonacci component. Taken together, these studies indicate that the Fibonacci-based *physiology* of animals' apparati of mentation and perception is intimately related to their Fibonacci-based *processes* of mentational impulse transmission and perception. If that is true, then perhaps we should be open to the idea that a *product* of impulsive mentation, i.e., the Wave Principle, has a Fibonacci-based form. The golden spiraling aspect of the Wave Principle (see Figure 2-29) is certainly compatible with the way the nervous system uses the spiraling physiology of the senses to translate reality into golden-spiral constructs and from there into mental perceptions. We might postulate at this point that when a number of individual human nervous systems interact in a social setting, individual differences, which are ruled primarily by the rational cerebral cortex, cancel out so that the collective net result is an unconscious Fibonacci-based spiraling and fractal progression of emotions and activity that reflects what all human nervous systems share in common: a set of Fibonacci-based spiraling and fractal structures and processes. Chapter 12 will bring these ideas to their culmination.

NOTES

1 According to Professor Guido Pincheira, when the researcher who measured these lengths in DNA was asked if he thought that with better measurements, the actual ratio of angstroms would be .618, he replied (off the record), "Of course!"

2 Stanley, H.E., et al. (1993). "Fractal landscapes in physics and biology." *Growth patterns in physical sciences and biology.*

3 The researchers calculated the correlation α of Figure 10-1 as follows: "We calculated a from the slope of double logarithmic plots of the mean square fluctuation $F(\ell)$ as a function of the linear distance ℓ along the DNA chain for a broad range of representative genomic and cDNA sequences across the phylogenetic spectrum. In addition, we analyzed other sequences encoding a variety of other proteins as well as regulatory DNA sequences. We discovered that remarkably long-range correlations ($\alpha > 1/2$) are characteristic of intron-containing genes and non-transcribed genomic regulatory elements. In contrast, for cDNA sequences and genes without introns, we find that $\alpha \cong 1/2$ indicating no long-range correlations. Thus, the calculation of $F(\ell)$ for the DNA walk representation provides a new, quantitative method to distinguish genes with multiple introns from intron-less genes and cDNA based solely on their statistical properties. The finding of long-range correlations in intron-containing genes appears to be independent of the particular gene or the encoded protein — it is observed in genes as disparate as myosin heavy chain, beta globin and adenovirus. The functional (and structural) role of introns remains uncertain, and although our discovery does not resolve the "intron-late" vs. "intron-early" controversy about gene evolution, it does reveal intriguing fractal properties of genome organizations that need to be accounted for by any such theory." [ref: Stanley, et al., "Fractal landscapes in physics and biology." *Growth patterns in physical sciences and biology.*]

4 Pincheira, G. (1997, November 27). Speech: "In the genome, symmetry seems to code symmetry."

5 If the head continues to grow through evolution, subsequent species may look even more like starfish (or Coneheads)!

6 Ricketts, R.M. (1982, May). "The biologic significance of the divine proportion and Fibonacci series." *American Journal of Orthodontics,* Vol. 81, No. 5, pp. 351-370.

7 My source is Dr. Glenn Freisen of Amarillo, Texas.

8 Weibel, E.R. (1962). "Architecture of the human lung." *Science,* No. 137 and (1963) *Morphometry of the human lung.*

9 West, B.J. and Goldberger, A.L. (1987, July/August). "Physiology in fractal dimensions." *American Scientist,* Vol. 75.

10 Doczi, G. (1981). *The power of limits.*

11 Stanley, H.E., *et al.* (1993). "Fractal landscapes in physics and biology." *Growth patterns in physical sciences and biology.*

12 Coveney, P. and Highfield R. (1995). *Frontiers of complexity,* p. 289.

13 Penrose, R. (1994). *Shadows of the mind.*

14 McIlvride, B. (1986, March 10-16). *MIU Review,* Vol. 1, No. 27.

15 Personal letter from F.A. Hottes to R. Prechter, August 21, 1996.

16 Schwartz, E.L. (1980). "Computational anatomy and functional architecture of striate cortex: a spatial mapping approach to perceptual coding." *Vision Res.,* Vol. 20, pp. 643-669. And (1980) "A quantitative model of the functional architecture of human striate cortex..." *Biol. Cybern.,* Vol. 37, pp. 63-76.

17 Experiments by Mario Markus of the Max Planck Institute for Molecular Physiology and Jack D. Cowan reveal that people experiencing hallucinations or who are under the influence of LSD often perceive spirals. Apparently, neurons' electrical impulses at such times bypass the brain's mapping function, thereby failing to translate the spirals into straight lines. [ref: Cowan, J.D. (1982). "Spontaneous symmetry breaking in large scale nervous activity." *International Journal of Quantum Chemistry,* No. 22, pp. 1059-1082.]

Chapter 12:

Mentational Connections to the Fibonacci Foundation of the Wave Principle

A Fibonacci Influence in Individuals' Decision-Making Tendencies

Do our Fibonacci-structured neurons and microtubules and our Fibonacci-spiraled systems of perception and mental mapping in fact participate in Fibonacci patterns of mentation? Perhaps the most rigorous work in this area has been performed by psychologists in a series of studies on choice. G.A. Kelly proposed in 1955 that every person evaluates the world around him using a system of bipolar constructs.[1] When judging others, for instance, one end of each pole represents a maximum positive trait and the other a maximum negative trait, such as honest/dishonest, strong/weak, etc. Kelly had assumed that average responses in value-neutral situations would be 0.50. He was wrong. Experiments show a human bent toward favor or optimism that results in a response ratio in value-neutral situations of 0.62, which is *phi*. Numerous binary-choice experiments have reproduced this finding, regardless of the type of constructs or the age, nationality or background of the subjects. To name just a few, the ratio of 62/38 results when choosing "and" over "but" to link character traits, when evaluating factors in the work environment, and in the frequency of cooperative choices in the prisoner's dilemma.[2]

Psychologist Vladimir Lefebvre of the School of Social Sciences at the University of California in Irvine and Jack Adams-Webber of Brock University corroborate these findings. When Lefebvre asks subjects to choose between two options about which they have no strong feelings and/or little knowledge, answers tend to divide into Fibonacci proportion: 62% to 38%. When he asks subjects to sort indistinguishable objects into two piles, they tend to divide them into a 62/38 ratio. When Adams-Webber

asks subjects to evaluate their friends and acquaintances in terms of bipolar attributes, they choose the positive pole 62% of the time on average.[3]
When he asks a subject to decide how many of his own attributes another
shares, the average commonality assigned is 0.625.[4] When subjects are
given scenarios that require a moral action and asked what percentage of
people would take good actions vs. bad actions, their answers average 62%.[5]
"When people say they feel 50/50 on a subject," Lefebvre says, "chances
are it's more like 62/38."[6] If this is so, then *the Wave Principle may be a
product not only of a herding impulse prompted by human interaction but
also of a summation of a Fibonacci tendency in decision-making within
individuals.*

Lefebvre concludes from these findings, "We may suppose that in a
human being, there is a special algorithm for working with codes *independent of particular objects*."[7] This language fits MacLean's conclusion and
LeDoux's confirmation (see Chapter 8) that the limbic system can produce
emotions and attitudes that are independent of objective referents in the
cortex.[8]

In pursuing the question of "whether we can quantify belief," Lefebvre has devised an ingenious quantitative model of the opinion function.[9]
He proposes that human reflexion is multi-tiered, so that a person can have
no image of himself, an image of himself, or an image of himself plus an
image of himself imaging himself, and so on. A person can also have no
image of another person, an image of another person, or an image of another person plus an image of the other person having an image of him, and
so on. According to the bipolar model, each of these tiers of image can be
either positive or negative. Lefebvre shows that when the tiers are com-
bined, his model in neutral situations predicts imaging ratios between .6172
and .6180, depending upon the theoretical constraints employed. This prediction is consistent with the experiments that produce this ratio. His model
also predicts the net results of judgments when the images of those being
judged are skewed toward "good" or "bad." The mean result of these skewed
tests, involving an equal number of good and bad images, is .618, showing
that even in taking account objective data, subjects still skew their judgments positively, on average, by *phi*.

When subjects are asked to rate objects in between valueless poles,
phi shows up in an even more interesting way. For instance, one might
presume that if subjects were asked to evaluate the "lightness" of gray
paper against solid white and solid black, that the results would produce a

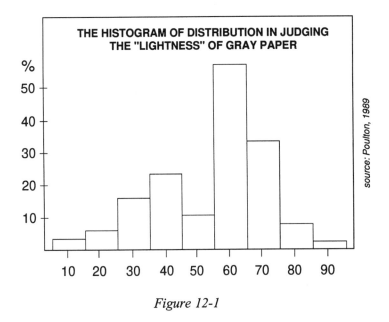

Figure 12-1

bell curve. In fact, however, subjects persistently avoid the middle of the spectrum and tend to mark it either 62% or 38% light.[10] (See Figure 12-1.)

Chapter 9 discusses the phenomenon of habituation, which is the process of becoming familiar. As it turns out, the very process of mental habituation skews people's positive judgment *in favor of the known* by *phi*.[11] When American subjects are asked to guess whether supposed (but actually fake) Chinese characters represent positive or negative attributes, they rate those characters to which they had previously been exposed a number of times as "positive" 63% of the time.[12] Lefebvre posits that when subjects have any excuse at all to do so, they create a bipolar mental construct weighted by the Fibonacci ratio. In this case, subjects divide the characters into two classes: "very well known" and "not very well known," *because that is the only difference between them that they can discern.* They then judge their positivity accordingly, assigning the "known" characters a positive value, on average at the 0.63 point along the scale, even though this aspect of the objects is irrelevant to the question they are attempting to answer. Simple familiarity, then, is enough to predetermine a positive evaluative skew. Chapter 8 discusses the tendency of animals and people to favor individuals who are like themselves, in other words, familiar. This experiment shows that this bias is weighted by *phi*.

Fibonacci bipolar weighting is independent of the faculty of visual perception. When subjects first move an object a certain distance and then are blindfolded and asked to move the same object half that distance, they move it on average to a spot that is 0.615 of the original distance.[13] As Lefebvre concludes:

> The experiment demonstrated that the phenomenon of the golden section is related not to the primary processing of visual information, *but rather to the work of the central processor* operating with "generalized information."[14]

This is the same "central processor" that is involved in the production of Elliott waves.

If these statistics reveal something about human thought, they suggest that in many, perhaps all, individual humans, and certainly in an aggregate average, *opinion is predisposed to a 62/38 inclination*. With respect to each individual decision, the availability of pertinent data, the influence of prior experiences and/or learned biases can modify that ratio in any given instance. However, *phi is what the mind starts with*. It *defaults* to phi whenever parameters are unclear or information insufficient for an utterly objective assessment.

This is important data because it shows a Fibonacci decision-based mentation tendency in *individuals*. If individual mentation reflects *phi*, then it is less of a leap to accept that the Wave Principle, which also reflects *phi*, is one of its products. To narrow that step even further, we must be satisfied that *phi* appears in *group* mentation in the real world.

Fibonacci in Collective Mentation, Including the Stock Market

Does Fibonacci-patterned decision-making mentation in individuals result in a Fibonacci-patterned decision-making mentation in collectives? Data from the 1930s and the 1990s suggests that it does.

Lefebvre and Adams-Webber's experiments show unequivocally that the more individuals' decisions are summed, the smaller is the variance from *phi*. In other words, while individuals may vary somewhat in the *phi*-based bias of their bipolar decision-making, a large sum of such decisions reflects *phi* quite precisely. In a real-world social context, Lefebvre notes by example, the median voting margin in California ballot initiatives over 100 years is 62%. The same ratio holds true in a study of all referenda in America over a decade[15] as well as referenda in Switzerland from 1886 to 1978.[16]

In the early 1930s, before any such experiments were conducted or models proposed, stock market analyst Robert Rhea undertook a statistical study of bull and bear markets from 1896 to 1932. He knew nothing of Fibonacci, as his work in financial markets predated R.N. Elliott's discovery of the Fibonacci connection by eight years. Thankfully, he published the results despite, as he put it, seeing no immediate practical value for the data. Here is his summary:

> Bull markets were in progress 8143 days, while the remaining 4972 days were in bear markets. The relationship between these figures tends to show that bear markets run **61.1 percent** of the time required for bull periods.... The bull market['s]...net advance was 46.40 points. [It] was staged in four primary swings of 14.44, 17.33, 18.97 and 24.48 points respectively. The sum of these advances is 75.22. If the net advance, 46.40, is divided into the sum of advances, 75.22, the result is **1.621**. The total of secondary reactions retraced **62.1 percent** of the net advance.[17]

To generalize his findings, the stock market on average advances by **1s** and retreats by **.618s**, *in both price and time.*

Lefebvre and others' work showing that people have a natural tendency to make choices that are 61.8% *optimistic* and 38.2% *pessimistic* directly reflects Robert Rhea's data indicating that bull markets tend both to move prices and to endure 62% relative to bear markets' 38%. Bull markets and bear markets are the quintessential expressions of optimism and pessimism in an overall net-neutral environment for judgment. Moreover, they are created by a very large number of people, whose individual differences in decision-making style cancel each other out to leave a picture of pure Fibonacci expression, the same result produced in the aggregate in bipolar decision-making experiments. *As rational cogitation would never produce such mathematical consistency, this picture must come from the impulsive paleomentation of the limbic system, the part of the brain that induces herding.*

While Rhea's data need to be confirmed by more statistical studies, prospects for their confirmation appears bright. For example, in their 1996 study on log-periodic structures in stock market data, Sornette and Johansen investigate successive oscillation periods around the time of the 1987 crash and find that each period (t_n) equals a value (λ) to the power of the period's place in the sequence (n), so that $t_n = \lambda^n$. They then state outright the significance of the Fibonacci ratio that they find for λ:

The "Elliott wave" technique…describes the time series of a stock price as made of different "waves." These different waves are in relation with each other through the Fibonacci series, [whose numbers] converge to a constant (the so-called golden mean, 1.618), implying an approximate geometrical series of time scales in the underlying waves. [This idea is] *compatible with our above estimate for the ratio $\lambda \cong 1.5$-1.7.*[18]

This phenomenon of *time* is the same as the one that R.N. Elliott described for *price* swings in the 1930-1939 period as recounted in Chapter 5 (see Figure 5-2).

In the past three years, modern researchers have conducted experiments that further demonstrate Elliott's observation that *phi* and the stock market are connected. The October 1997 *New Scientist* reports on a study that concludes that the stock market's Hurst exponent,[19] which characterizes its fractal dimension, is *0.65.*[20] This number is quite close to the Fibonacci ratio. However, since that time, the figure for financial auction-market activity has gotten even closer. *Europhysics Letters* has just published the results of a market simulation study by European physicists Caldarelli, Marsili and Zhang. Although the simulation involves only a dozen or so subjects at a time trading a supposed currency relationship, the resulting price fluctuations mimic those in the stock market. Upon measuring the fractal persistence of those patterns, the authors come to this conclusion:

> The scaling behavior of the price "returns"…is very similar to that observed in a real economy. These distributions [of price differences] satisfy the scaling hypothesis…with an exponent of $H = 0.62$.[21]

The Hurst exponent of this group dynamic, then, is *0.62.* Although the authors do not mention the fact, this is the Fibonacci ratio. Recall from Chapter 11 that the fractal dimension of our neurons is *phi*. These two studies show that the fractal dimension of the stock market is related to *phi*. *The stock market, then, has the same fractal dimensional factor as our neurons, and both of them are the Fibonacci ratio.* This is powerful evidence that our neurophysiology is compatible with, and therefore intimately involved in, the generation of the Wave Principle.

Lefebvre explains why scientists are finding *phi* in every aspect of both average individual mentation and collective mentation:

The golden section results from the iterative process. ...Such a process must appear [in mentation] when two conditions are satisfied: (a) alternatives are polarized, that is, one alternative plays the role of the *positive pole* and the other one that of the *negative pole*; and (b) there is no criterion for the utilitarian preference of one alternative over the other.[22]

This description fits people's mental struggle with the stock market, it fits people's participation in social life in general, and it fits the Wave Principle.

It is particularly intriguing that the study by Caldarelli *et al.* purposely excludes all external input of news or "fundamentals." In other words, it purely records "all the infighting and ingenuity of the players in trying to outguess the others."[23] As Lefebvre's work anticipates, subjects in such a nonobjective environment default to *phi, which Elliott's model and the latest studies say is exactly the number to which they default in real-world financial markets.*

Phi Dimensionality as a Property Only of Robust Fractals

Clouds and mountains, which are indefinite fractals, have a Hurst exponent near 0.8. The studies cited in the previous section show that neurons (which grow as arbora) and the stock market (which grows as waves) have a Hurst exponent related to *phi*. These studies prompt me to suggest the hypothesis that fractal objects that manifest as arbora or waves, i.e., the fractal objects of growth and expansion, will have a Hurst exponent related to *phi*, setting them apart from other fractal objects, which will have other Hurst exponents. What this means is that *robust fractal objects split the difference between two Euclidean dimensions by .618*, while other fractal objects do not.

Putting the Fibonacci Data Together

Chapter 11 concludes that the Fibonacci-based biological structure of animals' apparati of perception and mentation are related to a Fibonacci-based logarithmic conformal mapping process that translates input from the senses into mental images via the golden spiral. At this point, we can add that in turn, all of these aspects appear to be involved in producing *a Fibonacci-based form of both individual and collective mentation.*

Now we come to the concluding point of the last three chapters. We know that both in their arboral form and in the range of their pulsating electrical charges, our neurons have Fibonacci properties. We know that our spiraling apparati of perception and their paths of transmission via microtubules have Fibonacci properties. We know that our process of perception, i.e., the translation of reality into mental images via logarithmic conformal mapping, has Fibonacci properties. We know that our individual mentation, in the form of decision-making biases, has Fibonacci properties. We know that our collective interaction in a social setting has Fibonacci properties. We have the work of R.N. Elliott, who discovered, *before any of the above was known*, that the form of mankind's evaluation of his own productive enterprise (i.e., the stock market) has Fibonacci properties. Finally, we have my work and resulting contention, which will be explored in Part IV of this book, that the stock market is a direct recording of social mood change, which is the engine of social action, which in turn produces events that constitute history. This means that ultimately, the growth pattern of mankind has Fibonacci properties.

Throughout nature, countless animate forms and processes involved in growth and decay as well as inanimate forms involved in expansion and contraction are governed by *phi*. Given the findings of modern science here collected, it should no longer be considered speculative, much less mystical, to propose that mankind's pattern of progress through history is following this same law of nature. I would like to add that, given the chain of connection elucidated in this chapter, the natural and social sciences should nevermore be considered as distinctly different as traditionally thought.

NOTES

1 Kelly, G.A. (1955). *The psychology of personal constructs*, Vols. 1 and 2.

2 Osgood, C.E., and M.M. Richards (1973). *Language*, 49, pp. 380-412; Shalit, B. (1960). *British Journal of Psychology*, 71, pp. 39-42; Rapoport, A. and A.M. Chammah (1965). *Prisoner's dilemma*.

3 Adams-Webber, J. and Benjafield, J. (1973). "The relation between lexical marking and rating extremity in interpersonal judgment." *Canadian Journal of Behavioral Science*, Vol. 5, pp. 234-241.

4 Adams-Webber, J. (1997, Winter). "Self-reflexion in evaluating others." *American Journal of Psychology*, Vol. 110, No. 4, pp. 527-541.

5 McGraw, K.M. (1985). "Subjective probabilities and moral judgments." *Journal of Experimental and Biological Structures*, #10, pp. 501-518.

6 Washburn, J. (1993, March 31). "The human equation." *The Los Angeles Times*.

7 Lefebvre, V.A. (1987, October). "The fundamental structures of human reflexion." *The Journal of Social Biological Structure*, Vol. 10, pp. 129-175.

8 **More Evidence of Fibonacci in Human Relationships:** Even in the relationship between men and women we find the Fibonacci ratio. For instance, according to the U.S. Department of Labor, the (relatively) free market in the United States tends to pay women, on average, about 62% of the wages that it pays men for an hour of work. This is probably an expression of the difference between their proclivity for productivity. Feminists who deny differences of economic value between the sexes advocate male chauvinist conspiracy theories to explain the discrepancy. Without debating such theories, if they are true, its advocates must still concede that women let themselves be railroaded to that extent, which brings us back to the fact that there is a Fibonacci difference between the sexes of *some* type. Applying either theory, the productivity difference is a function of a difference in attitude either toward production or toward bullying by the other sex. The average earnings ratio, we must keep in mind, does not speak to either sex's *total* value, just its value in the productive context. Given the evidence in this book, we might expect to be surprised if the average difference in male and female attitudes and abilities were *not* phi.

9 Lefebvre, V.A. (1990). "The fundamental structure of human reflexion." In H. Wheeler, *The structure of human reflexion* (pp. 5-70). and Lefebvre, V.A., "A rational equation of attractive proportions," *Journal of Mathematical Psychology*, 36, 100-128.

10 Poulton, E.C., *et al.* (1968). "Response bias in very first judgments of the reflectance of grays." *Perception and Psychophysics*, Vol. 3, pp. 112-114.

11 Zajonc, R.B. (1968). "Attitudinal effects of mere exposure." *Journal of Personality and Social Psychology.* Monograph supplement, 9, No. 2, Part 2, pp. 1-32.

12 Lefebvre, V.A. (1997). *The cosmic subject.*

13 Bigava, Z.I. (1979). "A character of setting effects in various moving problems." In: Nadirashvili, S.A. (Ed.), *Voprosy Inzhenernoy I Socialnoy Psychologii (Problems of Human Factor and Social Psychology, in Russian)*, ii Tbilisi: Metsniereba.

14 Lefebvre, V.A. (1997). *The cosmic subject.*

15 Lefebvre, V.A. (1992). *A psychological theory of bipolarity and reflexivity.* and Lefebvre, V.A. (1997). *The cosmic subject.*

16 Butler, D. and Ranney, A. (1978). Referendums Washington, D.C., American Enterprise Institute for Public Policy Research.

17 Rhea, R. (1934). *The story of the averages.* (See discussion in Chapter 4 of *Elliott Wave Principle* by Frost and Prechter.)

18 Sornette, D., *et al.* (1996). "Stock market crashes, precursors and replicas." *Journal de Physique I France* 6, No.1, pp. 167-175.

19 The Hurst exponent (H), named for its developer, Harold Edwin Hurst [ref: Hurst, H.E., *et al.* (1951). *Long term storage: an experimental study*] is related to the fractal, or Hausdorff dimension (D) by the following formula, where E is the embedding Euclidean dimension (2 in the case of a plane, 3 in the case of a space): $D = E - H$. It may also be stated as $D = E + 1 - H$ if E is the *generating* Euclidean dimension (1 in the case of a line, 2 in the case of a plane). Thus, if the Hurst exponent of a line graph is .38, or ϕ^{-2}, then the fractal dimension is 1.62, or ϕ; if the Hurst exponent is .62, or ϕ^{-1}, then the fractal dimension is 1.38, or $1 + \phi^{-2}$. [source: Schroeder, M. (1991). *Fractals, chaos, power laws.*] Thus, if H is related to ϕ, so is D.

20 Brooks, M. (1997, October 18). "Boom to bust." *New Scientist.*

21 Caldarelli, G., *et al.* (1997). "A prototype model of stock exchange." *Europhysics Letters*, 40 (5), pp. 479-484.

22 Lefebvre, V.A. (1998, August 18-20). "Sketch of reflexive game theory," from the proceedings of *The Workshop on Multi-Reflexive Models of Agent Behavior* conducted by the Army Research Laboratory.

23 Caldarelli, G., *et al.* (1997, December 1). "A prototype model of stock exchange." *Europhysics Letters*, 40 (5), pp. 479-484.

Chapter 13:

From Long Waves to Rapid
Vibration: The Motor of Life?

The Long-Term Transmission of Cultural Images

In Chapter 5, we saw that the Wave Principle operates over decades. In Chapter 9, we read theories of how ideas, images, hopes and fears propagate through a population. Can we tie these two facts together?

How is it that social wave structures develop over the *very long term*? After all, the people who were participating actively in society many decades ago certainly are not doing so today. How can something that people did years or decades or even centuries ago have anything whatsoever to do with what is going on in the society now? Before formulating an answer, I would like to present a paragraph from a newspaper column on the aftermath of a football game from sportswriter Mark Bradley that will illustrate my answer. In November 1984, the Florida Gators won the Southeastern Conference football championship for the first time in the fifty-year history of that university's participation in the SEC. Here is how Bradley described the scene:

> And when the scoreboard clock struck zero, five decades of frustration burst into five minutes of glorious joy. Gerald Wilkins, a reserve linebacker, sprinted to midfield, flung himself to the turf and writhed in ecstasy. Elaine Hall, the coach's wife, leaped to kiss Lomus Brown, the defensive tackle, on the cheek. On the chilled sideline, Alonzo Johnson bent at the waist and clutched his belly with his hands, trying to hold the moment inside. When he straightened up, it was clear he had failed: the rough, tough Florida linebacker was crying, weeping not only for the SEC championship the Gators had won, but for the fifty others they hadn't. Fittingly, it didn't come easy. To have waited fifty years and then won easily wouldn't have purged Gator souls the way Saturday's victory did.[1]

What on earth was going on here? These players were kids, nineteen or twenty years old. They had not even been alive for most of the previous games. They had been playing football at the university an average of only two years, so were unassociated with 96% of the previous seasons. The people in the stands, many of whom were students, could not have gone to every game for fifty years and cried over the losses. What happened?

Think about Bradley's phrase, "purged Gator souls." What had taken place was a cultural transmission of the experiences of the University of Florida's football team through fifty years to all the associated students, commentators, university officials, coaches, players and fans. Anyone who became involved with the university had been fully indoctrinated with the history of the team, undoubtedly in a matter of months. Each person readily incorporated and assimilated all of that information, and his limbic system processed it into a gut emotional feeling. *The sum total of those feelings erupted orgasmically at the end of the 1984 season with such energy and emotion that it was as if each participant had personally lost or witnessed the loss of every one of those championships until that year and had experienced the anguish that went with it.*

I think that in the same way, transmission of all kinds of cultural experiences and values takes place over the years, over the decades, and even over the centuries. Social mood and experience has a memory. That is why waves continue to form at the highest observable degrees. Their antecedents provide the raw material for each new impulse and correction. Waves, then, represent a kind of forward-weighted summation of the human experience.

Waves In Evolution

Now let us expand the time horizon even further and investigate whether the Wave Principle governs not only the progress of *societies* but the overall progress of *all life on earth*. The September 1997 issue of *Nature* recounts a study by Per Bak, along with physicists Ricard Sole and Susanna Manrubia of the Polytechnic University of Catalonia in Barcelona and geologist Michael Benton of Bristol University, that concludes that the dynamics of species extinction have the same self-similar structure as earthquakes. "Massive extinctions happen far less frequently than tiny ones," reports the magazine, "but a graph showing the frequency of extinctions versus size closely follows a power law."[2] The researchers conclude from this fact that major extinctions can happen *without a catastrophic outside cause.*[3] In other words, evolution is a self-regulating complex dynamical

THE NUMBER OF FAMILIES OF PALEOZOIC FAUNA

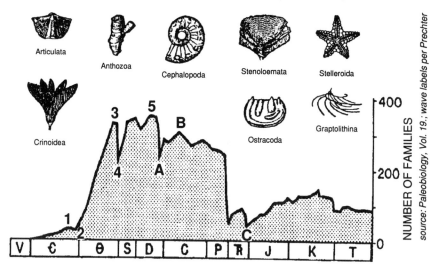

Figure 13-1

THE NUMBER OF FAMILIES OF MODERN FAUNA

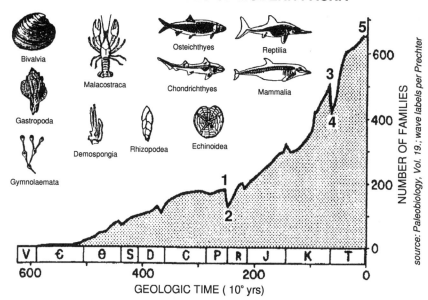

Figure 13-2

system[4] that fluctuates in a fractal pattern, just as the stock market and human society in general.[5] What kind of fractal pattern of fluctuation does it produce?

Figure 13-1 is from J. John Sepkoski, Professor of Geophysical Science at the University of Chicago. It is his depiction of the estimated numbers of families of Paleozoic fauna that have existed through time. I have added wave numbers to his graph. As you can see, after five waves up, the number collapsed in three waves, with the requisite subdivisions in waves B and C. Of more interest to us, perhaps, is Figure 13-2, showing the estimated total number of families of *modern* fauna, which began to expand at the end of the Cambrian period. As you can see, it forms an excellent five-wave pattern as well. If you look closely, you can see that even the subdivisions have five waves. The occasional mass extinctions have simply been corrections in the wave-patterned progress of life on earth.

Figure 13-3 is a depiction of the total number of families of marine species throughout earth's biological era, as compiled by M.J. Benton. It shows a fair amount of detail that in turn reflects the Wave Principle. As

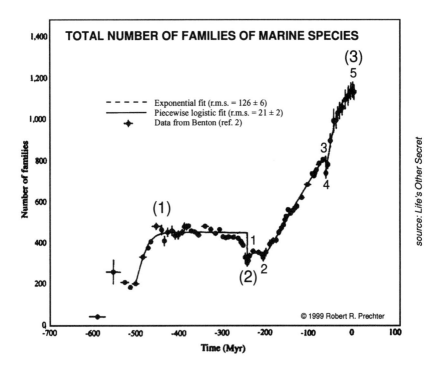

Figure 13-3

you can see by the wave labels that I have applied to the graph, particularly the advance from 250 million years ago shows the classic five-wave form, complete with an extension in wave three.[6] From collective life's extreme micro-scales to its extreme macro-scales, there is the Wave Principle, time and again.

It is not that surprising to me that evolution develops according to the same principle that governs social systems. Societies and evolution share the essential traits of self-regulating complex dynamical systems. I contend that evolution *is* a social phenomenon, as it involves the constant intermingling of life forms. On this basis alone, I am inclined to postulate that the Wave Principle applies to *all* interactive systems of life, not just the human.

The Wave Principle in Individual Life Forms

The Wave Principle may be an even more fundamental aspect of life than that. There is evidence that it governs not only the progress of societal systems but of *individual* life forms as well. Chapters 2, 3, 10, 11 and 12 show that individual plants and animals are, or contain, fractals, golden spirals and many Fibonacci-related forms and processes. The Wave Principle *per se* is a bit more difficult to detect in individuals, but there are clues to its presence.

For instance, most animals have 5 major appendages, their overall form therefore being ruled by the same number that primarily governs the Wave Principle. The appendages of the human body reflect the Wave Principle's 5-3 progression. Of the 5 protrusions from the body, all but the head have 3 subdivisions. The final subdivisions (hands and feet) have 5 appendages. Each appendage, with two exceptions (the thumb and big toe), has 3 subdivisions. The entire structure is based upon a 5-3-5-3 alternation, just like the Wave Principle. It is as if the human body is expanding into space the way a wave advances on a graph.

There may be an expression of the Wave Principle in the development of individual plants. Germany's famous poet Johann Wolfgang von Goethe also considered himself a scientist. Whether he was a good one is a subject of controversy, but he certainly was a consummate observer with an eye for detail that rivaled R.N. Elliott's. Goethe was fascinated by nature's constant display of creation, destruction and recreation and the possibility of finding "the ultimate secret of nature." To that end, he built a private botanical garden and closely studied the growth pattern of plants. His essay, "On the Metamorphosis of Plants," published in 1790, initiated the science of floral morphology, as well it should have. Two hundred years ago, Goethe's descriptions of plant morphology and adaptability included both their fractal aspects (see first paragraph below) and implications of evolution (see second paragraph). Pertinent to our discussion, we find that it also included a description of individual plant development that is nearly identical to a description of the Wave Principle (see third paragraph). The following is a summary of Goethe's conclusions:

> In a flash, he realized...that *all* the lateral outgrowths of the plant were simply variations of a single structure: the leaf. He saw that each organ, though outwardly changed from a similarity to a dissimilarity, had a virtual inner identity.
>
> Goethe saw in the changeableness of all the external characteristics of plants nothing but appearance; he drew the conclusion that...it might be possible to develop all plants from a single one. This small conceit was destined to transform the science of botany, indeed the whole concept of the world: with it came the idea of evolution. Metamorphosis was to become the key to the whole alphabet of nature. [Said Goethe,] "The plant forms around us are not predetermined, but are happily mobile and flexible, enabling them to adapt to the many conditions throughout the world, which influence them, and to be formed and re-formed with them."[7]
>
> Goethe also recognized that the process of development and refinement of form in plants worked through a threefold cycle of expansion and contraction. *The expansion of foliage was followed by a contraction into calyx and tracts; there followed a splendid expansion into petals of the corolla and a contraction into the meeting point of the stamen and stigma; finally there came a swelling into fruit followed by a contraction into seed. This six-step cycle completed, the essential plant was ready to start all over again.*[8]

That last paragraph is a stunning description to someone who knows the Wave Principle. It details *five waves* of progress in the form of *expansion-contraction-expansion-contraction-expansion*, which in turn is followed by a *larger contraction back to a starting point, from which the process repeats*. Even the nuances are compatible. The middle expansion into flowering is described as "splendid," which is exactly what I observed years ago about the character of third waves. ("Third waves are wonders to behold." – Frost and Prechter, 1978) The final expansion is a "swelling into fruit," which is an excellent description of the social product of fifth waves, as shown in Figure 18-6, when society reaps, in the form of peace, abundance and goodwill, all its effort has sown during the advance. Then, the larger contraction, which follows the entire five-wave expansion, returns a portion of the plant to the starting point, just as a corrective wave returns social mood back to the starting point of a new five-wave sequence. Like the patterns in the stock market, the propagation of plants is not a cycle, but a wave to successive heights. The original plant remains intact, so the formation of new seed is much like the starting point *at a higher level* that occurs after a correction under the Wave Principle. The only apparent difference between the two processes is that the final contraction Goethe describes is a single event, whereas corrective Elliott waves subdivide into a three-wave contraction-expansion-contraction sequence.[9]

Might the same progression occur in animals, including humans? We already know from Chapters 2 and 10 that plants and animals share the presence of fractals, from Chapters 3 and 11 that plants and animals share the presence of spirals and Fibonacci mathematics. All these correlations indicate that the mathematics of the growth and form of plants and animals are not that different. Do humans also develop in five waves? Let us give it a try.

Highly speculative as it may be, I can describe human development the same way that Goethe described the development of plants. There are the first two years of growth, then a setback in the "terrible twos" (particularly in boys), a longer period of flowering in the child, the emotional setback of the early teens (particularly in girls), and the final maturation, both mentally and physically, the "swelling into fruit" of the adult, containing the seeds of the next generation. When that person has a child, the cycle begins again.

This five-wave pattern of progress and setback, which fits both plant and human life, admits the possibility that the Wave Principle governs not only the pattern of progress for living *aggregates* but also the pattern of progress for *individual life forms*, thus covering the entire spectrum of life. Indeed, Goethe concluded that he had outlined "the manifold specific phenomena in the magnificent garden of the universe back to *one simple general principle. ...The same law can be applied to everything living.*"[10] The purpose of this book is likewise to show that there is one simple general principle that can be applied to everything living, and to describe it. I do not believe it to be coincidence that in its essence, *the description of the principle in each case is the same.* On this basis, I am inclined to postulate further that the Wave Principle governs the progress of *all* forms of life, not just societal systems.

The Implication of Continual Wave Subdivision

In the first part of this chapter, we examined the progression of waves over the very long term. Now we will examine the other end of the spectrum.

In Chapter 1, we saw that the Wave Principle operates over very *brief* times, as in Figure 2-1, which is a graph of every single incremental price change in the stock averages, the smallest scale of our data. In Chapters 10 and 11, we saw that our neurons have a fractal and Fibonacci-based construction and function. Can we tie these two facts together?

How is it that social wave structures develop over the *very short term*? In a 1987 speech, I provided this description of a five-minute trading pattern on the floor of the exchange:

Let's say that there has been a bear market going on for a week. Now, to a pit trader, that's a major bear market: five straight trading days of declining prices, with small rallies along the way. It's already worn him out. One day, the traders are watching the tape, and it's kind of slow because volume has receded during the decline. Suddenly, the market seems to be stalled out. A couple of traders who have been there the longest, you know, the grizzled old guys that really know the game, who have been there for almost two whole years, are watching the tape from the back of the room, and they say, "buy me ten, buy me fifty, buy me a hundred." A few heads turn because these are pretty good-sized lots. Sure enough, the market starts to tick up a little bit. Then it stops again and starts to recede very slowly. Most people are saying, "Ah, it's the same old stuff, a rally and a decline; it's going to come back to new lows just like it's been doing for a week. Forget it." They take another bite of their sandwiches and keep half an eye on the board. This is the point of lethargy and conviction that marks a second wave. Soon they notice that the market isn't making a new low; it's holding at a higher bottom. Well, to traders, that's a fundamental news event. They start watching more closely, and all of a sudden, they get a bit excited, and one or two orders pop out. Then the floodgates open. They are screaming and yelling buy orders, and sure enough, prices are roaring up. It's a broad, powerful third wave. It goes on for a full minute and a half but ends abruptly, and another reaction sets in. Guys who bought late have a small loss. It is the fourth wave's "surprising disappointment." Now, behind the scenes, over in the corner, there are some younger traders, who have been trading for only about a week and a half. They have been keeping an eye on this action, saying to themselves, "Man, look at that wild move! Look at the money we could have made just then! If I'd only been long! I tell you what, if this market starts up again *one more time*, I'm gonna buy. I'm getting ready." They're watching closely, eyes riveted on the board. Sure enough, the market starts up again. Those young guys start to yell in their orders: "Buy me one! Buy me one!" The market jumps to a new high. Orders from Merrill Lynch finally make it down to the floor, ending the flood as the fifth wave culminates. The old guys who started it all croak from the back, "Sell me ten, sell me fifty, sell me a hundred," and the five-wave move is over.

That chain of events is descriptive for a five-minute period, but it does not carry far enough. What about a five-*second* period? The compound construction of the Wave Principle implies, and perhaps demands, that the tiniest waves that we can plot in turn subdivide, and those in turn subdivide, and so on. Ultimately, it suggests that men's minds, in concert with others, must be *vibrating* in wave patterns between impulse and correction at the minutest scales of mental activity.

Is this implication sensible, or does it lead to an absurdity? We know that the nervous system both controls and is run by electrical impulses whose positive and negative charges appear to be in Fibonacci proportion. We know that these impulses travel via Fibonacci-organized microtubules as "*waves* of differing electric polarization states of the tubulins."[11] So the *electrical impulses* in the nervous system as well as the *physiological path they travel* in the form of *vibrating waves of polarization* are suffused with Fibonacci properties. Is it not possible that some of those waves at the minutest scale are also suffused with Fibonacci properties, i.e., that they vibrate in a 5-3 pattern that ultimately generates the Wave Principle? Perhaps this hypothesis could be stated more crisply, but at least there may be enough here to justify designing an experiment to test the idea of Fibonacci-patterned neurological vibration.

Since I have been speculating quite wildly, I might as well go all the way and suggest that infinitesimal Elliott waves of patterned electrical vibration may be the essence of consciousness, or perhaps even of animation. If so, the Wave Principle may govern not only the *progress* of all forms of life but *the essence of life itself.*[12]

In Chapter 21, we shall investigate astronomer Andrei Linde's proposal that the entire universe is a robust fractal and psychologist Vladimir Lefebvre's observation that certain astronomic activity mimics an aspect of human mentation. In the context of his suggestion that different universes may have different physics, Linde asks,

Does this mean that understanding all the properties of our region of the universe will require, besides a knowledge of physics, a deep investigation of *our own nature*, perhaps even *including the nature of our consciousness*? This conclusion would certainly be one of the most unexpected that one could draw from the recent developments in inflationary cosmology.[13]

The Wave Principle, which describes the social product of interactive unconscious mentation, is a crucial aspect of that proposed investigation. Since the Wave Principle influences collective animation (see Chapters 15 and 16) and, as we saw in this chapter, may even be the essence of individual animation, it is unquestionably a crucial aspect of the investigation into the essential nature of our mental function.

NOTES

1 Bradley, M. (1984, November 18). "At long last, Florida wins an SEC title." *The Atlanta Journal-Constitution.* Sentences are slightly rearranged.

2 Sole, R.V., *et al.* (1997, August 21). "Self-similarity of extinction statistics in the fossil record." *Nature*, Vol. 388, pp. 764-767.

3 The mechanism is as follows: Species that live on the lower end of the adaptability and viability scale die off. Upon occasion, after a number of marginal single species have died off, the number hovering at that lower end of the scale, particularly if they have a high degree of interdependence, is very large. A small environmental change can then result in many extinctions.

4 Such processes are said to display "punctuated equilibrium," a term coined in 1972 by Niles Eldredge of the American Museum of Natural History and Stephen Gould of Harvard to denote periods of stability interrupted by dramatic leaps or setbacks. However, equilibrium may not mean stasis. Land masses may be said to be at equilibrium in the absence of earthquakes, but as with evolution, the forces are never motionless. The stock market is always moving, to the point that it is difficult to designate any periods as "stable."

5 For the record, James W. Kirchner and Anne Weil of the University of California at Berkeley convincingly challenge Sole and Bak's findings with respect to the claim that extinctions follow a power law. [ref: *Nature.* (1998). No. 395, pp. 337-338. Published letter from James W. Kirchner and Anne Weil.] However this argument resolves, the graphs make my case that evolution follows the Wave Principle.

6 For a wave analyst, the implication of this pattern is obvious, though not comforting, as five waves up portends in the relatively near future the largest extinction since the one that occurred 300 to 250 million years ago. If this were a graph of the stock market, I would add that the slowing of upside rate of change in the past forty million years is a classic precursor of a reversal, which is strong support for the case that five waves are indeed ending.

7 Goethe, J.W. (1790)."On the metamorphosis of plants."

8 Tompkins, P. and Bird, C. (1973). *The secret life of plants.*

9 The fact that Goethe's description came from a man obsessed with empirics, coupled with the fact that (as far as I can tell) science has not expanded upon his description, suggests once again that intense empirical observation and inquiry of the type R.N. Elliott and Goethe practiced is a crucial, and perhaps neglected, aspect of modern science.

10 Goethe, J.W. (1790)."On the metamorphosis of plants."

11 Penrose, R. (1994). *Shadows of the mind.* (quoting Hameroff).

12 This idea recalls Eastern philosophical notions that existence *is* a tension between opposites. Perhaps we can suggest to these mystics that the opposites of yin and yang are not equal but related by *phi*, so that opposing values of .618 and .382 make the whole.

13 Linde, A. (1994, November). "The self-reproducing inflationary universe." *Scientific American.*

PART IV

AN INTRODUCTION TO SOCIONOMICS

Part IV provides only an introduction to socionomics. I have written much more about it than is here. I hope that these chapters will present enough of a case to establish its central ideas. My next big project will be to write a more comprehensive book on the subject.

Chapter 14

Components of Mood

I hereby state at the outset of this short chapter that the ideas herein are not fully developed. It will, I expect, take another ten years to construct a full theory of the components, aspects, processes and structure of social mood. Waiting to resolve these questions would delay this book too much, so I beg your indulgence in these pages. Chapters 15 through 17 show the *results* of social mood trend so clearly that I think you will "get it" even if there is some vagueness in what it is we are "getting." I am still working on a hierarchy of terms and a more comprehensive explanation, but in the interests of getting some of these ideas out, I will present the following thoughts, which I would categorize as observational summaries at best, not yet a hypothesis.

Aspects of Social Polarity

R.N. Elliott said only that "human emotions...are rhythmical" and that their waves govern "all human activities, whether it is business, politics, or the pursuit of pleasure."[1] "Human emotions" is not a precise term. What does it really mean to say that the social mood trend is trending "up" or "down" at a particular degree? Specifically, what characteristics and emotions do waves reflect? What actual human feelings comprise social mood?

There appears to be a social polarity that underlies all social interaction. We can refer to these opposites as "positive" and "negative," not simply to represent polarity but also to imply a value judgment with respect to the net social experience (though not to every aspect of it).

A good deal of empirical observation and historical investigation prompts the following list: A waxing positive social mood appears to correlate with a collective increase in concord, inclusion, happiness, forbearance, confidence, supportiveness, adventurousness, ebullience, daring, friskiness, optimism, skepticism, benevolence, sharpness of focus, practical thinking, a search for joy, an interest in love over sex, constructiveness, a desire to provide for oneself, a desire for power over nature, feelings of homogeneity with others, clarity of thinking and emotion, embrace of effort, and feelings of alignment with others. A waxing negative social mood appears to correlate with a collective increase in discord, exclusion, unhappiness, anger, fear, opposition, protectionism, depression, defensiveness, somberness, pessimism, credulity, malevolence, dullness of focus, magical thinking, a search for pleasure, an interest in sex over love, destructiveness, a desire for self-deprivation, a desire for power over people, feelings of heterogeneity with others, fuzziness of thinking and emotion, avoidance of effort, and feelings of opposition toward others. The list below summarizes these polarities.

Positive mood/Negative mood

   adventurousness/protectionism
   alignment/opposition
   benevolence/malevolence
   clarity/fuzziness
   concord/discord
   confidence/fear
   constructiveness/destructiveness
   daring/defensiveness
   desiring power over nature/desiring power over people
   ebullience/depression
   embrace of effort/avoidance of effort
   forbearance/anger
   friskiness/somberness
   happiness/unhappiness
   homogeneity/heterogeneity
   inclusion/exclusion
   interest in love/interest in sex
   optimism/pessimism
   practical thinking/magical thinking
   search for joy/search for pleasure
   self providence/self deprivation
   sharpness of focus/dullness of focus
   skepticism/credulity
   supportiveness/opposition

While I present these traits here in list form, I am certain that the correct depiction of these attributes and the things they cover is a tree. For instance, "clarity vs. fuzziness" has under it practical thinking vs. magical thinking styles as well as a preference for angular vs. rounded automobile styles. Similarly, "constructiveness vs. destructiveness" has under it stock market and business trends as well as trends in art and music. However, I have not fully developed this idea, which will require its own entire book, anyway. This chapter is just to give you the flavor of the two poles of social mood.

The tendencies listed above have concrete results. Here are a few examples:

(1) *Concord/Discord*: A rising mood leads to a substantial consensus in politics, culture and social vision; a falling mood leads to a divided, radical climate. After the social mood has risen for a number of years, the society tends to be peaceful; after it has fallen for a number of years, it tends to become involved in wars.

(2) *Inclusion/Exclusion*: A rising mood leads to feelings of social brotherhood and acceptance among races, religions and political territories, as well as toward animals, plants and proposed aliens. A falling mood leads to apartheid, religious animosity, cavalier cruelty, secession, independence movements and images of aliens as monsters.

(3) *Forbearance/Anger*: A rising mood leads to social expressions of acquiescence, apology and tolerance. A falling mood leads to social expressions of resistance, recrimination and intolerance.

(4) *Confidence/Fear*: A rising mood leads to speculation in the stock market and in business. A falling mood causes risk aversion in the stock market and business.

(5) *Embrace of effort/Avoidance of effort*: In a rising mood trend, people are disposed to expending effort, both mental, which elevates the use of reason, and physical, which elevates the ideal of fitness. In a falling mood trend, they are disposed to avoiding effort, which leads to magical thinking and physical laziness.

(6) *Practical thinking/Magical thinking*: Practical thinking manifests itself in philosophic defenses of reason, self-providence, individualism, peacemaking and a reverence for science. Magical thinking manifests itself in philosophic attacks on reason, self-abnegation, collectivism, witch hunts, war-making and a reverence for religion.

(7) *Constructiveness/Destructiveness*: The impulse to build shows up in the construction of record-breaking skyscraper buildings at social-mood

peaks. At troughs, few buildings are built, and many of those already in place may be burned or bombed out of existence.

(8) *Desiring power over nature/Desiring power over people*: Desiring power over nature leads to a naturalistic mindset, political freedom and peaceful technological advances. Desiring power over people leads to a socialistic mindset, political repression and technological advances in warring.

The Wave Principle suggests that mankind has within its nature the seeds of social trend and social change. Men are animated by, or are animated to create, change. They desire it, or at least bring it about, even when it appears superficially that they would be better off if things stayed as they were. For example, adversity eventually breeds a desire to take responsibility, achieve and succeed, while prosperity eventually breeds irresponsibility, complacency and sloth, regardless of whether the change, considered rationally, would be a good thing.

Inclusion vs. Exclusion

To give you an idea of the far-reaching effects of a single polar continuum, let us examine just one of them: inclusion vs. exclusion. A waxing positive social mood accompanies increased inclusionary tendencies in every aspect of society, including the cultural, moral, religious, racial, economic, national, regional, social, financial and political. A waxing negative social mood accompanies increased exclusionary tendencies in every aspect of society. With that realization, you can predict increasing cooperation and acts of brotherhood in all those areas in bull markets and the opposite in bear markets.

For example, in bull markets, most people like similar styles of music; in bear markets, the dominant types are often very different. In bull markets, politics tends to be middle-of-the-road; in bear markets, radical positions gain acceptance, and the electorate becomes polarized. Free trade is encouraged in bull markets; protectionism is demanded in bear markets. Racial harmony is promoted in bull markets, racial separation in bear markets.

Here are some concrete examples. Apartheid was made official South African policy in the 1940s at the end of the last Supercycle bear market (using inflation-adjusted prices; see Figure 15-2 or 16-6) near the peak of negative mood. It has been eliminated in the bull market of the 1990s near the peak of positive mood. A 1997 newspaper showed black and white African leaders, enemies for decades, clasping hands over their heads in the spirit of brotherhood. As another manifestation of exclusion and inclusion, religious wars were common in the Dark Ages and for awhile afterward, but have been a minor concern in the past eight centuries of rising long-term trend. Indeed, Catholic, Jewish and Arab leaders have all been apologizing, finding common ground and shaking hands publicly in the 1990s, an unprecedented spectacle. Similarly, nationalism was the political theme in the 1940s during a bear market; as this bull market has been peaking out, we have a new European Community with a unified currency, shadowy talk of a New World Order, and plans for the former Communist countries of Eastern Europe to join NATO. In the 1940s, the U.S. and Russia began a "cold war." In the 1990s, leaders of the U.S. and Russia, enemies for decades, clasped hands over their heads in the spirit of cooperation, reflecting the classic bull market sentiments of social inclusion.

The Correct Orientation toward Such Events

Each time one of these grand events occurs, whether viewed as good or evil, observers tend to see it as a turning point for mankind. Such observations are true, but because people think conventionally in terms of the direction of causality (see Chapters 18 and 19), it is a turning point in *precisely the opposite direction from what they assume it to be*. Conventional observers take each event "at face value" and assume that each positive event marks a turning point for the better and each negative event a turning point for the worse. However, every negative event mentioned in the above section indicated the approach a turning point for the better, while every positive event indicates the approach of a turning point for the worse. Lacking socionomics, conventional social observers are always entirely unprepared for the next chain of events. In contrast, observing what events reveal about extremes in social psychology prepares the socionomist for coming changes.

Anticipating the Character of Social Behavior

Once you incorporate these ideas, you can predict, probabilistically, many types of social behavior. You can test yourself on the following questions.

When would a society be more likely to have peaceful gatherings as opposed to hostile gatherings? In the 1940s, after over a decade of bear market, hundreds of thousands of men gathered in Europe and the Far East to kill each other. In 1996, after five decades of social mood rise, the United Nations managed, for the first time ever, a full attendance of world leaders

Some Cultural Expressions of Social Mood Trends

AREA OF CULTURE	RISING TRANSITION	PEAK POSITIVE MOOD	FALLING TRANSITION	PEAK NEGATIVE MOOD
CAMPUS TRENDS	Work hard, have fun	Positive-minded save-the-world social concern	Rebellious, angry social concern	From riots to sudden quiet
CREATIVITY	Positive mood creativity	Positive mood creative trend fully realized	Negative mood creativity; lack of creativity	Negative mood creative trend fully realized; destruction
DANCE	Partners together, tempo speeds up, partners separate	Partners apart, fast tempo	Partners come back together; tempos slow down	Partners together
FAMILY LIFE	Babies popular, family orientation, marriage	Trend reaches extreme	Children a negative value, divorce, "single" life preferred	Trend reaches extreme
FASHION (color)	Colors emerge	Bright colors dominate	Drabness emerges	Drab colors dominate
FASHION (covering)	Men's ties narrow	Bodies exposed, short skirts, bikinis for women, tight pants for men	Men's ties widen	Bodies covered; floor-length dresses, baggy pants
FASHION (style)	"Correctness" stressed	Flamboyant individuality for men and women	Anti-fashion fashions	Conservative dress returns
FITNESS/HEALTH	Healthy lifestyle, physical fitness practiced, encouraged	Body admired. Body-building peaks. Smoking, "junk" foods taboo	Fitness fanaticism wanes rapidly. Social concern replaces concern with self	"Working out" is out of fashion.
GOOD vs. EVIL	Bad guys vs. good guys (movies, pro wrestling). Heroes celebrated	Everybody's a good guy	There are no bad guys and no good guys. Heroes trashed	Everybody's a bad guy
JUDGMENTS	Answers are black and white	There is good in all	Who's to judge?	There is evil in all
MOVIES/TV/LITERATURE	"G" rated themes, adventure	Celebrate life; upbeat, entertaining themes	Social concern, symbolism, heaviness, anti-heroes	Horror, dead-end themes
NOSTALGIA	Nostalgia for black-and-white values	Focus on now	Nostalgia for mythical simpler times (back to the earth)	Focus on now
POETRY	Structured	Lyrical	Anarchic	Ugly

© Robert R. Prechter 1985/1999

Table 14-1a

Some Cultural Expressions of Social Mood Trends *(cont'd)*

AREA OF CULTURE	RISING TRANSITION	PEAK POSITIVE MOOD	FALLING TRANSITION	PEAK NEGATIVE MOOD
POLITICIANS (perceptions of)	Strengths magnified, weaknesses overlooked, forgiven or denied	Politicians revered (Camelot, "Teflon")	Weaknesses magnified, strengths overlooked or denied	Politicians hated or deified
POLITICS	Relative stability	Desire to maintain status quo	Old styles fail	Radical parties and solutions
POP ART	Structured, traditional	Colorful, wild, "alive"	Anarchic --anything goes	Deliberately ugly, heavy, sedate
POP MUSIC (Arrangement)	Simplicity peaks, complexity returns		Complexity peaks, simplicity returns	
POP MUSIC (Image)	Dirty, happy	Clean, happy	Clean, angry	Dirty, angry
POP MUSIC (Lyrics)	Any non-negative theme OK	Joyous celebration and love songs	Anxious, socially conscious themes emerge	Songs of despair, hate, violence; also happy denial
POP MUSIC (Melody)	Melody emerges as a key ingredient	Lilting, complex, inventive melodies and harmony	Melody is eclipsed by various elements: rhythm, arrangement	Little melody or chord structure
POP MUSIC (Mood)	Upbeat, major keys	Upbeat, major and minor keys	Minor keys, downbeat, arty	Distorted sounds, atonality, dissonance
POP PHILOSOPHY	Achievement is possible and desirable	Love will save the world	Achievement is a waste of time	Hate and destruction will give the world what it deserves
RELIGION	Conservative religion but increasingly subdominant	Religious tolerance and inclusiveness	Religion is openly questioned and passionately reintroduced	Powerful fundamentalist religions and cults
SEXUAL IMAGES	"Masculine" men and "feminine" women	Heterosexual images peak	"Feminine" caring men; "masculine", liberated women	Focus on alternative sexual styles
SPORTS	Clean "good guy" sports		Rough "bad guy" sports	
STOCK MARKET (popular valuation of productive enterprise)	Rising	Topping	Falling or correcting	Bottoming
WAR	Old wars fought and concluded	Little conflict	More conflict; new wars begin	New wars begin or intensify

Table 14-1b

© Robert R. Prechter 1985/1999

for a friendly photograph. In 1967-1969, after over two decades of social mood rise, hundreds of thousands of people gathered in Monterey, California, Woodstock, New York and other locations for big parties known as music festivals. In 1970, after a year and a half of bear market, angry students gathered in huge numbers to protest the war in Vietnam. In August 1987, after five years of bull market, thousands of advocates of world peace convened in a "harmonic convergence" celebration.

When would a society be more likely to sport adventurous, frisky fashions as opposed to similar, conservative dress? Colorful clothes, short skirts, and diversity in appearance are typical of social mood peaks. Dull colors, long skirts and uniforms are common at social mood troughs.

When would a society progress toward free trade, and when would it restrict it? In the 1920s bull market, free trade was encouraged. In 1929, at the start of the bear market, Congress passed protectionist tariffs despite widespread knowledge that such policies are destructive.

When would a government be more likely to produce an atomic bomb (anger, fear, opposition, protectionism) and when would it be more likely to send a man to the moon (confidence, adventurousness, sharpness of focus)? The U.S. government dropped the first atomic bomb after 16 years of bear market (in inflation-adjusted terms); it put a man on the moon after 20 years of bull market.

When is a society more likely to develop science and technology and when is it more likely to focus on mysticism? The Commercial, Scientific, Industrial, Technological and Information Revolutions took place during positive social mood trends. The pace of religious conversions tends to be the greatest near the end of negative social mood trends.

I could go on for a hundred pages, but I trust you get the idea.

The table on the previous two pages shows a scattershot collection of observations along these lines that I made over thirteen years ago. This table is meant to be roughly representative, not precise or conclusive.

The social mood is always in flux at *all degrees of trend*, moving toward one of the polar opposites in every conceivable area, from hope for the future to fear of it, from a desire to speculate to a desire to conserve, from a preference for heroic symbols to a preference for antiheroes, from joy to cynicism, from a desire to build to a desire to destroy. There is so much more to say about how the historical characters of the arts, sciences, technology, religion and philosophy all parallel social mood trends, but that discussion will await a book dedicated to socionomics.

Aggregations and Their Interconnection

As implied in this book so far, society has *overall* mood trends. Statistics that reflect the society as whole, such as voting totals, the national economy, the society-wide popularity of different types of entertainment, etc., reflect that social mood. Within societies, there are countless *smaller* aggregations, each of which has its own waves. An aggregation that trades corn, copper, baseball cards or stocks has its own waves. Each city, state, political movement, religion and sport has its own waves. Smaller aggregations are embedded within larger ones. People can be members of several aggregations at once. The socionomist must obtain as much data as possible to isolate each phenomenon he studies, as each one has its own wave structure. An aggregation may be highly independent from or strongly influenced by the overall social mood, depending upon how widely shared their respective concerns are. Together, all the waves of all the aggregations weave the fabric of social life. Chapter 17 includes some examples of smaller aggregations. The next two chapters focus on the overall social mood and its influence with respect to what I consider the most accessible socionomic subjects.

NOTES

1 Elliott, R.N. (1938). *The wave principle*. Republished: (1994). *R.N. Elliott's Masterworks — The Definitive Collection*, p. 92.

Chapter 15:

Popular Cultural Trends as Manifestations of Social Mood Trends[1]

If stock market trends reflect social mood trends, the emotions associated with those trends must have other manifestations. An examination of the major areas of social mood expression where data are available shows that they do, as popular cultural trends peak and trough coincidentally with the stock market in their joint reflection of the popular mood.

Any activity that quickly reflects changes in how people in general feel is a coincident indicator of social mood change. A person communicates his mood when he chooses a piece of music, decides what clothes to wear, buys a work of art, selects a movie, casts a vote, decides what sporting event to see, or chooses a book to read. Trends in music, movies, fashion, literature, television, popular philosophy, sports, dance, heroic images, commercial product styling, mores, gender-related ideals, family life, campus activities, religious activity, politics and poetry all reflect the prevailing mood, sometimes in subtle ways. The availability of numerous books, theaters, recordings, sports, fashions and political candidates is a requisite for the production of reliable data. The direction and extent of the relative popularity of various styles of these modes of expression reflect the direction and extremity of the dominant mood.

A record of these overall societal changes says nothing necessarily about how an individual or a specific group might feel or act but is an indication of the net mood of the society at large. For changes in mood to express themselves, *some* particularly susceptible people must undergo a *substantial* change in mood and/or *most* people must undergo *some* change in mood. I believe the mechanism is a function of both processes. As the mood dynamic progresses, those individuals whose state of mind is on the cusp of change can be stirred to a new expression as a result of just a slight change in mood, which pushes them past the threshold. The further the swing in public mood carries, the larger will be the number of people stirred to the new expression.

While all avenues of cultural mood expression tend to ebb and flow in concert, we cannot expect *particular* forms of expression necessarily to lead the charge. Different media may be more dominant in the culture at different times. As an example, audio and video entertainment have a golden age at every social mood peak, but it does not show up as strongly in every subcategory. In the audio category, jazz music reached a pinnacle of popularity in the late 1930s at the top of wave I, rock music reached a pinnacle of popularity in the late 1960s at the top of wave III, and country music has reached a pinnacle of popularity in the 1990s as we approach the top of wave V. All three styles fall under the category of popular music. In the video category, films reached a quality peak in the late 1930s, television reached a quality peak in the 1960s, and computer games may be reaching a quality peak in the late 1990s. History repeats in *mood*, but not necessarily *mode*.

Noticeable changes in slower-moving mediums such as the movie industry more readily reveal changes in larger degrees of trend, such as Cycle. More sensitive mediums such as television change quickly enough to reflect changes in the Primary trends of popular mood. Intermediate trends are paralleled by current song hits, which can rush up and down the sales charts quickly as people change moods. Of course, *all* of these media of expression are influenced by mood changes of all degrees. The net impression communicated is a result of the mix and dominance of the forces in all these areas at any given moment.

The timing of the careers of dominant popular entertainers, whether movie stars, television stars or pop music stars, is closely aligned with the peaks and troughs in the stock market. At major social mood turning points, the dominant stars quickly fade into obscurity to be replaced by stars that reflect the newly emerging mood. For example, the Cycle degree social mood peak of 1966 coincided with a large number of long-running TV programs going off the air and the retirement of countless happy-mood pop music representatives. As Philip Norman said in *Shout*, in the matter of a single year, "the latter-day Mersey groups had all gone home to settle down as pork butchers and damp course engineers [construction workers]."[2] The next peak in December 1968 was the last gasp of the old trend, as shortly thereafter, droves of formerly dominant stars and their venues became passe. Many broke up (as in pop groups), were canceled (as in TV shows), retired or died. This has been true at every major turn.

Sometimes trends rely on which wave is in force. For example, as a manifestation of fifth waves' attempt to relive the glories of the third wave, *nostalgia* becomes widespread. During wave V, fashions have reprised looks from the 1940s, 1950s and 1960s. The songs of the 1960s began flooding the airwaves in the 1980s as "oldies" became the most lucrative format in radio. Since then, there has hardly been a singer or group from the 1960s that has *not* returned to tour, record or appear on television. Elvis Presley, the Beatles, Frank Sinatra and even Benny Goodman have enjoyed adoring retrospectives. In TV land, the Nickelodeon channel has thrived running TV shows from the 1950s and 1960s. Old films have been colorized, restored and rereleased in theaters. The American Movie Classics channel has succeeded by running old black-and-white movies. Nostalgia is far less effective in powerful third waves and in bear markets because at such times people are far more interested in, or concerned with, the present than the past.

While analyses of such trends might appear important only to entertainment companies, they are relevant to almost every industry. It would help auto makers to know, for instance, that angular styles sell well in bull markets while rounded lines sell better in bear markets. Styling and color affect almost every product.

The biggest problem in proving the correlation that I propose in this chapter is a dearth of data. Unfortunately, there is today little demand and no central clearinghouse for such data. It will take a multi-year research project to gather and graph it all. Data unavailability is not the only problem. Given the limited introductory scope of this book, this chapter presents only a portion of what I know about the subject. My one small section on nuances in a single film genre provides just a glimpse of how close is the marriage between mood trends and the timing of related cultural events. For now, I hope that a few generalized examples and observations will suffice to convey the idea.

Trends in Hemlines

Harvard graduate Ralph Rotnem, a researcher at the Harris Upham brokerage firm, originated the so-called "hemline theory," which is the recognition that women's skirt lengths tend to rise and fall in tandem with the Dow Jones Industrial Average. Though this idea is often dismissed as frivolous, socionomics explains why there is a correlation. The trends of stock prices and women's hemlines are a function of social mood. When people feel bold and frisky, they buy stocks and wear more revealing clothes. When they feel threatened and conservative, they sell stocks and wear more concealing clothes. It is that simple.

Because skirt lengths have limits (the floor and the upper thigh respectively), the reaching of a limit implies the concurrence of an extreme positive or negative mood. As Figure 15-1 illustrates, hemlines were very low at the stock market bottom of 1921. They rose to miniskirt brevity in the late 1920s and late 1960s, peaking with stock prices both times. Hemlines plunged to maxiskirt floor-lengths in the 1930s and 1970s, bottoming with stock prices both times. Today, as we head into 1999, skirts worn by

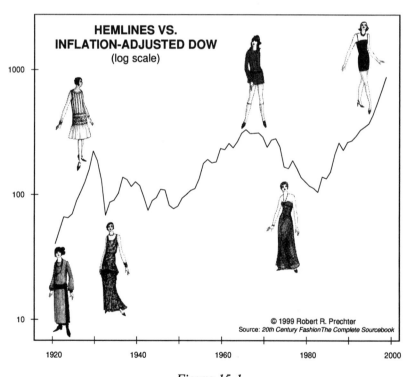

Figure 15-1

models and celebrities are extremely short (one runway featured what looked more like a wide belt), while those worn by the general public are just shy of 1968's minidress length.

Trends in Movies

The timing of the production and success of film genres is instructive as to social mood expression. Figure 15-2 plots the inflation-adjusted Dow-Jones Industrial Average marked with the acknowledged classics in two types of film entertainment: Disney cartoons and horror movies. If you are with me so far, you can probably guess in which direction of social mood trend each style of film has been innovative and popular.

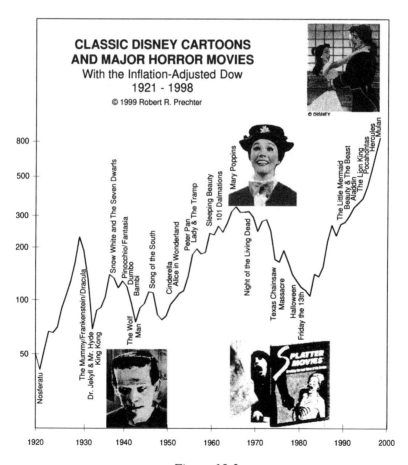

Figure 15-2

The Walt Disney Company released its first feature-length cartoon in 1937, the year of the top of a roaring five-year bull market that accomplished the fastest 370% gain in U.S. stocks ever. As shown here by the titles listed on the top side of the graph, these films stayed popular for thirty years, culminating with the ultra-sunny *Mary Poppins* in 1964, and to a lesser degree, *The Jungle Book* in 1967. The end of this period of success was essentially coincident with the great stock market top of 1966. For the next sixteen years, as stock prices fell along with social mood, most people thought Disney's feature cartoons were silly and sentimental. Indeed, the studio's productivity fell by more than 50%. With the possible exception of *The Jungle Book*, not one cartoon film from this period is considered a classic. When the bull market returned in the 1980s and 1990s, so did feature-length Disney cartoons that have been both acknowledged classics and box-office blockbusters. In the last eleven years of bull market, Disney has produced ten feature cartoon films. In the briefest possible terms, Disney cartoons are bull market movies, reflecting the shared mood of both their creators and their viewers.

Now we will examine the other end of the spectrum, whose titles are listed on the bottom side of the graph. Horror movies descended upon the American scene in 1930-1933, the very years that the Dow Jones Industrials collapsed. Five classic horror films were all produced in less than three short years. *Frankenstein* and *Dracula* premiered in 1931. *Dr. Jekyll and Mr. Hyde* was released in 1932, the year of the great bear market bottom and the only year that a horror film actor (Frederick March, for that film) was ever granted an Oscar.[3] *The Mummy* and *King Kong* hit the screen in 1933, on the test of the low in stock prices and right at the trough of the Great Depression. These are the classic horror films of all time.[4] Ironically, Hollywood tried to introduce a new monster in 1935 during a bull market, but *Werewolf of London* was a flop. When film makers tried again in 1941, in the depths of a bear market, *The Wolf Man* was a hit. Producers made sequels to these films, featuring Frankenstein monsters, vampires, werewolves and undead mummies, for about a decade, into the bottom of wave II in 1942.

Shortly after the stock market bottom of 1942, films abandoned dark, foreboding horror in the most surefire way: by laughing at it. When Abbott and Costello met Frankenstein in 1948, it showed that horror had lost its power. The cheesiness, mildness and comedy of the horror-based films of the ensuing bull market years and the limited extent of their innovation, influence and popularity stand in stark contrast to the films of the bear market years. For example, 1957's *I Was a Teenage Frankenstein*, released in the middle of an extended Cycle degree bull market, earned "the somewhat dubious distinction of being named one of the worst horror films ever made."[5]

When social mood reentered a major bear trend in 1966, so did groundbreaking horror movies. *Night of the Living Dead* debuted in 1968, the year after the last of that era's Disney cartoon classics. It was so influential that it spawned two sequels (both produced during the bear market), several derivations and two books. A breakthrough in gore entitled *The Texas Chainsaw Massacre* was released in 1974, as stocks made their nominal price lows.

In 1974, the year of the low for wave IV, horror-writer Stephen King burst upon the scene with his first novel, *Carrie*. His novels provided fodder for a number of horror-movie scripts, including the Hollywood slasher movie, *The Shining*, in 1977. At the darkest extreme of the trend, when inflation-adjusted prices were approaching bottom in 1978, the industry introduced so-called slice-and-dice films, or "splatter movies."[6] *Friday the 13th* and *Halloween* were so influential that they have spawned many sequels, none of which are rated by critics as highly as the originals. Not to be overly outdone, Broadway introduced the slasher play, *Sweeney Todd, the Demon Barber of Fleet Street*, in 1979, the same year that King's *Dead Zone* sat for six straight months on the *New York Times* bestseller list.[7]

Since 1982, and particularly since 1984, a bull market has been in force. Since that time, horror films have once again become increasingly derivative, muted or comic, just as in the years following 1942.

Nuances

All the subjects discussed in this chapter have countless coincidences of parallelism with social trends. While we do not want to get lost in the nuances of popular culture, a few observations should communicate the richness of the correlation. Here are a few examples relating to this one genre.

I observed years ago, and have often remarked, that the initial deterioration in the stock market during the fourth wave sets the stage for the ultimate reversal (see "Wave Personality" in *Elliott Wave Principle*). Apparently, this is true across all manifestations of social mood, not just the stock market. For instance, the fourth-wave social-mood correction of one smaller degree immediately preceding the two major bear market periods illustrated in Figure 15-2 gave advance indications of the style of horror that would be produced in the ensuing bear market. In 1920 and 1921, at the bottom of the preceding Cycle degree bear market, *Dr. Jekyll and Mr. Hyde* with John Barrymore, and *Nosferatu*, the German vampire film that we all study in film class, presaged the monster movies of the 1930s and 1940s. In 1962, at the bottom of the preceding Primary degree bear market, *Psycho*, the famous Hitchcock knife-in-the-shower shocker, presaged the slasher movies of the 1970s.[8]

One pop record stands out in the annals of horror: "Monster Mash" by Bobby "Boris" Pickett. It became the #1 record in the country on October 20, 1962 and stayed there for two weeks. The exact date of the orthodox end of the three-year bear market labeled Primary wave ④ (see Figure 15-4) was October 23, 1962, another perfect coincidence of mood and expression. While this record echoed the old horror style, it was a comic treatment because mood in the larger trend was so elevated. The recording returned to the charts twice: in August 1970, right off the bottom of the deepest bear market in thirty years and again in May 1973 in the midst of the bear market of 1973-1974. (As that bear market deepened, the comic approach of "Monster Mash" became outmoded, and horror got serious again.)

Why was the Hammer Films company of England able to release a series of fairly successful horror films in that country from 1957 through 1974? The reason is that, unlike the soaring American stock market, the London stock market was in a mild bear market from 1959 to 1966. After a brief two-year rise, it joined with gusto the American downtrend from 1968 to 1974, suffering a decline nearly as deep as that of 1929-1932. Through the first half of the 1970s, as stocks and mood collapsed their hardest, Hammer released vampire films at five times the rate it did in the 1960s. As soon as the British stock market turned powerfully up in 1975, demand for Hammer's output fell so abruptly that the company folded. Was that the end of a nearly perfect social-mood parallelism? Perhaps not. Suddenly, after 23 years in which Hammer has languished as but a memory, advertising mogul Charles Saachi has purchased the name with the aim of transforming Hammer "from a debt-ridden relic into a global empire."[9] Says an on-line site dedicated to vampires, "The future for Hammer looks promising for the first time in more than twenty years."[10]

The correlation between bear markets and horror holds before the days of movies. For example, America's master horror writer Edgar Allen Poe flourished in the Supercycle degree bear market of 1835 to 1842, during which time, according to *The World Book Encyclopedia*, "he produced several of his finest tales."[11] Poe died in 1847, "after five years of illness," five years that just happen to coincide with a rapid rise in social mood that began in 1842. That uptrend in public mood was not as well suited to his style, and the dissonance between them may have pressured his already weak constitution.

We may presume, with reverse wave analysis (see Chapter 17), that Shakespeare's *Macbeth*, the first modern slasher play, debuted in a bear market as well. The history of popular horror has traversed from plays to books to films, as once again, history repeats in mood but not necessarily mode.

The two books on horror movies that I have on my shelf (*Horror Movies* and *The Horror Film Handbook*) were published in 1974 and 1982, the exact years of the lows for stock prices in Cycle wave IV in nominal and inflation-adjusted prices respectively. Also on my shelf is a ten-volume set of books entitled, "The Works of Edgar Allen Poe," which I find was published in 1933, the bottom year of the depression. These are the times that people are interested in such topics, and the writers and publishers oblige.

Trends in Popular Music Expression

As a 78-rpm record collector put it in a *Wall Street Journal* article, music reflects "every fiber of life" in the U.S. Accordingly, its themes and tones have been virtually in lock step with social mood as reflected by the major trends in the Dow Jones Industrial Average. Figure 15-3 shows one major stock market cycle and the styles of music that were popular in the uptrend vs. the downtrend.

In the 1950s and early 1960s, as a great bull market was underway, major pop music stars were young and energetic, and their lyrical theme was, "I feel good and I love you." By the end of the decade, paisley-clad popsters in the Summer of Love sang in essence, "Oh, wow, I feel great and I love everybody." The excerpts below give you a flavor of the lyrics of hit songs near the peak:[12]

"Life, I love you! All is groovy." (1966)

"'Scuse me while I kiss the sky." (1967)

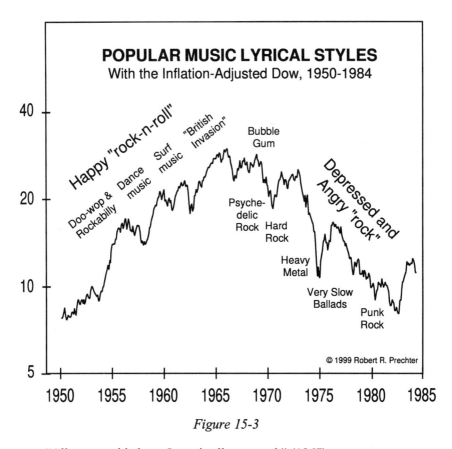

Figure 15-3

"All you need is love. Love is all you need." (1967)

"If we unite, it will all turn out right. Every awareness seems to bring us together. When you're happy, every place feels like home. You'll be happier yet. It's wonderful!" (1967)

"I think it's wonderful that people are finally getting together. Reach out in the darkness and you will find a friend." (1968)

"Put a little love in your heart, and the world will be a better place for you and me; just wait and see." (1969)

After decades of general uptrend, stocks peaked in 1966 in the Dow and December 1968 in the Value Line Index. Coincident with that high was a peak in popular musical creativity, the product of which was manufactured and released into the following year. A music industry executive flatly told *The Wall Street Journal*, "Rock peaked in 1969."[13,14]

The reversal of trend at the peak of the bull market brought such a dramatic change in the character of the music from upbeat to downbeat themes and tone that a #1 song on the subject from 1971 lamented, "Something touched me deep inside the day the music died."[15] As the deepest bear market since the early 1940s got underway, pop music stars became socially concerned, world-weary, angry and cynical, and their lyrical theme changed to, "I'm depressed and you're no good." Here are some sample lyrics of the time:[16]

> "When you're down and troubled, and you need a helping hand, and nothing, nothing is going right...I will be there to brighten up even your darkest night." (1970)

> "I rode a tank, held a general's rank, when the blitzkreig raged and the bodies stank. I shouted out, 'Who killed the Kennedys?' when after all, it was you and me." (1970)

> "Ticking away the moments that make up a dull day, you fritter and waste the hours in an offhand way. You run and run to catch up with the sun, but it's sinking. You're older, shorter of breath and one day closer to death." (1973)

> "Day after day I'm more confused, so I look for a light through the pouring rain. I'm beginning to think that I'm wasting time. I want to get lost in your rock and roll and drift away." (1973)

> "When I'm tired, I hide in my music, forget the day, and dream of a girl I used to know; I close my eyes and she slips away." (1976)

> "All we are is dust in the wind." (1978)

At the end of the decade, punk rockers communicated in violent fashion an amorphous, tortured, "I'm in agony and I hate everybody."

With the advent of the bull market in 1982, punk rock abruptly disappeared and the old depressed lyrical mood waned. In the 1980s and 1990s, pop music has been mostly happy again, including even previously-perennially-depressed country music! There is a mix (after all, this is a weaker fifth wave, not a strong third), but world-weariness among pop stars is mostly gone, and many of its players and singers are once again young and energetic.

Speaking of young and energetic, a sickly-sweet musical style called "bubble gum" music, aimed at ten-to-fourteen year olds, enjoyed a brief heyday in the late 1960s with the Archies and the Ohio Express. This style abruptly disappeared after the 1968 stock market high. Twenty years later, in 1987-1989, bubble gum returned with big hits by Debbie Gibson and

Tiffany. After another long absence, the Spice Girls and Hanson have reprised the genre in 1998. It has appeared at the end of each of three of the
four longest stretches of economic expansion in U.S. history. (The fourth
one lasted through 1944, when young bobby-soxers screamed for Frank
Sinatra.) In other words, *each time economists have warbled, "this is the
best of all possible worlds," teen songsters have warbled the same thing.*

The whole story of this period is not as simple as this brief discussion
suggests. For instance, the 1970s also featured upbeat, airy pop tunes, and
starting in 1975, "disco" dance music. There are two reasons for this divergence of trends. First, as listed in Chapter 14, bear market moods produce
social *opposition* as opposed to *alignment*. In the bull market of the 1950s
and 1960s, young people all listened mostly to the same music. The bear
market, in contrast, sported two distinct trends, the depressed and angry
one cited above and another that relentlessly pursued a sunny, singin'-in-
the-rain outlook. Fans of each genre hated the other with a passion. The
second reason is that from 1975 to 1982, though a bear market raged in
inflation-adjusted terms, a bull market was picking up steam in nominal
terms. This dichotomy fit the dichotomy in pop music. Once again, the
complexity, depth and wonder of this subject is to be found in the details,
which are too dense to present here. My 1985 essay, *Popular Culture and
the Stock Market*, goes into more detail on the 1950-1985 period.[17]

Lyrical theme is not the only aspect of musical expression that is correlated with social mood. It is easy to communicate lyrics in a print medium,
which is why lyrical theme is the focus of this section. However, I consider
it the least reliable aspect of pop music in communicating social mood.
Melodic connotation, harmony, dissonance, noise content, artistic self-con-
sciousness, the appearance and demeanor of the performers, implied
benignity or violence, and the simplicity or complexity of notes, chord
structure and arrangement appear to be even more reliably related to the
trends of social mood than lyrics.[18] All of these things are quantifiable, and
I hope to conduct proper studies on them someday.

Superstardom as a Reflection of Mass Emotional Release at a Social Mood Peak

When the social mood is overwhelmingly positive, people express
ecstasy. One way they do it is to revere public figures. Young people are
particularly prone to release ecstatic emotion by showering pop music per-

formers with adoration. Therefore, one manifestation of major degree ebullience is the excited and passionate idolization of pop musicians or singers by teenagers. Let us see how this idea has manifested itself this century.

There have been five major instances of crowd euphoria directed at pop music performers since the Supercycle low in 1932. Every one of them occurred in a bull market, and in particular, when a Primary or short Cycle degree advance was maturing. Figure 15-4 displays their positions within the wave structure.

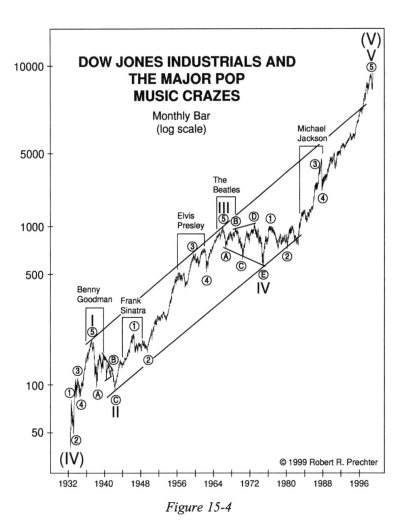

Figure 15-4

The first craze, which took place near the top of wave I, focused on Benny Goodman from 1935 to 1938. Goodman's "swing" music created such excitement that teenagers jammed concert halls and touched off riots. His moniker was the "King of Swing." The second craze was over Frank Sinatra in 1943-1946, near the top of wave ①. Teenaged girls known as Bobby Soxers suddenly swarmed and swooned over "The Voice." The third craze centered on Elvis Presley toward the end of wave ③ in the second half of the 1950s. His moniker was the "King of Rock 'n' Roll." The fourth craze surrounded The Beatles from 1963 to 1965, near the top of wave ⑤. They were dubbed "the Fab Four" and their music precipitated "Beatlemania." The fifth craze developed around Michael Jackson in the 1980s, in wave ③ of V. Jackson was crowned the "King of Pop." Here are some quotes that exemplify these social experiences and reflect their similarity:

1935-1938; peak year, 1937:

> The Goodman band became an overnight sensation at the Palomar Ballroom in Los Angeles in August 1935. [It] carried to unprecedented heights of success, reaching an apex in sheer popularity with the famous 1937 Paramount Theater engagement and the 1938 Carnegie Hall concert...[but] by 1938, the Goodman band had reached an artistic nadir, clearly reflected in its recordings.[19]

Note: This could just as well be a description of the rise into the peak and subsequent collapse in the stock market from 1935 to 1938.

1943-1949; peak year, 1944:

> Frank Sinatra's rise to become the most popular singer in the U.S. in 1944, accompanied by the loud screams of mostly female teenage fans, has often been compared with the outpourings of affection that accompanied the national appearances of Elvis Presley and the Beatles. ... The peak of the craze [was] probably the Columbus Day riot on October 12, 1944, when thousands of teens ran through Times Square after realizing that their compatriots inside the Paramount were staying for show after show (there were five a day) and they'd never get to see their hero.[20]

Note: This euphoric mayhem burst forth despite the raging of World War II. The bull market in social *mood* had to express itself regardless of social *events and conditions*, which were the result of the *preceding bear market* (see Chapter 16).

1955-1963; peak year, 1957:

It was the largest paying crowd ever to see an entertainer perform in Dallas (Elvis took home $18,000 out of a $30,000 gross), and from the moment Elvis appeared, waving to the crowd from the back of a Cadillac convertible as he circled the field, a kind of high-pitched, earsplitting, seismic wail went up, there were "screams of anguish" and "shrieks of ecstasy," the papers reported, that never wavered or stopped. The musicians couldn't hear a thing, apart from the crowd, said drummer D.J. Fontana. "All you could see was just thousands of bulbs going off. I thought, What's this guy done?"[21]

1963-1969; peak year, 1964:

According to Mark Lewisohn's survey of local newspaper coverage, "Beatles-inspired hysteria had definitely begun by the late spring [of 1963], some six months before it was brought to national attention by Fleet Street newspapers." Nonetheless, the national media's sudden saturation coverage could not help but amplify the underlying frenzy, creating a self-reinforcing process whose immediate effect was an absolutely tumultuous welcome at Heathrow Airport when the Beatles returned from a quick tour of Sweden on October 31. The Beatles themselves cited this event as the beginning of Beatlemania. The spectacle of many thousands of screaming fans jamming the airport made news across the land, and for the next three years photos of the Beatles' well-attended departures and arrivals at Heathrow were a staple of British media coverage. ...In each country, the scenes of uncontainable mass excitement were similar enough to have been scripted by a single invisible master of ceremonies: boisterous airport welcomes, clamoring crowds outside the Beatles' hotels, shrieking audiences at their shows, all magnified by virtually nonstop media coverage.[22]

Note the wonderful phrases, "self-reinforcing process" and "mass excitement similar enough *in each country* to have been scripted by a single invisible master."

1983-1991; peak years, 1983/1987:

Michael Jackson's popularity was such that one of his record albums produced both more hit singles and more sales than any other in history. Premiers of his music videos were treated as global media events. His Pepsi ads attracted more viewers than the TV shows that bracketed them. Viewers of the American Music Awards on television in January 1989 saw film clips of Jackson's 1987-1988 world tour, held in stadiums. It attracted 4.4 million people, dwarfing every previous such event in terms of attendance and income. News clips showed cheering, screaming, sighing, crying, fainting, swooning, dancing, rioting teenagers, all over the world. An ecstatic English woman gushed, "It was just like this with the Beatles."[23]

Lesser idolizations along the way notwithstanding, these five clearly achieved the summit of fan adoration in the field of pop music. Why did it happen? Was it simply due to inordinate talent? If so, why have even better talents been less feted? Was it handsomeness? If so, why have more handsome singers failed? Some observers have come close to the answer. Writer Bill Holland said this in his discussion of the Sinatra phenomenon:

> Magnetism and charisma are still human mysteries. Why humans are riveted and mesmerized by watching, listening or being in the presence of certain persons is a phenomenon that has been studied by philosophers and scientists over centuries. It has never been explained. ...Somehow, through the mystery that personified itself every time [Sinatra] took to the stage, most of the time we, the audience, gladly gave ourselves to him because he carried us to *a certain emotional state* which we all recognize, desire and crave.[24]

George Harrison made this blunt comment about Beatlemania: "The world *used us as an excuse* to go crazy, and then they blamed it on us. But we were just in the middle."[25] Said Ringo Starr: "The problem with the Beatles is that *it didn't matter what we did*, we'd get the same applause."[26] As one contemporary performer said about the concertgoers of 1968 in general: "There were huge crowds everywhere, full of *mindless* adulation."[27] Says Robert Goldberg in explaining superstardom: "The more familiar you become, the more you are appropriated by your audience: *You cease to be a person* and become *a mirror in which fans read their own lives*."[28] These descriptions reflect what happens in financial booms and swoons as well: Values and shares become meaningless as investors construct their own social fantasy to take their place. In other words, these performers not only appeared *in* a bull market, but their public personas *were* a bull market, driven by the mass cooperation of millions of limbic systems. *Each time it happened, it came at a similar point in the wave structure of a major advance in stocks*, when fear melted away and ebullience took its place. Simply put, these singers and musicians were the focal point for an outpouring of social ecstasy, which was clearly registering on the thermometer of social mood, the Dow Jones Industrial Average.

Such entertainers, because of their role in personifying social ecstasy, are the beneficiaries of more adulation than any other social figures of their day. The deaths or breakups of popular artists of this magnitude are widely and intensely mourned because people associate their intense memories of the joy of the bull market mood with the singers and musicians who best reflected and symbolized it.[29] The gratitude expressed toward the discoverer of a new technology or a cure for disease is nil compared to the gratitude showered upon these performers, the fondness of the memories associated with them and the agony experienced over their passing. Since positive social emotion is the engine of social productivity (see Chapter 16), perhaps that gratitude is not so ill-placed.

Do not presume that such reactions are only modern phenomena. This is timeless social behavior. The bull market of the 1830s, for instance, produced the same results with respect to the great pianists Chopin and Liszt, particularly the latter. Read Harold Schonberg's description of a typical Liszt concert:

> When Liszt played the piano, ladies flung their jewels on the stage instead of bouquets. They shrieked in ecstasy and sometimes fainted. Those who remained mobile made a mad rush to the stage to gaze upon the features of the divine man. They fought over the green gloves he had purposely left on the piano. One lady fished out the stub of cigar that Liszt had smoked. She carried it in her bosom to the day she died. Other ladies came away with priceless relics in the form of broken strings from the piano he had played. These *disjecta membra* were mounted in frames and worshipped. Liszt did not give mere concerts; they were saturnalia. The bemused Heine tells of a concert he attended at which two Hungarian countesses, contending for Liszt's snuffbox, threw each other on the ground and fought until they were exhausted. Heine once asked a medical man whose specialty was women to explain the nature of the hysteria that Liszt created. The physician, wrote Heine, "spoke of magnetism, galvanism and electricity; of contagion in a sultry hall filled with innumerable wax lights and some hundred perfumed and perspiring people...."[30]

Does this differ materially from a Sinatra concert in 1944, an Elvis concert in 1956, a Beatles concert in 1964 or Michael Jackson's world tour in 1987?[31]

"Contagion" is a key word in the good doctor's diagnosis, as we explored in Chapter 9 the idea of its role in the propagation of social mood.

"Magnetism" is the same word employed by Bill Holland in a 1998 article about Sinatra. Magnetism may just a vague analogy implying attraction, but it specifically involves the alignment of numerous particles in the same direction, which is almost exactly what is going on socially with millions of limbic systems under these circumstances. Recall from Chapter 8 MacLean's observation that the limbic system can generate emotions that do not necessarily have a referent based in reality. What is the limbic system to do with excess ecstasy? It bestows it upon the most popular attractive object that happens by. Charisma provides the excuse, and popularity allows unbound expression. No person would consider acting *alone* in the same way that he or she does at an ecstatic pop music concert (can you imagine being the only one wailing, weeping and screaming as others sit quietly?), but behavior is not bizarre when all others are doing the same thing. Dare we doubt that there were similar phenomena in ancient Roman, Greek and Egyptian times?

Data Required for Socionomic Study

Although the stock market will probably remain the single best indicator of social mood and mood change because of its precise measurement and long data history, socionomists should begin to detail, quantify, graph and study other cultural phenomena. A quantification of sporting event attendance figures, themes of popular entertainment, the number of notes and note changes in popular melodies, the lyrical content of popular songs, hemline lengths, tie widths, heel heights, the prominence of various colors in fashion and pop art, the angularity vs. roundness of automobile styling, average highway driving speed, sales of convertible cars, crime rates, religious activity, the construction of various architectural styles, and a host of other reflections of the popular mood, all weighted according to the volume of production and sales, would allow us to read charts of the public mood in the same way that we read charts of aggregate stock prices now. Any such data that followed the Wave Principle could be used to forecast trend changes in their own fields.

I believe that a plot of the net existence and dominance of these various popular cultural elements would produce charts closely paralleling those of aggregate stock prices. By comparing the evidence to stock price movement, we could test this empirical conclusion. If the data were indeed to show parallel trends, then we could use them in turn to forecast the stock market.

Coincident vs. Lagging Correlation

The trends in the stock market and such activities as described in this chapter are *coincident* because they reflect social mood trends *directly*. As positive mood waxes, many people buy stocks, watch Disney films, prefer music that expresses joy, and bestow their overflowing ecstasy upon pop stars. When the negative mood waxes, many people sell stocks, watch horror movies, prefer music that expresses dissatisfaction, and have little ecstasy to bestow.

In contrast, most trends that are deemed important to history, such as those economic and political, *lag* trends in social mood. The reason, I contend, is that while social mood trends are the cause of social action, the latter requires time to undertake.

The Greek philosopher Plato suggested a connection among cultural events 2400 years ago when he said, "When the mode of the music changes, the walls of the city shake." Or, according to another source, "When the modes of music change, the laws of the State always change with them." In other words, the trends of music and politics are connected. I propose that *all* cultural trends are so connected, via social mood. Chapter 16 will explore the more concrete results of social mood trends.

NOTES

1 Much of this chapter, along with parts of Chapters 14 and 16, was originally published in my 1985 paper, "Popular Culture and the Stock Market," some of which was excerpted in *Barron's*. [ref: Prechter, R. (1985, September 9). "Elvis, Frankenstein and Andy Warhol..." *Barron's*.] Ideas herein have since been appropriated at least twice without attribution.

2 Norman, P. (1981). *Shout: the true story of the Beatles.*

3 *Dr. Jekyll and Mr. Hyde* was produced three times this century: in 1920, 1932 and 1941, within one year of the three biggest stock market bottoms of that 21-year period.

4 The message of these monster movies appeared to be that people had an inhuman, horrible side to them. Hitler was placed in power in 1933 (an expression of the darkest public mood in decades) and fulfilled that vision. In discussing Fritz Lang's *M* (1931), "the first film to feature a serial [child molester/]killer as its protagonist," *The Atlanta Journal-Constitution* of October 7, 1997 said, "Even more chilling is the way Lang presages an encroaching horror that left thousands of children dead in Hitler's camps." Indeed, that is the chronology. Films reflect mood change concurrently and mood change results in action later (see Chapter 16).

5 Frank, A.G. (1974). *The movie treasury — horror movies.*

6 Different sources disagree slightly on the year-dates from some of these films. If you have a definitive source that proves any of these dates incorrect, please let me know.

7 King's horror output remained wildly popular through 1984, the last year of extreme social fear (see bond market discussion in Chapter 6). Since then, his style has softened, so he has remained popular, though much less so.

8 In inflation-adjusted terms, Supercycle wave (V) ended in 1966. Zombie movies became big immediately thereafter. The first zombie movie ever was *White Zombie*, released in 1932, at the low of Supercycle wave (IV). Once again, an event at the previous fourth wave low hinted at the trend to come after the end of the fifth wave.

9 Harlow, J. (1997, May 18). "Saatchi revives gory glory days of Hammer." *The Sunday Times* (London).

10 Web site: www.pathwaytodarkness.com

11 (1992). *The World Book Encyclopedia.*

12 (1) "59th Street Bridge Song (Feelin' Groovy)" by Paul Simon. (2) "Purple Haze" by Jimi Hendrix. (3) "All You Need Is Love" by Lennon/ McCartney. (4) "It's Wonderful" by Cavaliere/Brigati. (5) "Reach Out in the Darkness" by Friend and Lover. (6) "Put a Little Love in Your Heart" by Jackie DeShannon.

13 Source unavailable.

14 Read this excerpt from *The Swing Era* about **1937**: "...For one fine moment in American musical history there was an alliance between national popular taste and a *creative music* called jazz...." This is exactly the way my generation feels about **1968** (+ and - one year): For one fine moment in American pop music history, there was an alliance between national popular taste and a creative music fusing blues, country, r&b, jazz, folk, latin, pop and classical influences, arranged and played with artistry and virtuosity. Each of these years is a Cycle degree top in the stock market.

15 MacLean, D. (1971). "American Pie."

16 (1) "You've Got a Friend" by James Taylor (1970). (2) "Time" by Mason/Waters/Wright/Gilmour (1970). (3) "Sympathy for the Devil" by Jagger/Richards (1973) (4) "Drift Away" by Mentor Williams (1973). (5) "More Than a Feeling" by Tom Scholz (1976). (6) "Dust in the Wind" by Walsh/Livgren (1978).

17 We hope to publish this essay as part of a book entitled *New Frontiers in Market Analysis* in the year 2000.

18 Prior to the 1970s bear market, there was never in American pop music an abrasive chordal relationship in a big-selling song like the G to C# progression in Black Sabbath's "Black Sabbath" or as much noise as there was in punk rock. The last time any music produced this much dissonance was Bartok's during the bear market of the 1930s.

19 Schuller, G. (1989). *The swing era.*

20 Ruhlmann, W. (1998, June 19). "Celebrating Sinatra." *Goldmine.*

21 Guralnick, P. (1994). *Last train to Memphis – the rise of Elvis Presley.*

22 Hertsgaard M. (1995). *A day in the life.*

23 Dick Clark Productions. (1989, January 30). *16th Annual American Music Awards.*

24 Holland, B. (1998, June 19). "The mystery of Frank Sinatra." *Goldmine.*

25 Smeaton, B. (1996). *The Beatles Anthology.* (Videotape series).

26 Gunderson, E. (1989, July 21). "Drumming up a super Starr tour." *USA Today,* p. D1.

27 Roeser, S. (1993, October 15). "Ginger Baker: anyone for polo?" (Comment from Steve Winwood, then with the band Blind Faith.) *Goldmine.*

28 Goldberg, R. (1995, November 20). "The fab four 25 years later." *The Wall Street Journal,* p. A12.

29 Upon his death, Frank Sinatra received 13 minutes of coverage on CBS Nightly News, far more than any other entertainer in the history of the program. Newspapers routinely featured the story in the top half of page

1.[ref: Holland, B. (1998, June 19). "The mystery of Frank Sinatra." *Goldmine.*] Elvis's death is mourned annually by millions, and he is periodically spotted alive and occasionally treated by the devout as a savior. John Lennon's death caused mass mourning and is still remembered in annual pilgrimages. His passing is often characterized as the death of a great cultural dream, as indeed it was. Michael Jackson may not be quite so idolized, as his popularity was in a fifth Cycle wave, which is usually a weak echo of the more powerful third wave, but it is unlikely that he will be forgotten.

30 Schonberg, H.C. (1987). *The great pianists from Mozart to the present.*

31 Liszt stayed nearly this popular through half of the wave (B) advance within the 1836-1859 bear market, then abruptly ceased doing paid concerts. He was revered throughout his life, and even as late as the 1870s, pianists wanted to "play like Liszt." Today, rockers are still trying to become the next Elvis or Beatles.

Chapter 16:

Historical Impulsion: Events that Result from Social Mood Trends

Le Bon surmised, "The memorable events of history are the visible effects of the invisible changes in human thought."[1] Indeed, major historic events that are often considered important to the future (i.e., economic activity, lawmaking, war) are not causes of change; they are the result of social mood changes that have already occurred. To put it succinctly, the stock market is a *thermometer* of public mood and a *barometer* of public action.

The *primary* cause of each type of action is the same: social mood trends. The difference is in the time it takes to translate thoughts into results. The mechanics of this difference apply even to mood changes within individuals. For instance, a person whose ebullience crosses a particular threshold may decide on the same day to purchase a stock, wear a bright tie, build a house and expand his business. Results of the first two decisions can be fully realized in a matter of minutes. The results of the latter two decisions would take months to become fully realized. The first two would be recorded directly in cultural data. The latter two would show up later in data on activities that lag the initial impulse which produced them.

A reason that collective action in particular is a lagging indicator of aggregate mood change is that while an individual can initiate action immediately upon a mood change, a society requires a good deal of time for an extensive swing in mood to spread throughout the populace before it is positioned to initiate coordinated collective action. For instance, to motivate a body that represents the society to undertake an action such as creating a sweeping new law, electing a new regime or starting a war, the necessary mood must have taken root throughout much of the society and reached extreme proportions. Then, just as with individual economic decisions, the ultimate manifestation must further await the mechanics of implementation.

If we were to plot very precisely statistics on the economy, war activity and election results, i.e., the products of social mood trends, they should produce plots that reflect, with a short time lag, the trends in the stock market. Let us examine some major areas of activity that the stock market, in its barometric function, foreshadows.

Economic Consequences of Social Mood Trends

Social mood trends have economic consequences. Men produce more goods and services when the dominant social mood trend is positive rather than negative. The reason for the lag between *mood* (as tracked by the stock market) and *result* is that it takes time for people to put their new-found energy to work and then to reap the fruits of its employment, or on the other hand to reverse one's forward momentum and witness the results.

If this is true, then economic trends should lag stock market trends. This is indeed an established fact, as the National Bureau of Economic Research in Cambridge has found that, year after year, the S&P Composite index of 500 stocks of major corporations is the single best indicator among the dozen that the Commerce Department uses to foreshadow broad economic trends.[2] In other words, no one has found a better advance indicator of the economy than the stock market. When we plot the history of recessions, depressions and economic booms against the stock market, we see this correlation at work. As we look at a few examples, notice that in each case, the economic change does not precede and cause mood change; it follows mood change. In fact, *the bigger the mood change, the bigger the effect*.

Figure 16-1 examines the big history-making stock market declines. As you can see, *the four largest declines in the stock market* over the past 250 years preceded *four of the largest depressions* in U.S. history, those of 1790-1794, 1840-1843, 1857-1858 and 1929-1933.The single largest stock drop (1929-1932) produced the single biggest depression. The multiple stock panics of 1795-1813 produced multiple depressions. The economic contractions of 1874-1879, 1884-1885, 1893-1894, 1896-1897, 1907-1908, 1920-1921 and lesser ones along the way all developed *after* downturns in stocks.

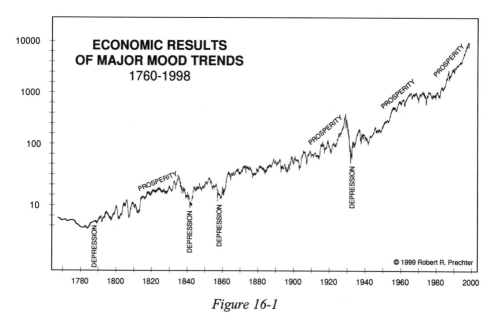

Figure 16-1

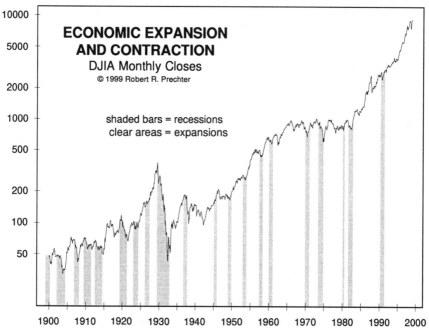

Figure 16-2

As you can see in Figure 16-2, every economic contraction in the 20th century also followed a stock market decline except for the recession of 1945. Every stock market decline did not produce a recession, but *every corrective wave* of at least Primary degree did, whether in wave A or C or both, as detailed in Figure 16-3. For example, in the corrections of 1937-1942 and 1959-1962, recessions occurred in the "A" waves but not in the "C" waves. In the corrections of 1946-1949, 1966-1970, 1976-1980 and 1987-1990 (as reflected by the Value Line Index per the inset), recessions occurred in the "C" waves but not in the "A" waves. There are even two relatively rare "E" waves of triangles on this graph: 1946-1949 (in inflation-adjusted prices; see inset and Figure 16-6) and 1973-1974, both of which produced recessions.[3] A socionomist, then, has the Wave Principle to make the stock market indicator of recession more accurate. Rather than saying simply that recessions often follow setbacks in the stock market, I have refined the indicator as follows: *A recession results from any negative mood trend (stock market correction) of Primary degree or higher,*

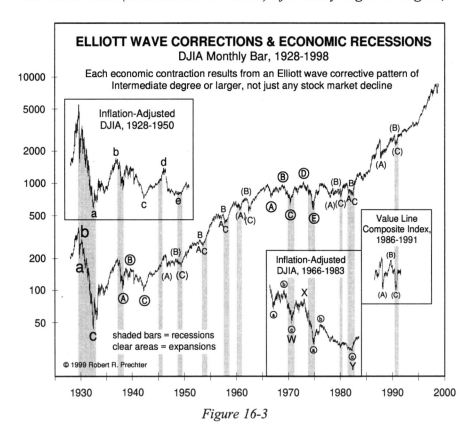

Figure 16-3

typically after the start of at least one of its declining subwaves of one lower degree. Sometimes a recession occurs after the start of more than one subwave. This tendency is increasingly likely at Cycle and Supercycle degree and inevitable at Grand Supercycle degree and above.

Now take a closer look at the *lesser* changes over the past two decades, which are plotted against the 12-month rate of change in the DJIA in Figure 16-4. Even in this crude rendition of annual economic output, one can see the *lagging* results of *leading* changes in mood. The stock market's decline into *August* 1982 reflected lower energy levels among people, the result of which was less production into *November* 1982. The averages topped in *1983* after the *fastest one-year rise* in forty years. This rapid change toward positive mood caused a higher energy and greater output, which peaked the following year, in *1984*, at a 6.8% rate, *the highest annual output* of the past two decades. As mood continued to *wax, though at a lesser rate*, the economy continued to *expand, though at a lesser rate.* The stock market, and therefore mood, went into a "correction" from 1987 to 1990, as expressed most clearly in the Value Line stock index (see inset in Figure 16-3). The waxing negative mood finally produced a drop in productivity figures in 1991, the year *after* the correction ended.[4] Stocks rose sharply during the 1991 recession, leading the economy out of its slump.

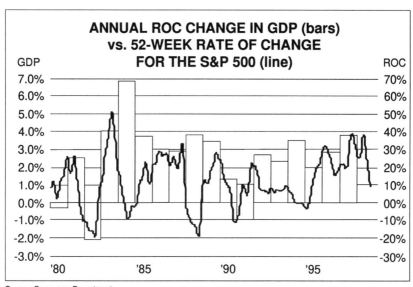

Figure 16-4

The next major corrective pattern in the stock market will lead to the next recession, and if it is of large enough degree, to a depression. This train of causality is unceasing.

Supporting my thesis both of social mood causality *and* the direct-recording mechanism of the stock market is the inescapable observation that *the extent of expansion or contraction correlates with the degree of the preceding trend change in the stock market.*

Many economists brush off the tight correlation between stock market trends and economic trends by endlessly repeating the joke that "the stock market has called fifteen of the last ten recessions" or some such quip. This is myopia, and it is due to two things. The first reason is the lack of knowledge of the Wave Principle. One must know what corrective *patterns* are in order to observe the right correlation between those patterns and economic activity. Second, a bureau has established an "official" definition of a recession, which requires at least six months of contraction. If the economic statistics do not fit into that formula, then it is not considered a recession. However, *all* changes in the economy are relevant to investigating their correlation to the trends in the stock market. Sometimes the larger uptrend in mood is so powerful that a decline in stock prices produces only a brief contraction or just a *slowdown* in productive gains. The result is still recessive, but not a "recession." Like the intensity of social mood itself, the *effects* of social mood are a function not only of the size of mood change but also of its *position within the overall wave structure*, which injects nuances into the study.

As a final comment, I would add that any method that calls fifteen out of the last ten recessions is immeasurably more successful than any economist on record and infinitely more successful than economists in the aggregate (see Chapter 19). It is unfathomable that serious professionals can poke fun at such a record. Moreover, when we take the Wave Principle into account, corrective patterns have announced *every* recession this century but one (1945).[5]

Stock market trends also predicate trends in corporate earnings, as shown in Figure 19-3. I have more work to do to show how closely stocks and economic output track each other, but I believe there is enough evidence here to establish my hypothesis of the social mood causality of economic trends. We will now examine some *political* effects of social mood.

Peace

The latter portions of major bull markets are always relatively peaceful times. For instance, the latter bull market periods of 1815-1835, 1875-1892, 1921-1929, 1954-1965 and 1982 to today have been almost entirely free of U.S. war involvement.

Major advances in mood invariably produce overtures of reconciliation and treaty. In 1928-1929, at the top of Supercycle wave (III), President Hoover pursued the Kellogg-Briand peace pact and presided over a contraction in U.S. armed forces. Lesser degree social mood peaks bring lesser expressions of peace. For example, in January-February 1966, right at the top of Cycle wave III, President Johnson pushed a "peace offensive" in Vietnam, which soon melted into an escalation of the war as the ensuing bear market unfolded. On January 23, 1973, days after an all-time high in the DJIA that held for ten years, President Nixon concluded a peace agreement that ended the Vietnam War. In 1987, as the stock market reached a zenith, the Soviet Union pulled out of Afghanistan, which it had engaged in war at the stock market bottom in 1982. At the same time, President Reagan, who had been referring to the Soviet Union as the Evil Empire, reached a major missile ban agreement with the Soviets in mid-September, a few weeks from the high. (It was signed as a treaty on December 8, a lagging result of the previous mood trend.)

In the late 1990s, we are approaching the top of wave (V), which will also mark a Grand Supercycle degree top, the largest in over 2½ centuries. Coextensively, during this time there have been almost too many peace initiatives to count. Olive branches have been offered in the political, religious, racial and social realms worldwide, many of which have addressed grievances and soothed conflicts that have existed for centuries. Here is a partial list: the Prime Minister of Israel and the Chairman of the Palestine Liberation Organization, enemies (symbolically speaking) for millennia, executed a historic peacekeeping handshake for the press; 117 nations signed the North American Free Trade Agreement (NAFTA) and the General Agreement on Tariffs and Trade (GATT); after decades of violence, the Irish Republican Army ceased military operations in Northern Ireland, and the English and Irish Prime Ministers signed a peace treaty; the Catholic Church entered into an accord with the Jewish state in which the Vatican and Israel, enemies symbolically for nearly 2000 years, officially recognized one another for the first time; Russia, Ukraine and the U.S., after 40 years of mutual nuclear threat, promised in a treaty to stop aiming warheads at each other; China and Russia, enemies for decades, signed a peace pact vowing not to use force against one another; Presidents Clinton and Yeltsin met in a summit that was described as a "virtual lovefest" by *USA Today*; Yeltsin stated flatly in a speech at the Library of Congress: "We will never fight the United States";[6] France invited Germany to parade its soldiers down the Champs-Elysees in Paris on France's biggest national holiday in a symbol of postwar reconciliation; a European Union was consummated following 1500 years of repeated conflict in the region. Some elements of this list are depicted in Figure 18-6. This multi-year pageant of apology, concession and agreement and the concurrent wonderful atmosphere of international peace and cooperation are consistent with my Elliott wave case that an uptrend of *Grand* Supercycle degree is ending.

War

Major mood retrenchment produces war, as humans finally express their collective negative mood extreme with representative collective action. As with economic output, the size of a war is almost always related to the size of the bear market that induces it. Figure 16-5 is a depiction of the

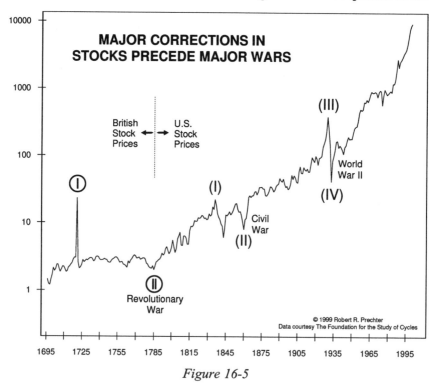

Figure 16-5

U.S. stock market (spliced to the English one prior to 1789) for the past 300 years. As you can see, the three biggest wars involving North Americans followed the three largest stock market declines. The Revolutionary War began near the end of the 64-year bear market in British stock prices that began in 1720. The Civil War followed the 24-year bear market of 74% that ended in 1859. World War II began six years after the 89% collapse in stock prices that bottomed in 1932 and during a 50% drop into 1942.

The Revolutionary War was arguably an English war that resulted from England's bear market, and the lack of an efficient technology for transporting troops across the Atlantic Ocean kept casualties relatively low. Regardless, it is the case that all wars involving United States soldiers have typically produced American casualties in proportion to the size of the mood retrenchment that led to the war. Some statistics are remarkably reflective of this tendency. In World War I[7] and the Vietnam War, which accompanied or immediately followed corrections of *Cycle* degree, deaths among U.S. military personnel totaled 53,402 and 47,378 respectively. In the Civil War and World War II, which accompanied or immediately followed corrections of *Supercycle* degree (one degree larger), deaths caused directly by war activity totaled 294,900[8,9] (including Confederates) and 291,557 respectively. In the wars that accompanied or immediately followed corrections of *Primary* degree, such as the Bay of Pigs fiasco and the Gulf War, only a few U.S. military personnel died.[10]

The Importance of Wave Labels to Bellicose Action

I must mention something here that is rather more technical than any other discussion in this book but which is too important to relegate to an endnote. Conflict results from a contraction in mood, but the appearance of conflict is *not* strictly a function of the size of the contraction. *It is a function both of its position in the wave structure and its size.* To predict conflict, then, one must know the Wave Principle. The most intense conflicts, such as wars, are not associated with all large bear markets but *typically occur during or immediately after the largest C waves in corrective processes of Primary degree and higher.* **A** waves, regardless of extent, rarely result in war.

Figure 16-6 is the same graph as Figure 16-5 except that it is adjusted for inflation, which allows us to see some different nuances in the 20th century. I have labeled all pertinent A-B-C corrections and overlaid a thick, dark line over the C waves. As you can see, the huge A wave crashes in

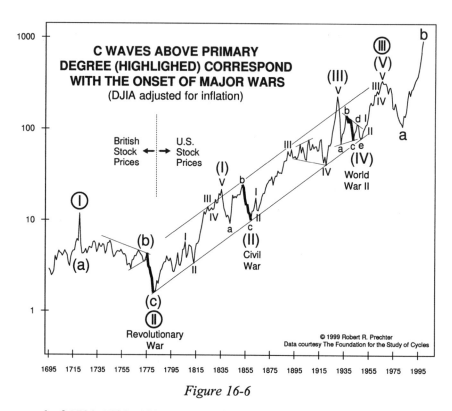

Figure 16-6

mood of 1720-1722, 1835-1842 and 1929-1932, despite their monstrous severity, *did not produce wars*. The C waves that followed each of them *did*.

 Let us go through each of these three bear markets to see the development of events. When the last Grand Supercycle bear market began in 1720 with a devastating two-year stock market collapse for wave **(a)**, no major war followed. The Revolutionary War broke out in the *late* 1700s during wave **(c)** of the (a)-(b)-(c) corrective process. When Supercycle wave (II) began in 1835 with a seven-year collapse for wave **a**, no war occurred. The Civil War began in 1861, two years after the end of wave **c**. When Supercycle wave (IV) began in 1929 with a record-breaking three-year collapse for wave **a**, no war followed. World War II began in 1938, one year after the start of wave **c** of (IV). (All of these declines were "C" waves in nominal terms as well, the only difference being that the last one was wave Ⓒ of II, as shown in Figure 5-12.)

 Even the smaller bear markets exhibit these characteristics. (The following three examples are not illustrated.) The War of 1812 did not break out with the panic of 1807 in wave Ⓐ but during the *second* declining phase, in wave Ⓒ. The Spanish-American War did not take place in wave Ⓐ of IV in 1890, but in 1898, two years after the end of wave Ⓒ of IV. World War I did not begin with the panic of 1907, but during the *second* declining phase of the corrective pattern from 1910 to 1914. The Vietnam War, which began uncharacteristically early with regard to Elliott Wave patterns,[11] nevertheless reached its greatest intensity and saw its strongest domestic opposition (in the form of "May Day"1970 campus riots, which resulted in the shooting of students at Kent State University at the month of the stock market low) during Primary wave Ⓒ of IV (refer to Figure 16-3). The Gulf War did not break out after the 1987 crash, which was wave (A) in the Value Line index (see inset in Figure 16-3), but in January 1991, right after the end of wave (C) in October 1990. Like the record for recessions, the record for wars has one exception. The Mexican War, a brief encounter in 1848, took place near the top of wave b within a 24-year bear market. The Vietnam War is at least a partial exception. Overall, this evidence indicates *that wars are almost always the product of "C" waves in a corrective process* of at least Primary degree, not merely any severe decline in stock prices and social mood.[12]

Apparently society handles the first retrenchment in social mood, no matter how severe. "A" waves surprise optimistic people, who are unprepared and unwilling to wage war. After the monstrous crash of 1720-1722, in fact, not only was there no significant war, but major powers arranged a "détente" (partly to deal with the debt under which so many of them labored). It is the second drop that makes a sufficient number of increasingly stressed people angry enough to attack others militarily.[13] "C" waves are apparently the "last straw" psychologically for those who suffered once in the "A" wave.

The Importance of Wave Position to Social Acts of Construction and Destruction

Advance-decline statistics in the stock market during third waves and "C" waves show broad participation by a great number of *stocks* (see discussion in Chapter 7). Likewise, in third waves and "C" waves, a broad cross section of the *populace* is apparently influenced or affected by the social mood trend. The ethic of achievement that is rooted throughout a society in a third wave up induces the fulfillment of *constructive* social goals, such as the interstate highway system and the space program that were executed in the U.S. during wave III (or the Great Pyramid of Egypt or the roads and aqueducts of the Roman empire undoubtedly as well). On the other hand, the wide spread of anger, fear and deprivation throughout a society in a "C" wave decline induces the fulfillment of *destructive* social goals through actions such as waging war.

War between nations is not the only consequence of large C waves down in mood. Bear markets of sufficient size appear to bring about a desire to slaughter groups of successful people. In 1793-1794, radical Frenchmen guillotined countless members of high society. In the 1930s, Stalin slaughtered Ukrainians. In the 1940s, Nazis slaughtered Jews. In the 1970s, Communists in Cambodia and China slaughtered the affluent. In 1998, after their country's financial collapse, Indonesians went on a rampage and slaughtered Chinese merchants.

Such undertakings, particularly when sponsored by the state as most of them are, require immense cooperation. It might be postulated that major "C" wave declines are times when *destructive social goals are achieved with wide cooperation*, just as third waves on the upside are times when *constructive social goals are achieved with wide cooperation*.

I include this section because it makes the larger point that *a rigorous practice of socionomics depends upon an understanding of the details of the Wave Principle*. While elsewhere this book meticulously avoids discussing Elliott wave nuances to keep from bogging you down in detail, it is important to understand their utmost importance.

Nuclear Testing as a Function of Worldwide Social Mood

If you take the time to read the history of wars, you will find that the statements and events that lead to tensions that lead to conflict and then to escalation often quite faithfully reflect mood changes recorded by the DJIA. For example, the Mexican War resulted from tensions that began in 1835, the year the bear market started. The Civil War resulted from tensions that built throughout the bear market of 1835-1859.

While we do not have graphs of warlike thinking or preparation to show how well they would correlate with the smaller ebbs and flows of social mood, we do have one that comes close. Figure 16-7 is a graph of the number of annual worldwide nuclear weapons tests in the past twenty years plotted against the DJIA. Note the extreme parallelism. This relationship makes the point that smaller waves of mood change result in responses that are sometimes far more subtle than warring, *but they take place nevertheless*.

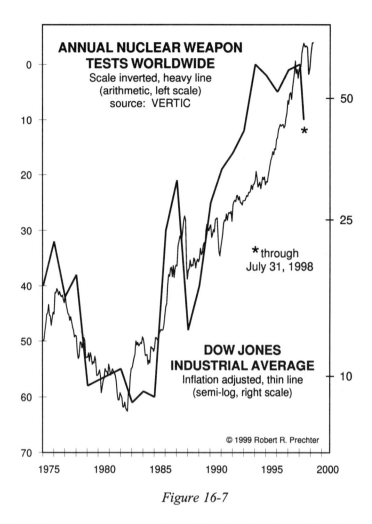

Figure 16-7

Political Freedom as a Function of Worldwide Social Mood

Figure 16-8 is a graph of worldwide political freedom over the past 200 years plotted against U.S. stock prices.[14] Note the general parallelism. This relationship suggests that advancing waves tend to lead to political freedom, while retrenchments tend to lead to political repression. As social mood becomes more positive, more territory moves from dictatorship to representative government. As social mood becomes more negative, more territory falls to dictators. For example, communists took over Russia at the social mood low of 1917. Fascists took over Germany at the social

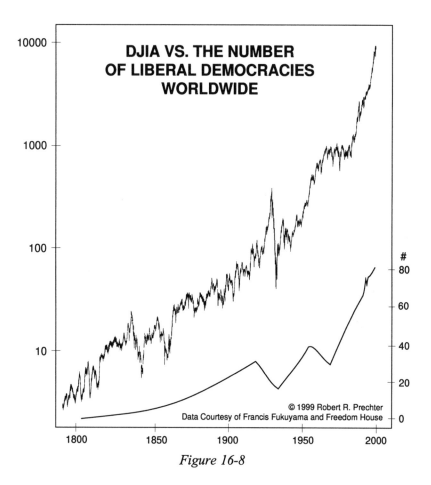

Figure 16-8

mood low of 1933. Russia took over Eastern Europe over the course of the 1946-1949 bear market, which ended the 20-year-long Supercycle wave IV corrective pattern in inflation-adjusted terms (see Figure 16-6). Mao took over China right at the end of wave e of the pattern, in 1949. Pol Pot took over Cambodia in 1975, immediately after the low of Cycle wave IV. In contrast, the Communists voluntarily *relinquished* power over Russia and Eastern Europe at the social mood high of 1989.[15]

Electoral Consequences of Social Mood Trends

The social psychology that accompanies a bull or bear market is the main determinant not only of how voters select a president but also of how they perceive his performance. Correlation with the stock market, consumer confidence, economic performance and other measures suggests that social mood is by far the main determinant of presidential popularity.

What a leader does is mostly acausal with respect to the public's opinion of him. There are two reasons for this fact. First, his actions, despite their endless analysis in the press, do little to affect his popularity. Second, his popularity is dependent upon a social mood and economy over which he can exercise no countertrend influence. If you are new to these ideas, they may be hard to swallow. Aren't some presidents fools or rogues and others statesmen? Don't some presidents affect the economy for good or ill? As to the first question, the answer is, certainly there are presidents of high or low character and ability. However, that does not affect their popularity. For example, President John Kennedy blew the only military conflict in which he engaged the country, attacked the steel industry out of pique to no result, and continually committed adultery. He is revered. Why? Because the country was in a state of euphoria for all but a few months of his term, euphoria that morphed three months later into Beatlemania. As to the second question, the answer is, certainly presidential actions affect the economy. However, the president is not the one who is in control of his social efficacy. For example, the laissez-faire and low-tax policies of President Ronald Reagan helped spur the economy in the early 1980s, but they did not help spur the economy in those ways in 1979 *because he was not elected in 1976*. Social mood called the shots on when it was time for a change. When most of the population wanted lesser taxes and regulation, they got it.

First we will examine the electoral fortunes of some U.S. political figureheads both at extremes in social mood trends as well as in more moderate times. As we shall see, social mood determines their perceived efficacy, legacy and fate.

Near lows of major bear markets, incumbent presidents have suffered their greatest defeats. Apparently, the populace blames the rapid mood change toward the negative and its associated events (such as economic contraction) on the incumbent, so voters overwhelmingly reject him and the party he represents.

For example, Martin Van Buren was ousted by a landslide in 1840 near the low of wave **a** of (II); Herbert Hoover was ousted by a landslide in 1932 at the low of wave (IV), Jimmy Carter was ousted by a landslide in 1980 near the low of wave ② in nominal terms and a major low in inflation-adjusted terms. An interesting victim of dramatic market change to the downside was Richard Nixon. He was elected by a landslide in 1972, two months before the price *peak* of wave IV in nominal terms, then had to

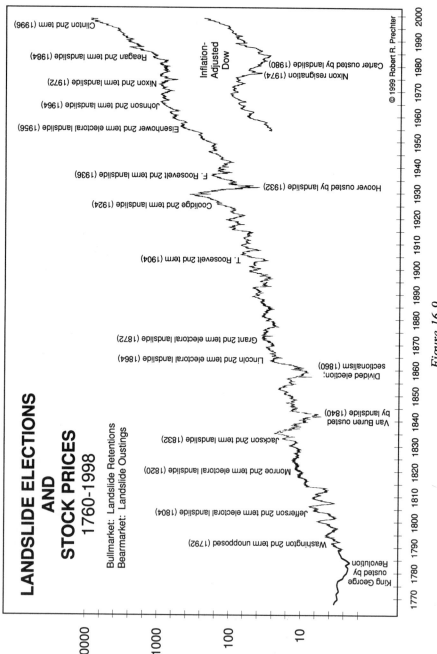

Figure 16-9

resign his office amidst a barrage of social hatred two months before the price *low* of wave IV less than two years later. Figure 16-9 shows the timing of these events. (See Figures 16-5, 16-6 and 5-12 for wave labels.)[16]

The extent of the political reversal is related to the degree of the bear market. The most dramatic defeats of incumbent U.S. presidents have occurred near lows within Supercycle degree bear markets. Lesser ones have occurred near lows within Cycle degree bear markets.

The larger the degree of the market reversal, the longer the party newly elected at its end holds power afterward, since that party is credited with causing the turnaround. After the Supercycle wave (II) low of 1859 when a Democrat had been in office, Republicans won six elections in a row. After the equivalent Supercycle wave (IV) low of 1932 when a Republican had been in office, Democrats won five elections in a row. (For wave labels, see Figure 16-5.) The one-degree-smaller Cycle low of 1828 gave Democrats a comparatively lesser three elections in a row, just as the similar lows of 1896, 1920 and 1980 (see Figure 16-6) each gave Republicans three elections in a row. The key determinant is *not* the politics of the party, but which one is blamed for the preceding downward social mood trend.

The *second* election in a new bull market produces a landslide in favor of the party, and typically the candidate, already in power. In 1832, a landslide retained Andrew Jackson in office. In 1864, a landslide retained Abraham Lincoln in office. In 1924, a landslide retained Calvin Coolidge in office. In 1936, a landslide retained Franklin Roosevelt in office. In 1956, an electoral landslide retained Dwight Eisenhower in office. In 1984, a landslide retained Ronald Reagan in office. Every one of these was a retention in a new bull market.

In each developing fifth wave of Cycle degree, that candidate's *party* also won a third election. In 1836, within one year of the peak of wave V of (I), Martin Van Buren was elected by a substantial margin (though smaller than his predecessor, since the peak had occurred a year earlier), securing a third consecutive term for the Democratic party. In 1928, within one year of the peak of wave V of (III), Calvin Coolidge wisely declined to run (he would have won the election but lost the respect of history), and Herbert Hoover was elected by a substantial margin (a landslide, since the uptrend was still in force), securing a third consecutive term for the Republican party. In 1988, in wave V of (V), George Bush was elected by a substantial margin (though smaller than his predecessor, since a temporary peak had occurred a year earlier), securing a third term in a row for the Republican party. These examples show that fifth waves of *Cycle* degree to date have guaranteed *two* additional elections to the recently elected party, usually by large margins. Fifth waves of *Primary* degree appear to guarantee one additional election.

Presidents are also retained by landslides in elections that take place near major stock market tops. Grant won a landslide in 1872. In 1964, Lyndon Johnson, who had presided since Kennedy's death, won in a landslide. In 1972, Nixon won reelection in a landslide.

The implication is clear: In the first case, nervous voters want society to "stay the course" in its new-found good fortune. In the second case, they want to maintain the euphoria that they feel at a social mood peak. In both cases, they think that reelecting a president or maintaining a political party will have the desired effect. The cause-and-effect relationship, however, is in the opposite direction.

Nuances

Once again, I will explore nuance briefly, just to communicate how closely history repeats at similar times in the wave structure. As one example, Cycle degree fifth waves have produced a remarkably similar sequence of elections and background conditions in the past two hundred years. Wave V of (I) occurred from 1828 to 1835. Republican Andrew Jackson was elected by a large margin (178 to 83 electoral votes), was retained in office by a landslide victory (219 to 49), enjoyed an endearing nickname, "Old Hickory," and presided during a debt-fueled speculative boom in stocks and land. He was succeeded by a member of the same party. Wave V of (III) occurred from 1921 to 1929. Republican Warren Harding was elected by a large margin (404 to 127); Calvin Coolidge took over when Harding died in office, was retained in office by a landslide victory (382 to 136 and a margin of 1.9:1 in popular vote, the largest ever), enjoyed an endearing nickname, "Silent Cal," and presided during a debt-fueled speculative boom in stocks and land. He was succeeded by a member of the same party. The liftoff portion of wave V of (V) occurred from 1982 to 1987. Republican Ronald Reagan was elected by a large margin (489 to 49), was retained in office by a landslide victory (525 to 13), enjoyed an endearing nickname, "The Great Communicator," and presided during a debt-fueled speculative boom in stocks and land. He was succeeded by a member of the same party. 1988 was the first time that a sitting Vice President was elected since 1836 and the first time that the Republicans had won three in a row since 1928, each of those being near the previous fifth wave peaks of Cycle degree.

If an uptrend in social mood persists for a long time, it eventually becomes taken for granted. Then voters' patterns change because *they no longer assume that they must keep a particular person or party in power to maintain what they now regard as normal conditions.* However, they change exactly in a way that reflects their increasing ebullience and confidence as the positive mood reaches extremes. A typical result is the election of politicians more willing to express social feelings of abundance by supporting or initiating social programs. For instance, after electing the conservative Eisenhower twice during the initial phase of a long bull market, the public voted in a moderate Kennedy and then a liberal Johnson near the top. Similarly in the 1980s, after electing the conservative Reagan twice during the initial phase of the bull market, the public voted in a moderate Bush and then a liberal Clinton.

Given that Cycle wave V of (V) is ending a much larger *Grand* Supercycle, a second president, Bill Clinton, has enjoyed the benefits of an extension of wave V's debt-fueled uptrend in stocks and land. As befits the relative weakness of a fifth wave of a fifth wave, the quality of the luster is off substantially. He did not win his second term in a landslide, and his nickname is a far less endearing "Slick Willie." (To see my comments and forecast regarding President Clinton's fortunes, see Chapter 17.)

There may be a connection between fifth waves of Supercycle degree as well. 1998 has marked the first year since 1928, near the end of wave V of (III), that each of three consecutive elections has produced Republican domination of both houses of Congress.

Even Near-Term Trends in Mood and Politics are Correlated

Major trends, then, are quite clear in their electoral influence. What about trends that last mere months? Join me on a roller coaster ride with President George Bush.

The *Time* magazine cover of August 1989 read, "How Bush Decides: He's smarter than Reagan, less driven than Carter and savvy like Nixon"! Gallup polls of January 1990 showed that Bush sported a phenomenal approval rating of 80% at the end of his first year in office compared to Reagan's 40%, Carter's 55%, and Nixon's 61%. The only higher first-year approval rating recorded was in 1961 when President Kennedy enjoyed the euphoria of all-time stock market highs after the extended Primary wave

③ of the 1950s. *The Wall Street Journal* on April 20 called Bush "a man for the season" who "wins praise" and "rides a huge current of political popularity." On May 1, a political cartoon showed Bush rejoicing that the U.S. had turned "into a one-party system!"

A *single quarter* made a tremendous difference. When the Dow slid 21% from mid-July to mid-October 1990, the Value Line index fell nearly to its 1987 low and the Dow Transports finished a collapse of 47%, the press no longer regarded Bush as a political genius. In October and November, they bombed him with derisive headlines and comments such as, "Bush May Have Lost 1992 Already," "From Sizzle to Fizzle," "Bush Faces a GOP Revolt," "The Bush Blueprint Bombs," "The Carterization of Bush," "Is Bush Presidency Headed for Doom?," and "a quagmire of indecision and ineptitude which could take him the rest of the Presidency to dig out." The direct effect of the social mood change on the perception of national leaders extended around the world:

1) England's Margaret Thatcher resigned under pressure after serving for eleven years, the longest term for a British Prime Minister this century.

2) The Prime Minister of Singapore, the longest serving democratically elected head of state, resigned.

3) The President of France, according to headlines of the time, was "fighting to stay in power" as his administration fell apart.

4) The President of Brazil's political honeymoon came "to an abrupt end eight months after he came to power," said *The Wall Street Journal*.[17]

Just four months after the press unleashed its blizzard of derision, the Dow had soared back at 3000. George Bush's approval rating soared right with it, to 91%, the highest in the history of the records. The media loved him again.

Now the most popular president ever, George Bush was considered unbeatable in the 1992 elections. Prominent Democrats refused to run, so a pack of relative unknowns took to the hustings. You may recall the end of the story. For the rest of 1991, corporate earnings, as a result of the bear market in mood that ended in 1990, plummeted in their sharpest drop since the 1940s. The unemployment rate, which was near 5% when Bush took office, jumped to nearly 8% (see Figure 16-10). Both of these measures of economic well-being were recovering in late 1992, but too sluggishly to

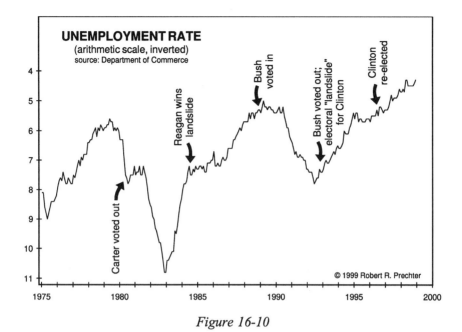

Figure 16-10

cheer the now-disillusioned public. Just eighteen months after his record-setting approval rating, Bush lost the election.

Did this fantastic roller-coaster ride reflect *anything* but social mood? It is absurd to think otherwise. George Bush, as an *individual*, did not in three months metamorphose from a genius to a buffoon, then five months later from a buffoon to the greatest president ever, then in the next eighteen months to a pitiable loser. His change of mind on taxes, for instance, would have been hailed as "statesmanlike" in an uptrend. His handling of the Gulf War, seen first as brilliant as stocks soared, was later found wanting after stocks languished for a year and the economy slowed. At no time did Bush's essential character or moderate, pragmatic political philosophy change. At each turning point in the wave structure, it was not Bush, but the focus and perception of him, that changed.

We have the records for Bill Clinton as well, and they show the same ebbs and flows with stocks and the economy as did those for George Bush. For some details, see Chapter 17. Analyst Paul Montgomery presented two charts (Figures 16-11 and 16-12) of President Bush's and Clinton's popularity vs. the Dow Jones Industrial Average, each over an eight-month period. These periods included intensely emotional events, the Gulf War and a sex scandal, respectively. As you can see, even such visceral subjects and war,

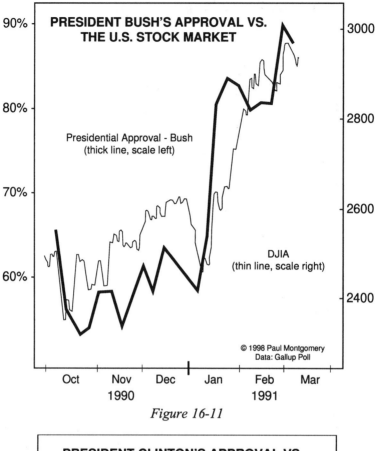

Figure 16-11

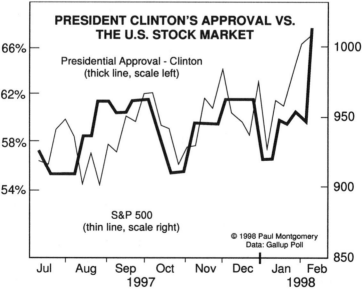

Figure 16-12

sex and scandal cannot be shown to have a claim on the people's view of the president. Only their aggregate and *independent* mood, as reflected by the trends in the DJIA and its results as reflected by economic statistics, unquestionably does.

There are times when these lines diverge, but when they do, it is always in the direction of the lagging economic statistics. It is never due to the president's actions *apart* from those.

Herding and Leader Selection: Two Results of a Single Cause: Social Mood, Which Follows the Wave Principle

Dr. Paul MacLean concludes from his research, "The reptilian brain in mammals plays a crucial role in...selecting leaders."[18] This is the same portion of the brain that produces the herding impulse. While one might surmise that even in the most primitive portion of the brain, apparently different functions such as mood, herding and judging leaders might be distinct from each other, Figures 16-11 and 16-12 show that this is not the case. I conclude from this parallelism that the latter two operate as a *single impulse*, apparently directed by fluctuations in mood. The connection of social mood specifically to *the* leader is further evident upon observing that voters always associate their feelings primarily with the president, not Congress. If the president during a stock market collapse is of one party while Congress is dominated by the other party, the president's party gets the blame. During the 1929-1932 crash, for instance, Democrats controlled Congress and even passed the Smoot-Hawley tariffs, which many economists warned were economically dangerous, yet the president's party, the Republicans, paid the price. Opposition Congresses bedevil(ed) both Nixon and Clinton, but the president in both cases has received the credit or blame for social moods. Obviously there is little rational thought attached to the very visceral connection among mood, herding and the assessment of leaders. Certainly, however much there is cannot dent the collective expression of the reptilian complex.

In January 1998, *USA Today* summed up the influence of a persistent positive social mood trend on the image of the leader when it said, "President Clinton is the most resilient survivor of scandal in modern American history."[19] The "Teflon coating" that has allowed scandalous allegations of all kinds to slide off his back is simply the sheen of a positive social mood deep in people's minds, which is reflected in rising stock prices. Many observers see Clinton's new all-time highs in popularity amidst countless scandals as a paradox. Montgomery lucidly explains that it is not:

It constitutes a paradox only if one expects our [collective] opinions regarding our leaders to be rational. As neuroscience, much less casual observation, makes clear, the feelings we have for our leaders are the product not of our highest, but rather our lowest, cortical processes.[20]

Montgomery makes another observation, which summarizes how the lowest cortical processes operate:

President Bush's popularity as measured by the Gallup Poll moved in an exquisitely precise Elliott wave pattern and followed perfect Fibonacci proportions.[21]

Obviously, if the stock market follows the Wave Principle, and if the public perception of the leader mirrors the stock market, then the public perception of the leader follows the Wave Principle.

The Extent of Impulsivity in Political Action

To produce the results we have examined in this section, it is not necessary that all people vote impulsively. In fact, many do follow a political philosophy. Vote totals over the past two centuries suggest that perhaps 1/3 of the populace consistently votes toward one end of the left-right spectrum and 1/3 votes toward the other, while 1/3 is mostly rudderless, voting with the current mood rather than by consistent thought. However, even those who are consistently left or right tend to fluctuate in the *intensity* of that orientation, thus also participating in cycles of social expression.

The left-right spectrum itself is utterly prerational, as it mostly represents (1) the survival impulse among producers to keep the means of their sustenance vs. the survival impulse among nonproducers and their sympathizers to appropriate it, and (2) the impulse among some people to direct others' behavior vs. the impulse among others to do as they please. Only the up-down spectrum, between individual liberty and authoritarianism, has differences that may be regarded as philosophical.

The Inevitability of Change in the Mechanics of Events when Social Mood Changes

Each Elliott wave pattern has implications both for its own development and for coming events that it causes. The more one works with the Wave Principle and studies history as it relates to similar pattern junctures, the more one is able to forecast specific developments outside the market (see Chapter 17). Yet it is important to understand that events always fall into place to reflect the trend of the market, and thus of social mood, *whether we can describe them in advance or not.*

As an example, when Frost and I originally forecasted the great bull market of the 1980s, we had no idea where the vehicles for speculation would come from. Five years later, in 1983, *The Elliott Wave Theorist* pointed out a number of emerging conditions associated with the bull market:

> With sentiment, momentum, wave characteristics and social phenomena all supporting our original forecast, can we say that the environment on Wall Street is conducive to developing a full blown speculative mania? In 1978, an Elliott analyst had no way of knowing just what the mechanisms for a wild speculation would be. "Where is the 10% margin that made the 1920s possible?" was a common rebuttal. Well, to be honest, we didn't know. But now look! The entire structure is being built as if it were planned. Options on hundreds of stocks (and now stock indexes) allow the speculator to deal in thousands of shares of stock for a fraction of their value. Futures contracts on stock indexes, which promise to deliver nothing, have been created for the most part as speculative vehicles with huge leverage. Options *on* futures carry the possibilities one step further. And it's not stopping there. Major financial newspapers are calling for the end of any margin requirements on stocks whatsoever. "Look-back" options are making a debut. S&Ls are leaping into the stock brokerage business, sending flyers to little old ladies. And New York City banks are already constructing kiosks for quote machines so that depositors can stop off at lunch and punch out their favorite stocks. Options exchanges are creating new and specialized speculative instruments — guess the CPI and win a bundle! In other words, the financial arena is becoming the *place to be.* And, as if by magic, the media are geometrically increasing coverage of financial news. Financial News Network is now broadcasting 12 hours a day, bringing up-to-the-minute quotations on stocks and commodities via satellite and cable into millions of homes.[22]

At the same time, services that rate analysts and fund managers were just coming into being, and the mutual fund industry began its greatest expansion in history.

Not only did these market-related factors develop, but economic conditions improved in response to the rise. Interest rates declined, inflation receded, employment grew, unemployment fell, production expanded, and a business-friendly political environment predominated. In essence (and also in many specifics; see Chapter 17), *those conditions were forecasted years ahead of time by the simple prediction that wave V in stocks lay ahead.*

Forecasting such specifics is an immense challenge because major social mood changes bring about unbelievably radical social changes. For instance, in 1929, with the Dow at 381, who could have said specifically that in ten years, war and holocaust would begin in Europe, that in twelve years, Japanese aircraft would attack Pearl Harbor, and that within twenty years, the most populous country in the world, as well as half of Europe, would be taken over by Communists? The *character*, or *tenor*, of each of these actions was utterly consistent with the developing wave structure at the time. Specifics, however, cannot be forecasted at the outset, only surmised. As social trends develop, we can anticipate more and more specifics and formulate plans in time to take advantage of blossoming developments or to avoid the trouble spots.

The Occasional Imposition of Structural Rigidity

In some cases, extremes in mood cause actions that impose structural rigidity on a society. The effects of such institutionalization continue for a long period because it takes time to play out the consequences of the rigidity imposed at the extreme point of mass mood. Once a restrictive political policy is put in place, it can most definitely affect such things as economic output. For instance, the imposition of a mild rigidity in the form of wage and price controls or a substantial rigidity such as communism or fascism has always served to dampen a country's economic progress thereafter regardless of a later upswing in mood.

As an extreme example, the collective mood in Germany in July 1932 was so negative that its expression produced Adolf Hitler's peak of popularity, exactly concurrent with the month of the low in stocks. Although the underlying public mood as reflected by stock prices was changing toward the less negative from July 1932 forward, and although Hitler's popularity was accordingly waning, he remained just popular enough to be granted the reins of power. The consequences of the social action taken just after the social-mood low took thirteen years to play out because the representatives of the negative popular mood gained such great political power. The collective mood in the United States also reached a negative extreme in 1932-1933. One manifestation of that mood extremity was the increased enrollment in and disruptive activity by the Communist Party in the U.S. In contrast to the German experience, however, the most extreme political forces never achieved political control, so the improving mood was allowed to express itself in the years that followed.

Policies are relevant, but they are not the *fundamental* cause of conditions. Governments institute policies in response to the prevailing (or sometimes the immediately preceding) social mood trend, so it is the public's mood that is ultimately responsible for the change. Furthermore, it is a change in the trend of mood that ultimately causes authorities to ditch the policy or people to ditch the authorities.

History and the Socionomic Hypothesis

All of history flows from the fact that men have a nature, that this nature includes unconscious patterns of interaction, and that these patterns produce results in human social action. Humanity might have produced a history without the unconscious herding impulse. However, it would not have produced the passionate, collective history that we do have, with its wars, treaties, construction, migrations, governments, religions, societies and cultures. Elliott waves, like them or not, are the first cause of history. Since waves are governed by mathematics, history has a mathematical basis. Since waves are governed by *Fibonacci* mathematics, then the mathematics with which nature is most intimate are behind the tenor and events of history.

The mathematics of robust fractal geometry (see Chapter 3) also account for both the repetitiveness and uniqueness of history. The Wave Principle provides a scientific explanation for the observation, "History repeats in the generalities but not in the details." Because fundamental Elliott wave patterns are limited in number while their manifestations have substantial variability, and because the continual expansion of degree imparts uniqueness to every wave, interactive human mentation and behavior, which produce history, are continually repeated, but not precisely. Once again, empirics and hypothesis are compatible.

NOTES

1 Le Bon, G. (1895). *The crowd.*

2 Malabre, A.L. (1987, February 23). "The stock market and the business cycle." *The Wall Street Journal.*

3 Elliotters should note that W, Y, and Z are used to label certain other types of corrections.

4 The 1991 recession, which followed this three-year Primary degree bear market, also precipitated the Gulf War and induced Hollywood to award five Oscars, including best picture, to *Silence of the Lambs*, a film about a brutal cannibalistic serial killer.

5 Even this one might be seen as the lagging result of the bear market that ended in 1942, but that seems too substantial a time lag to assert definite causality.

6 Nichols, B. (1994, September 28). "Warm fuzzy summit." *USA Today.*

7 Overall, World War I was a larger war than the associated bear market appears to have warranted. However, it was clearly preceded by a long bear market environment of increasing social frustration. The stock average in 1914 was little higher than it was in 1889, a full 25 years earlier. During that time, stock indexes had three major setbacks of 40% to 60%.

8 Another 284,000 died of disease indirectly caused by the war, making the total of Civil War-related deaths 578,900.

9 Price, William H. (1961). *The Civil War handbook.*

10 The Korean War of 1950-1953 is not so easily categorized by degree. It immediately followed the last low (wave e) in the *Supercycle* degree triangle pattern in inflation-adjusted terms (see Figure 16-6), which was a low only of *Primary* degree in nominal terms (see Figure 5-12 or 15-4). Accordingly, the total number of U.S. deaths, from both battle and other causes, at 54,246, was between the numbers associated with each degree exclusively.

11 The fact that the Vietnam War took place during a bear market that was simultaneously wave (a) in inflation-adjusted terms (see Figure 16-6) and which included two advances back to the level of the prior bull market's high in nominal terms may bear upon why it was unpopular. Much of the society was still in a socially positive mood, and simply did not feel like fighting.

12 Notice in Figure 16-6 that the current wave position implies wave c directly ahead. While this decline, should it unfold, could be dangerous in terms of war potential, it is unlikely to produce a "World War III" type

worldwide conflict. The reason is that the approaching wave c is not the *largest* wave c due in the pattern. It is expected to be only wave c of (a) of a larger (a)-(b)-(c) flat correction or (a)-(b)-(c)-(d)-(e) triangle. This wave labeling will soon bring the inflation-adjusted DJIA back to the same position as the nominal DJIA, which now faces the start of wave (a). For more on this topic, see Chapter 5 of *At the Crest of the Tidal Wave.*

13 People's anger shows up in countless ways. For example, while labor-management relations are harmonious in bull markets, they are acrimonious in bear markets, precipitating disputes and strikes. Even the U.S. homicide rate has quite well paralleled major inflation-adjusted stock trends in data from 1960 to the present.

14 Actually, this graph should probably be constructed as a percentage of worldwide population, as the number of countries could, depending upon circumstances, be meaningless.

15 In extremely rare cases, political repression at a social mood low leads to a war that the repressors lose, a prime example being the Revolutionary War.

16 Landslide oustings at major "A" wave lows appear inevitable, as the populace is shocked by the dramatic social mood change toward the negative. "C" wave elections are less predictable, often because by then social conditions are so unstable. The election of 1860, near the end of wave c of (II), reflected extremely negative sentiment. It certainly saw the ousting of the previous president, Buchanan, but the vote was close precisely because the political scene was so divided that the nation was not voting as a whole (the winner, Lincoln, wasn't even on the ballot in ten states), but by section (North vs. South), thus hardly reflecting contentment with the status quo. Social conditions during wave c of (IV) in inflation-adjusted prices were clearly chaotic as well, as World War II raged. The public image of Franklin Roosevelt had already benefitted from the greatest momentum kickoff of the century (see Figure 7-1) and the gains made thereafter. He then benefitted from the calendar. Had his third election taken place in 1942 near the low of wave II, he may have lost, even with a war in progress. However, he had the good fortune that elections were scheduled two years on either side of the low, both during stock market rallies.

17 Kamm, T. (1990, November 16). "Brazil's president, after eight months, finds roar of crowd is now against him." *The Wall Street Journal.*

18 MacLean, P.D. (1990). *The triune brain in evolution.*

19 Page, S. (1998, January 22). "President's resilience faces biggest test." *USA Today.*

20 Montgomery, P.M. (1998, February 4). *Universal Economics.*

21 Montgomery, P.M. (1991, March 15). "Neurophysiology, presidents and the stock market, part III." *Universal Economics.*

22 Prechter, R.R. (1983, August 18). "The superbull market of the '80s: has the last wild ride really begun?" *The Elliott Wave Theorist,* Special Report.

Chapter 17:

Forecasting Success Supports the Validity of Socionomics

Chapters 5 through 7 showed that the Wave Principle is unique in providing a basis for forecasting markets. This chapter, to the extent possible for this extremely young science, aims to demonstrate a broader application of socionomics to social forecasting.

If mass mood change is the cause of coming social events, then evidence of mood change or coming mood change is the single most important area of discovery for those who wish to peek into the future of social events. The practical value of the Wave Principle is that it provides, for the first time ever, a context for disciplined market analysis, economic analysis and social analysis. A proper identification of the patterns imparts an immense amount of knowledge about society's position within its behavioral continuum and therefore about its probable ensuing path.

As implied in this book so far, there are two types of socionomic forecasting:

   (1) predicting trends in social phenomena based upon waves within the phenomena themselves, and
   (2) predicting economic, political, social, cultural and other trends based upon the wave position of indicators of overall social mood such as the stock market.

Aside from an initial orientation, the rest of this chapter presents actual socionomic forecasts issued over the past two decades. I have examples of both type one and type two forecasts and end with examples of applying them to individual experiences in the social realm. Please take the time to reflect on their uniqueness. It is not a matter of, say, half of economists calling for an up quarter and the socionomist happens to be on the lucky side. Each of these forecasts has a character that only socionomics makes possible.

Waves in Social Phenomena Other than Financial

Chapters 5 and 6 give several examples of the first type of forecasting as applied to financial markets. Yet that is not the only realm in which it can be applied. Before reviewing past predictions, let us look at one example of waves in other social phenomena.

Take a close look at Figure 17-1, which is the per capita consumption of cigarettes in the United States throughout this century. As you can see, this data traced out a fairly classic Elliott wave advance over nine decades. Writers discussing this graph attempt all sorts of guesses about the reasons for both the advancing trend and the reversal, noting such supposedly causal events as "World War II." We all know that cigarettes were popular in World War II, but is that a *reason* they were popular? The reversal in 1963 appears even more mysterious. The Center for Disease Control and Prevention and the National Cancer Institute report, for example, that over the

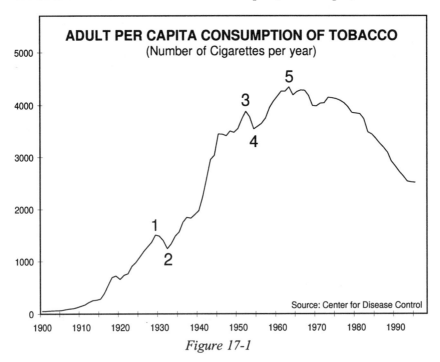

Figure 17-1

twenty-two years up to the time of the report in August 1995, smoking among black teenagers dropped dramatically from 26% to 4.4%. Says the director of the Office on Smoking and Health at the CDC, "It's a public health success story that we can't take credit for because we didn't do it. We can't [even] explain it."[1] Feeling compelled nevertheless to do so, people interviewed for the article go on to cite six retrospectively-conjured "theories" of why it happened, every one of which demands its own explanation.

A socionomist can go directly to the heart of the matter. Smoking is a social phenomenon. As such, its popularity has followed the Wave Principle. In the two dozen years after the peak came the Surgeon General's report, a broadcast ad ban, the beginning of a "nonsmokers' rights" movement and higher federal cigarette taxes. Of course, these are presumed to be causes of the change in attitude, but actually, they are results. Every trend carries within it the seeds of its own demise. Surgeons General would not have bothered to look into the health aspects of cigarettes if over 40% of adult Americans weren't smoking them. The government never could have gotten away with an ad ban or tax hikes without public support. The nonsmokers' rights campaign was a backlash reaction to widespread smoking. Decades prior to the Surgeon General's report, it was widely reported that cigarettes probably caused lung cancer. In the 1940s, they were called "coffin nails," in the 1950s "cancer sticks." When I was a kid in the 1960s, everyone knew that smoking was harmful, but it still looked cool. In the 1970s, I heard the term "death sticks," essentially the same slang term used thirty years earlier. Medical knowledge did not stop the uptrend. What did stop the uptrend? Five waves, that's what, complete with equally-sized waves 2 and 4, an extended wave 3, suggestion of the proper subdivisions within waves 1 and 3 even in this crude data, and a slowing upside rate of change in wave 5. The bear market that ensued is replete with incidents of social reaction toward cigarettes. To many teenagers, smoking is not even cool any more. It is not really accurate to say that such differences in action and attitude caused the trend change; they *are* the trend change.

At this point, the downtrend has lasted 34 years, which is .618 of the approximately 55-year long uptrend, and per capita consumption has fallen by about 2/5. At least one cigarette company has taken an aggressive pro-freedom stance in its advertising in reaction to what it sees as the harsh puritanism of the anti-smoking zealots. A socionomist, then, should be on the lookout for signs of a reversal.

This is an example of a nonfinancial social trend that could have been forecast, not one that was. Since the very idea of attempting to perform such forecasting occurred to me only a few years ago, and since normally we would have to make a determined effort to seek out such fairly obscure data, and since long-term forecasts take time to play out, I have only two examples of attempts at such forecasting for which there has been time enough for at least a partial resolution. The first was made by a novice.

PREDICTING SOCIAL TRENDS BASED UPON
WAVES WITHIN THE PROCESS

A Forecast of the U.S. Savings Rate

Here is a social forecast made on October 18, 1990 by Robert E. Burt, an *Elliott Wave Theorist* subscriber, who sent in the following commentary along with the graph shown in Figure 17-2:

> Enclosed is a *Wall Street Journal* clipping you may not have noticed. The chart shows the U.S. savings rate since 1970. What struck me was how it is a nearly classic example of the first four steps in a five-step long-term downtrend. I have included a blowup with my [wave] numbers drawn in. ...If one assumes wave 5 falls as far from the recent high as wave 1, then one has a...savings rate of 0.6%, occurring some time in late 1992 or early 1993. If one notes that the bottom of wave 3 is almost

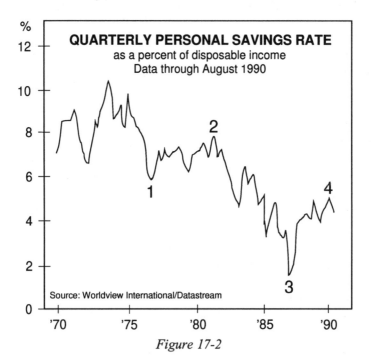

Figure 17-2

twice as much below the top as wave 1, a case can be made for an even more catastrophic *negative* savings rate of around -3.1% at that time.[2]

Figure 17-3 would show the same graph updated through today, except that the ensuing downtrend so upset the government that the keepers of the figures (perhaps justifiably) changed the formula to include money-market funds, which pushed the ratio to higher levels. Regardless of this change in scale and some resulting differences in the curve, you can see that not only did Mr. Burt's general expectation for a new low come to pass, but so did his specific call for a drop to minus 3.1%, which is about where Figure 17-3 would show the current rate to be had statisticians maintained the old formula. The forecast took longer to play out than expected because wave 3 in this data lasted an additional two years.[3]

The uniqueness of this forecast in calling for a trend reversal is its most remarkable feature. The savings rate had just soared from 1% to 5% in less than two years, yet the forecast did not extrapolate; it called for a downturn to *new lows*. It would be very surprising if any conventional economist said anything like it at the time.

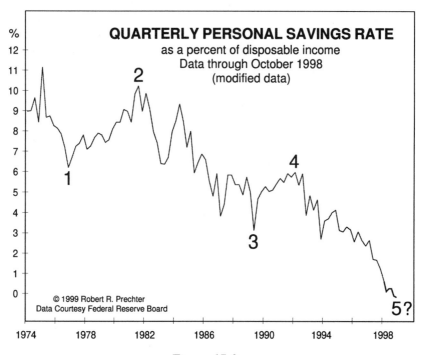

Figure 17-3

A Forecast for Baseball

I have found parallel trends between many different types of social activities and the stock market. Predicting some social trends might appear frivolous, but to the industry involved, correctly anticipating trend changes would be worth millions of dollars.

Immediately following the 1992 baseball season, *The Elliott Wave Theorist* published an analysis and forecast for the fortunes of that great American game, along with practical advice for collectors, players and team owners. The following quotes are excerpted from issues of *The Elliott Wave Theorist* published on the dates listed:

October 30, 1992

> **A Top in Baseball?** The first World Series game was held in 1903. This year was the Fibonacci 89th World Series. The *emotion* surrounding the 88th and 89th World Series games was huge. The 1991 series was widely described as "the best World Series ever." It brought together two "worst-to-first" teams, a battle of underdogs (who are always popular). Fans were chanting and "tomahawk chopping" like college fraternity lunatics. The games attracted a high 24.0 share of TV viewers. The teams were greeted by throngs totaling nearly a million people at post-series hometown parades. The 1992 series was similarly emotional, particularly in Canada, as the Toronto Blue Jays took on the symbolism of national pride. Indeed, the Atlanta Braves were the only team ever to have been magically groomed for such a setting by a decade of billing as "America's Team." It was the first nationalistic World Series ever.[4]
>
> *There is reason to believe that baseball players' salaries, as well as baseball cards and other memorabilia, have just made a "spike top" along with fans' emotions.*
>
> You may recall that our "Popular Culture" Special Report of 1985 concluded that baseball is a bull market sport.... When the first World Series was played in October 1903, the Dow was making a low at 43. It was never lower during another World Series, enjoying an 89-year net uptrend. If stocks are topping in a major way as the Wave Principle argues, so is the uptrend in baseball's popularity. In the past few years, Hollywood has idolized baseball in *Field of Dreams*, *The Babe* and *A League of Their Own*. The widespread popularity of such sentiment toward a subject often coincides with a peak in interest among the population.

Could baseball be in for a 55-year period of decline in public favor? Signs of a turn are there. *If you're an investor, take profits on baseball cards. If you're a player, sign a long-term contract. If you're an owner, sell your club.* Kids will soon be trading in their bats for helmets (or hockey pucks, soccer balls, or equipment for a more violent sport yet to come). If you're a real fan, you'll still find yourself griping about baseball some time in the 1990s.

Result: A few months later came these dramatic reports of a sudden change of fortune for the prices of baseball cards and their manufacturers' stocks, both of which collapsed:

THE WALL STREET JOURNAL
January 27, 1993

New York – Baseball-card stocks were hit by news that market leader Topps Co. will report its first quarterly loss in more than a decade.

Topps – which experienced strong insider selling last year – sank 31%, to $8.50 from $12.25, on seven times its usual volume.

The announcement sent shares of several companies in the sports-memorabilia business south yesterday. Among them was Marvel Entertainment Group, the comic-book giant that purchased card manufacturer Fleer Corp. last September. Shares of Marvel, which according to analysts gets roughly half its revenue from Fleer, slid $3.25, or 11.5%, to $24.875 on five times its normal volume.

"The speculative bubble has burst in the new cards," said....

ROCKY MOUNTAIN NEWS
April 7, 1993

SPORTS TRADING CARDS: Market has started to fall apart

The market is crumbling. Manufacturers are laying off employees as their stock tumbles and they cut back on production. Retailers are going out of business. Prices on goods are slashed. Card collecting exploded in popularity in the 1980s and turned into a highly profitable business. Card brands increased from one in the 1970s to 40. Then came the crash of '92-93. Pro Set filed for Chapter 11 bankruptcy. Topps, the trading card leader, lost 30% of its stock value in one day after it reported an expected quarterly loss.

January 29, 1993

[Elliott Wave International's] Pete Kendall has just obtained the data on baseball attendance during this century. As you can see by [Figure 17-4], the figures appear to have traced out an exceptional Elliott Wave, ending with the 1992 season. Notice that the 1981 strike brought attendance back to the preceding fourth wave, just as it was scheduled to do. When the data is plotted on semilog scale (not shown), the entire rise from the World War I low in 1916 forms a wedge, which has bearish implications. At minimum, then, baseball faces its *largest percentage drop in attendance since it became the national sport*. At junctures such as this, it is even appropriate to consider that it may fall far enough out of favor in coming years to cease *being* the premier national sport.

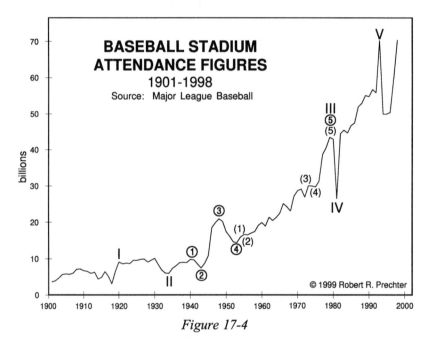

Figure 17-4

Result: 1993 was another record-attendance year, as fans bought season tickets on the strength of their overwhelming enjoyment of the previous two years. In 1994, baseball players called a strike. It closed down the season, causing the largest drop in attendance since the beginning of baseball in arithmetic (but not quite in percentage) terms. In 1994, there was no World Series for the first time ever. Fans' bitterness extended the low turnout into 1995. The following article revealed the immense pressure on the trading-card industry resulting from this change in fortunes:

USA TODAY
March 23, 1995
Strike is 'another nail' in trading cards' coffin

In limbo because of the major league players' strike, the baseball trading-card business faces a grim question: How low can it go? Not much lower, says Steve Myland, a wholesaler in Phoenix: "The strike has had a profound effect. The industry is collapsing." Joe Bosley, a dealer in Reisterstown, Md., says sales of baseball cards issued in recent years are down 90%: "It's another nail in the coffin." Myland estimates 20-30% of card retailers have folded since the strike began, as have four card publications. Topps says its production is at its lowest level in 30 years. Upper Deck says it cut back by 75%.

Was it luck that the players' strike happened after our forecast? It might have been. However, there are two reasons to think otherwise. First, it is definitely incorrect to presume that the strike was an "outside cause" that struck the baseball industry out of nowhere. I would argue that the strike, which was called by players making multiple millions of dollars who thought they were worth even more, was a consequence of baseball's affluence, which in turn was a consequence of its popularity. The entire event was internal to baseball and its fortunes, and it occurred right after one could identify five waves up in the attendance figures. Since then, the popularity of baseball has waxed again in tandem with the continuation of the bull market in stocks. However, it still significantly lags its pinnacle of 1991-1993 in terms of emotion, trading card values, television viewership and stadium attendance per team.

In 1996, despite record home-run statistics and a World Series match-up of the American and National leagues' most popular franchises, attendance was still off 14% from that of 1993, while television ratings for the World Series showed the third lowest percentage viewership ever. In 1997, attendance again remained moderate. In 1998, home-run statistics of several players set all-time records (record home runs are a bull market phenomenon, but that's another topic), two new teams were added to the leagues (another consequence of affluence typical of tops), the country felt as affluent as ever, stocks made new all-time highs, the economy was in the seventh year of an expansion, and America liked baseball again. This resurgence in the sport's achievements and popularity is a direct reflection of the resumption of the bull market in stocks after 1994. Despite all that, the 1998 World Series attracted the lowest television viewership *ever*. The two new teams added to the total turnout, which matched the peak of 1993, but turnout per team has yet to exceed that peak.

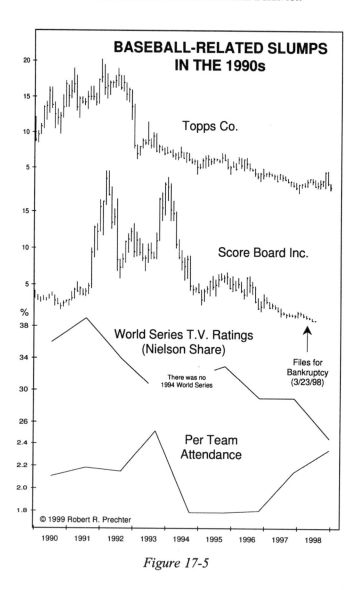

Figure 17-5

Most forecasters would simply extrapolate the multi-decade uptrend into the future. Maybe the uptrend will continue; there is no *guarantee* that wave 5 has ended; it could subdivide and last decades longer. However, if my thesis is correct that baseball is a bull market sport, and if my wave interpretation is correct that a Grand Supercycle bull market is nearing its end, then baseball's fortunes are due for a reversal on that basis (see next section for a discussion of this type of forecasting) as well as all those listed above. Time will tell, but at least you can see that my forecast for a multi-year decline in the popularity and fortunes of baseball is actually that, not a description of present conditions tagged with the title of a forecast.

PREDICTING DEPENDENT SOCIAL TRENDS FROM WAVES IN THE STOCK MARKET

I noticed the relationship between the stock market's trends and subsequent social events in the 1970s but did not realize how intimate the relationship was to both popular culture and social history until the 1980s. That is why, to date, we have very little of this type of socionomic forecasting on record. However, what is on the record has an even more accurate history than Elliotters' financial market forecasting. I have made few socionomic forecasts of this type that have *not* worked out, at least in a general sense.

Forecasting a Macroeconomic Trend

The first three years of the 1980s contained the most months of officially recognized economic contraction since the Great Depression bottomed out in March 1933. Stocks' advance on powerful upside momentum in August-October 1982 signaled the start of the recovery. On November 8, precisely at the end of the contraction, *The Elliott Wave Theorist* changed its front page summary from RECESSION IN PROGRESS to RECOVERY BEGINNING, stating flatly, "The stock market has given a powerful signal: the current very deep recession is ending." The January 10, 1983 issue announced RECOVERY UNDERWAY, which was then amended to ECONOMIC BOOM on March 7. This forecast was based on one thing: an understanding of the *degree* of the upturn in the stock market. The start of a bull market of Cycle degree implied a long period of economic expansion. What indeed began the very next month was the longest uninterrupted economic expansion since 1961-1969.

This forecast also maintained historical consistency with the developing long-term wave structure shown in Chapter 5. For example, because the expected bull market was specifically to be Cycle wave V of Supercycle wave (V), it would be the cousin to Cycle wave V of Supercycle wave (III), i.e., the 1920s. That is why in April 1983, when *The Elliott Wave Theorist* reiterated that "a period of economic stability has just begun," it added that its onset had a "parallel with late 1921."[5]

As for the ultimate *end* of the new long-term expansion, the December 1985 issue explained that my approach toward identifying it would be the same:

> We should keep the ultimate probability of an economic crash and financial calamity in mind, but it is still *too early* to prepare for it. Legions of super bears have warned of impending monetary collapse, imminent full-scale banking crises, and so forth for years. Although they continue to warn that such events could occur "out of the blue," "at any time," and "without warning," *history shows that a substantial decline in the stock market has always provided an early warning to such conditions. As long as the stock market is trending upward, there is no reason to harbor such fears.*[6]

Conventional economists, in contrast, had no means by which to predict a long expansion, much less comment on its position within the multi-decade trends of the U.S. economy.

Forecasting Macroeconomic Nuance

Fifth waves are weaker than third waves, both in terms of their intramarket ("technical") performance and their extramarket ("fundamental") results. This simple truth has immense value in applied forecasting. Chapter 7 presented some useful intramarket comparisons. This section covers some extramarket comparisons.

The idea that there is a difference in quality between the macroeconomic trends that manifest from a *third* wave and those that manifest from a *fifth* wave has been a part of the Wave Principle for twenty years. Our 1978 book, *Elliott Wave Principle,* described third waves as "wonders to behold" as they deliver on the promise of rising stocks with "increasingly favorable fundamentals." In contrast, "the fifth of the fifth [wave] will lack the dynamism that preceded it." This description is useful because contrasting periods of economic performance can confirm or contradict a wave interpretation. However, it can also be the basis for *forecasting the quality of economic trends.* For example, by labeling the March 1942 to February 1966 bull market wave III, Frost and I in 1978 established the extramarket vitality of the 1950s and early 1960s as a standard that the forecasted wave V bull market would not surpass. *The Elliott Wave Theorist* reiterated the expected relationship between the two periods with this description in the August 1983 report on the upcoming "superbull market":

This fifth wave will be built more on unfounded hopes than on soundly improving fundamentals such as the U.S. experienced in the 1950s and early 1960s. And since this fifth wave, wave V, is a fifth within a larger fifth, wave (V) from 1789, the phenomenon should be magnified by the time the peak is reached.[7]

This is an unusually specific forecast. The very idea of commenting on the relative strength of a projected multi-year recovery is so unusual that no economist has ever attempted anything of the kind. Once you understand that economic trends fit the overall Elliott Wave structure, you can understand how I could presume to do it. How has this prediction fared?

Observe from Figure 15-4 that each of the two great post-Depression expansions accompanied a bull market in stocks that has lasted 24 years, from 1942 to 1966 in the first instance and from 1974 so far through now (1998) in the second. The percentage gain in the DJIA over the course of the latter has been *55% greater* (so far) than over that of the former. On that basis alone, one might assume that wave V should have produced a stronger economy than wave III. On the contrary, the progress and foundation of wave V have failed to measure up to those of wave III to a glaring extent, exactly as forecast. Figures 17-6 contrasts the economic strength of wave III vs. wave V through June 1998. Figure 17-7 highlights the difference in GDP between the latter half of both waves. Combining the GDP and Industrial Production figures, we may generalize that the economic power of wave V has been 62% of that of wave III.

To grasp the full measure of the underlying weakness of wave V's "fundamentals," one must look beyond economic figures to the corporate, household and government balance sheets that underlie production. Figure 17-8 shows the glaring contrast between waves III and V in eight such measures. Add to these the remarkable fact that at the end of wave III, the U.S was a net *creditor,* while today, near the end of wave V, the U.S. is a *debtor* of unprecedented scope, owing a record $1.3 trillion more to foreigners than it is owed.

The forecast included this phrase: "The phenomenon should be magnified by the time the peak is reached." In other words, the economic expansion would wane even further as wave ⑤ of V progressed and further as wave (5) of ⑤ progressed. True to expectation, the economic expansion has slackened further in the latter stages of wave V. Real GDP growth has been 21% *less* so far in the 1990s during wave ⑤ than in the 1980s during wave ③.

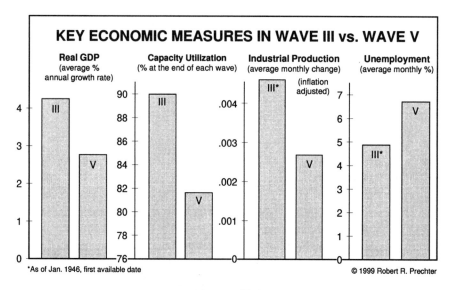

Figure 17-6

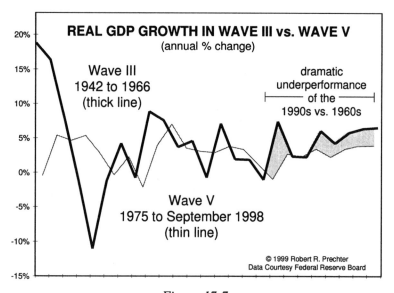

Figure 17-7

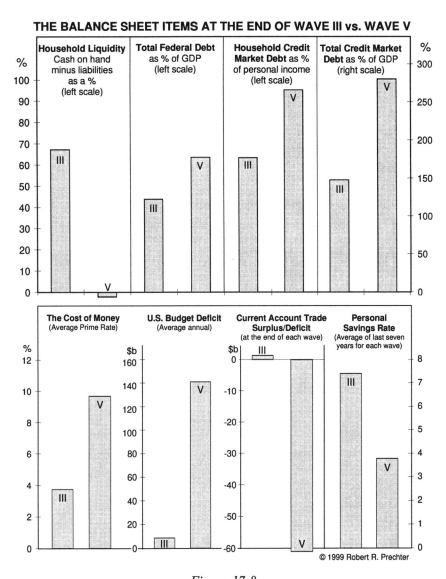

Figure 17-8

The juxtaposition of sky-high expectations (as represented by the highest stock market dividend valuation of all time) and the actual persistent slowing of economic growth is a revelation about the immense strength of social optimism near a fifth wave peak as compared to its inability to produce commensurate real results.

An objective contrast of the quality of the macroeconomic and fiscal aspects of waves III and V shows that wave V has been a weaker performance in terms of *every relevant measure*. Yet probably because background conditions since 1982 have been so much better than those in the *1970s*, conventional observers miss this very important long-term distinction. In contrast, the Wave Principle provides the basis for a profound insight regarding the relative character of the economic environment of the 1980s and 1990s. What's more, it is available not only as a useful latter-day observation (which even today is utterly lacking in current conventional economic discourse) but as a *prediction*, made fifteen years ago.[8]

Forecasting a Specific Monetary Trend

The spiraling inflation of the 1970s finally culminated in January 1980. In its final year, dozens of experts, including economics professors, congressmen, senators, cabinet members, scientists, institute spokesmen and even the president of the United States, specifically predicted that gasoline would reach $2 to $3 a gallon, both inevitably and soon.[9]

Such luminaries, needless to say, are usually unqualified in any predictive methodology to forecast commodity prices, yet such facts never seem to impose an impediment to issuing unqualified opinions. Had these particular forecasters expressed precisely the opposite sentiments, they would have been correct. It is now twenty years later, and gasoline still has not reached those forecasted prices. In fact, the inflation-adjusted cost of gasoline today is the lowest in decades. The true meaning of this blizzard of prognostications calling for higher prices is that they reflected the extremity of the emotional trend and therefore signaled the *end* of the rise in gasoline prices.

One forecaster did take a different view, right in the heat of the intense panic over inflation. As far as we know, there is not a single comparable commentary from that time. This is a remarkable fact given that there are thousands of forecasters of monetary trends.

In December 1979, *The Elliott Wave Theorist* spelled out its expectations for the major sea change that was at hand. *Commodities* (now *Futures*) magazine published my comments in its January 1980 issue. Here is an excerpt:

The incredible conjunction of "fives" in different markets [gold, silver, interest rates, bonds, and commodities] all seem to point to the same conclusion: *The world is about to begin a phase of general disinflation* [i.e., decelerating inflation]. As I see it, a pattern of several disinflationary years leading to a deflationary trend later on would be a perfect scenario for the Elliott outlook for stocks. A gradual disinflation would create an optimistic mood in the country and lead to the conclusion that we may have finally licked the inflation problem. This sentiment would support a bull market in stocks for several years until the snowballing forces of deflation began to take over. At that point, a major deflationary crash would be impossible to avert, and the Grand Supercycle correction would be underway.

As you can see in Figure 17-9 and 18-3, the inflationary trend that had accelerated for 13 years ended abruptly that very month. Indeed, the above paragraph spelled out ahead of time, just weeks before the reversal of trend, the experience of the past nineteen years. It may also spell out the next experience as well, but that remains to be seen.

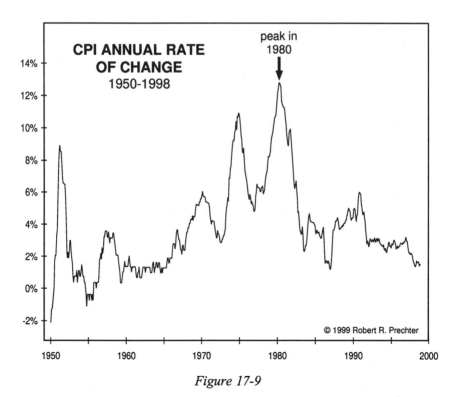

Figure 17-9

There were additional nuances to this forecast that you are welcome to review in Chapter 14 of *At the Crest*, which also attempts to forecast the next macro-monetary event. As with the economic outlook, monetary forces are part of the Elliott wave continuum, so the termination of each phase always has inescapable implications concerning the next one.

Forecasting Peace

Given the Elliott wave outlook in 1982 for a Cycle degree bull market, which portended an increasingly gentle social atmosphere, *The Elliott Wave Theorist* made this assertion on October 6, 1982:

> The confirmed status of the long-term trend of the stock market has tremendous implications. It means[, for instance], *no international war for at least ten years*.

That forecast was both comforting and accurate.

Forecasting the Fortunes of National Leaders

Watching the precision with which the level of presidential popularity had tracked the Dow and its rate of change, I began attempting to anticipate the fortunes of presidents of the United States. Below are excerpted summaries of my three forecasts to date, followed by the outcome.

Ronald Reagan

January 5, 1987

> Politically speaking, President Reagan will almost certainly survive the Iran "Contra"versy. His "Teflon" (a slick surface) coating, to which the press continually refers and off of which all potential difficulties slid until 1986's fourth wave correction, is simply the popular goodwill provided by a bull market. (Contrast that to what bear market presidents Hoover, Nixon and Carter experienced.) Given the Elliott Wave outlook for the stock market going into 1988, the Teflon will undoubtedly return, and President Reagan (assuming he lives through his term) will eventually exit as the most loved president in U.S. history.

Result: Reagan survived the controversy. His exit in January 1989 coincided with the top quarter in 1980s GDP growth, which was the lagging byproduct of the 1980s bull market. The last sentence above was hyperbolic, but when Reagan finally rode into the sunset, the headline in the (admittedly partisan) *Wall Street Journal* in a December 1989 article crediting him with the death of communism read, "Man of the Decade? Man of the Century!" Reagan is easily the most revered president since Kennedy and the most respected since Roosevelt.

George Bush

Chapter 16 recounts the extremely high public approval ratings that George Bush enjoyed in his first year of office. Nevertheless, with Republicans having upon his election won 21 of the 34 presidential elections (a Fibonacci 61.8%) since it first fielded a candidate in 1856, it was apparently time for the GOP to find itself on the losing side of the ratio.

July 27 and September 28, 1990:

EWT is already on record as forecasting a collapse in George Bush's popularity from the highest ratings ever for a President to a level that will ensure the impossibility of his reelection in 1992. Over the remainder of his term, look for a persistent, unrelenting change in the general assessment of his performance, which increasingly will be seen as inadequate, and eventually as downright lousy. There are only 2 1/3 years until the next election. Bush's approval rating remains at historically high levels. Regardless, I am more than willing to retain this radical forecast.

July 31, 1992

...George Bush will lose the election, as predicted by *The Elliott Wave Theorist* when he sported a 89% (91% according to one poll) popularity rating just one year ago.[10] At this juncture, with Bush's approval rating at 34% (having declined from one Fibonacci number to another), it appears that Bill Clinton, the Doonesbury candidate, will win in November.

October 30, 1992

As late as last July, 69% of portfolio managers polled by *Barron's* predicted a Bush victory, only 9% a Clinton victory (22% called for Perot). Regardless of the outcome of Tuesday's vote, EWT's forecast on this issue illustrates the value of the Wave Principle particularly well. Three years ago, and even six months ago, there was literally no one in print predicting a loss or even a close race for George Bush in the 1992 presidential election. Top-level Democrats, you may recall, refused even to run, because George Bush was believed to be unbeatable. That's the main reason why Governor Bill Clinton finds himself with a strong shot at the White House.

Forecasting like this can be worth quite a bit if you place bets with Ladbroke's in London. But it could mean everything to the right politician. Clinton has numerous negatives (earning the nickname, "Slick Willie"), but a top-name Democrat running from the start with confidence would have been a shoo-in.

With the S&P having rallied in the past three weeks almost back to its all time high, Bush could still beat Clinton, but if he does, he'll wish he hadn't. Richard Nixon won the 1972 election at a nearly identical market juncture, and two years later, he was forced by scandal to resign.

Result: George Bush had taken office at the high quarter in the S&P's earnings per share. He exited a few quarters past the end of the biggest drop in earnings since the 1940s, which was a consequence of the three-year bear market (as reflected by the Value Line index; see Figure 16-3) from 1987 to 1990. Bush, the most popular president *ever* a year and a half earlier, lost the election. The winner was the man who ten out of eleven portfolio managers predicted would lose and who *The Elliott Wave Theorist* predicted "will win in November."

Bill Clinton

December 2, 1994

The Nixonian parallel is playing out closely. The guideline of alternation dictates the difference this time around. While it was the liberal press that exploited Nixon's weaknesses, today it is the conservative press that is exploiting Bill Clinton's weaknesses. Even after the massive Democratic party defeat [in 1994], however, almost no one entertains the idea that Clinton might not make it to 1996. Yet, pressures will soon build that could force Clinton out of office. The main social forces keeping the Clintons' various scams and affairs from full disclosure have been the cooperation of mostly sympathetic media (which in the U.S. have ignored the stories that make headlines in Europe), and a still mostly benevolent public mood as reflected by a high Dow Jones Industrial Average.

September 1, 1995

As for the political arena, though only sixteen months remain in the presidential term, *The Elliott Wave Theorist* remains on record forecasting the removal from office of President Clinton, probably by impeachment or resignation, but at least by vote, as a result of these same forces. Public heroes are of their times, and their images become vulnerable when the wind changes.

December 1, 1995

After the correction had ended in late 1994, Clinton's approval rating was down near 40%, and even some Democrats were publicly denouncing his policies. In February, *The Wall Street Journal* noted that the presidency was in "free fall." Since then, however, Clinton has charged back with a Teflon coat that would make Ronald Reagan envious. His approval rating is at 52%, an 18-month high. The social mood controls the image of the social leader. In this case, the mood is sky-high, and his image is the recipient of its benefits. When the bear market begins, all of this will change, and the atmosphere will become like that of 1973 when the American Civil Liberties Union was running ads explaining "How To Impeach President Nixon." When the trend turns down, the White House press corps will become as thirsty for blood as it was in 1973 and 1974.

July 28, 1996

As one headline noted, "Character Bullets Are Bouncing Off Clinton." ...As outrageous as our outlook sounds today with Clinton leading Dole in the polls by an all-time record amount as recently as May (a gap that historically no challenger has been able to close), we still expect that the bear market in public mood will change President Clinton's Teflon to Velcro and cause his downfall, probably before the November election.

November 1, 1996

The Elliott Wave Theorist inaccurately forecast four years ago that a falling stock market would make Clinton an unpopular president. We were wrong about Clinton because we were wrong about the stock market. ...This situation is a replay of 1972, when an incumbent, supported by a social euphoria reflected by all-time highs in the Dow Jones Industrial Average, won in a landslide. He was then hounded out of office less than two years later. The public's lack of interest in Whitewater, the travel office scandal, Filegate, campaign finance violations, Bimbogate, Vince Foster's death, etc., has a flustered Dole asking, "Where is the outrage in America?" Pundits assure us that "character is a dead issue" in 1996, which it is, for now. A recent NBC poll says that 73% of Americans feel it is more important for a President to understand their problems ("feel their pain") than to be of high moral and ethical character....Dole can console himself with the fact that he won't be in the White House when the market turns down and the public's outrage is unleashed. When that happens, there will be an acute interest in the Clintons' dirty laundry.

...We are so near the crest of this historic bull market that we also predict that Clinton will be forced out of office. The degree of the bear market further suggests that the scandal that will oust him will dwarf anything in the history of U.S. presidential politics. One of his terms may not be in office; it may be in jail.

January 31, 1997

According to a Gallup poll, Bill Clinton is the most admired man in the country. His approval rating has risen past 60%, its highest level ever. *USA Today* celebrated his inauguration by publishing an entire section on the President's upcoming term. As one would expect with the Dow so close to its all-time high, most Americans are satisfied with their lives and optimistic about their children's futures. Clinton keeps saying he will model his second term on that of Theodore Roosevelt. We think the analogy could turn out to be more accurate than he realizes. Roosevelt's second term was rocked by the crash of 1907. While Roosevelt served his term out, Clinton will find it much harder to do so, as negative social moods are a natural chemical for ripening scandals, and the taste for them.

January 30, 1998

What are the odds that any president will be forced from office? Out of [41 previous] U.S. presidents, only Richard Nixon was forced from office, placing 40-to-1 odds on any such expectation. Yet even before Clinton was elected, our working analogy for whoever did win the office was the presidency of Richard Nixon....The Nixonian analogy has been working out even more closely than we imagined. Like Nixon, Clinton survived and then thrived in his first term by deftly riding a wave of positive mass emotion. Nixon's approval rating topped out at 67% within a month of his second inauguration in January 1973, when the Dow hit a record high of 1,051.69. Clinton's Gallup poll rating hit a high of 62%, also within days of his second inauguration. From the January 1973 high, the market began a two-year fall of 45%, and scandal slowly engulfed the Nixon White House. The first year of Clinton's second term was far better than Nixon's, although near the lows of last April's correction, an AP story did make the first reference to a "Watergate echo," noting "similarities" linking "Washington's atmosphere in the spring of 1997 to the spring of 1973." For the most part, however, it was smooth sailing by a "brilliant politician." Last summer's Whitewater hearings lacked the drama and public fascination of the Watergate hearings in the summer of 1973 because the stock market was still trending upward. Key to our fledgling social science is that Clinton's perceived dexterity in avoiding outrage last year paralleled the market's run to record highs on August 6 (DJIA) and December 5 (S&P) 1997, driving Clinton's popularity to another high in September....The problem Clinton faces in this regard is that the public's mood has enjoyed a rocket ship ride since 1994, and its outlook on stocks (34% per year for the next decade, according to polls) reflects that fact that Americans expect their mood and speculative fortunes to continue waxing at historical-record speed. Anything less will disappoint. Anything less, we would add, is inevitable. The critical factor for Clinton is therefore not if, but when it happens. Andrew Jackson survived personal scandals as he negotiated his way through Cycle wave V of (I) in the 1830s, a cousin of today's Cycle wave V of (V). It was his successor, Martin van Buren, who rode the downwave and suffered deep unpopularity as a result. Clinton could survive politically if the bull market were to continue through his term. However, we see that as so unlikely that we stick with our original forecast for the ultimate outcome.

Naturally, many observers feared that market weakness would *result* from the situation: "An escalating scandal could trap stocks," says one article; "Clinton's Problems Could Bring Damage to Markets," says another. These efforts to gauge stocks' prospects based on the president's popularity are misguided. The market will do what it will, and social events will follow. The latest scandal's heat is a *result* of five months of corrective psychology. The causality is actually the inverse of the way these newspaper comments read. In fact, as the ink dried on them, the market began a rally, revealing once again that *it* is in charge, not the scandal. If the market soars again, the public is likely to retain a positive image of Clinton no matter what investigators uncover. If the stock market suffers a significant setback, it will reflect a social mood change toward dissatisfaction, and the strongest pillar of support for the president will give way.

July 31, 1998

Yesterday, *USA Today* called Monica Lewinsky's immunity deal on Tuesday a "*seismic shift*" in the legal and political pressure on the White House. We would apply the same term to what is happening in the stock market. Like the stock market, the Clinton team has used every stall tactic in the book. Their fortunes are linked, and both have run out of time.

Result: President Clinton has become the second U.S. president in history to be impeached. His behavioral history had provided the information necessary to identify his area of vulnerability. Then, all it took to trigger this fallout was a 20% drop in the DJIA (from July 20 to October 8) and a 30% drop in the average stock, as represented by the Value Line index. As far as I am concerned, this outcome is sufficient to demonstrate the value of an insight provided by the socionomic approach.

Even the weekly sequence of events has reflected the sociological dynamic. Clinton avoided political trouble for years until the 1998 stock market setback, which was the biggest since 1990. Congress finally acted on *October 8*, the exact day of the bottom in stock prices, voting 258 to 176 in favor of an impeachment inquiry. This set machinery in motion that could not be stopped, so despite the subsequent full recovery of the blue chip averages to previous highs, Congress finally impeached Clinton on Saturday, December 19, but with dramatically waning enthusiasm. The voting margins on the four articles of impeachment were 228/221/205/148 to 206/212/229/285, averaging 200.5 to 233. The voting averages on the two articles that passed were 224.5 to 209, much less than the voting margin of October 8. This difference reflects the waning of negative mood forces as reflected by the stock rally. As of December 20, the S&P Composite index has made a new all-time high, *and Clinton's popularity has reached 73%, also an all-time high.* In other words, despite everything else, *the stock market and the economy are in complete control of his public image.* Knowledge about his flawed character and behavior count for nothing against that background. Paul Gigot asks in *The Wall Street Journal*, "Why is lying less offensive in the 1990s than it was in the 1970s?"[11]

Virginia Postrel asks in *Reason*, "How is it that Bill Clinton is holding at about 60 percent support in public opinion polls — a lot better than he has done in a presidential election — while the political establishment sees him as an utter disgrace? It has been the year's great mystery."[12] Contrast the 1973-1974 bear market with the 1990s bull market, and you will see the answer to these mysteries.

It cannot be stressed strongly enough that the popularity of leaders, whether Reagan, Bush, Clinton or ones to come, is a direct reflection of social mood, which is governed independently and unconsciously by co-operating limbic systems. Character, morality, policies and events are meaningless to this portion of the brain. It does not reason; it generates feeling. It is fortunate for socionomics that the Clinton saga is so dramatic, as it demonstrates clearly that sociometers such as stock prices and presidential popularity move together even when events that conventional reasoning would assume are contrary to those trends are of historic proportion.

The main point with respect to socionomics is not whether the social image of these various public figures is *true*, but its *timing*. *Secretly immoral or incompetent public figures are protected by bull market psychology regardless of the facts, and truly upstanding or talented public figures are ravaged by an emerging bear regardless of the facts.*

A Forecast for Basketball

In the middle of the 1996-1997 basketball season, Peter Kendall of Elliott Wave International wrote a detailed socionomic study of the 100-year history of professional basketball and forecasted a dramatic reversal for the fortunes of the profession. Said Kendall:

> This examination of [basketball's] history shows the dominant influence of social mood on an American sport. The game's structure, rules and fortunes have developed in a manner that is totally consistent with the ebb and flow of the bull market in stocks.[13]

The 1997-1998 season and climax were euphoric, rivaling baseball's of 1991. "We were allowed up to Olympus,"[14] said *The Wall Street Journal* about Michael Jordan's performance in the final game.

Just a few months since that time, as I prepare this book, a major portion of the 1998-1999 season has been canceled. This action is the result of a strike that developed as a consequence of the social mood retrenchment (as reflected by the stock market decline) that ended in October. The cancelation is a first-time event in the half-century history of the

National Basketball Association. It is costing players, retailers, arenas and cities millions of dollars per missed game. This reversal is not unlike a crash from the pinnacle in a financial market. In December, the women's American Basketball League, which was formed in 1996, folded. Team owners who read Kendall's report had one full season to sell out gracefully before the debacle. Owners of Nike stock, which Kendall specifically cited as a short sale, had two months to sell, as the stock topped at 75 in February 1997 and has since fallen to 30. "How," asks the *Atlanta Journal & Constitution*, "could a business that brings in $2 billion [per year] have reached the point of self-destruction?"[15] The answer is, because it reached a pinnacle.

Whether this reversal in basketball's fortunes is the start of the long decline that Kendall envisions remains to be seen. Once again, however, the socionomic approach appears to have provided a most interesting insight into a unique situation.

APPLYING SOCIONOMICS TO INDIVIDUAL EXPERIENCES IN THE SOCIAL REALM

Individuals who become the focus of public adoration can survive the inevitable cooling of public acclaim if they understand that the immediate maintenance of their fame and social efficacy rests less on their actions than on public attitudes. Napoleon said quite accurately, "While my star is rising, nothing can stop me; while my star is falling, nothing can save me."[16] I do not know why he came to that conclusion, but a public person can reach it much easier if he knows about the Wave Principle.

Anticipating the Peak in a Public Persona from its Waves

Financial gurus are a social phenomenon like pop stars, which makes their fates somewhat forecastable. My knowledge that person and persona are different saved me from taking too seriously the market guru "round trip" that I experienced in the 1980s. I knew exactly what was happening at the time and even plotted the path and position of my "star." Figure 17-10 shows the monthly total of active subscriptions to *The Elliott Wave Theorist* in the 1980s. As wave 5 of the advance began to slow, I knew that the end of the ride was near. One day in September 1987, about twenty reporters with notepads and cameras crowded into a small hotel room in New York City to hear what the guru had to say. Although anyone else in that position would have used that scene as an opportunity for massive public-

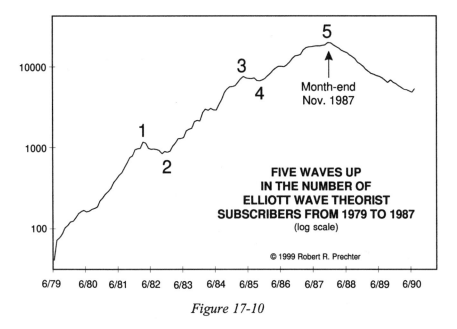

Figure 17-10

ity, I decided to do the opposite. I gave worthless, noncommittal answers to every question, and soon the room was empty. I didn't want my persona to have to fall from an even higher plane than it had already achieved. Yet that still was not quite the peak. Less than a month later, after being bullish since the 1984 low, I turned bearish on October 5, 1987, at the top of a rally less than 90 points from that year's high. Many papers, including *The New York Times,* reported the change. In October and November, reporters called ceaselessly and even parked their vans out on my street. Several people reported to me a rumor that Air Force One had landed on a nearby highway. These events were even stronger evidence of a top in my persona's fortunes. My subscriptions continued to reach new all-time highs through November.

In the midst of this frenzy, I foreshadowed the change with this comment to *USA Today*, published October 9: "There will be times when people will focus in on my 70 percent record for good calls...and there will come a time that people will focus on the bad calls. "[17]

Hoping to back out of the situation with the least personal damage, I suggested a new guru, Elaine Garzarelli, in my November 2 issue.[18] Upon plotting the first downtick on the graph in January 1988, I immediately ceased booking new speeches and media appearances, honoring only commitments for that year that were already made.

Sure enough, despite the fact that 1988 was one of my best forecasting years,[19] some members of the media had had enough of Prechter and began to attack the persona that their colleagues had overinflated. Some media people decided that my sell recommendation of October 5, which was the highest-level sell of any monitored advisor, was not good enough. According to them, I should have specifically predicted 900 points down in two weeks, and anything short of that was failure. The star fell, as it was destined to do, being a product of social mood and focus, which are as fleeting as limbic whims. Garzarelli became the new temporary hero. Then, just as economics follow markets and "fundamentals" follow mood, I entered a long period of relatively poor forecasting.[20]

Calling Reversals for Public Icons on the Basis of Extreme Events

Even though one may not have charts of superstars' waves handy, sometimes events are so extreme as to serve as a top signal. However, just because someone receives an award does not mean that his persona is peaking, and just because he is the subject of a negative article does not mean that his persona is bottoming. To serve as such a signal, an event must truly be an extreme social assessment of value.

I have made two forecasts on this basis. In 1992, Elaine Garzarelli's image was so attractive that she began appearing on television in panty hose commercials. On January 31, 1992, I presented the following assessment of her persona:

> Based on the typical progression, I would conclude that 1992 will witness the peak in her heroic public image, and the media will begin to shift focus toward some of her errors. It is the same natural flow of social psychology that produces bull and bear markets.

Within a few months, the press savaged her money management results, and her firm let her go.

Chapter 15 discussed the wave positioning of pop music superstars. Michael Jackson enjoyed a long superstardom, which led to an extreme event that signaled the reversal of his persona. Here is my assessment from March 29, 1991:

> It would be reasonable to assume that the astounding value of the contract that Mr. Jackson signed with Sony on March 19, as noted in the article that follows, is a sign of a peak in his valuation.

USA TODAY
March 21, 1991

Jackson hits billion-dollar note

Michael Jackson and Sony signed a partnership deal Tuesday that Sony says is worth a potential $1 billion to him.

"A national treasure" is how Columbia chairmen Jon Peters and Peter Guber describe Jackson.

The planet's top star gained unprecedented success, first with 1982's *Thriller*, which sold 40 million copies to become history's best seller, then with 1987's *Bad* (25 million copies). [21]

Within a year of that event, Jackson's image began slipping. Reviews of his records became mixed to critical, and his sister ridiculed him in public. That was wave A down. Then came a wave B bounce, when Jackson performed for the Super Bowl halftime show in January 1993. By the end of that year, his image was collapsing in a powerful wave C. The list of indignities that year is stunning. He was accused of child molestation. An estranged sibling and fired former employees (paid to appear on tabloid TV shows) were alleging conduct suggestive of guilt. He was hospitalized with a drug problem. He had to cancel the remainder of a world tour. Two major companies terminated their commercial relationships with him. He was sued for millions by promoters for cutting short his tour. He was sued for millions by two songwriters who claimed he stole their material. A high profile university reneged on giving him a prestigious award. Police ordered pictures of his genitals to verify testimony, and it was rumored that they were being peddled to publications. Certainly his behavior in those months, good or bad, had not *changed*; it was the public's *focus* that changed. Moreover, whether Jackson actually committed wrongdoing that warrants the collapse of his image is irrelevant to the dynamic. Unlike most, the following newspaper comments actually stated his situation quite accurately:

> The self-proclaimed king of pop has enjoyed a lucrative reign, but that kingdom is eroding and in danger of collapse. In rushing to exploit dubious evidence of wrongdoing (Jackson reading *Child* magazine, for instance), the media seem oblivious to the concept of presumed innocence. Is this rush to judgment fair? Probably not, but you can't expect restraint when the stakes are so high and the drama so gripping. A be-

loved musical hero of children is a confessed drug addict and suspected child molester. A global icon may retreat from view forever. Guilty or not, Jackson is a tragedy unfolding. If the boy's story holds up, if a jury convicts him, we'll witness a fall from grace as indelible as Richard Nixon's. Both involve admired men empowered by the trust of millions. No Hollywood scandal compares.[22]

Experiences of mass rejection are never easy for celebrated people. Nevertheless, as a result of understanding the Wave Principle and preparing for the change, I suffered a lot less psychological pain than other former market "gurus." So if you plan to be famous, plot your persona's progress and pay attention to the waves. If you know what is really going on, you will not end up bitter or dead at a young age or pine away your life wishing for a return to former glory. What's more, if you play your cards exactly right, you might be able to engineer a retirement from the fray at the top and be remembered in your peak state forever.[23]

Elliott Wave International has a number of other social forecasts pending. They cover everything from the success of professional basketball to the exercise craze, both of which we expect to reverse trend significantly in coming years. Perhaps we will investigate these areas of social experiences in a number of years to see how they work out.

NOTES

1 "Call it a miracle, or call it a mystery, but black youths shunning tobacco." (1995, August 13). *The Atlanta Journal-Constitution.*

2 Personal letter from R.E. Burt to R. Prechter, October 18, 1990.

3 Either that, or wave 4 is a flat correction. It is actually a too-common aspect of forecasts made by Elliotters that our time targets are too near in the future. I have many times been fooled by how much longer it takes for trends to play out than I anticipate.

4 The November 1, 1991 issue of *The Elliott Wave Theorist* included these additional descriptive words:

> Listen to baseball analyst Don Sutton, being interviewed before Game 3 of the NL playoffs:
>
> *Reporter*: "You normally see these kinds of crowds at college football games in the Southeast. It's hard to believe this is baseball and to see this sort of enthusiasm."
>
> *Sutton*: "Most of the time when people are really revved up and into it, it's from a negative standpoint and not from a positive standpoint. In 28 years of being around baseball, it has been the most remarkable phenomenon I've seen in baseball."
>
> The "tomahawk chop," the "Indian war chant" and "homer hankies" were continually displayed in unison by tens of thousands of people at a time. 40 year olds acted like 20 year olds. Drums beat for weeks, game or no game. People showed up hours early at the ballpark to soak up the supercharged atmosphere of the crowd. These upbeat social rituals directly involved hundreds of thousands of people. Millions were involved indirectly via television. Victory celebrations in Atlanta and Minneapolis (despite sleet) attracted 760,000 people. The victory parade in Atlanta, with floats and 16 bands, attracted the largest crowd ever to flood downtown for any event. As one observer said on TV prior to a game, "It's the Woodstock of sports."

5 Prechter, R.R. (1983, April 6). "A rising tide." *The Elliott Wave Theorist*, Special Report. For the full text, see the Appendix to *Elliott Wave Principle.*

6 As it turned out, I did harbor such fears prematurely. After correctly anticipating the economic contraction of 1990-1991, which followed on the heels of the 1987-1990 bear market (as best reflected by the Value Line index; see inset in Figure 16-3), I ignored rising stock prices thereafter and did not call for the expansion that ensued. This is obviously a psychological failure on my part but not on the part of the approach, which evidenced its continuing validity against my opinion!

7 Prechter, R. (1983, August, 18). "The superbull market of the '80s: has the last wild ride really begun?" *The Elliott Wave Theorist,* Special Report.

8 The multi-decade economic underperformance of the 1980s and 1990s vs. that of the 1950s and 1960s has important implications about the severity of the *next* economic contraction. Further, the underperformance of the rate of the economic expansion since 1932 as compared to that from 1857 to 1929 has even more important implications. For details on both these differences and the resulting outlook, see Chapters 9, 12 and 13 of *At The Crest of the Tidal Wave.*

9 (1986, September 9). *Daily News Digest,* Vol.12, No.45. This publication produced a great list of dire quotes from such personages as Kenneth Arrow, Professor of Economics, Stanford University; Representative John Dingel, D-MI, Chairman, Subcommittee on Energy and Power; James Schlesinger, Secretary of Energy; President Jimmy Carter; Marshall Loeb, *Time* magazine; Leonard Silk, *The New York Times*; Senator Howard Metzenbaum, D-OH; Senator Dale Bumpers, D-AR; and Carter Henderson in the *Bulletin of Atomic Scientists.*

10 This all-time record high approval rating for a president of the United States in the late summer of 1991 coincided with what may have been the most euphorically emotional baseball season ever, as described earlier in this chapter.

11 Gigot, P.A. (1998, August 14). "Woodward and Bernstein lose their fastball." *The Wall Street Journal.*

12 Postrel, V. (1998, December). "The two faces of Bill Clinton." *Reason,* p. 4.

13 Kendall, P. (1996, December 16). "Basketball and the bull market." a Special Report of *The Elliott Wave Theorist.*

14 "Too Good." (1998, June 16). *The Wall Street Journal.*

15 Denberg, J. (1998, December 9). "A League's Fiscal Rift." *The Atlanta Journal-Constitution,* p. E1.

16 Ludwig, E. (1926). *Napoleon.*

17 Shaw, R. and Landis, D. (1987, October 9). "Prechter flees Wall St. for Georgia hills." *USA Today.*

18 The November 2, 1987 issue of *The Elliott Wave Theorist* said this:

> **Garzarelli for Guru**: It has come to light that New York analyst Elaine Garzarelli was blamed by some clients for causing the October 16 crash because she sent out bearish warnings the previous week.... Elaine clearly is bright, she has put in the time and effort to know what she is talking about, and she has the guts to say so. Elaine has my vote for Nu Guru.

That was a pretty good call. The media took to Ms. Garzarelli and focused only on her successes for the next 4½ years.

19 According to the newsletter rating service, *Commodity Traders' Consumer Report*, EWT was the second-best performer in stock market timing that year among all monitored publications.

20 On December 31, 1992, I published an analysis of one larger trend of the popularity of the Wave Principle in terms of my professional efforts, which contains a prediction yet to be fulfilled.[ref: "An application of the wave principle to business." *The Elliott Wave Theorist* special report.]

21 Gunderson, E. (1991, March 21). "Jackson hits billion dollar note." *USA Today*.

22 Gunderson, E. (1993, November 19). "Jackson faces the man in the mirror." *USA Today*.

23 Upon extremely rare occasions, when society is particularly sensitive to their achievements or they themselves are particularly sensitive to the social mood, very talented people have enjoyed comebacks that carry them back to or beyond previous extremes of public glory. However, the path to that position is rarely the same as it was the first time.

Chapter 18:

Thinking Socionomically

Renowned financier Bernard Baruch, who was as close to markets as anyone, saw a connection between economic trends and the herding impulse of animals. He also understood the crucial importance of that knowledge to a correct social analysis:

> All economic movements, by their very nature, are motivated by crowd psychology. Without due recognition of crowd-thinking...our theories of economics leave much to be desired....It has always seemed to me that the periodic madnesses which afflict mankind must reflect some deeply rooted trait in human nature — a trait akin to the force that motivates the migration of birds or the rush of lemmings to the sea.... It is a force wholly impalpable...*yet, knowledge of it is necessary to right judgments on passing events.*[1]

The Irrelevance of Outside Cause to the Self-Organization of Complex Systems, Including Social Systems

Let us revisit the fact, discussed in Chapter 13, that extinctions follow a power law. As Per Bak and his colleagues have discovered, catastrophic events such as asteroids striking the earth are unnecessary to the solution of why there are mass extinctions from time to time. The dynamics of evolution themselves are such that mass extinctions can, and probably do, happen simply as part of the operation of the system. Computer simulations bear out the results of an endogenous dynamic. Bak and Kim Sneppen, when they were at the Brookhaven National Laboratory in the early 1990s, developed an evolutionary model using the basics of Darwin's theory. They found that species, simply interacting with each other, evolved and became extinct in the model according to a power law; there were many small changes, fewer medium-sized ones, and a few huge ones, just as in actual evolution. They did not program asteroid impacts into the computer. Says Bak, "A huge extinction doesn't necessarily imply a corresponding cata-strophic cause."[2] This is a wonderful sentence because what Bak means is that there is no corresponding *outside* cause, which is what I have been saying about finance and macroeconomics for years. Bak and Kan Chen of Simon Fraser University (British Columbia) say as much about the economy in the January 1991 issue of *Scientific American*:

> Conventional models assume the existence of a strongly stable equi-librium position for the economy, whereby large aggregate fluctuations can result only from external shocks that simultaneously affect many dif-ferent sectors in the same way. Yet it is often difficult to identify the reasons for such large-scale fluctuations as the depression of the 1930s. If, on the other hand, the economy is a self-organized critical system, *more or less periodic large-scale fluctuations are to be expected even in the absence of any common jolts across sectors.*[3]

Two studies in particular have destroyed the idea that outside causal-ity is necessary to explain financial markets. Chapter 8 reported on a stock market simulation study from 1987 using a few dozen people at a time that "repeatedly created a boom-and-bust market profile." Chapter 12 reported on the latest stock market simulation study by European physicists Caldarelli, Marsili and Zhang, in which a limited number of participants bet on a currency relationship with "no real information input." Their aim was to observe financial market psychology "in the absence of external factors." Here is what they find with respect to causality:

> In spite of the simplicity of our model and of the strategies of the single participants, and the *outright exclusion of economic external fac-tors*, we...find a market which behaves surprisingly realistically. These results suggest that a stock market can be considered as a self-organized critical system: The system reaches dynamically an equilibrium state char-acterized by fluctuations of any size, *without the need of* any parameter fine tuning or *external driving*.[4]

Says Marsili, "The understanding that we got is that the statistics of price histories in financial markets can be understood as *the result of the internal interaction, and not the fundamental interaction with the external world*."[5] Adds Tony Chapman in reviewing the study, "*The outside world has no influence*, something that might surprise real traders who rely heavily on news from the economic world outside their trading floor."[6] In reviewing this model, the October 1997 *New Scientist* says the same thing about the stock market that Bak says about earthquakes, extinctions and economic contractions: "You don't need a crisis to trigger a financial crash."[7]

There is far more to the process than these tentative comments imply. It is not just the catastrophes that need no outside cause but the *entire process*. As a team member put it, "Our ultra-simplified model has *all* the major characteristics of a real market: bull runs, crashes and mini-crashes."[8]

This phenomenon applies to companies as well, whose structure is social and whose products' success depends upon aggregate human desires. A research team including Stanley and Michael Salinger of Boston University's School of Management has studied fluctuations in corporate success and setback. *New Scientist* states, "The group's results show a *universal pattern of growth* that holds for firms of all types, *whatever business they are in*."[9] This sentence is nearly identical to a hundred I have written over the years. Its sentiment permeates the literature on the Wave Principle.

The Impossibility of Outside Cause with Respect to Social Systems

The studies cited above are important because they show that no outside causes of financial market and macroeconomic behavior are *necessary*. To the extent possible, this book explains something even more important: why there *are not*, and *cannot be*, outside causes of financial, economic and social behavior. Think about it. When dealing with social events, what is an "external shock"? What is an "outside cause"? Other than the proverbial asteroid striking the earth, which presumably might disrupt the NYSE for a couple of days, or the massive earthquake or destructive hurricane that we already know does not affect financial market behavior in any noticeable way, there is in fact, in the social context, *no such thing as an outside force or cause*. Every "external shock" ever referenced in finance is in fact an *internal event*. Trends in the stock market, interest rates, the trade balance, government spending, the money supply and economic performance are all ultimately products of collective human mentation. Human minds create these trends and change both them and their apparent interrelationships as well. It is men who change interest rates, trade goods, create earnings and all the rest. All social events, whether a rise in interest rates, a drop in the stock market, or even a war, are the result of collective human mentation. To suggest that such things are outside the social phenomenon under study is to presume that people do not communicate (consciously or otherwise) with each other from one aspect of their social lives to another.

This is not only an unproven assumption but an absurd one. All financial events, indeed all social movements, are part and parcel of the interactive flux of human cooperation. All such forces are intimately commingled all the time. Yet to the conventional analyst, each is as detached a cause as a cue stick striking a billiard ball. It is this error that so profoundly undermines the conventional approach. As we have seen throughout this book, the Wave Principle shapes the trends in markets, economics, politics, cultural trends, the personas of social heroes and even evolution, implying a universal pattern of growth and decay for all social phenomena.[10] It is time to abandon the idea of outside causality for social mood and action.

The most extreme example that I can think of that could be argued as constituting an outside event that would affect societies is an epidemic or pandemic. After all, they kill thousands or millions of people. How could they fail to be an important social factor affecting mood?

The fact is that epidemics and pandemics seem to hit populations during major negative social mood trends. Perhaps it happens that way because people's psychological constitutions are weaker during bear markets. Perhaps it is because people's personal behavior, whether involving hygiene (as in the time of the plague or in recent years with respect to hypodermic needles used to inject drugs) or sexual promiscuity, is more conducive to spreading disease during social mood retrenchments. Perhaps it is because social mood retrenchment brings economic contraction, which makes people less able to afford the creature comforts that ward off disease and more apt to crowd into smaller, more affordable spaces. Whatever the reason, when we study pandemics of the Dark Ages or the Spanish influenza epidemic that broke out during the bear market of 1917 (which year also saw intense fighting in World War I and the Communist coup in Russia), there always appears to be a bear market in force, and the extent of the epidemic tends to correlate with the size of the setback in mood.[11]

R.N. Elliott observed that markets often travel within parallel trend channels.[12] Take a look at Figures 18-1 though 18-5 and observe how some of the most volatile markets in history, which operated in extremely diverse economic and social conditions, nevertheless traveled paths that reflect this fundamental aspect of collective behavior. These channels contain prices regardless of wars, energy crises, speeches, assassinations, Watergates, Peanutgates, Travelgates, Zippergates, jawboning or the weather. Financial markets, it appears, often know exactly where they are, where they have been, and at least in some respects, where they are going. The events

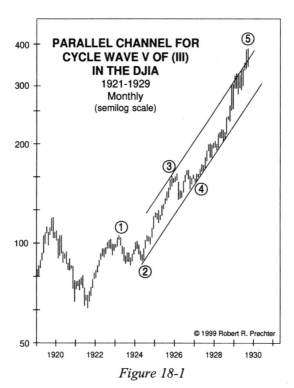

Figure 18-1

Figure 18-2

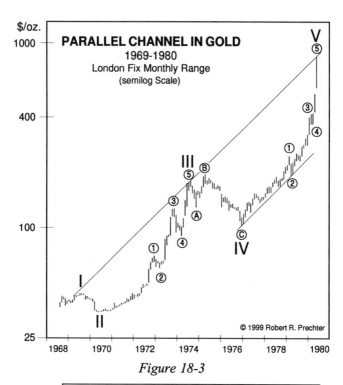

Figure 18-3

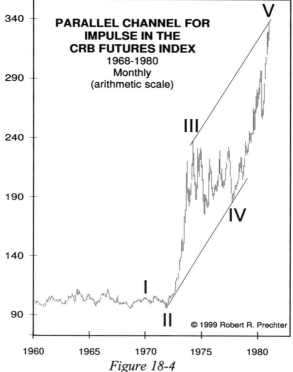

Figure 18-4

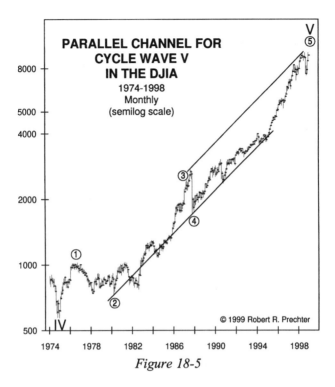

Figure 18-5

of economics, politics and history must mean nothing to them. Conventional views of social causality, chaos, randomness and unpredictability (see Chapters 19 and 20) are incompatible with this observation. The Wave Principle, on the other hand, subsumes it.

For over twenty years and throughout this book, I have argued that economics and politics are acausal to financial and system behavior. The reason is not only that outside causality is unnecessary, as modern studies are proving. It is because outside causality is *impossible* because financial markets are patterned according to the Wave Principle.

The Direction of Social Causality

If social mood is patterned, it cannot be the result of random social events, and there is no basis upon which to suggest that it is somehow the result of social events that are themselves perfectly patterned to produce the Wave Principle, which would require utter event determinism. Yet Chapter 16 shows an intimate connection between social events and mood. Therefore, the only possible direction of causality is the opposite of that popularly assumed. Events do not shape social mood; social mood shapes events. Mass psychological fluctuations are not simply correlated with mankind's actual progress and regress through history, but in fact are their engine. Collective mood shapes the character of social interaction, and thus of resulting actions and events.

The evidence of this fact is continually available. Just the past few months provide several dramatic examples. The financial collapse in Indonesia in October 1997 led to riots in April 1998 and the ousting of a previous popular ruler, Suharto, who had been president for 32 years. The financial collapse in South Korea beginning in October 1997, which brought its stock market to an 11-year low, led to massive labor strikes in April 1998. The collapse in the Russian stock market, the ruble and its government bonds in 1998, has led to "a profound political crisis." Financial uptrend precedes social euphoria, and financial downtrend precedes social crisis.

The Uselessness of News Even to the Clairvoyant

Champions of news causality truly have a fundamental problem, which is that no investor really knows the implication of any piece of news. This fact is hidden by the ease with which financial news writers can retrospectively pull out from the plethora of news on any given day a story that appears to justify whatever market movement occurred. The reverse order of things is not so accommodating. If you could construct a time-machine mailbox that would generate *The New York Times* a full day early but with news about the stock market omitted, you would be just as unable to forecast the next day's market action as if you had nothing at all to read. Riots, peace pacts, summits, earthquakes, destructive hurricanes, price changes in commodities, assassinations, triumphs of statesmanship and political scandals — nothing of this sort has more than a momentary effect on the stock market, much less any predictive value. This week, an economics writer for *The Atlanta Journal-Constitution* said quite accurately, "If history is any guide, the stock market could go either way today in the wake of the U.S. air strikes against Afghanistan and Sudan."[13] Correct! Kudos for an economic writer who bothered to look at the record before opining. (Now go back to Chapter 16 and review how reliably the market, as a thermometer of the social mood that triggers such events, tends to fall *prior* to military activity.)

In August, *The Atlanta Journal-Constitution* ran an article that reviewed a 42-year history of surprise news and the stock market entitled, "Identifying Sell-off Trigger Difficult."[14] That is to say, it is difficult *even in retrospect* to make any connection between dramatic surprise events and what the market does. The biggest decline in the period studied was the 1987 crash, about which the article quite accurately says, "*Scholars still debate the reasons why.*" Imagine scholars endlessly debating about things that history proves have no validity! That is what so many scholars do because their ideas of financial market causality, rationality and efficiency are all wrong, yet they see no alternative.

Once you understand that news is not causal, that even if you got it in advance, you could not forecast the stock market, then you realize that there is no satisfactory news-related explanation for the market's behavior on Black Monday, last Tuesday or next Thursday, either, or on any market day at all, or any week, month, year, decade or century. It does not take a dedicated market student long to observe the acausality of news to the stock market. A socionomist observes, and more important, *understands*, the reverse causality. As R.N. Elliott said, "At best, news is the tardy recognition of forces that have already been at work for some time and is startling only to those unaware of the trend."[15]

Reasoning from Conditions to Markets – in Advance

The belief that news affects the market is the lowest level of misunderstanding, and it is the most common. There is a higher level of misunderstanding, which at least pays tribute to the *fact* that the market moves ahead of events. Technicians say that the reason earnings lag stock prices is that smart investors anticipate, or "discount," the future, in other words, guess the future correctly.

While this position is a time-honored and valiant attempt to explain why events lag stock prices, I believe it is false. The idea of the mass of investors possessing near-omniscience about the economic future is difficult to defend. Nor does it explain why in 1928 the market foresaw nothing but blue sky, in 1929 very suddenly foresaw depression, and in early 1930 saw a recovery that never happened.

One might try to make a case that smart investors sell stocks when they get a whiff of trouble in their own businesses. If the economy typically turned before or even coincidentally with stocks, this argument might be plausible. But stocks lead the economy, normally by months. Then there is the problem that when you ask investors what they think, they express no inkling of coming economic changes. At the start of a bull trend, the vast majority is bearish, and at the start of a bear trend, it is bullish.

Because markets are patterned, the concept of near-perfect collective forecasting *must* be false. Otherwise, future events would have to be patterned according to the Wave Principle, and the collective would have to anticipate each nuance perfectly. This is an untenable position.

The truth is that the stock market does not see into the future, as the discounting concept suggests; it reflects instantaneously the *causes* of the future. Optimistic people expand their businesses; depressed people contract their businesses. The results show up later as an apparently "discounted" future. The actions of human beings spurred on by an increasingly ebullient or pessimistic social mood cause earnings to rise or fall. Rising earnings are the fruits of a bull market, and falling earnings are the result of a bear. The same thing is true of political action. Politicians do not turn the tide of a bull or bear market by enacting or abandoning policies. The mass emotional environment, as reflected by the market, forces them at some critical point to act.

Socionomics Reverses the Thinking Process Relating Markets and Events

While knowledge of current events and extramarket conditions has almost no value in predicting the stock market, knowledge about the position of the market can help predict changes in outside conditions. The Wave Principle provides a basis for speculating upon upcoming changes in market trends and therefore the events that result from the social psychology that the trend changes represent. This ability provides an opportunity to prepare for the coming character of events, and sometimes even actual events, before they are realized. It is worth knowing, for instance, that banks were closed by government decree in 1933 shortly after the low of Supercycle wave (IV) and that most of the banks in the country closed in 1857 as well, at the end of Supercycle wave (II). It is unlikely, therefore, that with regard to bank health, the next bear market of Supercycle or larger degree will fail to produce similar results. Most analysts work the other way around. For example, they wait until they have observed widespread bank failures and then declare their bearish meaning for the stock market, which is precisely the opposite of their true implication. With the Wave Principle, we have a tool that allows us to use the pattern of social mood objectively and properly rather than let *it* bend *us* to its design.

A conventional analyst asks, "What will the Fed's actions do for, or to, the stock and bond markets? The socionomist asks, "What will stock and bond market action do for (or to) the reputation of the Fed?" A conventional analyst sees a country's prime minister as standing "at the helm of the economy."[16] The socionomist sees social mood, and thus the market, and thus the economy, as standing at the helm of the prime minister's reputation. A conventional analyst asks how bills in Congress will affect the stock market. The socionomist asks what the stock market says about the kinds of bills that will be introduced and whether they will be passed. A conventional analyst points out that an election was *divisive*. The socionomist says it was *divided*. A conventional analyst says that the outbreak of war will make people fearful and angry. The socionomist says that angry and fearful people are prone to engaging in war. A conventional analyst asks how a federal government tax surplus will help the country. The socionomist asks when it is in the wave progression of social mood that budget surpluses typically occur and forecasts the surplus. A conventional analyst asks what the impact of revised corporate earnings estimates will be on the stock market. The socionomist watches the trend of stock prices and predicts in what direction analysts will revise their earnings estimates. Let us explore some concrete examples of this reversal of roles.

Throughout the 1950s, people built bomb shelters. They were responding to events that had *already happened*, in essence preparing for 1945 a decade late. In 1994, the Smithsonian Institution placed a bomb shelter in its collection as a relic. Observers, conventional analysts all, hailed it as reflecting the beginning of a new era of peace for mankind. What is the true importance of that occurrence as a reflection of social mood? It reflects a complacency common to developing major social mood tops. It suggests to a socionomist that the long-term positive mood trend is nearing an extreme and that worries about warfare will probably soon begin waxing again. Conventional thinkers waste time building shelters when they are unnecessary and then have no shelters when they need them the most. Socionomists do the opposite.

Here is another example. Major market uptrends eventually bring into fashion the recurring belief that market timing is passé and useless, if not counterproductive: "All one needs is good stock selection. Just stay in good stocks, and you will make money *and* be safe." When have we seen this sentiment widely expressed? Answer: 1928, 1968 and 1998. Few made this case in June 1984. No one made this case in December 1974. No one said this in 1932, 1942, 1859 or 1842. What socionomic conclusion can you draw when this opinion is pervasive? *It is a symptom of complacency about the trend of the overall market*, a complacency that people express only very late in uptrends. Now contemplate the kind of irony that we continually observe when thinking socionomically. *It is precisely the position of the stock market in its overall trend that induces people to say that the position of the stock market in its overall trend is irrelevant.* At the bottom of a bear market, *timing* becomes the new philosophy, which assumes its place on the pedestal just when it is actually time to concentrate on holding and selecting stocks.[17] Socionomists can observe and profit from such irony in the marketplace every day; conventional analysts produce irony every day without knowing it.

The Media as Reflectors of Consensus Mood

Socionomics shows why the media must always be wrong in the aggregate when reporting predictions about major social trends. Reporters usually are nonprofessional in the fields they cover, so the feelings of reporters in general mirror those of the public. Reporters often contact financial analysts who express their own feelings about markets, thus reflecting society's consensus feelings. A bullish analyst rarely gets a forum at a major market bottom, and a bear rarely gets one at a major market top. The media's *choice of times to quote* certain professionals typically shows those professionals retrospectively in their worst light.

James Stack of Investech undertook the tedious job of culling market-related articles going all the way back to the 1920s.[18] The resulting chronicle is a tragicomedy of never-ending wrongness. As John Rothchild sums up Stack's conclusions, "When they are predicting anything that involves money, economists, prominent investors and the reporters who quote them haven't been wrong on occasion; *they've been unerringly errant.*"[19] Paul Montgomery of *Universal Economics* and Ned Davis of *Ned Davis Research* have studied the timing of the covers of major news magazines, finding that whenever one of them takes a stand on the stock market, it is invariably an important turn in the other direction that typically lasts years.[20,21,22]

I have noted a sister phenomenon. When trends reach extremes, reporters no longer require the services of financial professionals to express an opinion; the continuation of the trend is so obvious to them that they become convinced that anyone can do it, and they take on the forecasting themselves. Error at such times is guaranteed.

Forecasting Implications of Extremes in the Character of Events

Though events are the result of social mood, even they have some predictive value when they reach extremes. Of course, that value is precisely the opposite of what is typically assumed (see Chapter 19). Baron von Rothschild encapsulated this truth when he said about investing, "Buy when blood is running in the streets." In other words, when things look darkest, it must be a low in mood and therefore a low in stock and bond prices. Here is an example. On November 12, 1857, right at the low of wave (c) of a 22-year bear market of Supercycle degree, a headline in the *Boston Globe* read, "Energy Crisis Looms — World To Go Dark — Whale Blubber Scarce." A few weeks earlier, in October, *Harper's Weekly* made this statement:

> It is a gloomy moment in the history of our country. Not in the lifetime of most men has there been so much grave and deep apprehension; never has the future seemed so incalculable as at this time. The domestic economic situation is in chaos. Our dollar is weak throughout the world. Prices are so high as to be impossible. The political cauldron seethes and bubbles with uncertainty. Russia hangs, as usual, like a cloud, dark and silent, upon the horizon. It is a solemn moment. Of our troubles no man can see the end.[23]

Perhaps no man could "see the end," but it was directly at hand. That month marked a low in stock prices and economic performance that was never breached and from which stock prices soared 3.5 times in value in six years and 47.6 times in 72 years.

The converse is also true. In 1928, the happy character of events and conditions reflected an extreme of positive social sentiment that hinted at a reversal. Similarly, in 1965, after 23 years of bull market, the United States had no war, no shortages, undisputed world power, cheap energy, a happy populace and a productive economy. The spirit of abundance and invincibility was so great that Congress and President Lyndon Johnson initiated the greatest expansion of government-sponsored social programs in history, including Medicare, the Voting Rights Act, Head Start, the Elementary and Secondary Education Act and the Housing and Urban Development Act. The government had launched The Great Society. Was it time to be optimistic or pessimistic?

In 1979, after 13 years of bear market, the U.S. had "uncontrollable" inflation, labor unrest and violence, slipping world power, shortages, expensive energy, stifling regulation, confiscatory taxes and had even lost a war for the first time ever. The Roper organization reported that for the first time in the history of its poll dating back to 1959, Americans rated the future as less promising than the present. President Jimmy Carter lectured the country on its "crisis of confidence." Was it time to be pessimistic or optimistic?

Extremes in conditions at Supercycle degree are even more dramatic. Political events were *scary and dangerous* in the Supercycle degree bear market (in inflation-adjusted terms) of the 1930s and 1940s. They included totalitarian takeovers of vast territory, war on an unprecedented scale, state-directed murders of forty million people, countless atrocities, the invention and deployment of atomic bombs and the annihilation of cities. These events reflected the negative social psychology of a Supercycle degree bear market. *That period also accompanied one of the greatest stock market lift-offs of all time.*

As you can see, an extreme character of social events implies nearness of a trend change in the opposite direction. In this way, social events, when their character is extreme, can be a contributory tool to socionomic forecasting.

Shall we apply this concept to today's environment as we enter 1999? The character of today's social events is as bright as any time in history. Look around and witness how a Supercycle upswing in mood has produced events during this decade that are so positive as to have been previously unimaginable. Officials have pronounced the forty-year-long Cold War officially over; the U.S.S.R. has freed Eastern Europe, creating what *The Wall Street Journal* called "a period of euphoria unequaled in the postwar era"; China appears to be on the long-term road to adopting capitalism and freedom; U.S. political leaders have promised a perpetually balanced Federal budget by constitutional amendment; the U.S. won its first war in 46 years; South Africa ended apartheid three and a half centuries after the Dutch arrival in South Africa and 45 years after its adoption as official government policy; and countless political and religious leaders have reached conciliation after decades, centuries and in some cases millennia of animosity, as listed in the "Peace" section of Chapter 16.

The response of today's conventional analysts to these conditions is as optimistic as it was in the late 1920s. For example, State Department Policy Planner Francis Fukuyama, in his widely praised *New York Times* bestselling book, declares "the end of history as such" because political risks have been obliterated by the global triumph of Western liberal democracy.[24] World officials agree, expressing joy that a new golden age of world peace and prosperity has begun. The public agrees; as a result of all this truly wonderful news, the Consumer Confidence statistic in 1998 approached its highest levels of the past 25 years. The vast majority of citizens, public and private, including all conventional futurists, economists and political analysts, are bullish on the stock market, the economy and the future as far as the imagination can project. However, you, as a reader of this book, have the basis for a more reliable perspective.

Understanding that "bullish" means that things will improve and "bearish" means that things will deteriorate, *are the events described above bullish or bearish?* Events of recent years, as chronicled above, are the *opposite* of the social spectacle of the 1930s and 1940s. Figure 18-6 details the colossal difference in political tone between the results of the Supercycle wave (IV) *bear* market and the results of the Supercycle wave (V) *bull* market. The photographs on the following pages communicate the difference in human terms.

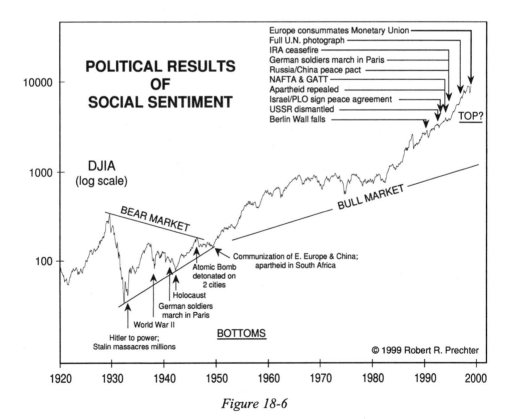

Figure 18-6

As perverse as it may seem, these photos represent an extreme in negative social mood and therefore a time to become increasingly optimistic

Hitler enters Danzig, September 1939

Atomic Bomb, July 1945

Buchenwald, 1945

As perverse as it may seem, these photos represent an extreme in positive social mood and therefore time to become increasingly pessimistic

Peacemaking handshake between
Prime Minister Rabin of Israel and PLO President Arafat

source: The Atlanta Journal-Constitution, 9/93

Historic day for South Africa
End of an era: Races equal under new constitution

source: David Brauchli, AP, 11/18/93

UK and Ireland plan for peace

source: Financial Times, 12/16/93

Pacts mark 'historic' day
BREAKTHROUGH IN RUSSIA All is warmth

source: Associated Press, Jan 1994

'no more war'
Jordan, Israel agree to seek permanent peace

source: USA Today, 7/26/94

A picture-perfect U.N.: 185 leaders side by side

source: Associated Press, 10/23/95

Are the latest events, deeply welcome as they are otherwise, consistent with events that accompany a social-mood bottom or top? Given your answer, should we anticipate an acceleration or long continuance of the trend we have enjoyed or begin anticipating a reversal?

If your answer is the same as mine, then you disagree with (to the nearest percent) *100%* of economists, who conclude that these events have created "favorable fundamentals" that are bullish for the indefinite future. According to *The Wall Street Journal*, 55 out of 55 economists polled in July 1998 say that the odds of a "recession or that the stock market will enter a bearish phase are slim."[25] Adds *The New York Times* on August 15, "not a single Blue Chip economist sees a recession."[26] *Business Week* magazine's August 31, 1998 issue features a cover story on the 21st century economy. A team of reporters and editors "examined every aspect of the economy" and have concluded that "all elements are in place for an era of long-term growth."[27] This conclusion would have been visionary in the fourth quarter of 1974 or 1982, when no conventional economist said it. Should a socionomist change his opinion because every conventional economist and futurist in the country disagrees with it? Chapter 19's discussion of economists' aggregate track record answers that question emphatically. The answer is no, whether our statement of probability (not certainty) turns out right in this particular instance or not.

Events look so good at a major top and so bad at a major bottom that few can envision any trend but a continuation, if not acceleration, of the one that brought them there. The point of this section is to communicate that *that very fact* implies an increased probability of change.

Keep in mind that event extremes are *relative*. Just because times are good does not mean that it must be a top. Similarly, just because times are bad does not mean that it must be a bottom. Both the Renaissance and the Dark Ages lasted a long time. The key, as always, is a proper perspective on the wave structure.

Predicting the Popularity of Socionomics Itself

A socionomist even has the advantage of being able to anticipate changes in the public's perception of his own value and the validity of his work. The reason is that social mood trends correlate with the waxing and waning of interest in such things as the very notion of cycles and waves of social mood. In uptrends, social cycles themselves are increasingly ignored, derided or declared dead as people credit policy makers with the power that brought about the uptrend. At tops, this sentiment is pervasive. For example, in September 1929, the president of the New York Stock Exchange, echoing the sentiments of bank presidents, economists and government officials, said, "It is obvious that we are through with business cycles as we have known them."[28] In 1991, a professor of political economy speaks for his entire profession in saying, "There are very few ideas in macroeconomics that serious economists agree on, but doubting the existence of the Kondratieff [cycle] is one of them."[29] In July 1998, an MIT professor declares that "this expansion will run forever" because we have "policy levers" to "keep the current expansion going."[30] At such times, the idea of social cycles is anathema to conventional thought.

In contrast, when negative social mood waxes and financial and economic changes become volatile, cycles become *de rigueur* as people search for causes of the dramatic events that caught them off guard. One such period was 1929 to 1949. R.N. Elliott was inspired to do his work by the 1929-1932 collapse, publishing books in 1938 and 1946. Nikolai Kondratieff sent his paper, "Long Economic Cycles," to Harvard in 1935. Harvard economics professor Joseph Shumpeter expanded upon the Kondratieff cycle (which he called "the single most important tool in economic forecasting") in his 1939 book, *Business Cycles*.[31] Edward R. Dewey started the Foundation for the Study of Cycles in the 1940s after the U.S. government asked him to explain the causes of the 1929 crash. He and Edwin F. Dakin finished *Cycles: the Science of Prediction* in 1945.[32,33]

Over the years, membership in the Foundation for the Study of Cycles fell when the stock market went up and rose when it corrected. In the 1960s' uptrend, cycles were again passé and interest waned. In the corrective period of the 1970s, both the foundation and the Kondratieff cycle returned to prominence. Books such as *Cycles – The Mysterious Forces that Trigger Events* by Dewey (1971), *The Kondratieff Wave* by Shuman and Rosenau (1972) and *Cycles* by Dick Stoken (1978) were strong sellers, and cycle-oriented financial newsletters flourished. In the 1990s, cycles are once again considered relics of the past. With that background, you should not be surprised to learn that in 1997 and 1998, after 15 years of relentless bull market, the Foundation for the Study of Cycles ceased issuing publications after over half a century of operation.

Why does interest in this subject fluctuate? The answer is that people equate uptrends with predictability and downtrends with unpredictability. The *Harper's Weekly* quote from 1857 includes the phrase, "never has the future seemed to incalculable as at this time." Translation: "The market has been falling for several years." The media constantly characterize market setbacks as injecting "uncertainty" into a picture of the future that presumably was previously as clear as crystal. I am not exaggerating when

I say that this foible is timeless. Just this month, after a three-month de-cline in the Dow and a six-month decline in the Value Line index, *The Wall Street Journal* says, "The prevailing sentiment among investors these days appears to be confusion. And confusion is costly after so many years of *predictability*."[34] Translation: "After going up for years, the market has trended down for several months." If uptrends are so predictable, then why didn't these same investors know that one had ended in April/July and another had already begun six days before the article appeared? The time-less conceit that uptrends are predictable explains why people ignore cycles in uptrends and embrace them in downtrends.

Today, after decades of advance, virtually no one is interested in cycles of human behavior. Once again, the majority believes that the market and the economy are "predictable" and the uptrend will persist because policy makers have engineered social retrenchments out of existence. This belief is a luxury of a neocortex that is not threatened by a limbic system in fear of, or desiring to escape blame for, a serious economic setback. Of course, the extremity of today's bemusement toward the outmoded idea of social cycles is yet another signal of an approaching major social mood reversal and the beginning of a trend back towards a general interest in patterns of social behavior. I hope this book contributes to that trend.[35]

Reverse Forecasting: Inducing Waves from Past Social Events

If society's actions are patterned over five minutes, five hours, five days, five weeks, five years and five decades, as the graphs in this book indicate, they might be patterned over five centuries and five millennia. Indeed, it is my contention that all of history can be understood from the standpoint of waves, and in fact *only* from that standpoint.

Because waves manifest themselves in events, we now have a basis for delving into the past, where no stock market prices have been charted, and using social events and conditions to induce the position of waves. Figure 18-7 is one possible categorization of the historical trends of West-ern culture since Roman times. We have market price data from the year 1690 forward, but the waves prior to 1690 in this depiction are constructed on the basis of social trends and events. The few notes on the illustration hint at the reasons behind my wave labels. In my opinion, Elliott wave patterns can be induced back to the start of the Bronze Age. This kind of analysis can provide a panoramic view of the past, and by implication, of the future as well. There is obviously much more to say on this subject as well, but that will wait for another time.

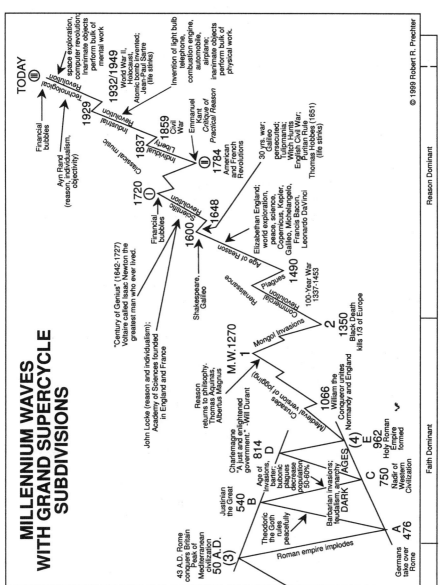

Figure 18-7

© 1999 Robert R. Prechter

NOTES

1 From Baruch's foreword to Mackay's *Extraordinary popular delusions and the madness of crowds.*

2 Bak, P. and Chen, K. (1991, January). "Self-organized criticality." *Scientific American*, pp. 46-53.

3 *Ibid.*

4 Caldarelli, G., *et al.* (1997, December 1). "A prototype model of stock exchange." *Europhysics Letters*, 40 (5), pp. 479-484.

5 *Ibid.*

6 Chapman, T. (1998, January-February). "Speculative trading: physicists' forays into finance." *Europhysics News.*

7 Brooks, M. (1997, October 18). "Boom to bust." *New Scientist.*

8 *Ibid.*

9 Buchanan, M. (1997, November 8). "One law to rule them all." *New Scientist.*

10 The invalidity of outside event causality may apply to more than the social sciences. Formological causality may apply to physical sciences as well, certainly biology.

11 AIDS might appear to be an exception, as this slow-moving epidemic has remained in force during the bull market years of the 1980s and 1990s. However, in inflation-adjusted Elliott wave terms (see Figure 16-6), a bear market pattern of Grand Supercycle degree began in 1966. The advance since 1982 is just subwave b. Moreover, during this advance, the epidemic has waned significantly, as AIDS today is no longer in the top ten causes of death in the United States, the rate halving in 1997 alone. [ref: Kim, L. (1998, October 8). "Fewer lives lost to AIDS." *The Atlanta Journal-Constitution*, p. A1.]

12 Sometimes channels manifest themselves on arithmetic scale, sometimes on semilog scale. They most commonly involve a line that connects the ends of waves two and four.

13 Walker, T. (1998, August 21). "Impact of air strikes on stocks uncertain." *The Atlanta Journal-Constitution*, p. E1.

14 Walker, T. (1998, August, 6). "Identifying sell-off trigger difficult." *The Atlanta Journal-Constitution*, p. F3.

15 Elliott, R.N. (1946). *Nature's law.*

16 Sakarui, J. (1998, July 10). "Japan goes with veteran at helm of wayward economy." *The Atlanta Journal-Constitution.*

17 On October 6, 1982, with the Dow in the 900s, *The Elliott Wave Theorist* said, "This bull market should be the first 'buy-and-hold' market since the 1960s. The experience of the last 16 years has turned us all into traders, and it's a habit that will have to be abandoned."

18 James Stack, Investech Research, Whitefish MT.

19 Rothchild, J. (1998). *The bear book.*

20 Davis, N. (1992). "Being right or making money." *Ned Davis Research Inc.*

21 Montgomery, P. (1986, March 8). "Volcker part III: The Godfather." And (1990, October 11). "Magazine covers and real estate." *Universal Economics.*

22 Montgomery, P. (1995, April 6). Presentations. "The logical primacy of immaterial mental states in the price structure of investments...." And (1996, May 17). "Economic theory and technical analysis...."

23 "The lesson of the day." (1857, October 10). *Harper's Weekly.*

24 Fukuyama, F. (1992). *The end of history and the last man.*

25 Ford, C.M. (1998, July 7). "Survey sees brunt of Asian crisis hitting U.S. soon." *The Wall Street Journal,* p. A2.

26 Nasar, S. (1998, August 15). "Cloudy blue skies." *The New York Times.*

27 "The 21st century economy." (1998, August). *Business Week.*

28 Source unavailable.

29 Angrist, S.W. (1991, August 8). "Believers in one wave theory see U.S. in deep trough soon." *The Wall Street Journal.* (quoting Allen Meltzer, professor of political economy and public policy at Carnegie-Mellon University.)

30 Dornbush, R. (1998, July 30). "Growth forever." *The Wall Street Journal.*

31 Schumpeter, J. (1939). *Business cycles.*

32 Dewey, E. and Dakin, E. (1945). *Cycles: the science of prediction.*

33 The key here is popularity. Both Kondratieff's original study and Spengler's book, *Decline of the West,* were published in 1926, but it was in the 1930s and 1940s that their views became food for discussion.

34 Ip, G. (1998, October 14). "Risk and uncertainty wreak havoc on stocks." *The Wall Street Journal,* p. C1.

35 In classic socionomic irony, the Wave Principle is likely to become better accepted just as it becomes particularly difficult to apply, in a Grand Supercycle corrective process.

PART V

FURTHER AFIELD

Chapter 19:

Problems with Conventional Approaches to Financial Markets, and Their Solution in Socionomics

As in Chapter 18, I deliberately use contemporary citations of conventional financial and economic thinking throughout this chapter to show that all one need do is open the newspaper on any given week to find examples of it. Most examples are from the second half of 1998 and were culled pretty much as I wrote the book.

Random Walk; Efficient Market Hypothesis

For years, some theoreticians[1,2,3] have argued that stock price movements are random. Their assertion under the Efficient Market Hypothesis is that all investors make informed and rational decisions, weighing more or less identically the meaning of various events and conditions that affect markets and immediately adjusting investment values accordingly. Since no one can predict random outside forces, markets fluctuate randomly. Statisticians have run tests on financial market prices to demonstrate that they follow a "random walk" and are therefore unpredictable. "For two decades," said *Fortune* magazine in 1988, "finance professors have taught EMH as if it were as indisputable as the laws of gravity."[4]

Go back to Chapter 4 and review the simple computer-generated model that Elliott Wave International designed to create a simulated market based upon the Wave Principle. Clearly every single movement in the model is utterly determined; after all, a simple formula produces it. Did you know, however, that the standard statistical methods of assessing the presence of determinism would find that the results of our model were *random*? How is this error possible? Stephen R. Cunningham, Assistant Professor in the Department of Economics at the University of Connecticut provides an answer. His research paper in the *Review of Financial Economics* reaches this stunning conclusion:

> Neither the Samuelson-Fama tests for efficient markets nor the popularly-used augmented Dickey-Fuller (1979) test for unit roots *can successfully discriminate between a fully deterministic time series, generated from a nonlinear (chaotic) process, and a random walk.* A researcher applying these methods to a simple nonlinear price process would be misled into believing that such a series is a random walk.[5]

This fact proves that the champions of EMH and random walk do not know, despite their claims, that markets are random. The failure of EMH researchers' statistical applications successfully to determine randomness in utterly determined chaotic data series invalidates the empirical basis of their work. This book, I hope, invalidates the theoretical basis of it, the idea that aggregate financial market behavior is based upon the efficient, rational processing (error #1) of extramarket information (error #2).

Standard-bearers for random walk smugly joke of producing random data series that look so much like stock charts that they fool people into thinking they *are* stock charts, as if this proves something. The *definition* of the word random is that the data can look like anything, so why shouldn't some of them look like stock charts? Similar charts of random data and stock prices no more prove that stock prices are random than they prove random data are stock prices. If randomly generated dots on a scale happened to produce music, it would hardly prove that music is random. In technical terms, as Paul Montgomery points out, such assertions commit the logical error of "affirming the consequent."[6]

A champion of random walk, still plying his axioms in the very latest issue of Bloomberg's *Personal Finance* magazine, uses this common argument in favor of market randomness: "More than 90 percent of professional mutual fund managers were outperformed by the S&P 500. If it were that easy to earn excess returns by exploiting the predictable patterns in the market, we should be able to find a substantial number of professionals who are able to do so."[7] This is nonsense, for several reasons. (1) In the past decade, most of the money in the stock market has been handled by professionals. To demand that professionals outperform themselves is to demand the negation of a tautology. (2) Using the S&P, one of the best-performing investments among all stock indexes, bonds and commodities in the entire world over the past 16 years, as a benchmark for money managers to *exceed* is an inverted straw-man argument. (3) To demand that professional investors beat a bull market is to create a negative-sum game and then insist that the majority win at it. Every manager has to have some cash, and every manager pays commissions. By definition, it is impossible for the majority to beat a bull market. Even random walkers must reject this cute ruse. It is quite certain that if we were to isolate a bear market period in which many money managers beat the market simply because many of them held some cash, random walk proponents would not then declare such performance as evidence against their model. (4) Beating the market is a false standard. To be consistent, random walkers should also insist that portfolio managers beat the market on the short side in bear markets. After all, market prices are simply ratios, making direction irrelevant. Carried to its extreme, their benchmark demands no less than constant outperformance in every market fluctuation, which is absurd. The only valid question is whether a manager makes enough money to make investing with him a good idea relative to what you would do as an individual. (5) Nonrandomness hardly means that earning excess returns should be "that easy." This is a blanket substitution of one idea for another. Chapter 8 explains why it is anything but easy. (6) If professionals are operating under false premises, the patterns they perceive would be inconstant and therefore inadequate for reliable forecasting. In this case, their failures would not prove randomness, but epistemological error. (7) The argument presents a false dichotomy, an "either-or" that is not necessary. Random walk is a possible answer to the more general question of why few people do well at investing but hardly a necessary one. Impulsive herding behavior would explain why most people do not perform brilliantly in financial markets. It also happens to be the actual reason.

As A.J. Frost and I said in our 1978 book, "the Elliott Wave Principle challenges the Random Walk Theory at every turn."[8] As the Wave Principle reveals, the overall pattern of stock price movement is nonrandom and indeed so formally constructed that price fluctuation cannot (as argued in Chapter 18) be the result of reasoned decisions by well-informed individuals dealing continually with new information, as is commonly assumed. It is my contention after closely observing the market and its participants for twenty years that few investment and trading decisions are based on reason, logic and knowledge gained from comprehensive research. Rather than tell my own stories or repeat the classic cases described by Charles Mackay in his indispensable tome, *Extraordinary Popular Delusions and the Madness of Crowds*, I will let Rita Koselka, writing recently for *Forbes,* describe what goes on in an everyday auction market like those in finance:

Lured by free food and wine, I went with some female former Harvard Business School classmates to attend what Sotheby's, the big auction house, advertised as a mock auction. Sipping our chardonnay, we were herded into the auditorium with several hundred other invitees— all business school graduates, each of us [with] $40,000 in fake credit. We proceeded to behave in ways that threw scant credit on our M.B.A.s. A blue-glaze Oriental vase sold for well beyond our supposed $40,000 limit.

The final item up for bid was tea for eight with Sotheby's president, Diana Brooks. But this time we were bidding real money. Figuring I could find some friends to chip in, I thrust my paddle in the air at $600. A quick nod of acknowledgment from auctioneer Hildesley and then I was forgotten. The tea sold at $1,200 to a zealous young woman two rows ahead. She had a determined air about her that said, No matter what you bid, I'll top it.

The one business lesson I came away with may not be the one Sotheby's intended: I've learned it's nearly impossible to behave rationally at an auction, so written bids left with the auctioneer in advance are the only way to go. (If the top bid at auction is less than your written bid, you'll pay the lower price.) Unless you are a lot more disciplined than most folk, stay away from the auction room.[9]

The above description of people's behavior in such environments is far closer to reality than academic models based on investor rationality, fully disseminated knowledge and random outside impetus. Emotions rule most of the players in an auction crowd; the more naïve and/or impulsive some of players are, the less rational is the bidding.

Such behavior is the focus of a newly developing area of scientific study called behavioral finance, whose champions have been conducting experiments that demonstrate the validity of technical (i.e., market behavioral) analysis and the invalidity of EMH. One example is the paper, "Simple Technical Trading Rules and the Stochastic Properties of Stock Returns" by William A. Brock, Josef Lakonishok and Blake LeBaron, published in the *Journal of Finance* in 1992.[10] It shows that two simple technical trading methods based upon moving averages and trendlines generate returns in excess of those predicted by models presuming randomness. Both of these tools rely on the almost embarrassingly simple fact that *markets trend*, but even that is a challenge to EMH.

What is the status of the rational man in a trending market or emotional auction? When herding stock market investors have the bit in their mouths, rational individuals are powerless to stop the stampede. In fact, *they often have no choice but to take the trend into account* regardless of how they would otherwise value stocks.

Might the rare nonherding professional fund manager rise above this dynamic? In most cases, he cannot. His choice is this: He can raise cash in a bull market and buy stocks in a bear market, which would be prudent investing, or he can stay in business. That is his choice. If he acts counter to the market's trend, then his customers leave in droves. They place their funds with managers whose policies reflect their feelings. Any mutual fund manager whose personal opinion counters that of the majority will tell you how frustrating it is to be in this trap. Rationality, to most managers, means getting rich giving customers what they want, not losing most of them with prudent investing. Regardless of the market outlook of any specific fund manager, then, the herding majority remains in complete control of the bulk of professionally managed money.

Why is EMH so popular? There appear to be two reasons. First, the isolation of many academics from the real world of finance explains why they are not immediately uncomfortable with the idea. As a writer for the *International Herald Tribune* put it in 1995 with well chosen words, "If you believe that markets and investing live in the chilly climes of abstract thought, you probably haven't spent too long tracking your investments through the ups and downs of raging, irrational bull runs or the weird, depressing illogic of a bear phase."[11] The second reason that EMH is popular stems from the fact that, like most people, academics lose money in markets. Less like most people, however, academics are quite sure that they are highly intelligent and adequately informed. They think, "If someone as smart as I, thinking logically, consistently loses money when I invest, then markets must surely be random." Sure, chuckle if you will. Then read this comment from an academic economist:

> I have personally tried to invest money, my client's money and my own, in every single anomaly and predictive device that academics [mistake #1] have dreamed up, and *I have yet to make a nickel* on any of these supposed market inefficiencies [mistake #2]. If there's nothing investors [here is the extrapolation to everyone else] can exploit in a systematic way, time in and time out [must it be *always*?], then it is very hard to say that information is not being properly incorporated into stock prices."[12]

Perhaps this conclusion would explain his failure if that were our only information, but how does it explain the monstrous, persistent success of futures trader Paul Tudor Jones? Obviously, it does not. Socionomics accounts for both of their experiences. Most people cannot escape the impulses of their limbic systems. A rare few can.

As I have vowed to refrain from blunt criticism in this book, I am indebted to James B. Rogers, adjunct professor of security analysis at Columbia Business School and an outrageously successful investor, for his summary judgment, "The random-walk theory is absurd,"[13] and to Yale economics professor Robert Schiller for his incautious outburst, "The efficient-market hypothesis is the most remarkable error in the history of economic theory."[14] A.J. Frost and I take some pride in having flatly denied the validity of the theory in our book as early as 1978.

Despite Schiller's passionate statement, truly the most remarkable error in economics and sociology is not EMH but its underlying bedrock belief in event causality, which is shared by nearly everyone. That is what this book is designed to correct.

Weak EMH

EMH started to run into problems when academics began pointing out patterns of market behavior. In 1985, for example, DeBondt and Thaler reported that stocks that underperformed the market for several years tended to outperform the market for several years thereafter.[15]

The study begins with data from 1933, which mask a flaw in it. In the half-dozen years prior to that time, weak stocks got weaker, and many ended up as wallpaper. Buying relative losers in those years resulted in disaster. Over the past fifteen years since 1983, a bit before the study was published, the market has produced the same apparent anomaly: Stocks that have outperformed for awhile have tended to keep outperforming, and vice versa. The reason for this difference is that the 1920s and 1982 to now are fifth waves, when breadth is weak (see Chapter 7) and investors narrow their focus to a decreasing list of big winners. The results of this study, then, are not a consistent fact but a function of the labels of the waves. They are also a function of the fairly persistent upward direction of the market, as the period of the study encompassed most of the Supercycle wave (V) bull market, skewing the results.[16] In most bear markets, by contrast, underperforming stocks just get weaker. Regardless of this data bias, this study does suggest inefficiency and/or nonrationality via persistence in market-related behavioral trends.

The authors' hypothesis is that investors occasionally "overreact" to news about companies. In other words, *they assume outside causality, the bedrock of EMH, as a starting point.* However, because company news lags stock prices, it is impossible that investors "react" to any such thing. If they do not react, then they cannot overreact.

Although this study has spawned a fair amount of follow-up work, its results are explicable as simply a function of directional waves: Any study looking for stocks that have gone one direction for a set length of time is bound to include many that are near the end of wave patterns. So during market environments when investors are willing to shift from sector to sector and stock to stock (which is most of the time), previously weak stocks will outperform for awhile and previous strong stocks will underperform for awhile. In this context, rational efficiency and the modification of it are irrelevant concepts. The good news here, though, is that researchers are at least *pointing out*, via statistics, that at least sometimes, markets trend in a way that contraindicates EMH.

There are times when markets are extremely volatile, and it is those times that are particularly difficult to sweep under the rug of rational efficiency. For example, William A. Brock of the Social Systems Research Institute of the University of Wisconsin states flatly, "In my opinion, *no satisfactory explanation* has been found [for] the most recent crash,...Black Monday, October 19, 1987."[17] In other words, there was no event or change in outside conditions to justify the violence of the change in people's rational decision making on that day (actually over a two-week period starting October 6). This is true, of course,[18] and damning to EMH. As another professor says, "The [1987] crash makes us realize that prices are not *entirely* efficient."[19]

All these professors are brave souls and deserve credit for challenging EMH orthodoxy. However, as Chapter 20 discusses in more detail, there remains no reason whatsoever to assert that the market is nonrational only briefly and occasionally, when it is volatile or falling or in a short-term trend, and rational the rest of the time, when it is calm or rising or engaged in a long-term trend. These are simply presumptions, and they derive from no science of which I am aware. All such views are simply accommodations of the Efficient Market Hypothesis, or at least its underlying presumption that market participants primarily "react" to outside events and news in the first place, which they do not.

On the belief that sometimes markets are inefficient, some analysts spend immense time searching for "pockets of inefficiency" in the market that the EMH dynamic has presumably yet to incorporate, which means essentially, "important information that others don't know yet." Even if such events *were* causal, the effort expended to find those elusive pockets would be a waste of time because most investors behave otherwise than rationally. As I argued in Chapter 16, social actualities are the *product* of social mood, so in terms of overall market trends, there is no such thing as valuable event-related information in the conventional sense.[20] The social mood that led to any such events has already been and gone.

Tautological Rationality

Perhaps the nth degree of dependence upon the rationality model has just been published in an article in the *Financial Analysts Journal*. It argues that *buying because prices are rising* is rational, so "rational behavior by individual investors can cause a market bubble," which is defined as "some self-reinforcing, self-perpetuating mechanism that prevents successive security prices from being random."[21] This stance essentially defines nonrationality out of existence. If this theory is correct, then market crashes are rational, too, and so is selling when they occur. Would anyone like to take the affirmative side of that one? The fact is that buying *only* because prices have been rising is *not* rational because rising prices mean that the market is that much closer to a top. For the same reason, selling *only* because prices have been falling is not rational, either.

The Idea of Intrinsic Value

For rationality to be the driving force behind markets, EMH must assume that the objects of financial speculation have an *intrinsic value*. However, value is not inherent in objects; the term value pertains only when human beings *desire* something. Human desire, particularly for investments, where the lure of gain and the fear of loss are so potent, is hardly constant. This fact pertains particularly to investment prices, which are governed almost entirely by the shifting mental states of those bidding and asking in an auction market. If all it took to discern the value of an investment were to compute it on a calculator, then investments would hardly fluctuate as dramatically as they do.

The stock market bestows greatly divergent values upon various real things at different times, the most important of these being (1) dividends, (2) the value of corporate assets, and (3) the yield on high-grade bonds. When it comes down to valuing stock certificates apart from their appreciation potential, these are the only values that matter. An investor trades his money for a quarterly payment called a *dividend* plus the guarantee that if the company had to, it could *liquidate* and divide up the proceeds among shareholders, and he takes this action in lieu of lending his money out at *interest* to a solid, healthy debtor. In just this century, the Dow Jones Industrial Average has yielded as little as 1.5% in dividends and as much as 17.4%. It has been valued as high as 5.6 times corporate book value (which is the value of assets on the firm's balance sheet) and as little as 0.5 times. It has yielded as much as 4.9 times as much as Treasury bonds and as little as 0.25 times as much.[22] These huge differences are due to one thing: people's opinion about the *capital gain potential* of stocks, i.e., the extent to which they are bullish or bearish. Therefore, such valuations are a direct measure of investors' optimism or pessimism. These mental attitudes do not pay enough attention to intrinsic value to give it the time of day.

Figure 19-1 shows the bond yield/stock yield ratio for Japanese investments over the past fifty years. In 1968, they were just about equal. In 1998, thirty years later, they are again just about equal. But look what

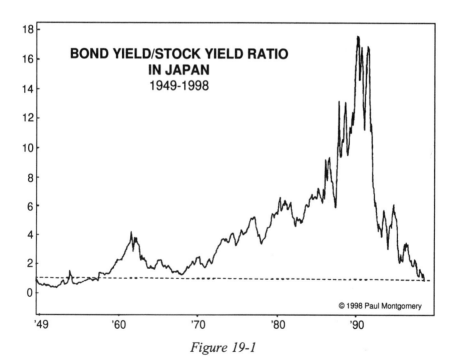

Figure 19-1

happened in between! The relative desire to own corporate shares over debt expanded by *18 times* and then contracted just as much. No valuation model that includes interest rates takes this difference into account because it is precisely interest rates that are factored out in the ratio. There is no way that changes in earnings can explain it unless one asserts that earnings changes compel irrational behavior. The difference is no small adjustment; it is the meat of the bull and bear markets that occurred over this period. As Paul Montgomery puts it, this ratio records changes in "amorphous states of mind" that make a mockery of the idea of intrinsic value.

How does one explain by way of "fundamental value" that baseball cards sold for one price in 1991 and one-tenth of that price in 1993? How does one account for the fact that President John Kennedy's rocking chair sold for $453,000 in May 1996 and less than two years later, in March 1998, sold for $23,000, 1/20th as much? Obviously these objects, like corporate shares, have no specific intrinsic value.

Some theoreticians construct models of what stocks "should" be worth. Obviously, there is no such thing. Even if the premise of such models were valid, the relentless uncertainly about facts *relating to value* coupled with the ever-present uncertainty about what the naive majority may do *without regard for value* is plenty enough to destroy the utility of attempting to invest with respect to "intrinsic value."

The "Too Popular" Theory and the "Self-Fulfilling Prophecy" Theory

One of the arguments used by random walkers, fundamental analysts, "contrarians" and others is that analysis of price patterns in markets cannot work because "people learn." If patterns work, goes the argument, then they will quickly become popular, at which time they will no longer work. There is no point in singling out price patterns as unworkable on this basis; if people learn to an extent that makes this objection valid, then *no* method can work, including whatever analysis the proponent of this theory proposes.

Does this mean that random walk defenders have a point? No. The very thought of the majority of investors actually learning the Wave Principle or any comprehensive approach to market analysis before investing is absurd. They would all have to quit their jobs to become market experts, in which case there would be no economy to support financial markets. So the objection is moot on a practical basis. It is invalid in theory as well. As LeDoux's laboratory work shows, rats whose cortexes have been removed can develop fears related to specific stimuli, but unlike rats with cortexes, they cannot learn to abandon them when the relationship between stimulus and result is dismantled.[23] This experiment proves that *the limbic system cannot learn*. This, along with the limbic system's immense power, is the reason that social patterns are immutable. Knowledge of any valid approach to market analysis, even among a substantial number of people, is not a cure for the continuance of patterns.

The above-cited objection further relies on the falsehood that knowing a market method is the same as knowing where the market is going. All analytical methods are tools only for *probabilistic* forecasting (see Chapter 20), leaving most investors chronically uncertain about the future no matter what their approach. This situation gives the limbic system all the room it needs in most people's psyches to operate exactly as it pleases.

The "too popular" objection has also been disproved by events. A national financial magazine dated October 1977 made this obligatory comment: "Over the last few years, the Wave Principle has gathered too much of a following and, therefore, it has less value today. Almost invariably, you can write off a technique when it gets too much of a following."[24] How does that statement look in light of the decade that followed, when the idea of the Wave Principle spread worldwide and had its greatest period of popularity ever?[25]

Finally and fundamentally, *the very claim that a market method can become popular enough to ruin itself reveals the reason why the claim is invalid*, as belief in this idea reflects the human trait of skepticism. When I have a period of good forecasting, some people say, "You have been right so long that you are due for a fall." When I have had a period of poor forecasting, the same people say, "See? It doesn't work." They do not remain consistent and tell me I am now ready for a period of brilliance. Whether I have been right or wrong, they are skeptical. So the mere fact that people ask the question, "If you or Elliott wave become too popular, won't that destroy the theory?" provides the answer to the question: Skepticism will not allow it to become "too popular."

Now let us examine the other side of this coin. In several cases after a successful forecast based upon the Wave Principle has come to pass, critics charge that the method itself has no value; it was simply that once a particular successful forecast had been disseminated, it became a "self-fulfilling prophecy;" people made it happen. This idea is absurd on several levels. First, the only way that one's forecast becomes widely disseminated is if he or she has been quite successful for awhile in the first place. Obviously *those* forecasts could not have been self-fulfilling prophecies. Second, if a popular analyst's forecasts did become self-fulfilling prophecies, then he would never fail thereafter, would he? Each new prediction would be taken as gospel and then fulfilled accordingly, forever. Obviously, subsequent forecasting errors disprove this theory. Third, consider the absurdity of even a single such event. If everyone knew that the Dow would bottom at 1087, why would anyone sell at 1100 or 1088? Wouldn't everyone buy more? If so, from whom would they buy? Finally, this hypothesis ignores the fact that forecasts are widely disseminated every day. Obviously all of them are not fulfilled; indeed most are proved utterly wrong. When does self-fulfillment come into play according to this theory? Only when one works. Now the claim is revealed as tautological.

Here we reach the fun part. The "self-fulfilling prophecy" theory is the *opposite* conclusion from the *same premise* that produces the "if it gets too popular, it won't work" theory. Both arguments begin with the idea that forecasts based upon a particular method might become popular. Then one concludes that therefore it cannot work, and the other concludes that therefore it will work perfectly! Each argument is nothing more than a quick *ad hoc* rationalization by people who believe that probabilistically accurate, objectively determined social forecasting is impossible.

Why are such bogus theories popular? A socionomist knows that the limbic system impels the neocortex to come up with reasons to avoid conflict with one's emotions. These two theories are classic examples, and I have little doubt that there are individuals who at different times have uttered them both.

The Wave Principle is a description of a fundamental aspect of the nature of human behavior. In order for society to continue going through wave patterns, it must be part of human nature to believe that theories of determined mass psychology are indefensible and not worth examining. People must be primed to accept bullish arguments at tops and bearish arguments at bottoms. This means that they have to be ever open to rationalization via bogus theories of market behavior. How else will they generate the patterns that fear, greed and hope forever produce?

Macroeconomic Formulae: Man as Machine

Economists devise today's macroeconomic formulations under the presumption that people react to outside stimuli like billiard balls following physical laws. Unlike physics formulae, though, the concepts represented by the variables in these equations are often imprecise. Many that are considered precise are not because they ignore the varying mental states of people. Often, the equations do not relate very well to the real world. The combination of vague definitions, improper assumptions and detached impracticality prompted Nobel prize winner Wassily Leontief of the Institute for Economic Analysis at New York University to say this in 1982:

> Year after year, economic theorists continue to produce scores of mathematical models and to explore in great detail their formal properties; and the econometricians fit algebraic functions of all possible shapes to essentially the same sets of data *without being able to advance, in any perceptible way, a systematic understanding of the structure and the operation of a real economic system.*[26]

In 1986, William Niskanen Jr. of the Cato Institute was more succinct: "Macroeconomic theory is in absolute shambles."[27]

The biggest flaw in macroeconomic formulations is their underlying assumption that the "billiard ball" has a fixed mental state. However, the mental states of people vary, so their "reaction" to a "cause" will be different at different times. For example, an increase in the money supply might lead to lower interest rates in some cases and higher interest rates in others, depending upon what people discern to be the meaning, if any, of the event. Because mental states change, the attempt to define a constant relationship is futile. This is certainly true in the stock market. In some stock market environments, rising bond prices are considered bullish; in others, bearish. In each case, there is always an apparently airtight logical argument in favor of the relationship. For instance, the conflicting arguments regarding stock and bond trends, offered depending upon the season, are: (1) Bonds compete with stocks for the investor's dollar, so when one market rises, the other falls. (2) Higher bonds mean lower interest rates, which helps the economy and makes speculative borrowing easier, so when one market rises, the other one rises. While each of these arguments appears true from time to time, that means the other is false. There is no macroeconomic formula that can express a *consistent* relationship.

A single discussion should concretize this point. Governments long operated under the assumption that the higher the tax rates they impose upon citizens, the higher their revenues will be. (Revenue = fixed social product x tax rate.) This would indeed be a consistent relationship if society were a physical system. However, people are not machines. Sometimes people increase their productive efforts when tax rates are high; indeed, that has been happening in recent decades in the U.S., as both parents of most families now must work to make up for the real income shortfall that high taxes have produced. At other times, people slow their productive efforts when most of their product is confiscated. This is one reason why communism fails. Thus, given a certain social mindset, higher tax rates can lead to *lower* revenues. In this case, *the end result is the opposite of the intended result.* Economist Arthur Laffer explained this phenomenon in 1980. He thereby proposed a different macroeconomic formula that relates tax rates to government income. The Laffer curve claims that one particular rate of taxation will return the greatest revenue to the government. If the rate is lower or higher than that, revenue will be less. (Revenue = predictably variable social product x tax rate.) This formula, too, relies on the assumption that society is a physical system like a machine that can be overburdened to such a degree that it slows down. Like its predecessor, it sounds sensible and could be applied with consistent results *if people were automatons.* However, suppose that this formula is accepted by a government that is taxing citizens above the supposed ideal level for maximum revenues. To achieve a goal of greater revenues, it lowers tax rates. Revenues rise. It works! Then after a few years, people begin to understand that lower taxes made them more prosperous. They agitate for further reductions in tax rates and elect politicians who will accommodate them. Taxes are lowered further. Government revenues fall. People begin to resent even the lowered tax rates as an impediment to their prosperity. Taxes are slashed; government revenue shrinks. *The end result is the opposite of the intended result.* Whether this would actually happen in any particular circumstance is perhaps debatable, but it *could* happen, and that is the difference between social and physical systems.

Coveney and Highfield are damning in their assessment of the formulae that have so long been taught in the typical undergraduate course in economics:

> It has taken economists a long time to recognize the inherent complexity of their subject. For decades, the central dogma of economics revolved around stale equilibrium principles in a manner entirely analogous to the application of equilibrium thermodynamics.... Many economists have sought to shoehorn all economics into theories whose merits are their mathematical simplicity and elegance rather than their ability to say anything about the way real-world economies work....Classical equilibrium-based concepts have been infecting the minds of generations of science and economics students with the dogma that the behavior of a complex system can be deduced by simply summing its component parts.[28]

I would disagree on only two points: First, economists for the most part have *not* recognized the error in their premises; only a few have. Second, the old economic theories are not elegant; they are ugly. In contrast, we have a truly elegant law in the Wave Principle, which is the bedrock principle of sociology and finance, and therefore ultimately of macroeconomics. The science of macroeconomics must drop the mathematics of physics and adopt the mathematics of sociology. Minds are not billiard balls or machines or computers; they are *minds*.

The "Potent Directors" Presumption

Virtually all conventional financial analysts and economists accept assumptions about certain men's ability to control the social future, be they presidents, treasury secretaries or central bankers. Last month, an article from *The Washington Post* entitled, "Key Players Control Money Supply," tells us that the Bank of International Settlements "helps keep the banking system steady in turbulent times...protects the world financial system...[and] focuses on *ensuring* that [a local] crisis doesn't threaten the world's intricate [banking] system."[29] The BIS, says the article, has "secret conversations that can shape the course of the global economy." This type of belief permeates practical economic discourse. It persists despite failure after failure of officials to control money, interest rates, commodity prices, retail prices, stock markets, and economic growth and contraction. The fact is that central banking authorities *never* reverse a financial spiral, in either direction. They participate in (and typically encourage) them in uptrends and flail uselessly at them in downtrends. As I type this sentence, I am looking at this headline in *The Wall Street Journal*: "Why the World Bank Failed To Anticipate Indonesia's Deep Crisis." The article opens with this salvo:

> The World Bank considered Indonesia's rise from poverty its greatest triumph. A shattering economic reversal is returning as many as half of its 200 million people to destitution. In some villages, they are unable to afford food...banks are on the ropes...[it's a] historic setback, in the words of the World Bank's top official here.[30]

How could the supposed generator of Indonesia's boom not only find itself unable to stop the collapse but be utterly oblivious to the fact that something untoward was developing? The subhead of the article explains all you need to know: "[It Got] 'Caught Up In [the] Enthusiasm'." Yes, bankers are human, too, and they, like most people, get swept up in the waves of optimism and pessimism so fully that they do not even realize that they are of, not above, the waves.

The Federal Reserve Board is believed to have godlike powers to propel or rein in economic growth in the United States by manipulating interest rates. Almost no economist disputes this "obvious" fact. Even distinguished scientists, who would never accept a casual assumption in their own fields, take this one for granted.[31] Yet consider: If central banks actually could regulate their economies, then the wild history of interest rates and economic behavior in the 20th century would not have taken place. Did the Fed manage the economy into the Great Depression? Did the Fed engineer the double-digit interest rates of the 1970s and early 1980s? Did the central bank in Japan program that country's debt crisis and developing depression of the 1990s? If a central bank's power to lower interest rates can turn an economy around, why did the U.S. crash into depression in the 1930s despite an aggressive lowering of the discount rate from 6% to 1.5% by 1931? Why is Japan still in recession after eight years of persistently lower discount rates from 6% to 0.5%? Neither policy designed to reverse these trends of deflation, bear market and economic contraction worked.

In truth, the Fed is not even in charge of interest rates. It is not the commander of the market but a puppet. If it were otherwise, then the federal funds rate would not have soared to 19.1% in 1981. Instead, the Fed would have kept rates at 4%, and the market would have dutifully followed. (If you believe *that*, I have a bridge to sell you.) So, anticipating the Fed's decisions on the discount rate as if a drama were unfolding is a waste of time and emotion. There is no need to monitor the look on members' faces for hints of their decisions. There is no need to hold one's breath when listening to the chairman announce the board's decision. A socionomist monitoring the T-bill rate can predict with fair accuracy what the Fed will do. No one monitoring the Fed's decisions can predict what T-bill rates will do.

Since 1913, when the Federal Reserve system was created to "maintain stability," the dollar has lost *94%* of its value,[32] an unconscionable appropriation of wealth. In recent days, newspapers have been reporting on the utter failure of the International Monetary Fund (IMF) to stave off financial collapse in Russia. It did succeed in one thing: It quickly blew over a hundred billion dollars in the attempt. Such is the utility of financial "policy."

Why do people fail to notice that authorities have no beneficial power? One important reason is that most of the time, *times are good*. It is easy then to presume that the authorities are doing their jobs just fine. It is only when markets fall, interest rates soar or economies implode that the truth is revealed, and such times are comparatively brief. Perhaps that is why examples of failure simply invoke rationalization. Economists can always cite supposed causes of the "aberrant" behavior. The 1930s? "The Fed was young then and didn't know what it was doing." 1974 and 1980? "The politicians messed things up and the Fed finally fixed them." Japan? "Its bank is not as smart as our Fed; it didn't make the right moves." Asians? "What do they know about macroeconomic management?" The rationalization is endless. Three weeks after the report of the latest World Bank debacle, the same newspaper published an editorial by an MIT economist who steadfastly maintains the conventional presumptions. Referring to the economic expansion of the past seven-to-eight (depending upon which statistics you use) years, he says, "This expansion will run forever. We will not see a recession for years to come,...as we have the *tools* to keep the current expansion going. *Policy levers [and] our policy team*...will keep it from happening."[33] Echoes the celebrated director of the Economic Forecasting Center at Georgia State University, "Another depression would require a degree of *policy stupidity* that would *never happen again*."[34]

Today we are also told that authorities can change the course of the stock market:

> It is known as the "plunge protection team," an emergency council of America's top financial officials that operates with its own special staff in the shadows of the U.S. Treasury....The purpose of the group, known officially as the Working Group on Financial Markets, is to avoid repeating the near-catastrophe of October 19, 1987....The permanent members include the chairman of the Federal Reserve, Alan Greenspan, and the heads of the Securities and Exchange Commission and the Commodity Futures Trading Commission....Decisions are made in conjunction with the National Economic Council at the White House, and the powerful governor of the New York Federal Reserve Bank. They have each other's telephone numbers at all times and are plugged into a sophisticated "market surveillance" system that helps them to anticipate trouble.... Each agency has a confidential crisis plan. At the SEC, this is known as the Red Book, or more properly, the Executive Directory for Market Contingencies. The team relies on "circuit breakers" to ensure an orderly fall in the markets, with intermittent halts in trading. It can extend open lines of credit, inject money into the system and cut interest rates....There is also speculation that it might intervene directly in the stock market, buying shares and futures contracts to prop up the indexes.[35]

That article appeared on September 2, 1998. Three weeks later, on September 24, came this assessment from *The Wall Street Journal* about the same team's attempts to deal with the financial crisis in Asia:

> With little notice, President Clinton summoned his top advisers to the Oval Office on Labor Day for a late-night huddle on the spreading global financial crisis....His anxiety about the adequacy of the U.S. response had been building for weeks. From vacation on Martha's Vineyard, Mass., he had phoned Treasury Secretary Robert Rubin, fly-fishing in Alaska, almost daily. On his trip to Moscow, he hectored top aides for new ideas. He and his political soulmate, British Prime Minister Tony Blair, talked about convening an emergency meeting of world leaders. ...Mr. Clinton wanted bold solutions as big as the problem. But Mr. Rubin wanted to be cautious; he worried that a meeting of world leaders would create unrealistic expectations.
>
> The year-long financial firestorm may be turning into a Vietnam for Washington's "best and brightest" economic minds....Through hubris, political clumsiness and the unintended consequences of well-meant policies, the Clinton administration and its allies at the International Monetary Fund have, so far, failed to contain what President Clinton now calls "the worst financial crisis in half a century."
>
> The power of the United States, in many ways mightier than ever, seems no match for international flows of money unleashed, in part, at the urging of the U.S. itself....It will be years before the world can fully understand what went wrong and whether different policies might have staved off some of the pain.[36]

The article is incorrect in saying that it will take years to understand what went wrong. Every sentence in the above excerpt screams out the absurdity of the project. The only question remaining is, How many years will it take before economists admit that such posturing does little more than provide a false hope that is viciously destructive to anyone who adopts it? It certainly has yet to happen, as faith in such things as "plunge protection teams" still abounds.

Is there any science to support my position? Thanks to recent research, there is. Experiments show that financial markets without central authorities behave no differently from those with them. Recall the financial market simulation model produced by Caldarelli, Marsili and Zhang, discussed in Chapters 12 and 18, which mimics the stock market with only a few participants and no outside information. The authors state, "Our model does not implement the many corrections [sic] which are taken in similar cases by central authorities in a real market."[37] Intentionally or not, this study shows that *actions of central authorities are irrelevant to whatever is essential to market behavior.* Such actions, therefore, are apparently not corrective of anything noticeable, so they are of no fundamental consequence.

Government agencies in particular not only do not, but *cannot*, affect such trends. The reason is that government does not act; it reacts. Moreover, it is always the *last* institution to react, because it is the ultimate crowd, every decision being made by committee as a result of pressure from a majority of voters. For example, the securities laws of 1934 were passed to prevent the crash that had already occurred and the depression that had already bottomed. Indeed, it was a lagging indicator that the bottom had passed. Similarly, the Monetary Control Act passed in December 1980 was designed to deal with the runaway inflation that had raged for a decade and had ended nearly a year before. Again, the passage of the act was a lagging indicator that the period of accelerating inflation was over. As you can see, any seeming successes of such government policies are reverse-causal. Both apparent social-policy stupidity and apparent social-policy brilliance are *results* of socionomic cycles, not causes.

People today almost unanimously believe that government, the IMF, the World Bank, the Japanese central bank and the Federal Reserve system have potent and magic powers to shape macroeconomic forces. The cause of this error is once again the belief in extramarket causality. In fact, it is the interaction of millions of people that sets interest rates and regulates the economy. The power of financial "authorities" to manage markets and economies is like the power of the Wizard of Oz: smoke and bluster. Faith in these wizards is little different from pre-civilized people's accordance of similar powers to witch doctors. Like the ministrations of a witch doctor, the typical result of "policy," if there is any result at all (after all, policy is a social phenomenon, too), is to make things worse. Complexity theory recognizes nature's processes of *self organization.* It is a short step to realize that *society operates the same way.* That is why free societies are more successful and productive than controlled ones. They self organize far more efficiently than any human directors could make them do. Just like the Communists who could never figure out who was directing the industrial success of the United States, conventional analysts keep trying to identify the "directors" that make everything in the markets and the economy happen, but the only actual director is the behavioral dynamic that governs human interaction. Every attempt at control, whether by communists, fascists, socialists or central bankers, can only misdirect energy and resources, thereby impeding the efficiency of the self-organizing process. So macroeconomic policies are not merely impotent, they are counterproductive.

In sum, mechanics and "tools" are of no assistance unless you are tinkering with a machine, and human society is not a machine. Harboring an illusion of being in control of the waves is a guarantee of getting caught up in them. This is yet another illusion that socionomics has the power to eliminate.

Presumed Mechanical Determinants of Market Movements

A variant of the approach that assumes society is a machine is the idea that the stock market is a machine. If it is running properly, the implied idea seems to go, then prices rise. If prices *fall*, the machine is broken. The trick, then, is to identify the weak cogs every now and then and fix them. The crash of 1987 was such a storm of mass emotion that it caused "market as machine" theorists to work overtime explaining the drop and figuring out how to "fix" the system. The theory that gained the most credence was that the crash was caused by so-called portfolio insurance computer programs, which in essence sold stocks as the market went lower. This process presumably fed upon itself. Unfortunately for the theory, it does not explain very well why markets around the world crashed simultaneously or why the decline stopped.[38] It is at an utter loss to explain why many indexes around the world that had *no* computer trading fell *further* than the DJIA. It also ignores the fact that throughout 1986 and 1987, market observers in an equally serious tone had continually explained why a stock market crash was impossible because of "the safeguards that are in place,"[39] safeguards such as portfolio insurance. In 1988, I had a lot of fun putting up a chart of the crash and then asking the audience how many felt that it would not have happened, or would have been mitigated, had there been no program trading. Usually half or more of the attendees would raise their hands. Then I would tell them the answer was unequivocally "no," and by the way, did I mention that this was a picture of the *1929* crash?

Inconvenient facts have no bearing on strongly held beliefs of mechanistic causality, as demonstrated in July by a major editorial in *The Wall Street Journal*. Addressing portfolio insurance and a few other mechanical aspects of the market, two finance professors of the highest caliber, reporting on the opinion of "the nation's leading academic scholars," explain,

"Sources of structural fragility [in the market] have been substantially, *if not totally*, corrected, [making] a repeat of the hair-raising events of 1987 highly unlikely."[40] In response to this presumption, I would say that to this day in evolutionary history, the emotional fragility of the human limbic system remains uncorrected. Until neocortexes evolve enough to dominate their primitive antecedents, the market shall ever rise, fall and occasionally crash.

Linear Extrapolation: "Predicting" the Present

Trend extrapolation is the crudest form of technical analysis, and it is employed by nearly all conventional analysts, though they rarely realize it. Mainstream social and economic forecasting has forever been a practice of extrapolating present and recent conditions and trends into the future. More specifically, apparent predictions are simply (1) descriptions of present conditions (2) multiplied by unconsciously calculated moving averages of the trends of those conditions. Obviously, in a *changing* world, this approach is doomed to fail. Because of this practice, both economists and futurists in general have always been notoriously optimistic at tops and pessimistic at bottoms, producing highly inaccurate forecasts of coming events. Now we know why. Because the forecasters have no reliable basis upon which actually to attempt a forecast, the prevailing social mood has full rein to affect the tone of their conclusions. The stronger the mood, the stronger their conviction, the more inventive their rationalizations, and the more extreme and confident their extrapolation. This means that the closer the social mood gets to the point of change, the greater will be conventional forecasters' conviction that it will *not* change, and the further into the future will be their extrapolation. (See the classic example from July 1984 in the bond market section of Chapter 5.)

This convention is demonstrated almost daily in the financial press. A new 1998 book that is "must" reading for stock market watchers contains the statement, "I predict that we are *soon going to see* the greatest economic boom in our history."[41] This would have been a useful forecast, in fact it would have been an *actual* forecast whether it had turned out right or not, back in 1982. Today, it is simply a description of what has happened in the past sixteen years, multiplied and extrapolated into the pervasive social dream of the moment. A recent favorite headline of mine, from *The Wall Street Journal*, is "Economists Forecast Mild Inflation of 2.5% Yearly Through 2008."[42] Is there *any basis whatsoever* for this decade-long year-by-year forecast? Obviously not. Like all such "forecasts," it is simply a statement of present conditions tempered by recent trends. It is a "prediction" of the present.

This wholly psychological phenomenon applies to virtually all people in all social fields. For instance, after Tiger Woods won the 1997 Masters tournament, a sports reporter explained how prior to the event he had been skeptical of Jack Nicklaus's opinion of Tiger Woods' abilities, but now he was declaring Nicklaus's opinion "an understatement," as there was no one to beat Woods over the next 30 tournaments.[43] Countless sports writers echoed this sentiment. To date, Woods has yet to win another tournament. The point is not that the forecasters were wrong twice. The point is that at neither time did they make a forecast, at least not with any tools that allow one to do so. They were simply describing the latest achievements of the man. Their *claim* that they were forecasting does not change that fact. Nor does the same claim do so for economists.

The natural, unconscious way of anticipating reality is to observe it over time and assume that trends will continue in the same way as they have in the past. While this approach is applicable to physics, it is improper to apply it to sociology. By succumbing to the natural tendency to extrapolate, forecasters become part of each wave rather than rise above it.

There is a greater irony. The very fact that people extrapolate trends in this manner, particularly when their fellow men support them by agreeing, is what creates extremes in social sentiment. Thus, the phenomenon that *produces* the turning points in social behavior is precisely the one that *masks* them.

Futurists in all social fields must abandon the practice of extrapolation and adopt a method of identifying sociological *patterns* and their concomitant indications of social trend *change*. Anyone can recognize, with the appropriate data, the state of the economy and its recent trend, which is the most that today's economists do. Without the proper tools, however, no one can anticipate changes in either. Anticipation is the reason for being in the economics profession. To know (even in probabilistic terms) in the midst of a recession whether that recession is ending or about to slip deeper into depression is worth a king's ransom. To know that the peak or trough of a major economic trend is nigh is of inestimable value to nearly everyone. To identify months after the fact that a turn has occurred is comparatively useless. After an upturn, the bargains are gone. After a downturn, your junk bonds are impossible to sell, business buyers have disappeared, and liquidity has dried up in the real estate market.

Conventional Reasoning from Event Causality

Conventional analysts study *extramarket* data, that is, events, conditions and processes outside the marketplace, which are deemed to be the factors, or "fundamentals,"[44] that drive the market. For example, people generally assume that the stock market is driven by interest rates, the economy, politics, corporate earnings and the Fed.

While a conventional analyst will insist that some event or other market (earnings, the economy, oil prices, debt levels, interest rates, liquidity, etc.) caused a movement in the stock market, if you ask him to *predict* the stock market on the same basis, he cannot give you an answer unless he predicts what the presumed causal factor will do. We have uncovered a secret, which is that conventional analysts must *predict their own indicators*. It is not good enough to say, for instance, that stocks will go up as long as earnings increase. You must predict earnings to arrive at a payoff. To do that, you need an indicator of earnings. And so on; the chain is endless. Furthermore, a conventional analyst cannot adjust for error. If earnings fall and stocks are going up, or if interest rates fall and stocks fall with them (as has been the case in Japan for the past half-decade), he has no basis upon which to modify his stance. He just stays wrong.

The belief in outside causality is so ingrained that people use its language to impart nonsense. One writer in August noticed that the stock market has risen 500 points "every time another woman comes forward telling [about] the President."[45] Rather than consider therefore that the bull market has been unrelated to the president's sex life, he opines that sex scandals must be *bullish*. He simply cannot imagine abandoning the false idea of news causality. A recent newspaper quotes an economist at a major brokerage firm who thinks he is giving a reason why the economy will continue to expand. He says, "The fundamentals that support the domestic economy remain good to excellent,"[46] fundamentals such as rising incomes, an abundance of jobs and the availability of credit. This is not an isolated *faux pas*, but a generic utterance. Can you see that this analysis is a tautology? A good economy *is* rising incomes, abundant jobs and expanding credit. He is actually saying, "The fundamentals that support the fundamentals..." or "the domestic economy that supports the domestic economy...." Describing the economy's current condition says nothing about the future, yet economists continually speak as if it does.

The error of belief in outside causality is not confined to economists. Even physicists who discover the impotence of this presumption cannot let go of it. For example, although Caldarelli, Marsili and Zhang demonstrate that a small group of traders can mimic the actual stock market without a single outside causal element, they still cling to the old myths. "By no means," they say, "can one conclude that our model captures all the relevant aspects of a real market....In a true economy, there are external driving factors, such as politics, natural disasters, human psychology, etc."[47] The first sentence is careful science; the latter sentence is pure assumption. It is also inaccurate to include "human psychology," which is not an external factor but the essence of what the researchers have studied. This leaves natural disasters, which have zero effect on the stock market (try to pick out one on a chart of the averages) and politics. To boil down their only presumed external factor, then, it is politics. Despite the dramatic implications of their study, the authors maintain the assumption that "authorities" can "correct" markets in the "real" world, as revealed by the quote cited earlier in this chapter. That hard-nosed scientists include these unsupported examples of outside event causality shows how deeply the underlying presumption is held.

The Faddishness and Unreliability of Purported Economic and Financial Relationships

This section undertakes a cursory review of the role that conventional economic discourse has played in influencing investors' views of what data is helpful in stock market forecasting. It should give you an idea of how lacking is a coherent framework from which to reason.

Throughout most of the 1980s, stock market watchers waited in fear of the weekly money supply report. It was widely and firmly believed that this figure would determine the course of stock prices. When that fixation died, the bond market became the key. Every tick in bonds was scrutinized for foreknowledge of the next short-term move in stocks. Later came the insistence that the near-term trend of the U.S. dollar held the answer to where stocks would go. In every case, economists had ready detailed explanations of the causal relationship involved. Investors *abandoned* each focus as readily as they assumed it, the *difference being the lack of any explanation for doing so and the lack of any notice that there wasn't one.*

How did each of these points of focus fare as keys to market behavior? The popular argument concerning the money supply was that a "high" figure is bearish because it might result in higher interest rates, which are bad for stocks. The only thing contradicting this conventional wisdom is the fact that the money supply roared throughout the 1980s bull market, and when the increases finally slowed, the market crashed. In other words, the correlation was the opposite of what popular economic wisdom supposed.

The "bond market indicator" became very popular by the mid-1980s on the theory that since declining interest rates are bullish for stocks and vice versa, and since everyone knows this, then every movement in U.S. T-bond futures prices would translate into a movement in the same direction in the stock market. In other words, a rise in bond prices means a drop in interest rates, which means less competition for stocks, which means stocks go up. The daily and weekly trends of stocks and bonds began to diverge about the time this relationship was popularized. They became almost entirely disconnected for months during mid-1987, when the most money was being bet on their prior lock-step relationship. Soon, daily commentators forgot about the whole idea.

The dollar's value was the next point of focus. The dollar had risen from 1979 to 1985. It was first viewed as a welcome event, evidence that inflation might be slowing and the U.S. was becoming strong again in the eyes of the world. Then economists said the dollar was "too high" because its value was supposedly hurting exports. Stock market followers initially welcomed the decline in the price of the dollar that began in 1985. That trend was dramatic and persistent as well, so it created full-blown worry by early 1987 that it had gone "too far," and what was worse, there had been little change in exports. All this hand wringing amounted to naught. Throughout this time and despite huge oscillations in the price of the dollar relative to other currencies, the DJIA continued to advance as if nothing about the dollar mattered to it. This was in fact the case. Eventually, people stopped watching the dollar, too. (But like all these points of focus, it will return.)

What do these fixations have in common? First, they reveal a desire among investors to have one simple indicator of the future course of stock prices. Second, not one of them is an indicator derived from market activity itself; each one is from outside the market and simply presumed to have an impact upon it. Third, all have apparently logical explanations. Fourth, intense scrutiny of each one of these "key figures" was in fact counterproductive to a correct assessment of the trend of the stock market. All served to keep investors' eyes off the ball. Finally, each new key-relationship claim appeared at first blush to sound reasonable, but it was never connected to enough, or any, history. Indeed, none of them was the least bit investigated, as in each case, a brief glance at a graph would have instantly debunked the claim. Nobody, it seems, ever bothered to look.

One reason why no one investigates these purported financial and economic relationships is that their purpose is to be tools not of understanding
but of rationalization. Each time, knowing too much would destroy the
utility of the tool. It is easier for the neocortex to rationalize when it does
not know or think too much. That is why one day in a bull market, it can be
found engaged in explaining why a *rise* in the Nikkei is bullish for U.S.
stocks ("It is a vote of confidence that the Japanese recession will not deepen
and so will not spread to the United States"), and the next day it can be
found engaged in explaining why a *drop* in the Nikkei is bullish for U.S.
stocks ("That money will have to flee to a strong market"). The same available duality of meaning holds for *all* of the above-mentioned "relationships."
Here is an example: "A falling dollar is good because it makes our exports
more affordable" and "A rising dollar is good because a strong currency
reflects a strong economy." Can you do it with the "money supply" indicator?

Two Detailed Examples: Corporate Earnings and the National Trade Balance

I could choose to detail examples of supposed causal relationships
that you would quickly accept as bogus ideas. Instead, I shall deliberately
investigate two ideas that most people hold very strongly and which they
have held for many years. If we can debunk these two time-honored cer-
tainties, we can easily debunk the next one that comes along.

Corporate Earnings

As I write this paragraph, today's newspaper sports this headline in
the business section: "Determining What Will Move Market Not Difficult
— But Forecasting Its Direction Is Harder." The "easy" part is no surprise,
since virtually everyone in finance agrees: "Earnings are the primary sources
of stock price movement, which accounts for Wall Street's preoccupation
with next month's earnings reports...."[48]

Is the indicator valid? Are stocks *driven* by corporate earnings? In
June 1991, *The Wall Street Journal* reported on a study by Goldman Sachs's
Barrie Wigmore, who found that "only 35% of stock price growth [in the
1980s] can be attributed to earnings and interest rates." Wigmore concludes
that all the rest is due simply to *changing social attitudes toward holding
stocks*. (Actually *all* of it is due to changing social attitudes, and earnings
are their *product*.) Says the Journal, "[This] may have just blown a hole
through this most cherished of Wall Street convictions."[49] This study shows

that *even in retrospect*, the "fundamentals" that most analysts are relying upon have little relationship to stock price movement.[50]

What about simply the *trend* of earnings vs. the stock market? Well, since 1932, corporate profits have been down in 19 years. The Dow *rose* in 14 of those years. In 1973-74, the Dow *fell* 46% while earnings *rose* 47%. 12-month earnings peaked at the bear market low. Earnings do *not* drive stocks. As Figure 19-2 illustrates and as Arthur Merrill showed years ago,[51] earnings *lag* stock trends. As shown in Chapter 16, the economy lags stock trends. It is therefore *impossible* for earnings or the economy to drive stocks. Forecasting the stock market is indeed impossible when the supposedly easy part is a wrong premise.

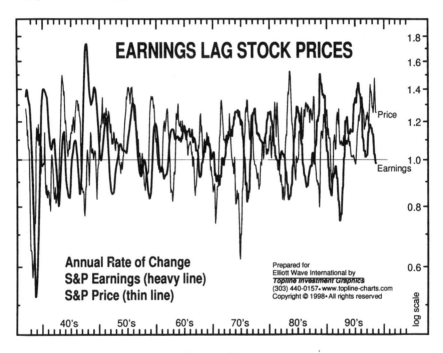

Figure 19-2

Trade Figures

In 1988, investors became "fixated" and "riveted," according to *The Wall Street Journal*, upon the monthly reported U.S. balance of trade with foreign nations. As with the other figures cited previously and now temporarily abandoned, this one appears to act as a simple indicator of stock prices. It is derived from outside the market. It has an apparently logical explanation: trade deficits (a negative value of U.S. exports minus imports) are bad for our country's "balance of payments," so they are bad for the country, so they are bad for stocks. There is only one problem: The facts are once again in direct opposition to the assumption.

Figure 19-3 reveals that in fact the trade gap has followed the rises and falls of the U.S. stock market and economy very closely, *but in precisely the opposite way that economists assume.* The bigger has been the deficit, the *stronger* have been the stock market and the economy, and vice

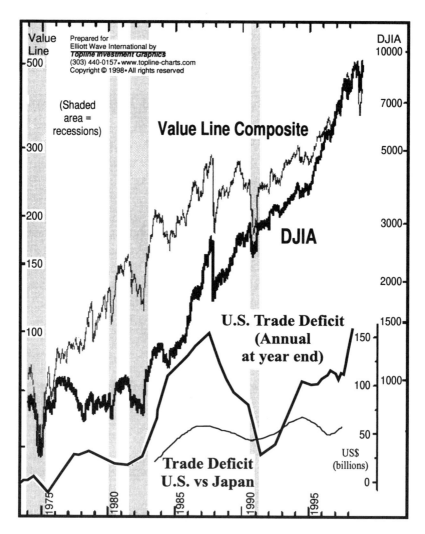

Figure 19-3

versa. Despite countless reports that "the trade deficit is slowing economic growth," statistics reveal the opposite experience for decades. A cursory perusal of Figure 19-3 reveals that the monthly trade deficit has expanded throughout most of the 1975-1998 bull market. Had the devil approached you in 1975 and given you the next 23 years of trade balance figures in exchange for your soul, you would have sold short right then and gone bankrupt ten times over as a result. The only periods that you would have been bullish (1978-1982 and 1987-1991), you would have made nothing.

As for the economy, the recessions of 1980 and 1982 followed a narrowing trade deficit. The next time the deficit began to narrow, in late 1987, it again led three years later to a recession, as the deficit shrank all the while. Those who followed the observations of economists and expanded their businesses in 1979 or 1989 on economists' predictions that the newly shrinking trade deficit was bullish got caught in *both* recessions.

In both cases, when the trade deficit began expanding again, so did the economy. Yet in 1994, the federal government, spurred on by economists, became apoplectic over the persistent trade gap and even risked a trade war over it. If the administration had somehow managed to force a further reduction in the trade gap, it would have derailed the economic recovery that came with its renewed expansion, reaping the opposite results that economists promised.

Today this erroneous theme remains alive and well. The Associated Press recently told us, "The Asian currency crisis hit America full force in March, pushing the month's trade deficit to a record."[52] What is the implication? "Analysts predict this year's overall deficit will easily be the *worst in history*," "worst" implying that it is a bad thing for the economy, despite 24 years of the reverse correlation. An economics writer for *The Atlanta Journal-Constitution* tells us, "The soaring trade deficit presents clear evidence that Asia's mess is starting to lap onto U.S. shores."[53] At any time the deficit was soaring during the preceding 24 years of a generally rising trend, did it present "clear evidence" of an Asian mess? No, because *Asia was not in a mess; it was booming. The supposed connection to any crisis in Asia does not exist.* As I write this paragraph, the figures for August have just been released. Concomitant with the new all-time high in stocks in July and the continued economic expansion, trade figures hit an all-time record deficit, showing that the trends remain in lock step. Needless to say, the chief economist at a "Washington think tank" says, "We have a lot of bad months ahead of us on trade...it wouldn't take a lot to push us into a recession."[54] If his forecast is for "bad months," i.e., higher deficits, then he should not be predicting a recession. If he expects a recession, then he should forecast a narrowing trade deficit. At least the writer of the AJC article admits this much: "It's hard to comprehend the story because the facts are so jumbled." The facts are *not* jumbled. It is the thinking that is jumbled because the wrong premise is unceasingly at war with the facts. The correct premise is that when the U.S. economy is strong, its citizens buy more goods from abroad, while citizens of other countries, most of which have a higher savings rate, save a portion of the money they receive rather than spend it. The trade balance does not cause economic trends; it results from them. This situation may change, but that is how it has transpired for at least the past few decades.[55]

A further irony of conventional assertion, after two dozen years of wrong-headed consternation over the rising trade deficit, is that when the U.S. economy contracts again (as it surely will), these same writers and analysts will be saying, "See, we told you that the big deficit was bad! Look what finally happened." Those of us watching the graph, however, will probably be observing a *shrinking* deficit along with the next contraction. We can further assume, until the relationship changes, that as the economy continues to shrink, the trade deficit will continue to shrink right along with it. Conventional analysts, meanwhile, will be saying that the new trend is bullish. Those who believe it will get caught in the developing economic downdraft for the same reason they were too cautious all the way up: a belief that the relationship of the trade balance to economic health is the opposite of what it actually is, both in causality and implication.

The Conflict Between Reality and False Premise

Even though most economists use the stock market as a leading economic indicator, they habitually present arguments reasoned in the other direction because they cannot imagine the proper chain of causality to be true. Conventional analysts try to reason from economics and political policy, which they call "the fundamentals," to mood (i.e., stock prices). This approach is backward, which is why it consistently fails at the most critical times. The so-called fundamentals are the caboose on the train. This approach appears successfully predictive occasionally when the train is on a long straightaway. Then the trends are the same. Those in the caboose, however, are unequipped to predict a coming curve in the track that will change the direction of the locomotive. However, those up ahead observing the direction of the locomotive can tell you quite reliably what the caboose will do. This is why an economist cannot predict the stock market, but a stock market observer can do quite well at predicting the economy.

The actual direction of cause and effect does not stop economists from continuing to assert its opposite. Six months after the stock and currency collapses in Thailand, the Associated Press on December 8, 1997 said, "The permanent closure of insolvent finance companies is expected to leave 5000 to 10,000 workers unemployed, rattle the already battered stock market and spark a further drop in Thailand's currency, the baht, which has lost more than 40% of its value against the dollar."[56] Observe that the stock market and currency collapsed *first*, precipitating the failure of companies and unemployment. Despite this chronology, experts interviewed by the press cannot help presuming that those events will be causal of stock market trends. If that were so, why did stocks bottom nearly a year before unemployment hit its peak in the Great Depression of 1933? Why didn't the highest number of business failures and workers unemployed in nearly a century then "rattle an already battered stock market"? The *Washington Post* likewise said on May 28, "...the latest display of labor unrest threatens to plunge South Korea into a new financial crisis."[57] However, there was no "labor unrest" or any other social crisis preceding the latest financial crisis, was there? Indeed, that country's social mood in the summer of 1997 was confident, ebullient, even downright giddy. But overwhelming contradiction is no deterrent to conventional analysts, where an erroneous underlying assumption stubbornly governs all commentary.

This foible is not new. Garfield Drew[58] and John Train[59] describe how investors of the late 1940s braced for a "typical postwar depression" that the majority of economists predicted would follow World War II. It never came. Nor should it have. A financial crisis in the 1850s *preceded* the Civil War. A financial crisis in the 1930s *preceded* World War II. While a deep recession did follow World War I, which is one of two apparent precedents that economists were using, the usual chronology is evident there as well in that before the war started, the stock market had been falling for two years, it was below its peak of eight years previous, and the economy had been in recession for an unprecedented four years out of five. While there is no tradition of postwar economic contraction, there is a very consistent precedent of prewar bear market. Because these facts do not fit the conventional prescription, they are ignored as meaningless.

Conventional Analysts Cannot Avoid Using Trend Extrapolation

Is there an internal logical flaw in using extramarket events for market forecasting? I think so.

If someone is bullish on stocks because interest rates have recently fallen, you are justified in asking, "How do you know that interest rates did not stop falling today, in which case stocks are about to decline?" He might respond, "well, the latest economic report shows a flat trend, which supports lower interest rates," in which case you are justified in asking, "How do you know that the economy didn't just turn up?" At some point, he must respond that he will wait for a change of some kind, a report of a stronger economy or a rate rise by the Fed. Then you can ask, "How do you know that the economic report you are waiting for will not reflect the *only* economic uptick or that the Fed will not raise rates *once* and then start lowering them again with the result that you will have sold your stocks at the bottom?" If he answers that he doesn't know, then he remains stuck with no basis for a forecast. If he continues to provide more causal indicators of his causal indicators, the chain is endless. Both of these answers are dead ends. His only way out of this dilemma is finally to provide a prediction based upon trend extrapolation. More often than not, an analyst pressed into this corner simply says that he sees no evidence of a change in trend for his supposed cause, an answer that relies on the fact that trends persist. The presumably trending cause (in this case the economy) will affect the trend of the next cause (in this case Fed policy), which will then affect a market (i.e., interest rates) that will affect the one he actually wants to predict (i.e., stocks).

Since the conventional analyst cannot avoid employing trend extrapolation at some point, might we ask him, "Isn't it far easier merely to extrapolate the trend of the market that you actually want to predict?" Instead of saying, "the trend of the economy is flat, which trend should continue, so the Fed should continue to lower interest rates, so stocks should continue to rise until the economic trend changes," he could simply say, "the trend of stocks is up until *that* trend changes." That way, he not only saves trouble but also avoids the pitfall of requiring his whole chain of causality to maintain itself. Because history shows numerous exceptions for each supposed relationship, each step removed from the market he wishes to forecast further weakens his market conclusion. In contrast, trend extrapolation works with equal effect and lack thereof with the market he is trying to forecast in the first place.

Conventional analysts would do far better to trash all of their supposed indicators and just trend-follow the market with a single moving average, like Dick Fabian[60] does. The chain of argument with a moving average trend indicator, as with Elliott wave analysis, is direct and finite. Indicators such as these speak to the future, and that's that.

Conventional Attempts Are Counterproductive to Anticipating the Future

I hope this book changes some economists' methods forever. Entrenched conventional economists may attack the thesis of this book. If they do so in a scholarly way, fine. If they disparage socionomics without much in the way of argument, it will be helpful for you to understand what legs they do not have to stand on.

Business Week summarized the state of modern economics in 1982 when it said, "[With] a dismal performance...economists revealed most clearly...the extent to which their profession lags intellectually."[61] Evidence of the failure of conventional forecasting methods is more than pervasively anecdotal. According to *The Wall Street Journal*, a study of its own surveys since 1982 of the country's top economists reveals that in the aggregate, these acknowledged experts predicted accurately the *direction* (forget the extent) of interest rates *only 22% of the time*, which is less than half the success rate that would be produced purely by *guessing*.[62] Conventional methods of economic prediction, then, produce worse than worthless results; they are typically *misleading*. As Paul Montgomery says bluntly, "Economic theory obviously fails abjectly at predicting interest rates over any time frame whatsoever."[63]

What about forecasting corporate earnings and stock prices? It is widely known by longtime market watchers (and shown statistically as well; see the study cited in Chapter 8) that both earnings estimates and buy/sell recommendations from brokerage-house "fundamental" analysts relentlessly lag stocks' price curves. The higher a stock goes, the more analysts in the aggregate adjust their earning estimates upward, so the more they insist on buying it. After a stock tops out, "strong buy" changes to "buy" when the stock is down 35%, then to "hold" when the stock is down 50%, then to "sell" at the bottom, when earnings estimates are finally revised downward. The lowest earnings reports and estimates come *after* the stock price recovers because as we have seen, earnings lag stock prices.

This persistent failure rate is not lost on economists. Most just play it safe by predicting growth all the time. *Business Week* said in 1996, "Over the past 25 years, economic forecasters have missed four of the past five recessions."[64] London's *Financial Times* likens economics to the businesses of "astrologers and quack doctors," whose clients nevertheless "continue to listen to them with extraordinary credulousness."[65]

Everyone knows *that* economists are almost always wrong. Now we need to understand *why* they are almost always wrong. In 1995, the London Economics consultancy analyzed predictions made by the U.K.'s top 34 economic forecasting groups, "including all the most quoted forecasters, [such as] the Treasury, the National Institute and the London Business School, [who use] elaborate econometric models of the economy."[66] John Kay, a professor of economics at the London Business School, reported on this study for the *Financial Times*. His cogent comments both describe the problem and hint at its cause. Read this description carefully:

> It is a conventional joke that there are as many different opinions about the future of the economy as there are economists. The truth is quite the opposite. Economic forecasters do not speak with discordant voices; they all say more or less the same thing at the same time; the degree of agreement is astounding. The differences between forecasts are trivial relative to the differences between all forecasts and what happens, [as] *what they say is almost always wrong*. It is clear from the analysis that there is a consensus forecast, which most forecasters cluster around to such a degree that it is barely worth distinguishing between one estimate and another. Yet the consensus forecast failed to predict *any* of the most important developments in the economy over the past seven years — the strength and resilience of the 1980s consumer spending boom, the depth and persistence of the 1990s recession, or the dramatic and continuing decline in inflation since 1991. Nor have the past four years been worse than usual for the forecasting profession. They did no better in the 1980s. And it is always safer to be wrong in a crowd. In large organisations, it is often more important to be wrong for the right reasons than to be correct. Even when they are proved wrong, forecasters see it as important to maintain the consensus in retrospect. For example, banks maintain as an article of faith that the depth of the recent recession and the magnitude of the property market collapse could not have been predicted. Looking more carefully at the figures in the tables, [we find that] the consensus forecast is easy to calculate, since it can be derived by taking the average of the present and the past. Yet the fundamental weakness in this approach is that it is incapable of identifying structural changes in the economy.[67]

These comments fit the thesis of this book. The relentless act of *herding*, which is due to fathomless feelings of *uncertainty*, which in turn is due to the application of methods that *do not work*, keeps the profession of economics in a perpetual fog. Chapters 10 and 11 of *At the Crest of the Tidal Wave* elaborate on the psychology behind conventional forecasting, revealing in more detail why it produces worse than random results.

Based upon their record, economists have no authority to complain about errors in the track record of practitioners of the Wave Principle. The pertinent question is, *"compared to what?"* Any approach that is *not persistently wrong* about future changes in trends and events is better than conventional methods. Any approach that has a rationale behind it is better, too. Socionomics wins on both counts.[68]

This is not to say that there are not legitimate gripes about how we fledgling socionomists conduct our craft. A crucial requirement of reliable forecasting is a thorough understanding of the limits of one's model. Although we are learning fast, we do not have those limits nailed down yet. Many Elliott wave practitioners are nonrigorous, sometimes too credulous, and often try to extract more from the principle than it will provide. Elliotters suffer from the same paleomentational impulses as economists, and sometimes it colors our predictions to the point of counter-productivity. Some of these problems result from the fact that socionomics is so new that there is no consistent line of inquiry, no cadre of supporters and no body of work to buttress our efforts. By necessity, practitioners of this new science are mavericks. We do, however, start with a stronger base because our premises are true. That is the reason for the great difference between our results and others'.

Why Does the Conventional Approach Remain So Entrenched?

If news is not the motor of market trends, and if outside forces are not causal to social mood and action, why do people assume that they are? There are two main reasons for the persistence of these myths.

As shown in Chapter 16 and discussed in Chapter 18, *economic and political news is not unrelated to the stock market; it lags the stock market.* One can be fooled by the proximity of market behavior and extramarket events because of a single important technical fact: *the market trends, and so does the news that results from the social mood change that propels it,* so the two are often going in the same direction. When conventional forecasters appear right, it is merely a reflection of the sociological fact that there *are* social trends. Economists' forecasts lag those trends, but for as long as the trend continues *past* the time that they first discern it, they can appear correct. The correlation between markets and news that does exist fools people into believing that there is empirical support for their apparently natural assumption that events are the causal factor. It also occasionally rewards economists and investors for their assumption about news, often for extended periods. Occasional reward is all it takes to reinforce the belief. Experiments show that lab rats will work much harder pushing a lever for an occasional randomly generated reward than a regularly predictable one.[69] In this situation at least, the same tendency appears to apply to people.

The second reason for the persistence of the belief in event causality is that it is so effortless. In Chapter 21, we explore astronomer Andrei Linde's theory that parts of the universe inflate exponentially in a self-replicating fractal, a process he calls "chaotic inflation." Linde muses on the long dominance of the "big bang" theory, saying, "One of the main reasons for the popularity of the old big bang scenario is that imagining the universe as a balloon expanding out in all directions is relatively easy. It is much harder to grasp the structure of an eternally self-replicating fractal universe."[70] I think that the "outside cause" paradigm has a firm hold on people's minds for the same reason. Like the expanding balloon analogy of the big bang, it is easy to imagine by simply extrapolating from physics.

Linde adds, "Once we began relaxing these [big bang] assumptions, we immediately found that inflation is not an exotic phenomenon invoked by theorists for solving their problems. It is a general regime that occurs in a wide class of theories of elementary particles." Similarly, when we delve into our subject, we find that the "general regime" of the Wave Principle "occurs in a wide class of theories" involving growth and life, while outside causality is more applicable to the behavior of billiard balls and balloons.

I assert that the matter is not simply that the purported causal relationships of macroeconomics are extremely complex or that they change at inopportune times but that in a fundamental sense, *there aren't any*. Markets follow the Wave Principle no matter what, and that is the only cause that is consistent. Once you can demonstrate to yourself that the stock market has a life of its own, you will begin to feel, as rightly you should, that it is the guys peering at and poring over each new statistic relating to the course of the economy or each new political nuance who are the real "tea leaves and entrails" bunch when it comes to anticipating the next move in the stock market. Conventional analysis is not a sound, reasonable approach; it is nonsense. It does not analyze the fundamental; it analyzes the extraneous.

"Economic forecasting," goes the old joke, "is like trying to drive a car blindfolded and following directions given by a person who is looking out the back window." With socionomics, we are no longer looking out the back window; we are facing forward. With the Wave Principle, we are no longer driving blind. We can see enough about the road ahead to negotiate the car.

NOTES

1 Cootner, P.H. (1964). *The random character of stock market prices.*

2 Firth, M. (1977). *The valuation of shares and the efficient-markets theory.*

3 Malkiel, B.G. (1985). *A random walk down wall street.*

4 Hector, G. (1988, October 10). "What makes stock prices move?" *Fortune.*

5 Cunningham, S. (1993, Fall). "Unit root testing: a critique from chaos theory." *Review of Financial Economics.*

6 Montgomery, P. (1996, May 17). Presentation. "Economic theory and technical analysis."

7 Malkiel, B. (1998, July/August). "Still on a random walk." *Bloomberg's Personal Finance.*

8 Frost, A.J. and Prechter, R.R. (1978). *Elliott wave principle — key to market behavior.*

9 Koselka, R. (1996, June 3). "The madness of well-heeled crowds". *Forbes.*

10 Brock, W.A., *et al.* (1992, December). "Simple technical trading rules and the stochastic properties of stock returns." *The Journal of Finance,* Vol. 47, No. 5.

11 Baker, M. (1995, October 7-8). "Investing: rhyme or reason?" *International Herald Tribune,* p. 6.

12 Malkiel, B. (1998, July/August). "Still on a random walk." *Bloomberg's Personal Finance* (quoting Richard Roll).

13 Klein, E. (1986, November). "Psychology meets the stock market." *Columbia.*

14 Donnelly, B. (1987, October 23). "Efficient-market theorists are puzzled by recent gyrations in stock market." *The Wall Street Journal.*

15 DeBondt, W. and Thaler, R. (July, 1985). "Does the stock market overreact?" *The Journal of Finance,* Vol. XL, No. 3, pp. 793-808.

16 It is very common for academic studies to have enough evidence to discover apparently constant market relationships such as this at just about the time they are ready to fail. The relationships are often valid, but only in context of the Wave Principle.

17 Brock, W.A. (1991). "Causality, chaos, explanation and prediction in economics and finance." *Social Systems Research Institute,* No. 387.

18 It is true despite some very inventive commentary from *The Wall Street Journal* that tried to blame it on a few words from the mouth of a government official, as if that were a rare event.

19 Hector, G. (1988, October 10). "What makes stock prices move?" *Fortune.*

20 Chapter 18 discussed the counter-intuitive exception.

21 Treynor, J. (1998, March/April). "Bulls, bears, and market bubbles." *Financial Analysts Journal.*

22 These ratios are derived from data provided by the Federal Reserve Bank of St. Louis (PO Box 442, St. Louis, MO 63166) and Ned Davis Research (2100 Riveredge Parkway, Atlanta GA 30238).

23 Goleman, D. (1989, August, 15). "Brain's design emerges as a key to emotions." *The New York Times.*

24 Kulkosky, E. (1977, October 15). "The Elliott wave's surprising message to investors." *Financial World.*

25 The Principle itself is probably on an Elliott wave of acceptance: three steps forward and two steps back.

26 Leontief, Wassily (1982, July 9). Letter to the editor. *Science.*

27 Brock, D. (1986, June 30). "Seeing the economy's future with a shattered crystal ball." *Insight.*

28 Coveney, P. and Highfield, R. (1995). *Frontiers of complexity*, p. 335.

29 Berry, J.M. (1998, July 6). "Key players control money supply." *The Washington Post.*

30 Brauchli, M.W. (1998, July 14). "Why the world bank failed to anticipate Indonesia's deep crisis." *The Wall Street Journal.*

31 For example, Harvard biologist Edward O. Wilson, who convincingly postulates a direct connection between genetics and culture in his book *Consilience*, nevertheless graciously accepts unchallenged the promise that "In the United Stated, the Federal Reserve Board now has enough knowledge and legal power to regulate the flow of money and prevent — we trust! — the economy from spinning into catastrophic inflations and depressions," irrespective of genetics, culture and six thousand years of economic history.

32 "Stand still, little lambs, and be shorn!" (1998, March). *Economic Education Bulletin.* American Enterprise Institute, Great Barrington, MA.

33 Dornbush, R. (1998, July 30). "Growth forever." *The Wall Street Journal.*

34 Ratajczak, D. (1998, August 30). "Global economy requires action." *The Atlanta Journal-Constitution.*

35 Evans-Pritchard, A. (1998, September 2). "'Plunge team' ready to spring into action." *Electronic Telegraph* (internet).

36 Wessel, D. and Davis, B. (1998, September 24). "How global crisis grew despite efforts of a crack U.S. team." *The Wall Street Journal.*

37 Caldarelli, G., *et al.* (1997, December 1). "A prototype model of stock exchange." *Europhysics Letters.*

38 Actually, many will whisper that the Fed bought S&P futures the day of the low, October 20. Had they not, we are then to presume according to the computer-causality model, the decline would have continued to zero.

39 This phrasing is from a January 1987 report from the Chase Manahattan Bank of London.

40 Litton, R.E. and Santomero, A.M. (1998, July 28). "Why a market correction won't replay 1987." *The Wall Street Journal.*

41 Dent, H.S. (1998). *The roaring 2000s*, p. 94.

42 "Economists forecast mild inflation of 2.5% yearly through 2008." (1998, May 26). *The Wall Street Journal.*

43 Sheeley, G. (1997, 14 April). "Runaway Tiger: Woods wins Masters by record 12 shots with 18-under total." *The Atlanta Journal-Constitution,* p. D1.

44 It is perturbing that conventional analysts have appropriated this word, as the actual *fundamentals* of market behavior are the unconscious forces that guide men in social mentation, the Elliott wave patterns that they produce, and at a deeper level the Fibonacci formology of nature's growth patterns.

45 Acker, L. (1998, August). "Why so bearish?" *3F Forecasts.*

46 "Economy surging behind spending." (1998, June 27). *The Atlanta Journal-Constitution.*

47 Caldarelli, G., *et al.* (1997). "A prototype model of stock exchange." *Europhysics Letters*, 40 (5), pp. 479-484.

48 Walker, T. (1998, June 21). "Determining what will move market not difficult — but forecasting its direction is harder." *The Atlanta Journal-Constitution.*

49 Lowenstein, R. (1991, June 6). "Goldman study of stocks' rise in '80s poses a big riddle." *The Wall Street Journal*, p. C1.

50 This is particularly evident in the 1980s and 1990s because the stock market has been in a *fifth* wave, whose product is weaker than that in a third wave (see discussion in Chapter 17).

51 Reference unavailable.

52 "Trade deficit soars to $13 billion." (1998, May 20). *The Atlanta Journal-Constitution.*

53 Geewax, M. (1998, June 21). "U.S. could become entwined in downturn." *The Atlanta Journal-Constitution.*

54 "Trade deficit hits record." (1998, October 21). *The Atlanta Journal Constitution.*

55 The full explanation is more complex. One of the many exports of the U.S. during its recent decades of economic strength has been dollars. Other countries' banks believe that this indefinable nonentity is a store of value, so they stock it as "reserves." One day, when U.S. economic soundness appears questionable, this socially shared mental image will dissolve, and many dollars will be desperately repatriated.

56 Horn, R. (1997, December 8). "Thailand starting big financial over-haul." *The Atlanta Journal-Constitution*, p. A12.

57 Jordan, M. (1998, May 28). "S. Koreans walk off their jobs...." *The Washington Post*.

58 Drew, G. (1955). *New methods for profit in the stock market.*

59 Train, J. (1994). *The money masters.*

60 Fabian Investment Resources, Huntington Beach, CA.

61 "A dismal performance." (1982, January 18). *Business Week*, p. 124.

62 Harman, T. (1993, July 6). "Economists look for moderate growth in second half...." *The Wall Street Journal*, p. A2.

63 Montgomery, P. (1998, February 4). *Universal Economics.*

64 Mandel, M.J. (1996, September 30). "Especially dismal at down-turns" *Business Week*, pp. 88-89.

65 Kay, J. (1995, September 29). "Cracks in the crystal ball." *Financial Times*.

66 *Ibid.*

67 *Ibid.* These sentences are substantially rearranged; I have omitted ellipses for reading clarity.

68 A rare few economists do pay homage to what matters at a funda-mental level. Clarence B. Carson says, "It is necessary to keep in mind throughout the study of economics the enduring nature of things. Only thus can we discover or be aware of the *principles*, the operation of cause and effect, *the order that underlies and endures* through change." [ref: Carson, C., (1990). *Basic economics.*]

69 Source unavailable.

70 Linde, A. (1994, November). "The self-reproducing inflationary uni-verse." *Scientific American*.

Chapter 20:

Some Key Fundamentals of Socionomics

Financial Man is Not the Same as Economic Man

It is universally presumed that the primary law of *economics*, i.e., that price is a function of supply and demand, also rules *finance*. However, human behavior with respect to prices of investments is, in a crucial way, the *opposite* of that with respect to prices of goods and services. When the price of a good or service rises, *fewer* people buy it, and when its price falls, *more* people buy it. This response allows pricing to keep supply and demand in balance. In contrast, when the price of an investment rises, *more* people buy it, and when its price falls, *fewer* people buy it. This behavior is not an occasional financial market anomaly; it always happens. Look at back at Figure 7-3, the graph of the dollar-valued trading volume in the U.S. stock market divided by the prevailing gross domestic product. As you can see, volume expands as stock prices rise and contracts as they fall. In economic matters, rising prices *repel* buyers; in investment matters, rising prices *attract* buyers. This difference is not incidental; it is fundamental.

Many market theorists argue that the law of supply and demand operates in finance but is simply "suspended" for periods of time because people "overreact" and "rationalize" with "elaborate arguments" why they should pay up for investments.[1] The difference between any such idea and what happens in markets for goods and services is irreconcilable by conventional economic theory. People never act in any such way with respect to goods and services. Most investors can quickly rationalize selling an investment because its price is falling or buying it because its price is rising, but there is not a soul who desperately rationalizes doing with less bread because the price is falling or who drives his car twice as much because the price of gasoline has doubled. In economic behavior, the law of supply and demand does not lie dormant *ever*. It is like the law of gravity; it works *all* the time. It cannot "fail to apply," even temporarily. Prices are the balance beam from which the scales of supply and demand hang. Changes in buying patterns are virtually instantaneous in responding to price changes for bread, cars, TVs and shoes.

In the same way, investment behavior has *its* iron law: the Wave Principle. This law governs unconscious, impulsive, collective herding behavior, while the law of supply and demand governs conscious, logical, individual economic decision-making. The former law governs prices for intangible values, whether associated with tangible goods or not; the latter law governs prices for utilitarian tangibles.[2] Attempting to apply the law of supply and demand to investment markets is akin to attempting to apply the laws of physics to falling in love. They do not pertain.

The law of supply and demand always produces *practical* behavior in the realm of economics. The Wave Principle (despite its apparent value for life and progress *per se*) produces *impractical* behavior in the realm of finance. In the *product* marketplace, the rational goal of survival leads to price stability and objectivity. In the *investment* marketplace, prerational impulses of survival lead to wild overvaluation and undervaluation. Time and again, observers, particularly those who understand the iron law of economics, complain that the stock market's action appears unreasonable. That observation is wholly correct. The decision to buy into rising prices and sell into falling prices is not governed by the reasoning neocortex but by the unconscious herding impulse, which generates inappropriate behavior in the financial realm as part of a generalized attempt to enhance the odds of survival. It is baffling only to those who insist that "supply and demand" rule finance.

It is not that reasonableness in finance is utterly absent; we are not talking about irrationality. People who invest in markets know through cold reason that they value their own lives and prosperity. Those who buy in bull markets are following the very reasonable desire to *enhance their sustenance*, while those who sell in bear markets are following the very reasonable desire to *survive*. Unfortunately, the portion of the brain that generates unconscious urges directs their behavior in this regard. The primitive mechanism employed is so inappropriate to the situation that instead of enhanced success, it produces guaranteed failure.

Because these desires *per se* are rational, they work just fine in the world of goods and services. In the product marketplace, the consumer wants prices lower while the producer wants them higher, and for the same fundamental reasons: survival and self sustenance. The process of mediating these identical goals between polarized dealers produces an objective, natural balance expressed as price.

In the world of investments, however, the consumer (who buys it) and producer (who creates and wants to sell more of it) *both want prices higher*. Rather than become excited to buy as prices *fall*, as consumers of goods and services do, investors become excited to buy as prices *rise*. Since desire and hope are entirely on the side of price rise, only fear and despair can be on the side of price decline. Thus, when prices fall, investors are pressured past endurance to sell. Both of these impulses are contrary to the way consumers behave with respect to goods and services.

The dynamics of the Wave Principle underlie financial markets and lead to nonobjective valuation. Individual investors who desire to be objective in financial speculation face the inescapable requirement of understanding that fact and its implications.

Direction, Volatility and Duration Do Not Determine the Source of Sociological Motive

Robert Schiller polled individual and institutional investors about why they sold stocks on October 19, 1987. Most of them admitted candidly that "they sold because others were selling,"[3] i.e., they were herding. It is welcome to have research telling us that the crash of 1987 was a "psychological event." However, no one ever thinks to poll investors about why they had *bought* stocks relentlessly throughout the preceding year. If any pollster did ask, *the truth would be exactly the same*, but he would find little honesty about that fact because in *rising* markets, people have plenty of time to let their neocortexes formulate all kinds of rationalizations for herding action. Panic is a faster-acting emotion than hope, and the neocortex is often stumped in coming up with an explanation for it. One of my favorite quotes in this regard, undoubtedly rushed out near press time, is this one from *The Wall Street Journal*: "The U.S. dollar continued to decline yesterday despite economic news that could have been bullish for the currency if traders' mood weren't so bearish."[4]

Market commentators often blame a declining trend on herding, but they virtually never ascribe a *rising* trend to herding. This convention is displayed so often that all one need do is read the papers for a few days to find an example. On June 2, 1998, the Dow Jones News Service quoted a brokerage firm's director of investment strategy after a few weeks of price decline in a broad list of technology stocks as follows: "The herd mentality is *taking over*." That is to say, herd mentality had nothing to do with the multi-year buying binge on all-time record volume producing all-time record valuation for technology stocks; *that*, we are to presume, was all fueled by the rational decision-making of independently minded individuals. On June 15, 1998, the morning after the intraday low of a correction in that index, *USA Today*, parroting economists, repeated, "the drop is based more on psychology than fundamentals."[5] A mere six trading days after that assessment was published, the NDX rocketed to a new all-time high. Once again, no experts claimed that that *rise* was due to psychology. As always, they found adequate "fundamentals" to explain the leap.

Direction is even presumed to affect the efficacy of fundamental indicators. Read this from October 9 of this year:

> Just 18 months ago in the midst of the steadily rising bull market, Wall Street's top strategists could start their computers, plug in the latest numbers for inflation, interest rates, dividends and corporate earnings, and come up with a reasonably plausible prediction of where the stock market was headed.

> But, my, how times have changed. Global financial markets are ricocheting. The usual relationships are gone. Stocks can't be counted on to move up as interest rates go down. The psychology of fear has become a big and changing factor, one that can't be plugged into economics-based models. No wonder the models are not much comfort any more.[6]

That is to say, psychology never interferes with these rational models of cause and effect when prices *rise*; it only happens when they fall. As you might guess, quick willingness to blame psychology only for declines is related to people's tendency, discussed in Chapter 18, to equate downtrends with unpredictability and uptrends with predictability. Of course, that the forecasts generated by the above-referenced models were any good on the upside is a myth; people simply felt comfortable and did not need to explain away all the errors. The market decline caused discomfort, evidence being that the above assessment was written on the exact day of the low following a three-month 20% decline in the S&P Composite index and a six-month 30% decline in the broader stock averages. (The limbic system is not only in charge of stock price trends; it is in charge of the timing of psychologically forced rationalization about them.)

The question is whether it is valid to assert, as it continually is, that psychology plays a part only in the crowd's stock-*selling* behavior and not its stock-*purchasing* behavior. The problem with the stance that advances are rational and declines are emotional is that market direction is simply a function of how the ratio of two assets is expressed. For example, one can plot stocks in terms of dollars or dollars in terms of stocks, or dollars in terms of yen or yen in terms of dollars. Stock prices express the value of stocks in terms of dollars (dollars per share), but they could just as well be inverted to show the value of dollars in terms of stocks (shares per dollar). Some of the graphs in this book depict the inflation-adjusted Dow, which expresses the value of stocks in terms of a pile of certain goods (goods per share). In each case, an uptrend in one expression of the ratio is a downtrend in the other. People are simply allowed a perpetual choice of whether to hold stocks or dollars, either of which can rise or fall in value with respect to the other. This means that *the engine of motivation for each direction cannot be different.* It is either rationality or herding behavior or some kind of mix, *all the time.*

A century ago, upon noticing that professional students of psychology made the same essential error in assigning only "bad" behavior to the herd mentality, Le Bon asserted the duality of crowd behavior:

> Without a doubt criminal crowds exist, but virtuous and heroic crowds, and crowds of many other kinds, are also to be met with. The crimes of crowds only constitute a particular phase of their psychology. The mental constitution of crowds is not to be learnt merely by a study of their crimes, any more than that of an individual by a mere description of his vices.[7]

The same is true of markets; one cannot understand herding behavior by studying only market crashes. He must study advances as well.

The direction of some markets does determine, for most people, *which* impulsive emotion is involved. This is particularly true for stock prices, in which most people are betting on the upside. That is why uptrends look different from downtrends on a stock market graph. Hope is the fuel for advances in stocks and fear the fuel for declines. Hope, fear and complacency express themselves differently. Hope tends to build slowly, while fear often crystallizes swiftly. Nevertheless, they are both still *emotions* and so derive from the same motivational engine.

In some markets, such as those for commodities, the price direction of these emotions is inverted. Commodity charts look different from stock index charts because their most violent movements, generated by fear (of drought, shortage, war, etc.) occur near tops instead of bottoms, and their lazier meanderings, generated by optimism, occur in mature downtrends instead of mature uptrends.

In some markets, direction has no such relationship because the two sides are equally opposed emotionally. For instance, a falling price of the U.S. dollar vs. the Japanese yen depicts, at the same time, an uptrend to a Japanese investor and a downtrend to a U.S. investor.

Regardless of which direction a market is trending, *all of its governing emotions are generated by the herding impulse*. In the most fundamental sense, the direction of prices does not change people's minds or their behavior. Their unconscious still follows the herd, expressing the form of the Wave Principle.

Neither does volatility determine the source of motive. As this book attests, there are many reasons to conclude that paleomentation rules even when financial markets appear calm and/or "reasonably valued," which times are merely transitional states along the emotional continuum. Herding and flocking animals are often calm for long periods when grazing or resting in a quiet field. When one begins to run or fly, however, panic throughout the group is a hairsbreadth away from being triggered. Similarly in the stock market, the reversal of a trend is due when just one extra change of mind is required to tip the balance. When that person makes his decision, the trend reverses, and the dynamic is played out in the other direction.

The duration of a trend is likewise irrelevant to the source of the market's motive. Some professors go way out on a limb to declare that *upon occasion*, and *in the short run*, financial markets become emotional rather than rational. One says, for instance, "In the *short run* (anything from a day to a few months), emotions and other biases may lead us to make a decision that may not be based on rationality."[8] The authors of the market simulation experiment discussed in previous chapters issue a similar explanation for the immutable patterns they have uncovered. Like governments after a crash, they attribute the results to technically oriented speculators as distinct from fundamentally oriented long-term investors: "Th[e results] suggest that the statistics we observe in real markets is mainly due to the interaction among 'speculators' trading on *technical* grounds, regardless of economic *fundamentals.*"[9] Elliott dispensed with this idea sixty years ago when he showed that markets are fractals. Mandelbrot again dispensed with this idea over a decade ago when he said about near and long-term market fluctuations, "the mechanisms don't seem to be different." The idea that "investors" trade rationally on external economic fundamentals while "speculators" trade emotionally on internal psychology is to assign a different motive to someone trading long term vs. someone trading short term. My own observations suggest no difference whatsoever other than time frame. When the public commits to investing "long term" after years of bull market, it is a purely psychological phenomenon that is analogous to a speculator committing to a rally a day or two before the top. As Chapters 5, 6, 16 and 18 attest, outside factors do not drive market behavior at *any* degree of trend.

We must recognize that rising markets have the same causal origin as falling ones, calm ones the same as volatile ones, and long-term ones the same as short-term ones. The Wave Principle reveals unequivocally that a structural dynamic, probably impelled by paleomentation, is in control of the aggregate stock market trend and level, and therefore social mood, *at all times.*

The Inapplicability of the Concept of Nonlinearity to Formological Systems

"Chaos" denotes physical processes that superficially appear random because of their immense variability of result but which in fact are patterned in hidden ways that adhere to mathematical formulae. Chaos theory made a great breakthrough in finding order in presumably random processes. Though utterly determined, chaotic processes are not predictable past a short time because the slightest variation in initial conditions changes the outcome.

"Complexity" denotes dynamical systems that generate paths of evolution. Complexity theory claims to have found only a vague order in self-organizing systems, one that is based upon structural influences but not fully determined. Complex systems are therefore presumed to be just as unpredictable as chaotic systems.

Both chaos and complexity are considered to be "nonlinear," which means that output is not proportional to input. In my opinion, it is incorrect to describe financial markets as nonlinear phenomena. The very concepts of linearity and nonlinearity depend upon the idea of cause and effect generated by "input" affecting the system. In a linear system, the same cause always produces the same effect, while in a nonlinear system, the same cause can have very different effects, such as the snowflake that finally causes the avalanche. However, financial market movements *cannot* result from a chain of incremental causes that trigger a reaction *because they follow the Wave Principle*. If the cause of a market's process is its form, then in a sense, the system *is linear*, or perhaps better said, *direct*. When the stock market completes a fifth wave, it retreats in corresponding degree. There is never an essential difference in result. This conclusion pertains to every system that progresses in waves. The concept of nonlinearity in such systems is therefore not paramount, and may not even apply.

For all systems that follow the Wave Principle, then, and perhaps for all systems that are robust fractals, the idea of nonlinearity may turn out to be an interim concept. It falsely presumes linear event causality *and* deduces unpredictability of result when in fact, (1) the results are not unpredictable, and (2) there is a direct cause to explain them. Such systems are not linear or nonlinear, as events are irrelevant. Such systems are *formological*, which means that they proceed relentlessly according to form. I propose the term *formological system* for such phenomena.

The November 1997 *New Scientist* suggests that some scientists may be edging toward this way of thinking:

> For hundreds of years, science has proceeded on the notion that things can always be understood – and can only be understood – by breaking them down into smaller pieces and by coming to know those pieces completely. Systems in critical states – and they seem to be plentiful – flout this principle.[10]

What the author means is that the structure of systems in critical states (see Chapter 3) is not dependent upon the properties of their parts and the directional causality of events perpetrated by those parts but upon a *form* that wells up within or imposes itself upon the system. The Wave Principle shows that *form,* not atomistic cause and effect, determines all social systems and perhaps all living systems. Chapter 21 further explores this theme.

The False Presumption of Unpredictability for Complex Systems

Belief in the inherent unpredictability of complex systems is entrenched. Part I of this book argues that there is far more order than currently believed in formological systems such as robust fractals, including waves and arbora. The following discussion shows how radical this idea is.

After obliterating the idea of randomness as fundamental to nature, chaos and complexity theorists quickly reenshrined it when they found that they were not immediately able to forecast specifics of the outcomes of their processes. Paul Davies, in *The Cosmic Blueprint*, states this conclusion succinctly:

> Typically, errors in ordinary dynamical systems grow in proportion to time (i.e., linearly). By contrast, in a chaotic system, the errors grow at an escalating rate; in fact, they grow exponentially with time. *The randomness of chaotic motion is therefore fundamental*, not merely the result of our ignorance. Gathering more information about the system will not eliminate it. *In other words, all power of prediction is lost.*[11]

The April 1997 *New Scientist* reiterates what complexity theorists currently believe: Even though we know that complex phenomena follow power laws, "it is *impossible to predict even roughly* the size of the next step"[12] in *any* system that follows a power law, be it earthquakes, bird flight or the stock market.

Chaotic systems, say scientists, are inherently unpredictable due to the "butterfly effect" (a phrase coined by MIT meteorology professor Edward Lorenz), which is the idea that small changes in "initial conditions" will result in massive changes later. For instance, a butterfly flapping its wings over Bolivia affects air currents, and if you do not take the butterfly into account, you cannot predict the weather in Siberia.

Articles, books and programs on social forecasting parrot the idea, erroneously applying it to formological systems as if it is a principle. Michael Barnsley on PBS says, "The thing that has come out of the Mandelbrot set...is that even in a utopian world, in practice you may not be able to predict the future; it can be deterministic in principle but not in practice."[13]

Edgar E. Peters, who in 1989 presented the idea of fractals in financial markets to *The Financial Analysts' Journal*, challenging EMH, nevertheless makes this assertion in the March-April 1991 issue:

> The further out in time we go, the less reliable our forecasts are. Th[is] point is particularly important. It means that, as with the weather, accurate, long-range economic forecasting is not feasible from a practical standpoint. Even if we were able to determine the equations of motion underlying the S&P 500, we would still not be able to forecast beyond a short time frame....[14]

The Fortune Sellers, by William Sherden asserts, "Complex systems have no natural laws governing their behavior at either their microlevel (individual humans) or their macrolevel (the economy); thus, complex systems cannot be scientifically predicted."[15] The *Dick Davis Digest*, summarizing the conclusions of several writers on the subject, states flatly, "The bottom line in applying chaology to financial markets is that forecasting is a waste of time; the chaotic nature of chains of events make predictions impossible."[16] John Liscio in *Barron's* says, "Any prediction that extends more than a month or so into the future is simply destined to fail."[17] "Simply" is exactly how this position is reasoned, as it first assumes the wrong causality (that events cause events) and then proclaims failure as therefore inevitable.

Fancy as it sounds, this idea, which permeates complexity discourse, is not new. Alfred Marshal, an English economist and John Maynard Keynes' teacher, noted in his 1890 book, *Principles of Economics*, that economic phenomena "do not lend themselves easily to mathematical expression." Philosopher Karl Popper said in 1957, "There is no doubt that the analysis of any concrete social situation is made extremely difficult by its complexity."[18] These long-running presumptions are valid only when one restricts his formulae to those applicable to physics and further presumes, as people still do today, that there are no mathematics distinctly applicable to social interaction. This long-standing error is understandable, as there has been little basis to assume otherwise until now. However, this does not excuse the arrogance and expressions of utter certainty that are typical of some modern proponents of this view.

The view expressed by these various quotations is wrong. To be sure, if one applies tools applicable to systems of linear causality to attempt to predict outcomes of formological systems, the result will be failure. The proper prediction of such systems is not in this approach. The key to predicting formological systems is in their *patterns*. I cannot reconcile the above view of market behavior, the "butterfly effect" view, with any experience I have had forecasting with the Wave Principle. What "errors" are they talking about? What randomness? What events? Randomness, events and error have nothing to do with the path of the stock market, much less are they fundamental.

In fact, there is not a shred of evidence that errors in forecasting the stock market escalate over time. Though two of the preceding quotations claim that predictions within "a short time frame" that extend only "a month or so" are reasonably expected to be accurate, there is no indication that any analyst depending upon event causality can predict the stock market over a month or so or even over a day or so or a minute or so. Because forecasting the stock market on this basis is *equally* impossible over all durations, the premise of event causality and chaotic error amplification must be false.

When applying the Wave Principle, the length of time into the future *per se* has nothing at all to do with forecasting accuracy. The fundamental determinant of forecasting accuracy is the *clarity of form*. The important question is, at what degrees have the developing patterns provided enough information to generate useful probabilities? Those are the degrees at which prediction will be the most reliable and accurate, whether they anticipate developments going out days or centuries.

In fact, contrary to all current views on the subject, it is the *long-term social trends*, the ones that chaos scientists say are impossible to predict, that are in fact *easier* to predict. Chapters 5 and 17 provide evidence of this fact. The reason that long-term trends are easier to forecast is that there are much more data to apply in one's analysis of form (such as breadth, volume, sentiment and behavioral statistics in markets, as described in Chapter 7) as well as a higher component of accuracy in the sociometer that one is using (for instance, aggregate stock prices).

The philosopher Kierkegaard, who correctly posited that progress is not smooth, was nevertheless similarly pessimistic about predictability. "In life, only sudden decisions, leaps or jerks can lead to progress. Something decisive occurs always only by a jerk, by a sudden turn *which neither can be predicted from its antecedents nor is determined by them.*"[19] The fact of the Wave Principle (1) affirms Kierkegaard's observation about progress and regress but (2) negates his assumptions about their unpredictability and (3) clarifies what antecedents do and do not determine the subsequent sudden turn.

Prigogine said resignedly in 1990, "I can never come up with an absolute theory of the stock market or of traffic flow because I can't read your soul."[20] The Wave Principle qualifies as an absolute theory of the stock market because it allows us to view, and to a great degree read, the soul of collective man.

Sherden adds this presumable *coup de grace* reason against economic predictability: "Complex systems are so highly interconnected with numerous positive and negative feedback loops that they often have counterintuitive cause-and-effect results."[21] Here are both the *reason* that herding takes place (feedback) and a correct observation that the typical outcome is *counterintuitive* to the neocortex's cause-and-effect presumption that actions and events cause actions and events. Despite the author's presumption, these observations do *not* speak to predictability, and they *are* compatible with the Wave Principle.

James Gleick said in a 1985 article, "Mandelbrot's mimicking of stock market and river charts *does not help in predicting* particular rallies and floods."[22] That is true, because he has mimicked only one very rough aspect of the stock market and flooding patterns: their fractal irregularity. He has not even considered, much less discovered, that they might exhibit forms.

The Wave Principle makes obsolete the idea that there is some kind of principle of inherent unpredictability in all complex systems. It presents a leap in scientific knowledge and value: Forecasting is possible in any system that displays the Wave Principle.

The Probabilistic Nature of Scientific Social Forecasting

An article entitled "Chaos" contrasts two long-standing views of the predictability of nature:

> The French mathematician Pierre Simon de Laplace [in 1776] proposed that the laws of nature imply strict determinism and complete predictability, although imperfections in observations make the introduction of probabilistic theory necessary. Poincare [in 1903] foreshadowed the contemporary view that arbitrarily small uncertainties in the state of a system may be amplified in time and so predictions of the distant future cannot be made.[23]

The Wave Principle says that both of these views are wrong, at least as they apply to nature's social trends, which are neither completely predictable nor utterly unpredictable in the distant future ("in the distant future" meaning, in modern expressions of this sentiment, "of any useful duration"). In fact, they are *highly* predictable in both *general* and *probabilistic* terms and *somewhat* predictable in *specific* terms. What is more, these facts pertain *regardless of the time scale*, as clarity of pattern is the prime determinant of predictability.

The Wave Principle guarantees reliable forecasting only of *probabilities*. It allows us to predict some aspects of the future and not others. For example, early in a new social mood trend, we can forecast society's coming *character* changes but not necessarily specific events. We can forecast that a major rising impulse wave will bring an increase in goodwill and productivity. The specific decisions that each man makes and the specific social actions and events that result depend upon countless details and are therefore chaotic. As the trend progresses, however, we can watch for signs to indicate such specifics and actually anticipate some of them quite well, as demonstrated in Chapter 17.

When predicting wave forms themselves, a comparatively difficult task, we might be able to anticipate, for instance, a five-wave advance of a certain relative size and duration, as various Elliotters did in the excerpts presented in Chapter 5. However, there is no known way to anticipate whether that advance will have an extended first, third, or fifth wave, or no extension at all or whether the movement will adhere to a parallel channel or whether an impulse will end with a diagonal triangle. (Figures 2-1 through 2-7 display the diversity of appearance in impulses.) Still, we do have immense knowledge of probabilities, as you can see from all the guidelines for impulses cited in Chapter 3. The good news is that such questions often do not matter. If we anticipate a five-wave structure, often all that is required is to observe its progress and decide when it is over. Given the fractal nature of the move, the fifth wave will subdivide into five smaller waves, and so on, providing a solid basis for making that decision.

Some people who come in contact with the Wave Principle dismiss it when they find out it cannot predict the future perfectly. This is like a blind man foregoing surgery to bring about sight in one eye because he would prefer to have sight in both. The probabilistic aspect of social forecasting is simply what is available; it is the reality of the situation, and nothing will change it. A search for the proverbial "holy grail" in finance or any other social science is as futile as the name implies.

It should not be too hard to get over this hurdle. In 1927, Werner Heisenberg discovered that subatomic particles' position and timing could be predicted only in terms of probability. If we must be satisfied with the fact that these *physical events* can be foretold only probabilistically, should we really gripe that predicting *social events* has the same restriction? We all accept that there are specific laws governing cloud formation, earthquakes and plant growth. We also accept that the *product* of these laws is immensely complex and variable, and predictable only in probabilistic terms. The same thing is true about human social mood and the history that it generates. So at times, we will know more than most people by understanding these laws, *and* we will often be able to anticipate the *character* of the next trend in social mood, *and* we will have a few very important, even crucial, insights about coming events, *but* there is no way we will know everything, or even most things, about the specific product of those laws. Similarly, we might be able to predict the conditions that will produce a jungle or a desert, and we might even be able to guess quite a few particulars thereof, but we cannot predict the future of every plant or the shifting of every sand dune. This degree of forecasting ability with the Wave Principle reflects what Yale professor of applied physics Roderick V. Jensen, in contrast to most of his colleagues, says is true of all chaotic systems:

> Chaotic dynamical systems are also like football games. Even with the largest imaginable digital computer, you could not predict the outcome with certainty.... Because of the complexity and unpredictability of chaos, direct numerical simulations of football games and turbulent flows are likely to remain impractical with even the largest supercomputers. *However, we can nevertheless compute reliable odds or probabilities for the outcomes of these processes.*[24]

Very recent work by Sornette and Johansen, published just months ago, supports this view. These authors call the stock market "a dynamical out-of-equilibrium...complex system," the same system that the legion of writers cited earlier say cannot be predicted at all. Yet they come to a rare conclusion:

> Crashes have their origin in the collective "crowd" behavior of many interacting agents.... The underlying cause of [a] crash must be searched years before it in the progressive accelerating ascent of market price[s].... The origin of crashes is...constructed progressively by the market as a whole. The main point of this paper is that the market anticipates the crash in a subtle self-organized and cooperative fashion, *hence releasing precursory "fingerprints" observable in the stock market prices.*[25]

In other words, there is an element of predictability in markets not despite their complexity but because of it.[26] This conclusion is along the lines of Coveney and Highfield's hesitant observation that "work... [involving]...evolutionary and nonlinear principles...provides all-important evidence that the complex behavior of financial markets *is* predictable to some extent."[27]

I see no reason why this view should be so tentatively advanced. Nature's laws generally produce predictable results, yet most scientists currently believe that complexity (1) is controlled by laws and (2) produces utterly unpredictable results. I believe that this view must be modified.

Systems that follow patterns are in fact highly predictable, within limits and in terms of probabilities. Ultimately, then, we can say that *laws of formological systems* lead to *utterly predictable results* within the confines of *probability statements*. That is how I view the Wave Principle, and its successful application in that light bears out that view.

Indeed, does it make sense that scientists quickly and emphatically posit randomness in any process for which we have yet to discover a law that applies? The word "universe" means "one order." So many assumptions of randomness have been disproved over the centuries and particularly over the past two decades that perhaps we would do better to begin with the opposite assumption. That is what Elliott did in his first published words about the stock market:

> No truth meets more general acceptance than that the universe is ruled by law. Without law, it is self-evident there would be chaos, and where chaos is, nothing is.... Very extensive research in connection with...human activities indicates that practically all developments which result from our social-economic processes follow a law that causes them to repeat themselves in similar and constantly recurring serials of waves or impulses of definite number and pattern.... The stock market illustrates the wave impulse common to social-economic activity.... It has its law, just as is true of other things throughout the universe.[28]

To put it in modern terms, there is no "butterfly effect" in social mood. There is no hurricane or earthquake effect. There is no peace or war effect. There is no exogenous effect, period. Social mood is formological, not reactive. On the other hand, minute details of the tangible actions that *result* from social mood are nearly infinitely variable and may indeed be subject to a butterfly effect. For instance, the precise outcome of a negative social mood manifestation such as war may depend upon whether there is a fog over the English Channel or whether the leader of one side is visited by a pneumonia bacterium.

The Value of Forecasting with the Wave Principle

With the caveat of immense specific variability within the known aspects of the Wave Principle, it is still the case that the practical value of all we know about it is immense. The first fantastic value that the Wave Principle provides is an amazing *perspective*, as you can see in Chapter 5. The second value is an occasionally remarkable *accuracy*, as you can see in Chapter 6. The third great value is that it provides a basis for assessing the past and analyzing the present in a *consistent context,* to which all the predictive literature on the subject attests. Finally, the Wave Principle indicates in advance the relative *magnitude* of the next period of social progress or regress. With all these gifts, we have a basis for informed, truly rational decision-making with regard to anticipating the tenor of future events. Its very nature forces us to look at the big picture, elevating our perceptions above the cacophony of daily news and providing the opportunity to make sense of the great social trend changes and the dramatic events that accompany them. As a result, the Wave Principle provides a basis for achieving a great sense of calm about the future, which no longer appears as a black cloud of unknowable chaos (sometimes just a grey cloud of partly knowable chaos).

The *general results* of social mood, i.e., economic trends, political trends, peace and war, etc., are fairly easy to predict, as they follow what has already occurred in social mood. Predicting social mood trends themselves, and their immediate reflectors such as stock index trends, fashion and entertainment trends, etc., is more difficult, but the Wave Principle at least provides a basis for doing so. With knowledge of how the patterns unfold, to the extent of our ability, effort and emotional detachment, we can enjoy success even at that daunting task.

Because the Wave Principle describes patterns of collective behavior, the accuracy of any resulting forecast depends upon (1) the reliability of the investing crowd's behavioral patterns and (2) the ability of an analyst to identify the relevant ones properly. In fact, the patterns, while varied, are more than reliable; within the bounds of their definitions, they are inviolate, a characteristic that makes wave analysis incalculably superior to other methods. An analyst's ability to identify the relevant patterns, interpret them properly and anticipate the ones to follow is another matter. *That* task is exceedingly difficult. Nevertheless, even on that score, the Wave Principle provides some advantages that most forecasting methods lack. For instance, it provides a method of conceiving and then ranking alternative scenarios. Perhaps most important, the Wave Principle provides a built-in mechanism for changing one's mind. The ultimate determinant of the objective analyst's opinion is the *market itself,* not a presumption about outside causes. This approach provides an objective basis for staying in tune with the developing trends and for changing one's opinion when necessary.

Social forecasting is an ability that has deftly eluded man throughout his existence and indeed has been considered as impossible as a perpetual-motion machine. The Wave Principle changes all that. Because of it, we finally have a way to forecast much about our social future, not with magic or revelation or astrology or sorcery or voodoo or mindless linear extrapolation, but with science.

Coveney and Highfield assert, quite generously given the state of conventional economics, that "economics straddles the divide between science and the humanities." With the Wave Principle, economics is now science, and with socionomics, even the humanities are tools of science.

The Role of Percepts in Forming an Accurate Concept of Human Social Behavior

Some critics quickly presume that the Wave Principle is "based on" a mathematical model, which would imply numerology and data fitting the market to the theory. Others presume it was "derived from" a grand analogy to nature's processes. Both of these assumptions are utterly false. If either were true, then the risk of theory shaping observation would be real. But the patterns were uncovered empirically with no preconceived notions whatsoever along either of those lines, which fact the literature proves unequivocally. Thus, the discovery of the Wave Principle *began* with percepts and it can be *reduced* to percepts. At bottom, we can point and say, *"Look."*

This fact is diametrically opposed to most of what passes for macroeconomic analysis, which too often advances formulas and theories irrespective of observation. For instance, in literally hundreds of instances, the media have reported an economist saying (usually when the stock market is down for a few weeks) that "the wide and widening U.S. trade deficit is bad for the economy and bearish for the market." It sounds logical at first blush, but look again at Figure 19-3. What do you *see*? You see that the trend of the trade deficit has waxed and waned in *precisely the opposite way* from what the theory presumes. *So what are you going to believe, a logical assertion, or your eyes?*

On this crucial question rests your chance for success. In the case of the trade deficit, the wrong answer *is* logical. If so, how can it be wrong? It can be wrong if the premise behind the logic is false. In this case, that is a fact that one can discern simply by looking. Your eyes come first.

What do you think happens when you show that graph to someone who believes otherwise? He evades it. He does not comment. He will not accept that trees are green if he thinks they should be blue. Paradox stymies him instead of igniting his mind to inquire. As Stephen M. Goldfeld once noted, "An economist is someone who sees something working in practice and asks whether it would work in principle."[29] More accurately, a conventional economist is often someone who sees something working in practice yet rejects its validity because it does not fit his model. As financier Mike Epstein jokes, "To an economist, real life is a special case."

Even if a conventional sociologist cannot see why something is true, he *must* place his perceptions of reality above his conceptions. Suppose an economist were confronted with the question of what would be the result of action by political forces to reduce the trade deficit by forcibly curbing imports or subsidizing exports with tax money. If he believes his eyes, he would conclude, even if he does not know why, that such actions might damage both the markets and the economy. Indeed, they would. So percepts can be valuable to economists in heading off political catastrophe, even if the mechanisms are not immediately clear. The great value in according importance to percepts is that they force you to examine and reshape your concepts until they conform to reality.[30]

It is on the question of perception vs. presumption that your assessment of the Wave Principle will depend. You have no choice if you are a scientist, but that does not mean it is easy. As the great A. Hamilton Bolton remarked about wave analysis, "The hardest thing is to believe what you see."[31]

While percepts are the bedrock of understanding aggregate financial behavior, the Wave Principle has a grand conceptual model as well, which was developed from those percepts. That is the essence of science, and we in this fledgling field are doing our inadequate best to perform it.

The Compatibility of Socionomics with Good Science

Socionomics has all four qualities that a science should possess. *Parsimony*: Human social mood follows the Wave Principle, which is succinctly represented in Figure 1-4. *Generality*: Socionomics subsumes all the social sciences as well as the character of the humanities. *Consilience*: Socionomics is compatible with, and derives from, the natural sciences. *Predictiveness*: Socionomics allows for better social prediction than any extant method.

Still lacking is the establishment of a *demonstrable, direct causal chain* from the Fibonacci aspects of biology and those of sociology. We have only the strong hints of their consistency, as detailed in Chapters 3, 11 and 12. Furthering this understanding is the province of natural scientists.

The Necessity and Goodness of Waves

Some people react to the Wave Principle with annoyance because it challenges the idea that men, through government or some other agency, can control collective behavior and the social future. They are sure that the government can "engineer" a recovery; they are certain that the central bank can "fine-tune" the money supply; they hope that cash infusions will "jump-start" a foreign economy. All of these beliefs are false.

However, the truth is actually more comforting. No, we cannot direct our social future, but the wild ride that we experience as a species is characteristic of systems that survive, grow and prosper. Ilya Prigogine won a Nobel Prize for discovering a most amazing fact: that ordered complexity and life *necessarily* arise in open systems. Entropy is not an antagonist in this arrangement but a partner, as the system takes in energy and exports entropy to the larger environment. The structures that dissipate entropy "are created by and thrive in a far-from-equilibrium, high-energy, unstable, even volatile environments,"[32] such as the stock market, such as society, such as life on earth. Says Michael Hutchison in *Megabrain*,

> Prigogine's vision of a universe of dissipative structures replaces the mechanistic view of a cosmos of "things" with a cosmos of *"process"*...[that is] unpredictable, self-organizing and evolutionary...*characterized by a series of leaps and bounds, or discontinuities*, rather than a gradual, incremental progression.... Prigogine's ideas...demonstrate that *periods of instability, perturbation, upheaval, collapse and chaos* are not to be seen as absolute evils *but instead as absolute necessities*, as phases through which every structure must pass *in order to evolve to higher levels of complexity*....[33]

This is an excellent description of both the style of progress under the Wave Principle and its message for mankind. It means that the type of behavior that the Wave Principle describes as the engine of the human social experience is both *necessary* and *good*, whether we happen to like its current expression or not. "Civilization," said Elliott, "rests upon change."[34] Philosophers from Lao Tzu and Heraclitus to Nietzsche and Goethe have celebrated opposing forces, strife, struggle, and cycles of creation and annihilation, all of which are different terms for the same underlying succession of change that is the secret engine of natural progress. The Wave Principle says that these philosophers' vague perceptions were correct. Even more valuable, it gives us a visual depiction of the form and progression of those opposing forces so that such philosophers' perceptions and sentiments no longer have to be vague.

Measured, recurring corrections of social trends are part of the natural robust fractal order of things. They have a purpose and are good, or they would not exist. Because human progress takes place in a "three steps forward, two steps back" manner, it is clear that the "two steps back" are required to put psychology and motivation in a condition to support the next geometric rise in material, social, cultural and intellectual progress. As implied in Chapter 13, corrections may be part of the mechanism of life itself. The very ultimate success of life may depend upon the occasional weeding out of those not intelligent enough to prepare, strong enough to fight, benevolent enough to avoid participating in the destruction of others, or unlucky enough to be in the wrong place at the wrong time. Yet, although we now know for a fact that the preservation and flourishing of living systems requires setbacks and calamities, the Wave Principle further communicates that such setbacks are only *partial* and that *the long-term trend is ever upward*. This knowledge is a welcome comfort in difficult times.

The Goodness of Socionomics

Socionomics allows us to understand and purge from our minds dangerous conceptual errors. An example is the idea that war creates prosperity. Now, if you really stop to think about it (ten seconds should suffice), you might conclude that any activity that destroys thousands or millions of lives and obliterates billions of dollars worth of property would actually be destroying prosperity, not creating it. In fact, that is exactly what war does. Unfortunately, the erroneous premise of event causality is so entrenched in economists' and historians' minds that the vast majority of them agree that war "stimulates the economy." How do they come to such a bizarre, even evil, conclusion? Simple: During wars, the downtrend in social mood that caused the war typically reverses, and production tends to rise along with the new uptrend. Economists presume that this chronology means causality. *Post hoc ergo propter hoc.*

Here is an actual and typical summary of prevailing economic wisdom: "World War I provided a quick fix to the economy.... If there ever was a great war for the economy, it was World War II.... The Vietnam War was at first positive in its economic effect...but impacted adversely on inflation...."[35] These are the views of an economic historian at The American University from an article entitled, "Is War Good For the Economy?" Having read statements like these countless times, I know that such notions are nearly unanimous among economists.

With the science of socionomics, we can understand that war is simply a social act that follows and expresses a negative social mood. It comes long after the onset of a major corrective wave because it takes that long for people to become angry enough to want to go to war and then arrange actually to wage one. The uptrend in mood that follows and the economic expansion that results are natural and unrelated to whether war actually breaks out. To put it in value-related terms, war is the result of negatives, not the cause of positives.

The value and goodness of this knowledge are immense. On the one hand, you have a socionomist who advises, "War is the result of a negative social psychology, which is why it occurs near the end of bear markets. I counsel you in such environments to watch potential enemies closely, particularly those whose societies have succumbed most thoroughly to the forces of the negative social mood. I also counsel you to beware the domestic impulse to wage war and do what you can to divert it. After all, war is *a bad thing* that should be avoided if it can be." On the other hand, you have a conventional economist who advises, "The economy tends to pick up during or after wars, so war must create economic expansion. If you want to pull this country out of recession, use every means, secret and overt, to insinuate your nation into a war. After all, net-net, war is *a good thing* that should be used to advantage." Who would you rather have advising your nation's leader or advising a rival country's leader when its economy is weak?

As related in Chapter 16, Adolf Hitler assumed the reins of power in 1933 as a result of the most extremely negative social sentiment in nearly a century. Stock markets around the world soared from that point forward, never seeing the level of those lows again. Following conventional assumptions and logic, an economist is forced to conclude that Adolf Hitler was *a good thing* for stocks and the world economy. A socionomist says that Hitler was put in power as a result of the most negative social psychology since 1859, which was *a bad thing*. Which explanation makes sense? Which explanation is *good*?

Determinism or Free Will?

It has been proposed that the novelty and diversity of nature are such that nature can be viewed as *self*-determined, as if it had free will.[36] It appears more accurate to say that nature's growth patterns are robust but deterministic, conforming without digression to waves, branches, spirals, or some other like expression of an underlying (apparently Fibonacci-based) fundamental form. The robustness of these patterns produces immense diversity. That diversity is (at least presently) unpredictable in terms of precisely forecasting all, or even many, specific attributes of the particulars. Still, unpredictability is not the same as saying that nature has a free will to do what it likes.

It is similarly clear that *collective systems do not possess or exercise free will*. Referring to the expansions and failures of publicly traded companies, *New Scientist* says that Eugene Stanley "has found power laws...even in systems in which the units have 'free will.'"[37] Quotation marks notwithstanding, if a system follows a power law, it is unlikely to be exercising free will. The dynamics of *aggregations* such as corporations, governments and societies are primarily determined by herding, which is impulsive and impelled by paleomentation. Certainly individuals at the head of such enterprises exercise great influence, but who chooses to put those particular individuals in such positions? The group does. They are appointed by boards, elected by voters or emerge as popular heroes. Their apparent power is actually a reflection of their ability to satisfy collectives of employees, customers or voters. This observation is compatible with Stanley's results; groups and societies are what the Wave Principle addresses. As the product of collectives dependent upon the public, corporate histories are exactly where we would expect power laws and the Wave Principle to show up. The Wave Principle form shows that a collective system is, like nature overall, robust but deterministic.

An individual man, on the other hand, does have the faculty of decision-making, conscious choice and an independent will to act in many, perhaps even most, matters. Free choice is a gift of the independent neocortex,[38] which can mull, consider and choose. Philosophically, there is no other rational position possible, as a full determinist has no business trying to convince anyone of anything. If he believes all thoughts are determined, then so are his and mine, so what is the point of discussion? The very presentation of his argument negates the argument.

The capabilities of a man's independent conscious mind include the potential to understand, recognize and to some degree mitigate or overcome some of the impulsive forces of his unconscious mind. While the Wave Principle structurally restricts the number of possible outcomes of *social* trends, it leaves the individual free, if he understands that the structure exists, to work to avoid to some degree his own tragic and/or comic unwitting participation in those trends. Indeed, he can sometimes profit from them. How can you succeed at this task?

As Francis Bacon explained, "Nature cannot be ordered about, except by obeying her." The tenor of the social future is like a law of physics; it cannot be ordered about. But you *can* manipulate your place in that future if you understand the forces at work. Knowledge of the Wave Principle dynamic is the only reliable basis upon which you can rise above the crowd and think, and act, independently of it. If you have the mental fortitude to do so, you can act independently of prevailing social illusions and resist being swept along by the social pressure to conform that they exert. Indeed, you can take advantage of the patterns of human sociology not only to survive but also to prosper. You can put yourself in a position to observe the crowd and thereby avoid or even profit from its excesses rather than become a part of it.

Unfortunately, independence is excruciatingly difficult for most people to assert in socially charged situations because the effects of the patterns are so pervasive and the power of the unconscious so strong. Hope, fear, denial and inertia are all part of the process. It is work to exercise and train your neocortex to overcome these influences and act independently. The number of consistently successful traders and investors is infinitesimally small compared to the total number of participants in markets. Indeed, after creating a valid method for market analysis, the main secret that successful professional traders (who are exceptionally rare people) learn through constant repetition of experience is how to resist or ignore emotional input from their limbic systems so as to allow their reason to prevail. This takes much time and practice, and even then, there is no guarantee that one's constitution can continuously take the heat.

Nevertheless, each person must do it to the extent possible. Living in harmony with social trends can make the difference between a happy, successful life and one in which time is spent futilely fighting the underlying tide. Failing to prepare for the next major trend can mean losing the opportunity of a lifetime, or it can be ruinous, and not only financially, but at times physically as well. At crucial turning points, an individual can act independently of the social flux if he has the knowledge and the will to do so. The rest of the time, he can hop aboard social trends and harness their power to his advantage. As the Easterners say, "Follow the way." As the Westerners say, "Don't fight the tape." In order to heed these nuggets of advice, however, it is necessary to know what is the Way, and which way the tape. There is no better method for answering that question than the Wave Principle.

NOTES

1 Pugsley, J. (1995). "Anthology of essential articles." *John Pugsley's Journal.*

2 Fad products such as art, fashion clothes, baseball cards, Pet Rocks, Cabbage Patch Kids, Beanie Babies, President Kennedy's golf clubs, etc., may be tangible, but they are not utilitarian. They satisfy intangible desires, thus fluctuate in price according to the Wave Principle rather than the law of supply and demand. Some such products can actually become viewed as investments, not goods, at which time they typically soar in price and then collapse.

3 Laderman, J. and Pennar, K. (1988, October 17). "Did the crash make a dent?" *Business Week*, p. 88.

4 I don't have the date, just the clipping. As the comment is so generic, I have not gone to the trouble to pinpoint this reference.

5 Rynecki, D. (1998, June 15). "Bull markets susceptible to anxieties." *USA Today.*

6 Henry, D. (1998, October 9). "High stakes guessing game: markets defy easy answers." *USA Today.*

7 Le Bon, G. (1895). *The crowd.*

8 Shomali, H.B. (1995, Winter/Spring). "Technical versus fundamental analysis: a view from academe." *MTA Journal.*

9 Caldarelli, G., *et al.* (1997). "A prototype model of stock exchange." *Europhysics Letters*, 40 (5), pp. 479-484.

10 Buchanan, M. (1997, November). "One law to rule them all." *New Scientist.*

11 Davies, P. (1988). *The cosmic blueprint — new discoveries in nature's creative ability to order the universe.*

12 Casti, J. (1997, April 19). "Flight over wall street." *New Scientist.*

13 Lesmoir-Gordon, N. (Producer). (1994). "Fractals: the colors of infinity."

14 Peters, E.E. (1991, March/April). "A chaotic attractor for the S&P 500." *Financial Analysts Journal.*

15 Sherden, W. (1998). *The fortune sellers.*

16 Davis, D. (1990, April 23). "Butterfly flap: chaology says no to market timing." *Dick Davis Digest,* Vol. 8, No. 190.

17 Liscio, J. (1998, March 2). "The seer syndrome." *Barron's.*

18 Popper, K.R. (1957). *The poverty of historicism.*

19 Reference unavailable.

20 Tindol, R. (1989, December 11). "Vanguard of a new approach to physical sciences." *On Campus.*

21 Sherden, W. (1998). *The fortune sellers.*

22 Gleick, J. (1985, December 8)."The man who reshaped geometry." *The New York Times.*

23 Crutchfield, J.P., *et al.* (1986, December). "Chaos." *Scientific American*, pp. 46-57.

24 Jensen, R.V. (1987, March-April). "Classical chaos." *American Scientist*, Vol. 75.

25 Sornette, D. and Johansen, A. (1997, November 1). "Large financial crashes." *Physica A – Statistical and Theoretical Physics.* This study cites *Elliott Wave Principle* as a source.

26 *Business Week* ran an article in its November 2, 1992 issue with this headline: "Chaos hits wall street — the theory, that is; an arcane market system is making waves." Well, this is cutesy, but perhaps in a few years, it will be inverted to read, "Waves are making over chaos theory."

27 Coveney, P. and Highfield, R. (1995). *Frontiers of complexity.*

28 Elliott, R.N. (1938). *The wave principle.*

29 Goldfeld, S.M. (1984, November). "Modeling the banking firm." *Journal of Money, Credit and Banking*, p. 611.

30 Let me provide an example in an unrelated area. A member of my family suffered from terrible migraines as a child. After studying the literature, we began looking for possible "triggers." To that end, we kept a diary of everything the child did, looking for triggers in food, sleep, stress, etc. The search appeared fruitless, as we found nothing preceding the migraines that correlated with them. Would the child have to eliminate *every* food and activity that preceded the migraines? That might be the answer of a conventional analyst who knows that outside cause must precede internal result. One day when reviewing the diary, I saw a consistent correlation between the migraines and events that happened *afterward*. Now, according to the conventional premise, any such correlation would be impossible. How could an event following a migraine trigger it? I had a choice. I could take the percept seriously or insist that it be coincidence because it did not appear to fit the model. Because I took the better route, this percept led me to the correct concept and therefore to a solution. I noticed that the events following migraines always involved some kind of responsibility on the part of the child. Ultimately, I realized that the trigger for each migraine was the child's

realization that directly ahead lay a stressful situation. Coming down with a migraine was a way to escape it. The child's *fears* preceded the migraines, but *events* followed them. This realization led us to a happy resolution to the crisis.

31   Bolton, A.H. (1960). *The Elliott wave principle—a critical appraisal.*

32   Hutchinson, M. (1987). *Megabrain.*

33   *Ibid.*

34   Elliott, R.N. (1940). "The basis of the wave principle." Republished: (1994). *R.N. Elliott's Masterworks — The Definitive Collection*, p.192.

35   DiBacco, T. (1990, August 24). "Is war good for the economy?" *Fort Myers News-Press.*

36   Jantsch, E. (1980). *The self-organizing universe.*

37   Buchanan, M. (1997, November 8). "One law to rule them all." *New Scientist.*

38   One of the areas of the brain responsible for some aspects of free will "appears to be located within or at least close to the anterior cingulate sulcus, on the inside of a fold of the cerebral cortex." [ref: Wilson, E. (1998). *Consilience*, p. 108]

Chapter 21:

The Kitchen Sink: Linking Physics to the Human Social Experience, A Principle Behind Ordered Complexity, Hints of Robust Fractals in the Heavens, the Fibonacci Foundation of Robust Forms, and Phimation as an Opposing Principle to Entropy

At the risk of going overboard, I will nevertheless take one more step. Put succinctly, I believe that we can link the Wave Principle to all of nature in a grand underlying theme.

The Wave Principle in Nonliving Processes?

Scientists see so much in the way of shared mathematics and behavior in living and nonliving systems that they are beginning to question whether there is that big a dividing line between life and nonlife; the continuum is smoother than they thought.[1] The Belousov-Zhabotinski (BZ) chemical reaction pulses like life. It also produces spiral waves that resemble the muscles in the heart and the electrical activity within our brains. Fire is animated, consumes organic material, and exudes waste. Water self-organizes into crystals when it is frozen, and silicone oil self-organizes into cells when it is heated, much in the way that the cells of slime molds self-organize into a super-organism when challenged for food or in the way that conditions on earth a few billion years ago appear to have been conducive to the self-organization of amino acids that are the foundation of life. Like living entities, inanimate entities produce spirals (galaxies and hurricane clouds) and arbora (river systems and chemical deposits). Can they produce Elliott waves as well?

Figure 21-1 shows the absorbance by cement slurry of each wavelength of infrared light, a property that is important for timing the hardening of cement for oil-well drilling operations. Why such a relationship should have *fluctuations* in it I have no idea, but those fluctuations do produce a pattern that I can label as Elliott waves. Wave 4 even falls to the territory of wave four of 3, following typical wave behavior. The entire plot even channels well on semilog scale (not shown). Whether this actually *is* an Elliott wave, as opposed to random data that happen to mimic one, I hesitate at this time to say.

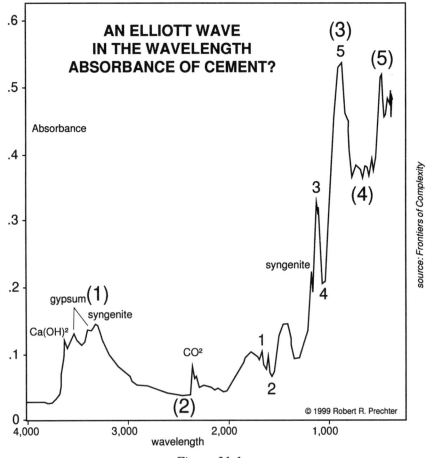

Figure 21-1

If inanimate processes such as this do produce waves, they would not be expected to compound for as long a time as waves of life. They would form what we call in commodity markets "contained waves,"[2] which need not build to ever loftier heights. The difference between commodity markets and the stock market is that stock market valuation reflects a phenomenon of persistent growth, while commodity prices need not.[3] The same difference undoubtedly applies to natural processes of life in general vs. natural processes of nonlife, which is why waves of the two would be expected to differ in this way. If Bak's sandpile (see below) were fed grain by grain forever, it would be an *unnatural* nonliving process that mimics life in its aspect of receiving a continuous input of energy. As a result, it would undoubtedly manufacture larger and larger avalanches the higher the pile extends, just as social man is doing.

On the slim evidence of Figure 21-1, I am hesitant to make one more suggestion, but will do so anyway. As postulated in Chapters 3 and 12, Fibonacci mathematics may come into play when nature constructs arbora, waves or spirals, whether living or not. It is also possible that the Wave Principle governs all kinds of self-organized dynamical systems that display fluctuation, i.e., active collectives of all types, whether they are living or not. To find out whether it does, we should investigate sandpiles, as well as rainfall, flooding and earthquake patterns, to see if they not only share with animate processes the properties of fractals, power laws, criticality and self-organization, but progress in Elliott waves as well.[4]

A Chain of Relationship From Physics to the Human Social Experience

"You can't extrapolate from physics or chemistry to human behavior," says Belgian theoretical chemist Ilya Prigogine, "but it is interesting to see the things they have in common mathematically."[5] It is particularly interesting to see what certain inanimate physical processes have in common with collective human mentation. For example, in studying sand piles, Bak and Chen found a phenomenon that I would characterize as very like herding behavior. Their machine dropped single grains of sand at regular intervals. A pile shaped roughly like a cone quickly developed. Then, at seemingly unpredictable times, a single grain added to the pile produced a slide of many grains down the side of the cone. As sand was added, the cone continued to grow. Landslides continued, and their sizes varied. Upon occasion, a particularly large slide occurred. Here is their summary of this behavior:

At criticality, the size of the landslide does not depend on the size or the number of new grains added. It depends on the holistic behavior of all the grains acting together. *The global behavior of the total pile transcends the behavior of the individual grains within it.* At criticality, every grain is interacting in complex ways with all its neighbors. *The motion of one grain on the slope can induce motion in thousands of others.*[6]

I would emphasize one implication in the above description. It is not only at criticality that the behavior of the sand pile is dependent upon the holistic behavior of all the grains acting together. It is just as true when sand grains hold each other up when the system is stable. Such interdependence holds true *all the time.* As I argued in Chapter 20, the ceaselessness of human interdependence and common influence persists whether the herd is excited and active or not. As it is with sand piles in this regard, so it is with plate tectonics, evolution and human social interaction.

Can we form a *chain of connection* linking physics and chemistry along a continuum all the way up to collective human mentation and activity? Stanley *et al.* relate the DLA model (see Chapter 3) to the underlying physical determinants of neuron growth (see Chapter 12):

The key point is that the growth follows rules that faithfully represent the solution of the equations for a diffusion-limited process, including the presence of stochastic noise. It has recently become established that the resulting clusters accurately describe a class of growth phenomena in which the diffusion equation or Laplace equation $\Delta^2 x = 0$ controls the essential physics. Thus growth phenomena governed by *chemical* gradients (in which case x is the concentration), by *electrical* gradients (x is an electrical potential), or by a *difference in viscosity* between the inside and outside of the pattern (x is the pressure) all are believed to be described by the DLA model. It is known that growing neurons respond to *chemical gradients* and *electric fields*, and it is also known that there is a *difference in viscosity* between the neuronal cytoplasm and the surrounding intercellular matrix. For this reason, it is not implausible that DLA might represent a zeroth order description of neuron growth.[7,8]

Since both the DLA model and neuron growth are suffused with Fibonacci properties, there must be Fibonacci-related forces hidden in the underlying physical processes of neuron formation. Hints of these forces may be found in Figure 2-26, which reveals a logarithmic spiral in the activity of subatomic particles, in Figure 2-23, which reveals a Fibonacci spiral embedded in the quasi-crystal, and in Figure 21-1, which depicts a possible Fibonacci-based Elliott wave in the infrared absorbance of cement slurry. For the most part, it is only those natural processes related to growth/decay and expansion/contraction that appear to manifest Fibonacci properties. We may surmise, then, that Fibonacci-related forces hidden in physics exert themselves particularly when called upon to generate or regulate *expanding or growing forms, including all life forms.*

We know that fundamental patterns of nature relating to growth or expansion, in forms as diverse as galaxies, DNA, and the paths of subatomic particles, have Fibonacci properties. We know that chemistry, fluid dynamics and electricity are involved in shaping our neurons, which have Fibonacci properties. By linking these observations to the studies cited in Chapters 10 through 12, we have less to muse about *extrapolating* from physics and chemistry to human behavior and more to link them *directly*. Taken together, all the studies and conclusions cited in Chapters 2, 3, 10, 11, 12 and here do nothing less than connect, via *phi*, the *physics* and *chemistry* within the mind to its *biology* to its *perception* to its *mentation* to its *behavior*, both individually and collectively. If chemistry, electricity and fluid viscosity are responsible for forming and energizing neurons, and if neurons are responsible for carrying thought, and if human thought processes produce patterns of decision-making, and if decision-making produces the Wave Principle, and if all of them share Fibonacci properties, then we have established a chain of relationship from the behavior of elementary matter and energy all the way up to collective human mentation and, as we saw in Chapters 15 and 16, from there to its manifestation in human interaction and thus ultimately to the very path of human social progress.

One may speculate, though not assert, that as chemistry, fluid physics and electricity serve to organize and energize microstructures in the nervous system, their Fibonacci properties may actually *influence* the development of Fibonacci-related forms in those structures, which in turn may influence the development of Fibonacci-related processes within the neurology of living entities, which in turn influence their style of mentation, which in turn influence their product. Thus, we might speculate that there is a chain of influence deriving from the minutest forms of matter all the way up to the cultural progress of man.

While such a chain of causality is an attractive explanation for nature's larger structures and perhaps correct, I would leave open the possibility that virtually everything that grows or expands in nature has Fibonacci properties more because of a formological imperative that permeates everything that progresses rather than because of a linear chain of influence. Unfortunately, this type of thinking has little science behind it. It does have some philosophy behind it, but as we are coming to the end of this book, we will leave such speculations for another time.

A Principle Behind Ordered Complexity

How does the simplicity of 5-3 wave alternation give rise to the complexity of the human social experience? As scientists have been discovering lately, that is, generally speaking, the way that the universe works. Here is a pertinent section from a 1996 article in *The New York Times*:

> Last week in the journal *Nature*, scientists at the University of Texas and the University of Santiago in Chile described a remarkable experiment in which they tapped into nature's self-organizing flow. Jiggling a layer of sand at just the right rhythm caused patterns of circular peaks and craters to emerge. *Sometimes these vibrating structures — dubbed oscillons — joined to form larger patterns, which came together to form still more intricate designs.* The photographs of this naturally arising order call to mind the process of subatomic particles combining to form atoms, and atoms to form molecules and crystals – science's Great Chain of Being.
>
> It is hard not to let the imagination run wild. Could real particles – the quarks and leptons of particle physics – be created from the jostlings of some kind of incredibly tiny subatomic sand? With the right rhythms, could scientists jostle their sandboxes so that the "molecules" combined to form cells, and the cells joined with other cells to produce some weird artificial life?
>
> These are the kinds of speculative leaps you sometimes hear when hanging out with complexity theorists. But behind the fantasies is a serious, sober effort to understand one of science's most engaging mysteries: how order emerges in the world. Experiments like the one described in *Nature* show that masses of identical tokens (like the sand grains), *each capable of interacting only with its immediate neighbors*, can spontaneously generate intricate patterns. Then these patterns become tokens in another game, consorting with one another to form the next level in an intricate hierarchy. Simplicity gives rise to complexity.

Instead of grains of sand, think of neurons in a brain, each communicating only with its neighbors and yet generating the far-reaching patterns of thought. Or think of traders buying and selling, each of these purely selfish exchanges giving rise to the blind, overarching forces of the marketplace, Adam Smith's invisible hand. In all these examples, there is no need of a Grand Conductor, looking down from above and orchestrating the flow. The order bubbles up from below, as though something universal were going on.

Is there a parallel between sand grains cooperating to form oscillons and quarks cooperating to form the particles that form the atoms that form jaguars? Stuart Kauffman...[of the] Sante Fe Institute believes that the laws we already know are not enough to understand these great towers of complexity. *Something extra is needed - a grand principle that would explain how order inexorably arises in the world.* In his view, it is not by chance that molecules in the primal sea came together to form the first self-reproducing cell, the grandparent of us all. *The chemistry was guided by yet-to-be-discovered laws of self-organization, laws that are as fundamental and irreducible as those of physics.*[9]

I believe that we have a piece of that "grand principle." The Wave Principle may not explain *how* ordered complexity arises in the world, but it certainly depicts at least one form of its progress. This chapter explores the idea that it operates "as though something universal were going on."

In Chapter 2, we noted the ubiquity of fractals, spirals and power laws in both animate and inanimate objects and systems. In 1970, Leo Kadanoff, then at Brown University, expressed an emerging realization that countless systems from magnetic to atomic to biologic can reach "critical states." He said that physical systems show "a kind of universal organization in which details of the original system get obliterated."[10] *What interacts doesn't matter. The simple fact of interconnection brings order and self-similarity all the way through the system.* This property is shared by both *animate* and *inanimate* systems. How far does this tendency permeate the universe?

Fractals and Degrees in the Heavens

Astronomers began realizing in the 1950s that the universe is patterned in a certain way. Stars cluster as constellations, constellations as galaxies, galaxies as superclusters. In the late 1980s, astronomers discovered a "super-supercluster."[11] Though the term was not in use at the time, it has become increasingly clear that the heavens are arranged as a fractal.

Is this an infinitely variable fractal, like a seacoast? No, there appear to be *distinct relative sizes to which we can attach names*, such as star, constellation, galaxy, cluster, supercluster and super-supercluster. In other words, the arrangement of matter in space may have the characteristic of specific *degrees*, just like arbora and the Wave Principle. Indeed, it is curious that the names chosen by astronomers are not unlike Elliott's nomenclature of degree: minor, intermediate, primary, cycle, supercycle, and grand supercycle. The astronomical arrangement of matter, it seems, has, in this regard, more in common with the robust fractals of waves and arbora than with the apparently indistinct relative scaling of seacoasts, clouds and mountains. Is there a more specific connection to robust fractals?

Arbora and Waves in the Heavens

In the past four years, two astrophysical theorists, armed with up-to-date observations of the universe, have proposed models that reflect not only fractals but waves as well. Stanford physicist Andrei Linde, in the November 1994 issue of *Scientific American*, proposes a *"self-reproducing inflationary universe*" in which the universe is "a self-generating... growing...fractal that sprouts other inflationary universes." He says that the result "appears to be both chaotic and homogenous, expanding and stationary." Linde says that his model solves six of the main problems with the "big bang" theory, including the flatness of space, the size of the universe, the timing and speed of the expansion, and the uniformity of matter distribution. Linde adds that along with gravitational waves, density perturbations, which affect the distribution of matter in the universe, imprint upon the microwave background radiation in such a way as to be is consistent with the "ripples in space," the "perturbations in temperature of the background radiation," found by the Cosmic Background Explorer (COBE) satellite. Now comes the interesting part from our point of view:

> One can visualize quantum fluctuations of the scalar field in an inflationary universe as *waves*. They first moved in all possible directions and then froze on top of one another. In some parts of the universe...these newly frozen waves increased the scalar field. Those rare domains where the field jumps high enough begin exponentially expanding....If the universe contains at least one inflationary domain of a sufficiently large size, it begins unceasingly producing new inflationary domains... producing a fractal-like pattern of universes....The total number of inflationary bubbles on our "cosmic tree" grows exponentially in time [and] indefinitely far away from the trunk of the tree (see Figure 21-2).[12]

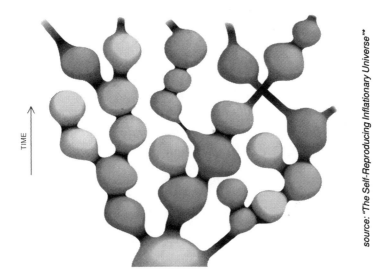

source: "The Self-Reproducing Inflationary Universe"

TIME

Figure 21-2

Needless to say, a *self-generating growing fractal* that appears *both chaotic and homogenous, expanding and stationary* is equally a description of human progress according to the Wave Principle. The idea that it is based on *waves* makes the two concepts even more compatible.

Says Linde, "One can interpret each peak as a new 'big bang' that creates an inflationary 'universe.'" In the same way, under the Wave Principle, one can interpret each new peak in a wave, or each new trough, as a "big bang" that creates a new social "universe" of experience. That is why there are eras in human society, for instance, the roaring 'twenties, the depressed 'thirties, the warring 'forties, the conservative 'fifties, the exuberant 'sixties, the schizophrenic 'seventies, the bootstrap 'eighties and the speculative 'nineties. Each is its own temporary universe that leads at a sudden point of change to the next one.

Linde is not alone in the character of his ideas. The January 9, 1997 issue of *Nature* reports that astronomer Jaan Einsasto of the Tartu Observatory in Estonia, in cooperation with astronomers from other nations, has evidence that superclusters of galaxies are distributed not randomly, as astronomers have assumed, but in a sort of cosmic crystal on a "three-dimensional chessboard." If so, says the team, then it could only have happened if there is "*some hitherto unknown process that produces regular structure at large scales.*"[13] Could this presumed law of physics, this unknown ordering process, govern at *all* scales and pertain not only to the universe itself but to countless processes within it? If so, it would be mightily compatible with the principle of waves discussed in this book. In fact, that is precisely the term that these astronomers use. Here is a report by *The New York Times*:

> Suspicions that there might be a pattern to these superclusters began to arise in the late 1980s. Looking out along a narrow line of sight in what is called a "pencil beam" survey, astronomers found that galaxies seemed to be bunched periodically, *as though stellar matter were somehow congealing on the crests of waves.*[14]

We are coming closer to an ordering principle in the distribution of matter in the universe. So far, we have evidence of *robustness, degree, arboration and waves*, four main aspects of the Wave Principle. Can we find the main determinant, *Fibonacci*?

Fibonacci in the Heavens

If Linde's description of the universe is accurate, then the universe is a branching structure. That branching structure could be an arborum. As shown in Chapter 3, arbora reflect *phi* both in the multiplication of their arba and in the most common angle of furcation, 36 degrees.

Behind Einsasto's description of the arrangement of superclusters as being like "a cosmic crystal" lies the possibility that their arrangement may actually be like a *quasi*-crystal. In the early 1980s, Daniel Shechtman of Technion in Haifa, Israel, discovered a type of crystal that contains spiral arrangements and is governed by Fibonacci mathematics. Initially believed impossible, the quasi-crystal has been verified by photographs made with an electron microscope (see Figure 2-23). The quasi-crystal exhibits "five-fold symmetry," which means that a single rotation of the crystal exposed to an X-ray produces a symmetrical scattering pattern five times.

While these are pure speculations, there is some concrete evidence of Fibonacci mathematics at work in our solar system. The September/October 1989 issue of *Cycles* magazine reports that the solar sunspot cycle of 10.88 years is skewed in time so that the average time from maximum to minimum sunspot activity is 6.80 years and the average time from there back to maximum activity is 4.08 years.[15] The ratios of each phase to the whole cycle are .625 and .375, which are 5/8 and 3/8, ratios of Fibonacci numbers.[16]

While there is considerable latitude in the ratios (.547, .656, .724 and .536), it is also the case that the average mean ratios of the distances of adjacent planets among the first six planets from the sun, excluding the Mars/Jupiter relationship, is .615, the Fibonacci ratio. The Mars/Jupiter separation is so great as to imply by this numerology that there is a missing planet between them. That is where the asteroids are located. The Titius-Bode Law, developed in 1766, recognized these relationships and correctly predicted the position of the next planet, Uranus.

In 1986, *The New York Times* printed a picture of the ten-mile-long nucleus of Halley's comet.[17] An alert subscriber of mine[18] noted its skewed appearance, measured its two lengths and found that they are in Fibonacci relationship, as shown in Figure 21-3.

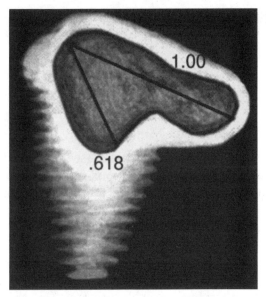

The phi *proportion in the nucleus of Halley's Comet*

Figure 21-3

The opposing polarities of the magnetism of solar wind may produce a "warped heliocentric current sheet" that serves as a boundary between the positive and negative sectors of the magnetic field. J.M. Wilcox and associates, in *Science* magazine, describe this sheet as a logarithmic spiral structure, as reproduced in Figure 21-4.[19]

source: Cycles Magazine, May/June 1983, Vol. 34, #4, p.107

Logarithmic spirals in the heliocentric current sheet

Figure 21-4

A Hint of the Universe in the Mind

If, as Prigogine and Vandervert assert (see Chapter 10), the mind is fractal and chaotic because the universe is fractal and chaotic, then the human brain and mind share fundamental aspects of form with the universe.[20] There is at least one aspect of astronomic behavior that reflects not just Fibonacci, but a specific expression of it that mimics the Fibonacci-weighted bipolar constructs of human mentation discussed in Chapter 12. The X-ray source MXB 1730-335, called the Rapid Burster, emits radiation in a quasi-periodicity. Dr. Lefebvre and Yuri N. Efremov of the Sternberg Astronomical Institute at Moscow State University have just reported that the two sets of overlapping frequencies produced by this irregular oscillation are related by *phi* both in terms of the frequency of the burst and the interval between them. Says their paper, "In sets of observations which give this ratio with a standard error equal to or less than 0.02, its average value is 1.61."[21] Both these and other astronomers have noted that the frequency system governing the output of the Rapid Burster appears at the beginning of the burst to "know how large the burst is going to be,"[22] much as a person must know at the beginning of a sentence what the entire sentence structure will be. Given the relationship of this phenomenon to Lefebvre's work with bipolar mental constructs (see Chapter 12), he and Efremov conclude that this finding "opens the possibility of *an intrinsic similarity between the RB activity and human cognition.*" In Chapter 12, I linked the *phi*-based physical structure of neurons to *phi*-related electrical charges to the *phi*-based apparati and dynamics of perception to the *phi*-based product of mentation. Apparently, this link may carry to the behavior of the Rapid Burster.

All of these observations might be coincidence. However, the coincidences are piling up. Given the context of our discussion, these are far more than curiosities; they may pertain to the essence of universal arrangement. How universal is Fibonacci to compound arrangement?

Fibonacci as Fundamental to Robust Compounding and Subdividing Forms

Paul Steinhardt, a theorist at the University of Pennsylvania, along with several colleagues, postulates that the structure of a quasi-crystal is based upon the mathematics of "tiling," which involves the fitting together of geometric shapes to fill space. Roger Penrose has recently demonstrated that a plane can be completely covered using two specific types of rhombus-shaped tiles (see Figure 21-5). He found the astonishing fact that no

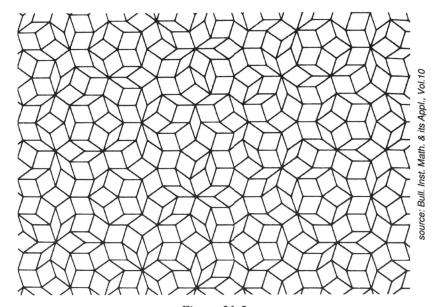

source: Bull. Inst. Math. & its Appl., Vol.10

Figure 21-5

pattern of tiles is ever exactly repeated, which means that patterns made by these two tiles are *infinitely robust*. *Infinite robustness within a process involving rigid restriction* is a property shared by arbora and Elliott waves, both of which are governed by Fibonacci. What governs Penrose's quasi-periodic tiling pattern? It turns out that both the *areas* of the tiles and therefore the *numbers* of the tiles in any given (large) area, are in *Fibonacci proportion*, the same proportion that governs both the numbers and sizes of motive vs. corrective Elliott waves. In addition, the *angles* of the rhombi are single, double, triple and quadruple multiples of 36 degrees, the ruling angle of the Fibonacci-based five-pointed star and of the DLA model of arboration discussed in Chapter 3.[23] This means that you can slide the 36 degree angle of one of Penrose's tiles into the nook of the average arborum.

Hans C. von Baeyer points out in *Discover* magazine that the Penrose tiling scheme is very like the Fibonacci sequence itself in that it contains no repeating patterns and is generated by two simple rules.[24] It appears that when nature produces patterns with infinite variance, whether animate or inanimate, it utilizes, and probably must utilize, Fibonacci mathematics to do so. In other words, Penrose's tiles suggest that *phi* is a fundamental property of forms that are self-identical in some ways yet infinitely variable in others, i.e., robust forms.

Taking a separate route, two high-school students from Connecticut have confirmed this same idea. The January 1997 issue of the academic journal *Mathematics Teacher* reports their solution to a mathematical puzzle that was first proposed by Euclid around 300 B.C., the puzzle of "regular partitioning."[25] The question is, "Is there a universal geometric principle for subdividing a line of any length into any number of equal smaller lengths?" The answer, illustrated in Figure 21-6, has been hailed it as "significant new mathematics." "The result," says *The Wall Street Journal*, "has impressed scholars like Robert Bryant, who typically ponders the calculus of curved objects at the Institute for Advanced Studies in Princeton, New Jersey, [who] says, 'it's pretty, no question about it."[26] It "exhibits what mathematicians call elegance," says University of Toronto mathematics professor Ed Barbeau. Actually, the mathematics is not new, because the answer lies in the application of the Fibonacci sequence, which has been known for millennia.

The students' discovery is important because along with Penrose's tiles, it raises the applicability of the Fibonacci sequence to the level of a mathematical principle that pertains universally to any process of structured yet infinitely variable *partitioning* and its inverse, structured yet

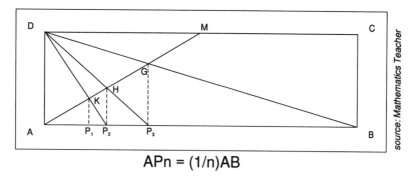

$$APn = (1/n)AB$$

Figure 21-6

infinitely variable *building*. Of course, the Wave Principle is compatible with this mathematical principle, as Fibonacci governs both the partitioning of waves into components and its building of waves into larger and larger structures.

The Universe and the Wave Principle

Taken together, these observations and theories make a tentative case that the universe produces *fractal waves of growth* that are governed by *Fibonacci*. What kind of wave system has fractal waves of growth governed by Fibonacci? Answer: the one described in this book. The Einsasto team's description of the universe as a latticework structure governing a fractal arrangement of matter congealing on the crests of waves is very like R.N. Elliott's description of the stock market, which is a latticework structure governing a fractal arrangement of collective mentational changes and trends that congeal in waves. The Lefebvre team's description of the Rapid Burster as representative of a Fibonacci aspect of human cognition supports R.N. Elliott's contention that collective human mentation follows a principle that is found throughout the universe. Is it reaching to propose that some fundamental Fibonacci form that underlies all robust fractals is at work in both cases, and probably in countless others? Says *The New York Times*,

> The Einsasto study, involving a much wider sweep of the sky than the pencil-beam surveys, is harder to explain away. Maybe, back in the beginning, the dice were loaded. *As the universe was unfolding, some unknown ordering principle might have been at work.*[27]

If so, what is the nature of this "unknown ordering principle"?

The Fundamentality of Form

When Frost and I wrote *Elliott Wave Principle* in 1978, the first word in the book that we italicized was the word *form*. Waves are variable in terms of extent and duration, but they never terminate until they complete a certain *form*. The discovery of the Wave Principle is a tremendous breakthrough for many reasons, not the least of which is that it reveals the importance of form in human life. The apparent fundamentality of form prompted several writers in the 1920s to develop and expand upon a theory of "morphogenetic fields," which supposedly account for the development of physical forms in nature.[28] In 1981, Rupert Sheldrake, in *A New Science of Life*, argued that such fields actively transmit a memory from foregoing entities to new entities that are influenced by a field of the same "probability structure."[29] Regardless of whether such ideas are valid, it is easy to understand some men's *passion* to account for the importance of form. Central to morphogenetic hypotheses is the true (in my opinion) observation that *there is something of paramount importance in form as such*.

The importance of form in the universe has received too little attention from scientists. One reason why science has gravitated away from detailed descriptions of forms may be the intricacy and therefore the required observational meticulousness of the task. Says Jochen Bockmuhl, leader of the Nature/Science section of the laboratory at the Goetheanum in Dornach, Switzerland, "A science [that] would approach concrete realities demands a faculty of observation which is *at home on several levels* and requires constant practice."[30] Descriptions so developed do not begin conveniently with mathematics; they end with them. One way to discover mathematical properties of nature, it seems to me, is with the most detailed empirically derived description one can create. That is how R.N. Elliott proceeded, and it led him to understand the underlying mathematics of financial markets. This approach also led Mandelbrot to understand the commonality of mathematics in fractals. Even in these fields, however, who on earth has studied minutely the patterns of lightning, rivers, blood vessels or coastlines as closely as R.N. Elliott studied the patterns in stock averages[31] or Goethe the patterns of plants?[32] The useful results of such undertakings should lead scientists to view such painstaking observation at least as a value, if not a fundamental one to science.

To find much serious thought about forms, we have to go all the way back to ancient Greece. Pythagoras saw the universe as a product of an underlying, ubiquitous mathematical order. Plato postulated archetypal forms that serve as generative *uber*models for less perfect and more variable forms that appear in nature. Aristotle saw form as a property that exists within, and determines the shape of, each individual entity.[33] These views are typically seen as opposing each other. While each of these men would probably argue well into the night about their differences, I think that *all* of them are correct: Order in the universe reflects the order of mathematics; growth in the universe is based upon a Fibonacci *uber*form that is ubiquitous and mathematically orderly; each entity deriving from that form contains within it the causal and variable instructions for its particular manifestation, which includes environmental adaptability.

Goethe, who may have discovered the Wave Principle in the progress of plant growth (see Chapter 13), also had something to say about the genesis and fundamental nature of form, as summarized in this description:

> Seeing that every part of the plant is a metamorphosis of the archetypal "leaf" organ, Goethe came to the conception of an *archetypal* plant, or *Ur-pflanze*, a supersensible force...which possesses within itself the capacity to take on manifold forms, and which at a particular time takes on that form which is best suited to the conditions of the external environing world.[34]

Goethe asserted that the sequence of development reflecting the Wave Principle that he described in plants "applied to everything living." Chapter 3 postulates that the primary patterns of natural growth and expansion — spirals, arbora and waves — are actually different expressions of a single underlying phenomenon of form, which is based upon *phi*. As Goethe's "archetypal plant" might behave somewhat like Linde's concept of the entire universe, as shown in Figure 21-2, *we should not neglect to consider and pursue the possibility that this phi-based principle may apply to everything growing, whether alive or not.*

The Engine of Formation: *Phimation* Against Entropy

If any of this is true, how does it come about? The second law of thermodynamics states that heat always dissipates into the environment, ultimately making any closed system (one that has no outside source of energy) heat-homologous and therefore dead. Entropy is the unavoidable winding-down of energy differentials. Open systems (which enjoy an input of energy) are a different matter. As energy flows into an open system, complex systems come into being, grow and thrive. Prigogine argues that the immense dissipation of entropy propels the formation of expanding structures and systems from the cosmological to the living and even propels the evolution of laws of nature to accompany the evolving systems. (Earlier in time, he argues, there were no laws of planetary motion or biology, as there were no planets or life.) Because robust fractals are so common in such systems and so similar, there is probably a law of formative development that governs them. I would bet that if there is a *first* law of growing, expanding or striving structures, including (if Linde is correct) even the universe itself, its governing ratio is *phi.*

Perhaps we can speculate, with inspiration from Prigogine's elegant explanation of how order arises from chaos, that there may be some kind of universal *force* or *field* that impels what is essentially a *striving against entropy.* This formative law is governed by Fibonacci mathematics, which is why manifest forms of growth and expansion are as well. (If it is a force, its persistence would account for the increasing order and complexity of related systems. If it is a field, it must have the same positive relationship to *time* that a gravitational field has to *mass*, which would also account for the increasing order and complexity of related systems.) Fibonacci formation, or, for want of a better expression, *phimation*, then, may be *an opposing principle to entropy.* It is the yin of growth and progress that opposes the yang of dissolution and decay. From it would flow all the lesser laws that govern its expression in terms of robust structures such as spirals, arbora, waves and whatever other forms it may subsume. One could hardly depict the concept of a measured, regulated striving against entropy more elegantly than with an Elliott wave, as shown in Figure 1-5. The opposition of entropy and phimation, I contend, is the grand underlying theme of nature.

If it is not already blatantly evident, I will state here that these ruminations derive from the furthest frontiers of my understanding and are far from socionomics, the only field in which I claim expertise. That will not stop me, however, from continuing.

A Principle of Universality

The Principle of Universality so far is only a hoped-for goal of being able to model and understand all complex systems with one formulation. If such a principle exists, it will unite the sciences and place many of the processes of the universe under a single name. The "unknown ordering principle" for which scientists are searching would have to pertain to far more than "just" the ordering of the stars in the universe, the pulsing of the sun or the arrangement of the planets in our solar system. It would have to pertain to everything from subatomic particle behavior to the structure of DNA to the essence of life to collective human behavior to the pattern of the cosmos, the very processes shown in this book to be related. *New Scientist* sums up the view required to embrace universality:

> From earthquakes to evolution, the notion of universality lies behind theories that are adding an extra dimension to our understanding of the world. But the consequences of the idea may ultimately be far more profound. For hundreds of years, science has proceeded on the notion that things can always be understood — and can only be understood — by breaking them down into smaller pieces and by coming to know those pieces completely. Systems in critical states — and they seem to be plentiful — flout this principle. Important aspects of behavior have little to do with the detailed properties of their component parts. Organization in a magnet, a company or an ecosystem isn't down to the particles, people or organisms that make it up.... "Without universality," says James Crutchfield, a physicist at the University of California at Berkeley, "each and every complex system would be a discipline to itself, and the very enterprise of science would be doomed from the start." With it, there seems to be a basis for a true "theory of collectives" of all sorts.[35]

To sum up today's scientific view, then, there is a basis for saying that there may exist a principle of collectives that underlies the self-organization of all self-organizing things, at all scales. This book says we have more than hope for that principle; *we have one aspect of the principle itself*, a structural principle that combines Fibonacci and growth in a marriage called the Wave Principle, which in turn may be a manifestation, like arbora and other robust fractals, of a more fundamental principle of collectives that may be termed phimation. Look back at Chapter 13 and observe again that evolution follows the Wave Principle. Look back at Chapter 5 and observe again that the stock market follows the Wave Principle. Recall Chapters 10 through 12 and consider that the brain and mind have fractal and Fibonacci properties, the key aspects of the Wave Principle. Reread in Chapter 13 the description of individual life forms following the Wave Principle. Go back to Chapters 15 and 16 and observe again that social action and all of history are products of the Wave Principle. Look back at Figure 21-1 and recall that even inanimate processes might follow the Wave Principle. The Wave Principle is connected to every phenomenon discussed in this book, uniting them all. As early as 1940, R.N. Elliott had seen enough about his discovery of a structure behind "the various moods of human behavior" to assert that it had as its cause "the immutable natural law...of change... that governs all things."[36] In 1946, he titled the Wave Principle "Nature's Law." He was not overstating the case. If there is a principle of universality for collective action, or of progress against entropy, this may be it. At the very least, I believe, it is a manifestation of it.

NOTES

1 One difference between objects and growth processes may be that when dealing with objects, we can say that for every action there is an equal reaction; within growth processes, we may be entitled to say that for every action there is a .618 reaction!

2 See Chapter 6 of *Elliott Wave Principle*.

3 In times of fiat money, commodity prices do, however, inversely reflect the phenomenon of persistent decay in the value of the purchasing medium, which allows their waves to compound over many decades.

4 Here is an idea for two experiments. Treat earthquakes as corrections. That makes the impulsive component a measure of stress. Plot stasis as a continuing *uptrend in stress*, steady over time, and earthquakes as reactions. After two (or four, in an extension) reactions of approximately equal size, is the next one larger? After two (or four) of those, is the next one larger still? If so, we can begin to predict earthquakes. If not, fine. Earthquakes are not living growth patterns, so there is no compelling reason to insist that waves must be there. As a second experiment more closely related to an animated growing system, plot each added sand grain in Bak's sandpile as an uptrend in growth, and sandslides as corrections. Does the overall process create an Elliott wave?

5 Tindol, R. (1990, December 11). "Vanguard of a new approach to physical sciences." *On Campus*.

6 Bak, P. and Chen, K. (1991, January). "Self-organized criticality." *Scientific American*, pp. 46-53.

7 Stanley, H.E., *et al.* (1993). "Fractal landscapes in physics and biology." *Growth patterns in physical sciences and biology*, p.134.

8 In the authors' expressions of the equation, they use the letter ϕ to represent the variable. Since it has no Fibonacci denotation in this context, I have replaced it with x.

9 Johnson, G. (1996, September 8). "From grains of sand: a world of order." *The New York Times*.

10 Domb, E. and Green, M. (1971). "Critical behavior: universality and scaling." *Critical Phenomena*, Vol. 5, p. 100. Also, private communication.

11 Peratt, A.L. (1990, January/February). "Not with a bang." *The Sciences*.

12 Linde, A. (1994, November). "The self-reproducing inflationary universe." *Scientific American*.

13 Einsasto, J., *et al.* (1997, January 9). "A 120-Mpc periodicity in the three-dimensional distribution of galaxy superclusters." *Nature.*

14 Johnson, G. (1997, January 19). "The real star wars: between order and chaos." *The New York Times*, p. 4.

15 Collins, C.J. (1989, September/October). "The effect of sunspot activity on the stock market." *Cycles.*

16 Thanks to EWT reader K. M. Manning for this insight.

17 (1986, November 1). *The New York Times*, p. 1

18 P. Kendrick of Falmouth, Maine.

19 Wilcox, J.M. (1980). "Origin of the warped heliospheric current sheet." *Science*, Vol. 209, pp. 603-605.

20 It may not be a new idea that the mind and the universe are reflections of each other. In ancient Egypt, the pharaoh Tutankhamen rested his head upon a curved alabaster pedestal. On each side was a figurine, one representing the guardian of the easternmost reach of the universe, the other the guardian of the westernmost. In the eyes of that culture, the mind of the pharaoh *was* the universe.

21 Lefebvre, V. and Efremov, Y. "Possible analogues of cognitive processes in the patterns of X-ray variability of the rapid burster" Astrophysical archive on the Internet (1998).

22 Kawai, N., *et al.* (1990). "Spectral evolution of type II bursts from the Rapid Burster." *Astronomical Society of Japan,* No. 42, pp. 115-133.

23 In viewing Penrose's pattern, one gets the distinct impression of a three-dimensional quality as if the pattern were a pile of regular and skewed cubes. Is the third dimension somehow a product of Fibonacci mathematics?

24 Von Baeyer, H.C. (1990, February). "Impossible crystals." *Discover.*

25 Litchfield, D. and Goldenheim, D. (1997, January). "Euclid, Fibonacci, and sketchpad." *Mathematics Teacher*, Vol. 90, No. 1.

26 Naik, G. (1996, December 9). "Teen math whizzes go Euclid one better." *The Wall Street Journal.*

27 Johnson, G. (1997, January 19). "The real star wars: between order and chaos." *The New York Times*, p. 4.

28 For a history of these theories, see Rupert Sheldrake's book, *A New Science of Life.*

29 Sheldrake, R. (1981). *A new science of life.*

30 Bockemuhl, J. and Suchantke, A. (1995). "The morphic movements of plants as expressions of the temporal body." *The metamorphosis of plants.*

31 This time-consuming task was facilitated by the fact that Elliott was physically debilitated for half a dozen years by a disease that nearly killed him. He was forced to cease his previous substantial mobility, which appar-

ently gave him immense time for quiet contemplation and study. For details of his life, see the biography in *R.N. Elliott's Masterworks.*

32 The rarity of Goethe's feat and approach is in keeping with the centuries-long direction of science away from studying forms and toward studying components. Andreas Suchantke informs us that "Goethe's discovery of the metamorphosis of plants has, until very recently, provoked no new research of any depth. ...Science has followed a path of development so different from Goethe's methods that bridging the gap thus opened up is now well-nigh impossible." [ref: Bockemuhl, J. and Suchantke, A. "The metamorphosis of plants as an expression of juvenilisation in the process of evolution" and "The leaf: 'the true proteus'," from *The metamorphosis of plants.*] For those interested, this short book is an excellent series of treatises on the formative motions of plants.

33 These summaries are my interpretation of descriptions from only one source. If they are inaccurate in any way, please let me know.

34 Tompkins, P. and Bird, C. (1973). *The secret life of plants.*

35 Buchanan, M. (1997, November 8). "One law to rule them all." *New Scientist.*

36 Elliott, R.N. (1940, October 1). "The basis of the wave principle."

If you would like to learn more about various aspects of the Wave Principle as listed below, please read the publications cited thereafter.

Details of the patterns, their application, and Fibonacci mathematics:
Elliott Wave Principle

Original exposition by, and a biography of, the Wave Principle's
discoverer: **R.N. Elliott's Masterworks**

History of the principle's application:
R.N. Elliott's Market Letters
The Complete Elliott Wave Writings of A. Hamilton Bolton
The Elliott Wave Writings of A.J. Frost and Richard Russell

Related studies of the 1980s and 1990s:
New Frontiers in Market Analysis (to be published in 2000)

Financial and economic outlook for the next century:
At the Crest of the Tidal Wave

Ongoing application to U.S. stock, U.S. bond, gold and silver markets:
The Elliott Wave Theorist

Ongoing application to all other markets:
(Request list from Elliott Wave International)

All books and periodicals listed above are available from
Elliott Wave International, Inc.

Mailing address: **P.O. Box 1618, Gainesville, GA 30503**
Site address: **Suite 400, 200 Main Street, Gainesville, GA 30501**
Phone: **800-336-1618, 770-536-0309**
Fax: **770-536-2514**
E-mail address for products: **customerservice@elliottwave.com**
E-mail address for comments: **bb@elliottwave.com**
Web site: **www.elliottwave.com**

Sources

"16th annual American music awards." (1989, January 30). Dick Clark Productions, Burbank, CA.

"A dismal performance." (1982, January 18). *Business Week*, p. 124.

Abzug, Robert H. (1985). *Inside the vicious heart: Americans and the liberation of Nazi concentration camps*. New York: Oxford University Press.

Acker, Larry. (1998, August). "Why so bearish?" *3F Forecasts*. Vol. 12, No. 8.

Adams-Webber, J. and Benjafield, J. (1973). "The relation between lexical marking and rating extremity in interpersonal judgment." *Canadian journal of behavioral science*, Vol. 5, pp. 234-241.

Adams-Webber, Jack. (1997, Winter). "Self-reflexion in evaluating others." *American Journal of Psychology*, Vol. 1110, No. 4. pp. 527-541.

Ahuja, Anjana. (1998, June 29). "The nature of numbers." *The London Times*.

Alexander, Garth and Smith, David. (1998, September 27). "Fund crash took world economy to brink of collapse." *The London Times*.

Angrist, Stanley W. (1991, August 8) "Believers in one wave theory see U.S. in deep trough soon." *The Wall Street Journal*.

Arneodo, A., Argoul, R. Bacry, E., Muzy, J.F. and Tabbard, M. (1993). "Fibonacci sequences in diffusion-limited aggregation." *Growth Patterns in Physical Sciences and Biology*, edited by Juan Manuel Garcia-Ruiz, Enrique Louis, Paul Meakin and Leonard M. Sander. New York: Plenum Press.

Bak, Per and Chen, Kan. (1991, January) "Self-organized criticality." *Scientific American*, pp. 46-53.

Baker, Martin. (1995, October 7-8). "Investing: rhyme or reason?" *International Herald Tribune*, p. 6.

Ball, R. and Bartov, E. (1996, June). "How naïve is the stock market's use of earnings information?" *Journal of Accounting and Economics*, Vol. 21, No. 3.

Begley, Sharon, Service, Robert and Underhill, William. (1992, May 25). "Finding order in chaos." *Newsweek*.

Bell, E.T. (1936). *Men of mathematics*. New York: Simon & Schuster.

Bergamini, David and the editors of *Life*. (1963). *Mathematics*. New York: Time-Life Books.

Berreby, David. (1993, March). "Chaos hits Wall street." *Discover Magazine*.

Berry, John M. (1998, July 6). "Key players control money supply." *The Washington Post*.

Bigava, Z.I. (1979). "A character of setting effects in various moving problems." In: Nadirashvili, S.A. (Ed.), Voprosy Inzhenernoy I Socialnoy Psychologii (Problems of Human Factor and Social Psychology, in Russian), ii Tbilisi: Metsniereba.

Bion, Wilfred. (1952). "Group dynamics: a review." *International Journal of Psychoanalysis*, No. 33, pp. 235-247.

Bisher, Furman. (1984, November 17). "The Gator grail, the hallowed hall." *The Atlanta Journal-Constitution*.

Bishop, Jerry E. (1987, November 17). "Stock market experiment suggests inevitability of booms and busts." *The Wall Street Journal*.

Bockemuhl, Jochen and Suchantke, Andreas. (1995). *The metamorphosis of plants*. Capetown, South Africa: Novalis Press.

Bolton, Arthur Hamilton. (1953). "Elliott's wave principle." Supplement to *The Bolton-Tremblay Bank Credit Analyst*. Republished (1994). *The Complete Elliott Wave Writings of A. Hamilton Bolton*. Prechter, Jr., Robert Rougelot. (Ed.). Gainesville, GA: New Classics Library.

Bolton, Arthur Hamilton. (1960). "The Elliott wave principle — a critical appraisal." Supplement to *The Bolton-Tremblay Bank Credit Analyst*. Republished: (1994). *The Complete Elliott Wave Writings of A. Hamilton Bolton*. Prechter, Jr., Robert Rougelot. (Ed.). Gainesville, GA: New Classics Library.

Bradley, Mark. (1984, November 18). "At long last, Florida wins an SEC title." *The Atlanta Journal-Constitution*.

Brauchli, Marcus W. (1998, July 14). "Why the world bank failed to anticipate Indonesia's deep crisis." *The Wall Street Journal*.

Briggs, John and Peat, F. David. (1989). *Turbulent mirror*. New York: Harper & Row.

Briggs, John. (1992). *Fractals — the pattern of chaos*. New York: Simon & Schuster.

Brock, David. (1986, June 30). "Seeing the economy's future with a shattered crystal ball." *Insight*.

Brock, William A. (1991). "Causality, chaos, explanation and prediction in economics and finance." *Social Systems Research Institute*, No. 387, a publication of the University of Wisconsin – Madison.

Brock, William A., Lakonishok, Josef and LeBaron, Blake. (1992, December). "Simple technical trading rules and the stochastic properties of stock returns." *Journal of Finance*, Vol. 47, No. 5.

Brooks, Michael. (1997, October 18). "Boom to bust." *New Scientist*.

Browne, Malcolm W. (1997, April 15). "Variations in stride." *The New York Times*.

Browne, Malcolm W. (1989, September 9). "A new solid that matters." *Toronto Globe and Mail*.

Buchanan, Mark. (1997, November 8). "One law to rule them all." *New Scientist*.

Buettner, Michael. (1995). "An evolutionary model of market growth: the Elliott wave principle." Unpublished paper.

Butler, D. and Ranney, A. (1978). Referendums Washington, D.C., American Enterprise Institute for Public Policy Research.

Caldarelli, G., Marsili, M. and Zhang, Y.C. (1997, December 1). "A prototype model of stock exchange." *Europhysics Letters*, Vol. 40, No. 5, pp. 479-484.

"Call it a miracle, or call it a mystery, but black youths shunning tobacco." (1995, November 20). *The Wall Street Journal*.

Carson, Clarence B. (1990, December). *Basic economics*. Foundation for Economic Education.

Casti, John. (1995). *Complexification*. New York: Harper.

Casti, John. (1997, April 19). "Flight over wall street." *New Scientist Magazine*.

"Chaos under a cloud." (1996, January 13). *The Economist*.

Chapman, Toby. (1998, January-February). "Speculative trading: physicists' forays into finance." *Europhysics News*.

Church, A.H. (1904). "Phyllotaxis in relation to mechanical law." London: Williams & Norgate.

Collier, P.F. (1985). *Collier's photographic history of world war II*. New York: Bonanza Books. (reprint from original 1946, NY: P.F. Collier, Inc.)

Collins, Charles J. (1989, September/ October). "The effect of sunspot activity on the stock market." *Cycles*.

Collins, Charles J. (1966). "The Elliott wave principle of stock market behavior." Supplement to *The Bolton-Tremblay Bank Credit Analyst.* Republished: (1994). *The Complete Elliott Wave Writings of A. Hamilton Bolton.* Prechter, Jr., Robert Rougelot. (Ed.). Gainesville, GA: New Classics Library.

Cook, Theodore. (1914). *The curves of life.* London: Archibald Constable.

Cootner, P.H. (1964). *The random character of stock market prices.* Cambridge, MA: MIT Press.

Coveney, Peter and Highfield, Roger. (1995). *Frontiers of complexity.* New York: Ballantine Books.

Cowan, J.D. (1982). "Spontaneous symmetry breaking in large scale nervous activity." *International Journal of Quantum Chemistry,* No. 22, pp. 1059-1082.

Crutchfield, James P., Farmer, J. Doyne, Packard, Norman H. and Shaw, Robert S. (1986, December). "Chaos." *Scientific American,* pp. 46-57.

Cunningham, Steven R. (1993, Fall). "Unit root testing: a critique from chaos theory." *Review of Financial Economics,* Vol. III, No. 1.

Dacosta, N.C.A. (1994, September). "Overreaction in the Brazilian stock-market." *Journal of Banking and Finance,* Vol. 18, No. 4.

Dauben, Joseph W. (1990). *Georg Cantor: his mathematics and philosophy of the infinite.* Princeton University Press.

Davies, Paul. (1988). *The cosmic blueprint — new discoveries in nature's creative ability to order the universe.* New York: Simon & Schuster.

Davis, Dick. (1990, April 23). "Butterfly flap: chaology says no to market timing." *Dick Davis Digest,* Vol. 8, No. 190.

Davis, Nathan E. (1992). "Being right or making money." *Ned Davis Research Inc.*

Dawkins, Richard. (1993, December 15). "Is religion just a disease?" *The Daily Telegraph.*

Dawson, Chester. (1998, July 4). "Japan: time's right for tax cuts" *The Atlanta Journal-Constitution.*

DeBondt, Werner F.M. and Thaler, Richard. (1985, July). "Does the stock market overreact?" *The Journal of Finance,* Vol. XL, No. 3.

DeMause L. (1982). *Foundations of psychohistory,* pp.172-243.

Denberg, Jeffrey. (1998, December 9). "A league's fiscal rift." *The Atlanta Journal-Constitution,* p.E1.

Dennett, Daniel. (1991). *Consciousness explained.* London: Allen Lane. p.202.

Dent, Harry S. (1998.) *The roaring 2000s.* New York: Simon & Schuster.

Dewey, Edward R. and Dakin, Edwin F. (1945). *Cycles: the science of prediction.* The Foundation for the Study of Cycles.

DiBacco, Thomas. (1990, August 24). "Is war good for the economy?" *Fort Myers News-Press.*

Dissanaike, Gishan. (1994, December). "On the computation of returns in tests of the stock market overreaction hypothesis." *Journal of Banking and Finance.*

Doczi, György. (1981.) *The power of limits.* Boulder, CO: Shambhala Publications.

Domb, Eds C. and Green, M. (1971). "Critical behavior: universality and scaling." *Critical Phenomena,* Vol. 5 p.100. Academic Press. Also, private communication.

Donnelly, Barbara. (1987, October 23)."Efficient-market theorists are puzzled by recent gyrations in the stock market." *The Wall Street Journal.*

Dornbush, Rudi. (1998, July 30). "Growth forever." *The Wall Street Journal.*

Douady, Stephane and Couder, Yves. (1993). "Phyllotaxis as a self-organized growth process." *Growth patterns in physical sciences and biology.* Garcia-Ruiz, Juan Manuel, editor, *et al.* New York: Plenum Press.

Douglas, Kate. (1996, August 10). "Arachnophilia." *New Scientist,* pp. 24-28.

Drew, Garfield. (1955). *New methods for profit in the stock market.* Republished 1966. VT: Fraser Publishing Co.

Dunham, William. (1990). *Journey through genius: the great theorems of mathematics.* New York: John Wiley & Sons.

"Economists forecast mild inflation of 2.5% yearly through 2008." (1998, May 26). *The Wall Street Journal.*

"Economy surging behind spending." (1998, June 27). *The Atlanta Journal-Constitution.*

"Edgar Peters' fractal market hypothesis: a new market theory." (1994, May 31). *Derivative Risk Analyst.*

Edgar, G.A. (ed.) (1993). *Classics on fractals.* Reading MA: Addison-Wesley.

Einsasto, J., Einasto, M., Gottlober, S., Muller, V., Saar, V., Starobinsky, A.A., Tago, E., Tucker, D., Andernach, H., and Frisch, P. (1997, January 9). "A 120-Mpc periodicity in the three-dimensional distribution of galaxy superclusters." *Nature.*

Eliades, P. (1998, May 4). "Danger: bear may be crossing." *Barron's.*

Elliott, Ralph Nelson. (1938). *The wave principle.* Republished: (1994). *R.N. Elliott's Masterworks — The Definitive Collection.* Prechter, Jr., Robert Rougelot. (Ed.). Gainesville, GA: New Classics Library.

Elliott, Ralph Nelson. (1940, October 1). "The basis of the wave principle." Republished: (1994). *R.N. Elliott's Masterworks — The Definitive Collection.* Prechter, Jr., Robert Rougelot. (Ed.). Gainesville, GA: New Classics Library.

Elliott, Ralph Nelson. (1941, August 11). "Market apathy – cause and termination." Educational Bulletin. Republished: (1993). *R.N. Elliott's Market Letters (1938-1946).* Prechter, Jr., Robert Rougelot. (Ed.). Gainesville, GA: New Classics Library. Also (1994) *R.N. Elliott's Masterworks — The Definitive Collection.* Prechter, Jr., Robert Rougelot. (Ed.). Gainesville, GA: New Classics Library.

Elliott, Ralph Nelson. (1941, August 25). "Two cycles of American history." Interpretive Letter No. 17. Republished: (1993). *R.N. Elliott's Market Letters (1938-1946).* Also (1994) *R.N. Elliott's Masterworks — The Definitive Collection.* Prechter, Jr., Robert Rougelot. (Ed.). Gainesville, GA: New Classics Library.

Elliott, R.N. (1946). *Nature's law: the secret of the universe.* Republished: (1994). *R.N. Elliott's Masterworks — The Definitive Collection.* Prechter, Jr., Robert Rougelot. (Ed.). Gainesville, GA: New Classics Library.

Elson, Lawrence M. and Kapit, Wynn (1992). *Anatomy coloring book.* New York: Harper Collins.

Engel, Stefan. (1962). *Lung structure.* Springfield, IL: Charles C. Thomas.

Evans-Pritchard, Ambrose. (1998, September 2). "'Plunge team' ready to spring into action." *Electronic Telegraph* (internet).

Fell, Barry. (1980). *Saga America.* New York: Times Books, pp. 327, 330.

Firth, M. (1977). *The valuation of shares and the efficient-markets theory.* London: The Macmillan Press Ltd.

Ford, Constance M. (1998, July 7). "Survey sees brunt of Asian crisis hitting U.S. soon." *The Wall Street Journal,* p. A2.

Frank, Alan G. (1974). *The movie treasury — horror movies.* London: Octopus Books.

Fraser, James L. (1984, June 6). "Unpopular independent action." *The Contrary Investor.*

"Frontiers of finance." (1993, October 9). *The Economist.*

Frost, Alfred John, and Robert Rougelot Prechter, Jr. (1978). *Elliott wave principle — key to market behavior.* Gainesville, GA: New Classics Library.

Frost, Alfred John. (1970). "The Elliott wave principle of stock market behavior." Supplement to *The Bolton-Tremblay Bank Credit Analyst.* Republished: (1996). *The Elliott Wave Writings of A.J. Frost and Richard Russell.* Prechter, Jr., Robert Rougelot. (Ed.). Gainesville, GA: New Classics Library.

Fukuyama, Francis. (1992). *The end of history and the last man.* New York: Avon Books.

Fund, John H. (1994, June 14). "Welfare: putting people first." *The Wall Street Journal.*

Gajdusek, D.C. (1970). "Physiological and psychological characteristics of stone age man," *Symposium on Biological Bases of Human Behavior, Eng. Sci.* 33, pp. 26-33, 56-62.

Gauquelin, Michel. (1970). *The scientific basis of astrology.* p. 23-24. (from French astronomer Paul Couderc's *la Relativité*, p. 28). New York: Stein & Day.

Geewax, Marilyn. (1998, June 21). "U.S. could become entwined in downturn." *The Atlanta Journal-Constitution.*

Gigot, Paul A. (1998, August 14). "Woodward and Bernstein lose their fastball." *The Wall Street Journal.*

Glazman, R.E. (1988, April). "Fractal features of sea surface manifested in microwave remote sensing signatures." *OE Reports.*

Gleick, James. (1985, December 29). "Unexpected order in chaos." *This World.*

Gleick, James. (1985, December 8). "The man who reshaped geometry." *The New York Times.*

Goerner, S.J. (1992). "Chaos as tip of an iceberg: the big picture of physics' revolution in understanding the order-producing universe." Paper presented to the Chaos Network Conference.

Goethe, J.W. (1790). "On the metamorphosis of plants."

Goldberg, Robert. (1995, November 20). "The fab four 25 years later." *The Wall Street Journal.*

Goldberger, Ary L., Rigney, David R. and West, Bruce J. (1990, February). "Chaos and fractals in human physiology." *Scientific American*, pp. 42-49.

Goldfeld, Stephen M. (1984, November). "Modeling the banking firm." *Journal of Money, Credit and Banking*, p. 611.

Goleman, Daniel. (1989, August 15). "Brain's design emerges as a key to emotions." *The New York Times.*

Goleman, Daniel. (1995). *Emotional intelligence.* New York: Bantam Books.

Grabbe, J. Orlin. (1995). *International financial markets.* New York: Prentice Hall.

Gunaratne, P.S.M. and Yonesawa, Y. (1997, August). "Return reversals in the Tokyo stock exchange: a test of stock market overreaction." *Japan and the World Economy.*

Gunderson, Edna. (1989, July 21). "Drumming up a super Starr tour." *USA Today.*

Gunderson, Edna. (1991, March 21). "Jackson hits billion dollar note." *USA Today.*

Gunderson, Edna. (1993, November 19). "Jackson faces the man in the mirror." *USA Today.*

Guralnick, Peter (1994). *Last train to Memphis – the rise of Elvis Presley.* Boston: Little-Brown.

Gutenberg, B. and Richter, C.F. (1949). *Seismicity of the earth.* Princeton, NJ: Princeton University Press.

Guyton, Arthur C. (1991). *Textbook of medical physiology.* (8th ed.). W.B. Saunders.

Hambidge, Jay. (1919). *The elements of dynamic.* Yale University Press.

Hanson, Gayle. (1990, October 8). "A world that is graphically real." *Insight.*

Harlow, John. (1997, May 18). "Saatchi revives gory glory days of Hammer." *The Sunday Times* (London).

Harman, Tom. (1993, July 6). "Economists look for moderate growth in second half but warn creation of jobs will remain sluggish." *The Wall Street Journal*, p. A2.

Hausdorff, Felix. (1919). "Dimension und äusseres mass." *Mathematische Annalen*, 79, pp. 157-179.

Hausdorff, Jeffrey M., Mitchell, Susan L., Firtion, Renee, Peng, C.K., Cudkowicz, Merit E., Wei, Jeanne Y., and Goldberger, Ary L. (1997). "Altered fractal dynamics of gait: reduced stride-interval correlations with aging and Huntington's disease." American Physiological Society. 0161-7567/97.

Hausdorff, Jeffrey M., Peng, C.K., Wei, Jeanne Y. and Goldberger, Ary L. (1996). "Fractal analysis of human walking rhythm."

Hawkins, Gerald S. and White, John B. (1965). *Stonehenge decoded.* New York: Delta Books.

Hector, Gary. (1988, October 10). "What makes stock prices move?" *Fortune.*

Hediger, Heini. (1950). *Wild animals in captivity.* London: Butterworth.

Henry, David. (1998, October 9). "High stakes guessing game: markets defy easy answers." *USA Today.*

Hertsgaard, Mark (1995). *A day in the life.* New York: Delacorte Press.

Hoffer, E. (1955). *The passionate state of mind.* Buccaneer Books.

Holland, Bill. (1998, June 19). "The mystery of Frank Sinatra." *Goldmine.*

Horn, Robert. (1997, December 8). "Thailand starting big financial overhaul." *The Atlanta Journal-Constitution*, p. A12.

Hotz, Robert Lee. (1997, October). "A study in complexity." *MIT Technology Review.*

Hurst, H., Black, R. and Simaika, Y. (1951). *Long-term storage: an experimental study.* London: Constable.

Hutchison, Michael. (1987). *Megabrain.* New York: Ballantine Books.

Ip, Greg. (1998, October 14). "Risk and uncertainty wreak havoc on stocks." *The Wall Street Journal.*

Janis, Irving L. (1972). *Victims of groupthink.* Boston: Houghton Mifflin.

Jantsch, Erich (1980). *The self-organizing universe.* Oxford: Pergamon.

Jensen, Roderick V. (1987, March-April). "Classical chaos." *American Scientist*, Vol. 75.

Johnson, George. (1996, September 8). "From grains of sand: a world of order." *The New York Times.*

Johnson, George. (1997, January 19). "The real star wars: between order and chaos." *The New York Times*, p. 4.

Johnson, W.A. (1986, September 17). "Remember warnings of $3/gallon gas?" *Daily News Digest.*

Jordan, Mary. (1998, May 28). "S. Koreans walk off their jobs: workers protest growing layoffs." *The Washington Post.*

Jung, Carl. (1959). *The archetypes and the collective unconscious.* (2nd edition, 1981) Princeton University Press.

Kamm, Thomas. (1990, November 16). "Brazil's president, after eight months, finds roar of crowd is now against him." *The Wall Street Journal.*

Kawai, N. *et al.* (1990). "Spectral evolution of type II bursts from the rapid burster." *Astronomical Society of Japan* No. 42, pp. 115-133.

Kay, John. (1995, September 29). "Cracks in the crystal ball." *Financial Times.*

Kelly, G.A. (1955). *The psychology of personal constructs.* New York: Norton.

Kendall, Peter. (1996, December 16). "Basketball and the bull market." *The Elliott Wave Theorist* special report.

Khinchin, A. Ya. (1964.) *Continued fractions.* University of Chicago Press, p. 36

Kim, James. (1998, July 24). "Traders seize PC power." *USA Today.*

Kim, Lillian Lee. (1998, October 8). "Fewer lives lost to AIDS." *The Atlanta Journal-Constitution.*

Klein, Easy. (1986, November). "Psychology meets the stock market." *Columbia.*

Knott, Ron. (1997, October 18). "The Lucas numbers." www.mcs.surrey.ac.uk/Personal / R.Knott/Fibonacci/lucasNbs.html.

Koselka, Rita. (1996, June 30). "The madness of well-heeled crowds." *Forbes Magazine.*

Kuhn, Thomas. (1970.) *The structure of scientific revolutions,* (2nd ed.) University of Chicago Press. (Original 1962)

Kulkosky, Edward. (1977, October 15). "The Elliott wave's surprising message to investors." *Financial World.*

Laderman, Jeffrey and Pennar, Karen. (1988, October 17). "Did the crash make a dent?" *Business Week.*

Larsen, William J. (1997). *Human Embryology.* New York: Churchill Livingstone.

Le Bon, Gustave. (1895). *The crowd.* (France). Republished 1960. New York: Viking Press.

Lefebvre, Vladimir. (1992). "A rational equation of attractive proportions." *Journal of Mathematical Psychology,* 36, 100-128.

Lefebvre, V.A. (1987, October). "The fundamental structures of human reflexion." *The Journal of Social Biological Structure,* Vol. 10, pp. 129-175.

Lefebvre, Vladimir. (1990). *The fundamental structures of human reflexion.* Peter Lang Publishing.

Lefebvre, Vladimir. (1992). *A psychological theory of bipolarity and reflexivity.* Lewinston, NY: The Edwin Mellen Press.

Lefebvre, Vladimir. (1997). *The cosmic subject.* Moscow: Russian Academy of Sciences Institute of Psychology Press.

Lefebvre Vladimir. (1998, August 18-20). "Sketch of reflexive game theory." Workshop on Multi-Reflexive Models of Agent Behavior. Army Research Laboratory, Los Alamos, NM.

Lefebvre, Vladimir and Efremov, Yuri N., (1998). "Possible analogues of cognitive processes in the patterns of X-ray variability of the rapid burster." Astrophysical archive on the Internet.

Leontief, Wassily. (1982, July 9). "Academic Economics." (Letter to the Editor) *Science,* Vol. 217, No. 4555.

Lesmoir-Gordon, Nigel (producer). (1994). "Fractals: the colors of infinity." Gordon Films (distributed by Films for the Humanities, Princeton NJ).

Liang, Y.G. and Mullineaux, D.J. (1994, Spring). "Overreaction and reverse anticipation 2 related puzzles." *Journal of Financial Research,* Vol. 17, No. 1.

Linde, Andrei. (1994, November). "The self-reproducing inflationary universe." *Scientific American.*

Lipsitz, Lewis and Goldberger, Ary L. (1992, April 1). "Loss of 'complexity' and aging – potential applications of fractals and chaos theory to senescence." *Journal of the American Medical Association,* Vol 267, No. 13.

Liscio, John. (1998, March 2). "The seer syndrome." *Barron's.*

Litchfield, D. and Goldenheim, D. (1997, January). "Euclid, Fibonacci, and sketchpad." *Mathematics Teacher*, Vol. 90, No. 1.

Litton, Robert E. and Santomero, Anthony M. (1998, July 28). "Why a market correction won't replay 1987." *The Wall Street Journal*.

Lowenstein, Roger. (1991, June 6). "Goldman study of stocks' rise in 80s poses a big riddle." *The Wall Street Journal*.

Ludwig, Emil. (1926). *Napoleon*. New York: Garden City Publishing.

Mackay, Charles. (1841). *Extraordinary popular delusions and the madness of crowds*. (London.) Reprinted 1980, Three Rivers Press.

MacLean, Paul D. (1990). *The triune brain in evolution: role in paleocerebral functions*. New York: Plenum Press.

Malabre, Jr. Alfred L. (1987, February 23). "The stock market and the business cycle." *The Wall Street Journal*.

Malkiel, Burton. (1985.) *A random walk down wall street*, 4th ed. New York: Norton.

Malkiel, Burton. (1998, July/August). "Still on a random walk." *Bloomberg Personal Finance*.

Mandel, Michael J. (1996, September 30). "Especially dismal at downturns." *Business Week*.

Mandelbrot, Benoit. (1988). *The fractal geometry of nature*. New York: W.H. Freeman.

Mantegna, Rosario N. and Stanley, H. Eugene. (1995, July 6). "Scaling behaviour in the dynamics of an economic index." *Nature*, Vol 376.

Marshal, Alfred. (1890). *Principles of economics*. New York: MacMillan & Co.

McGraw, K.M. (1985). "Subjective probabilities and moral judgments." *Journal of Experimental and Biological Structures*, Vol. 10, pp. 501-518.

McIlvride, B. (1986, March 10-16). "Dr. Robert Thatcher, leading neurophysiologist, visits MIU." *MIU Review*, Vol. 1, No. 27.

McKaig, Angie. (1996-1998). Website *Pathway to darkness*, www.pathway todarkness.com, Toronto, Canada.

Miller, Rich. (1998, February 2). "Economists: Asian storm about to hit U.S." *USA Today*.

Montgomery, Paul Macrae. (1986, March 8). "Volcker part III: The godfather." *Universal Economics*.

Montgomery, Paul Macrae. (1990, October 11). "Magazine covers and real estate." *Universal Economics*.

Montgomery, Paul Macrae. (1991, March 15). "Neurophysiology, presidents and the stock market, part III." *Universal Economics*.

Montgomery, Paul Macrae. (1991, March 19). *Universal Economics*. (untitled market commentary published and broadcast to clients.)

Montgomery, Paul Macrae. (1991, September 19). "Stocks and the irrational: possible sub-cortical influences on contemporary equity market pricing." Presentation to Grant's Fall Conference, Chicago, Illinois.

Montgomery, Paul Macrae. (1992, September 13). "Capital markets and the irrational: possible non-cortical influences on the price structure of investments." Presentation to the Elliott Wave International conference, Buford, Georgia.

Montgomery, Paul Macrae. (1995, April 6). "The logical primacy of immaterial mental states in the price structure of investments: or how to outperfom the markets in 10 easy minutes a week." Presentation to *Straw Hats in the Winter: An Overview of Behavioral Finance*, Cincinnati, Ohio.

Montgomery, Paul Macrae. (1996, May 17). "Economic theory and technical analysis: the unscientific nature of the 'rational' approach, versus the rational nature of the 'unscientific' approach." Presentation to the 21st Annual Market Technicians Association Seminar, Marco Island, Florida.

Montgomery, Paul Macrae. (1998, February 4). *Universal Economics*. (untitled market commentary published and broadcast to clients.)

Moody, Paul Amos. (1962.) *Introduction to evolution*. (2nd Ed.) New York: Harper & Row.

Naik, Gautam. (1996, December 9). "Teen math whizzes go Euclid one better." *The Wall Street Journal*.

Nasar, Sylvia. (1998, August 15). "Cloudy blue skies." *The New York Times*.

Nesmith, J. (1996, September 14). "The roots of personality: researchers are zeroing in on the biological and genetic foundations that determine who we are." *The Atlanta Journal-Constitution*.

Neuharth, Al. (1998, July 31). "'Ryan' movie misses the cause of WWII." *USA Today*.

Nichols, Bill. (1994, September 28). "Warm fuzzy summit." *USA Today*.

Nietzsche, F. (1886). *Beyond good & evil*. (Translated by Walter Kaufmann, 1989). Vintage Books.

Norman, Philip. (1981). *Shout: the true story of the Beatles*. New York: Simon & Schuster.

Ogburn, Charlton. (1984). *The mysterious William Shakespeare*. McLean, VA: EPM Publications.

Oglesby, Christy. (1998, August 18). "State unable to judge effect of welfare shift." *The Atlanta Journal-Constitution*.

Olsen, R. (1996, July/August). "Implications of herding behavior for earnings estimation, risk assessment, and stock returns." *Financial Analysts Journal*.

Osgood, C.E., and Richards, M.M. (1973). *Language*, Vol. 49, pp. 380-412.

Page, Susan. (1998, January 22). "President's resilience faces biggest test." *USA Today*.

Passell, Peter. (1989, August 25). "Dow and reason: distant cousins?" *The New York Times*.

Penrose, Roger. (1994.) *Shadows of the mind – a search for the missing science of consciousness*. Oxford University Press.

Peratt, Anthony L. (1990, January/February). "Not with a bang." *The Sciences*.

Peters, Edgar E. (1991, March/April). "A chaotic attractor for the S&P 500." *Financial Analysts Journal*.

Pigou, Arthur C. (1920). *The economics of welfare*. London: F. Cass.

Pigou, Arthur C. (1927). *Industrial fluctuations*. London: F. Cass.

Pincheira, G. (1997, November 27). "In the genome, symmetry seems to code symmetry." Presentation to the International Conference on the Unity of the Sciences, Washington, DC.

Planck, Max. (1949). *Scientific autobiography and other papers*. New York: Philosophical Library. (translated by F. Gaynor). pp. 33-34.

Popper, Karl R. (1957). *The poverty of historicism*. Boston: Beacon Press.

Postrel, Virginia. (1998, December). "The two faces of Bill Clinton." *Reason*, p. 4.

Poulton, E.C., Simmonds, D.C.V. and Warren, R.M. (1968). "Response bias in very first judgments of the reflectance of grays: numerical versus linear estimates." *Perception and Psychophysics*, Vol. 3, pp. 112-114.

Prechter, Jr., Robert R. (1982, September 13). "The long term wave pattern — nearing a resolution." *The Elliott Wave Theorist*. Republished: (1996) *Elliott wave principle — key to market behavior.*

Prechter, Jr., Robert R. (1983, April 6). "A rising tide — the case for wave V in the Dow Jones industrial average." *The Elliott Wave Theorist* special report. Republished: (1996) *Elliott wave principle — key to market behavior.*

Prechter, Jr., Robert R. (1983, August 18). "The superbull market of the '80s: has the last wild ride really begun?" *The Elliott Wave Theorist* special report. Republished: (1996) *Elliott wave principle — key to market behavior.*

Prechter, Jr., Robert R. (1985, September 9). "Elvis, Frankenstein and Andy Warhol: using pop culture to forecast the stock market." *Barron's.*

Prechter, Jr. Robert R. (1985, December 31). "1986: Another bull market for stocks." *The Elliott Wave Theorist* special report.

Prechter, Jr., Robert R. (1986, May). "The fractal design of social progress." Presentation given to the Market Technicians Association, Boston.

Prechter, Jr. Robert R. (1992, December 31). "An application of the wave principle to business." *The Elliott Wave Theorist* special report.

Price, William H. (1961). *The civil war handbook.* Fairfax, VA: Prince Lithograph Co.

Prigogine, I. and Stengers, I. (1984). *Order out of chaos.* New York: Bantam Books.

Prochnow, Herbert. (ed.). (1986). *The Public Speakers Treasure Chest.* New York: Harper & Row.

Prusinkiewicz, P. and Lindenmayer, A. (1990). *The algorithmic beauty of plants.* Springer-Verlag.

Pugsley, John (1995). "Anthology of essential articles." *John Pugsley's Journal*. Phoenix Communications.

Raghaven, Anita and Pacelle, Mitchell. (1998, September 24). "A hedge fund falters, and big banks agree to ante up $3.5 billion." *The Wall Street Journal.*

Rapoport, A. and Chammah, A.M. (1965). *Prisoner's dilemma.* University of Michigan Press.

Ratajczak, Donald. (1998, August 30). "Global economy requires action." *The Atlanta Journal-Constitution.*

"Reducing the health consequences of smoking: 25 years of progress." (1989). A report of the Surgeon General. DHHS Publication No. (CDC) 87-8411.

Rhea, Robert A. (1934). *Story of the averages*: a *retrospective study of the forecasting value of Dow's theory as applied to the daily movements of the Dow-Jones industrial & railroad stock averages.* Republished January 1990. Omnigraphi.

Richardson, L.F. (1961). "The problem of contiguity: an appendix of statistics of deadly quarrels." *General Systems Yearbook*, Vol. 6, pp. 139-187.

Ricketts, Robert M. (1982, May). "The biologic significance of the divine proportion and Fibonacci series." *American Journal of Orthodontics*, St. Louis, Vol. 81, No. 5, pp. 351-370.

Roeser, Steve. (1993, October 15). "Ginger Baker: anyone for polo?" *Goldmine.*

Rothchild, John. (1998). *The bear book: survive and profit in ferocious markets.* New York: John Wiley & Sons, Inc.

Ruhlmann, William. (1998, June 19). "Celebrating Sinatra." *Goldmine.*

Rynecki, David. (1998, June 15). "Bull markets susceptible to anxieties." *USA Today.*

Sakarui, Joji. (1998, July 10). "Japan goes with veteran at helm of wayward economy." *The Atlanta Journal-Constitution.*

Saleur, H. and Sornette, D. (1996). "Complex exponents and log-periodic corrections in frustrated systems." *Journal de Physique I France* 6, No. 3, pp. 327-355.

Samenow, Stanton E. (1984.) *Inside the criminal mind.* New York: Times Books

"Savings rate cut in 1990s." (1990, October 15). *The Wall Street Journal.*

Savit, Robert. (1990, August). "Chaos and economics." *New Scientist.*

Saxon, Edward, Utt, Kenneth and Bozman, Ron (producers), and Demme, Jonathon (director). (1991). *Silence of the lambs* (film). Orion Pictures.

Scholl, Jaye. (1998, September 28). "The big fizzle." *Barron's.*

Schonberg, H.C. (1987). *The great pianists from Mozart to the present.* New York: Simon & Schuster.

Schroeder, Manfred. (1991). *Fractals, chaos, power laws: minutes from an infinite paradise.* New York: W.H. Freeman & Co.

Schuller, Gunther. (1989). *The swing era.* Oxford University Press.

Schumpeter, Joseph. (1939). *Business cycles.* New York: McGraw-Hill.

Schwartz, E.L. (1980). "A quantitative model of the functional architecture of human striate cortex with application to visual illusion and cortical texture analysis." *Biol. Cybern.,* Vol. 37, pp. 63-76.

Schwartz, E.L. (1980). "Computational anatomy and functional architecture of striate cortex: a spatial mapping approach to perceptual coding." *Vision Res.,* Vol. 20, pp. 645-669.

Scism, Leslie and Browning, E.S. (1998, August 6). "In the battle of the stock-market gurus, bulls win a round." *The Wall Street Journal,* p. C1.

Scuoteguazza, Henry C. (1997, September/October). "Handling emotional intelligence." *The Objective American.*

Seagle, Gene Jay. (1993, October). "Time and tide." *MTA Newsletter.*

Sepkoski, Jr., J. John. (1993). "Phanerozoic taxonomic diversity." *Paleobiology,* Vol. 19.

Shalit, B. (1960). *British journal of psychology,* 71, pp. 39-42.

Shambaugh, Philip Wells. (n.d.) "The cultural theory of small group development." *Group Psychodynamics — New Paradigms and New Perspectives.* Chicago: Year Book Medical Publishers.

Shaw, Russell and Landis, David. (1987, October 9). "Prechter flees wall st. for Georgia hills." *USA Today.*

Sheeley, G. (1997, April 14). "Runaway Tiger: Woods wins Masters by record 12 shots with 18-under total." *The Atlanta Journal-Constitution.*

Sheldrake, Rupert. (1981). *A new science of life.* St. Martin's Press.

Sherden, William. (1998). *The fortune sellers.* New York: John Wiley & Sons.

Sherrington, C.S. (1940). *Man on his nature.* Cambridge University Press.

Shomali, Hamid B. (1994/1995, Winter/Spring). "Technical versus fundamental analysis: a view from academe." *MTA Journal.*

Showalter, Elaine. (1997). *Hystories: hysterical epidemics and modern media.* New York: Columbia University Press.

Siegfried, Tom. (1992, August 31). "Fractal patterns within DNA may encode mysteries of life." *The Dallas Morning News.*

Siegfried, Tom. (1993, March 29). "Healthy hearts have complex rhythm." *The Dallas Morning News.*

Smeaton, Bob. (1996). *The Beatles anthology* (Videotape). Hollywood, CA: Capitol Records.

Sole, R.V., Manrubia, S.C., Benton, M. and Bak, P. (1997, August 21). "Self-similarity of extinction statistics in the fossil record." *Nature*, Vol. 388, pp. 764-767.

Sornette, Didier, Johansen, Anders, and Bouchaud, Jean-Phillippe. (1996). "Stock market crashes, precursors and replicas." *Journal de Physiques I France* 6, No. 1, pp. 167-175.

Sornette, Didier, and Johansen, Anders. (1997, November 1). "Large financial crashes." *Physica A – Statistical and Theoretical Physics*, edited by Capel, H.W., Mulder, B., Stanley, H.E., and Tsallis, C. Vol. 245, Nos. 3-4.

Sornette, Didier. (1997, October 15) "Generic mechanisms for hierarchies." *InterJournal Complex Systems* No. 127.

Sornette, Didier. (1998, June 30-July 3). "Discrete scale invariance in turbulence?" Proceedings of the 7th European Turbulence Conference.

Sornette, Didier. "Discrete scale invariance and complex dimensions." *Physics Reports* No. 297, pp. 239-270.

Sornette, Didier. (1999). "Critical crashes." *Risk*, Vol. 12, No. 1.

"Stand still, little lambs, to be shorn." (1998, March). *Economic Education Bulletin*. American Enterprise Institute, Great Barrington, MA.

Stanley, H.E., Buldyrev, S.V., Caserta, F., Daccord, G., Eldred, W., Goldberger, A., Hausman, R.E., Havlin, S., Larralde, H., Nittmann, J., Peng, C.K., Sciortino, F., Simons, M., Trunfio, P., and Weiss, G.H. (1993). "Fractal landscapes in physics and biology." *Growth patterns in physical sciences and biology*. New York: Plenum Press.

Stein, R. Conrad. (1993). *The Manhattan project*. Chicago: Children's Press.

Stewart, Ian. (1998). *Life's other secret*. New York: John Wiley & Sons.

Stokes, William Lee. (1966). *Essentials of earth history*. (2nd ed.) New Jersey: Prentice-Hall.

"Tech stocks are hurt by uncertainty over Asia." (1998, June 2). *The Atlanta Journal-Constitution*.

"The 21st century economy." (1998, August). *Business Week*.

"The lesson of the day." (1857, October 10). *Harper's Weekly*.

"The mathematics of markets: a survey of the frontiers of finance." (1993, October 9). *The Economist*.

"The practical fractal." (1987, December 26). *The Economist*.

The World Book Encyclopedia. (1992). Chicago: World Book.

Thompson, D'Arcy. (1917). *On growth and form*. Cambridge University Press.

Tindol, Robert. (1989, December 11). "Vanguard of a new approach to physical sciences." *On Campus* (University of Texas staff publication).

Tompkins, Peter and Bird, Christopher. (1973). *The secret life of plants*. New York: Harper & Row.

"Too Good." (1998, June 16). *The Wall Street Journal*. (editorial).

Toon, John. (1988, April/May). "New technology uses fractals to transmit images." *Tech Topics*, publication of the Georgia Tech Alumni Association.

"Trade deficit hits record." (1998, October 21). *The Atlanta Journal-Constitution*.

"Trade deficit soars to $13 billion." (1998, May 20). *The Atlanta Journal-Constitution*.

Train, John. (1994). *Money masters*. New York: Harper Collins.

Treynor, Jack. (1998, March/April). "Bulls, bears, and market bubbles." *Financial Analysts Journal*.

Tuckman, B.W. (1965). "Developmental sequence in small groups." *Psychology Bulletin,* No. 63, pp. 115-133.

Vandervert, Larry R. (1990). "Systems thinking and neurological positivism: further elucidations and implications." *Systems Research,* 7, 1/17.

Vicsek, Tamás. (1993). "The fractal nature of common patterns." *Growth Patterns in Physical Sciences and Biology.* Garcia-Ruiz, Juan Manuel, editor, *et al.* New York: Plenum Press.

Vogel, H. (1979). "A better way to construct the sunflower head." *Mathematical Biosciences* #44, pp. 145-174.

Vollrath, Fritz. (1992, March). "Spider webs and silks." *Scientific American,* pp. 52-58.

Von Baeyer, Hans C. (1990, February). "Impossible crystals." *Discover.*

Voss, Richard. (1992, June). "Evolution of long range fractal correlations and 1/f noise in DNA-based sequences." *Physical Review Letters,* 68:3805-3808.

Walker, Tom. (1998, August 1). "Stocks conclude week on sour note." *The Atlanta Journal-Constitution.*

Walker, Tom. (1998, August 21). "Impact of air strikes on stocks uncertain." *The Atlanta Journal-Constitution.*

Walker, Tom. (1998, August 6). "Identifying sell-off trigger difficult." *The Atlanta Journal-Constitution.*

Walker, Tom. (1998, June 21). "Determining what will move market not difficult – but forecasting its direction is harder." *The Atlanta Journal-Constitution.*

Walters, Charles. (1993, June). "An interview with P.Q. Wall, analyst." *Acres, USA.*

Washburn, Jim. (1993, March 31). "The human equation." *The Los Angeles Times.*

Webster's Third New International Dictionary, 1976.

Weibel, E.R. (1962). "Architecture of the human lung." *Science,* No. 137.

Weibel, E.R. (1963). *Morphometry of the human lung.* Academic Press.

Weiss, Gary. (1992, November 2). "Chaos hits wall street – the theory, that is." *Business Week.*

Wessel, David and Davis, Bob. (1998, September 24). "How global crisis grew despite efforts of a crack U.S. team." *The Wall Street Journal,* p. A1.

West, Bruce J. and Goldberger, Ary L. (1987, July/August). "Physiology in fractal dimensions." *American Scientist,* Vol. 75.

Wilcox, J.M. (1980). "Origin of the warped heliospheric current sheet." *Science,* Vol. 209, pp. 603-605.

Wilson, Edward O. (1998). *Consilience: the unity of knowledge.* New York: Alfred A. Knopf.

Winter, Douglas E. (1986). *Stephen King: the art of darkness.* New York: Signet Books.

Witten, T.A. and Sander, L.M. (1981). *Phys. Rev. Lett.* 47, 1400. (1983). *Phys. Rev.* B 27, 5686; Sander, L.M. (1986). *Nature* 332, 789; Recent work on the dynamics of DLA growth is described in Schwarzer, S. Lee, J., Havlin, Stanley, H.E. and Meakin, P. (1991). *Phys. Rev.* A 43, 1134-1137 and refs. therein. A "void channel" model for DLA structure is described in Lee, J. Havlin. S. and Stanley, H.E. (1992). *Phys. Rev.* A 45, 1035.

Wright, K. (1997, October). "Babies, bonds, and brains." *Discover,* p. 78.

Zajonc, R.B. (1968). "Attitudinal effects of mere exposure." *Journal of Personality and Social Psychology.* monograph supplement, 9, No. 2, Part 2, 1-32.

Zipf, G.K. (1949). *Human behavior and the principle of least action.* Reading, PA: Addison-Wesley.

Index